AGAINST
WIND
AND TIDE

WALTER M. MERRILL

AGAINST WIND AND TIDE

A BIOGRAPHY OF

Wm. Lloyd Garrison

Cambridge, Massachusetts

HARVARD UNIVERSITY PRESS

1963

© Copyright 1963 by the
President and Fellows of Harvard College

Distributed in Great Britain by Oxford
University Press, London

Library of Congress Catalog Card Number 63-10871

Printed in the United States of America

"Every moral and religious reform . . . *is* . . . *struggling against the wind and the tide of popular clamor.*"

The Liberator, 10 September 1836

ACKNOWLEDGMENTS

My chief debt in the writing of this book is to the American Council of Learned Societies for two postdoctoral fellowships which allowed me two years of full-time research in the Boston area. I wish to acknowledge also research grants from Northwestern University and the University of Wichita.

I am grateful for the general cooperation and advice of the Garrison family, who furnished me with documents and information at that time unavailable in public collections. I would like to thank especially the following: Mr. and Mrs. William Lloyd Garrison III, Miss Eleanor Garrison, Mr. Frank W. Garrison, Miss Fanny Garrison, and Mrs. Hendon Chubb.

To numerous libraries I am indebted for the use of manuscript and newspaper resources, especially the Boston Public Library, the Houghton Library, the Massachusetts Historical Society, the Smith College Library, the American Antiquarian Society, the Newburyport Public Library, and the Library of Congress.

I am grateful to the *New England Quarterly* and the Essex Institute *Historical Collections* for permission to reprint in this book portions of articles originally published in those journals.

I also wish to thank Miss Genevieve Wood, my research assistant during the years of my fellowships; Mrs. John Boyd, my secretary while I was director of the Essex Institute; Mrs. Gene Smith, my present secretary; and my colleague Mrs. B. Bernard Cohen for research, typing, proofreading, and advice on both style and content.

W.M.M.

March 1963

CONTENTS

ILLUSTRATIONS

———————◆◆◆———————

INTRODUCTION

BECAUSE William Lloyd Garrison fought for the elimination of prejudice against the Negro and against woman, as well as for the freedom of the slaves, a full treatment of his life should be of special interest today when public opinion has grown sensitive to prejudice and discrimination. Indeed, Garrison can be appreciated today as the universal reformer, who protests against prejudice, against segregation, against war, against discrimination, against a thousand moral turpitudes as well as against the greatest sin of his own day, Negro slavery.

The present study was inspired by the author's discovery and acquisition of an extensive group of manuscripts relating to Garrison. This collection includes, in addition to some two hundred of Garrison's own autographs, all of the extant manuscripts of Garrison's mother, many letters by his wife and other members of the family, and sixteen diaries of Francis Jackson Garrison, as well as papers of Richard Davis Webb, Edmund Quincy, and other of Garrison's associates. It contains also all of the extant manuscripts of *Liberator* editorials (contradicting, incidentally, the often repeated claim that Garrison always composed his editorials directly in type), and the complete correspondence and records of the national testimonial to Garrison in 1866–67.

The current biography is based on a meticulous study of this private collection and, more important, of the available public collections of Garrison's papers. The largest of these is at the Boston Public Library, where there are approximately one thousand of Garrison's own letters in addition to several thousand letters written to Garrison by friends and associates. The Houghton Library has much pertinent material in collections like the Villard Papers, the Valentine Papers, the Garrison Family Papers, and the Charles Sumner Papers, which together contain approximately one hundred and fifty Garrison autographs. The Massachusetts Historical Society has in various collections about one hundred Garrison letters. The Smith College Library has recently acquired the papers of William Lloyd Garrison, Jr., as well as those of Mr. Francis Wright Garrison, Miss Eleanor Garrison, and Mrs. Hendon Chubb, including many of Garrison's own autographs. The New York Public Library has in the Philip McKim Garrison papers a substantial collection of Garrison letters as well as the memoirs of James Holley Garrison (edited by the author in 1954, under the title *Behold Me Once More*). The Library of Congress has some fifty Garrison letters scattered in various collections, the most important being the Lewis Tappan Papers. In addition, a few Garrison papers are preserved in various other libraries, such as the American Antiquarian Society, the Essex Institute, and the Maine Historical Society.

Intensive research in this material has led me to feel that a new biography of Garrison based on all available sources is needed to fill in lacunae in earlier studies, to re-evaluate the character and personality of Garrison the man, and to afford a solid basis for appraisal of his position in the American antislavery movement.

A number of significant books concerned with Garrison have appeared in the eighty-three years since his death. The four-volume life by his sons, Wendell Phillips and Francis Jackson Garrison, was published between 1885 and 1889. This exhaustive work preserves virtually in the form of a log a quantity of biographical material, including some letters no longer available in manuscript. But this material is rendered with such filial prejudice that even the editing is suspect. The authors, for example, were reluctant to publish the letters of Garrison's mother without cutting, polishing, and "improving" them generally. In presenting the letters of various abolitionists they omitted some of the passages most critical of their father. Garrison's own writings they edited to suit Victorian standards of good taste, thereby obliterating some passages indicative of his character. Moreover, they preserved such a vast quantity of material that the reader tends to become lost in the detail, so that he can hardly distinguish the significant from the insignificant. What might have been one of the most interesting parts of the work, the authors' analysis of their father's character, they relegated to a single chapter on traits at the end of the book. In short, the four-volume life is a chronological and not altogether dependable collection of source material rather than a biography of the man or a history of the movement.

INTRODUCTION

Lindsay Swift's conventional life of Garrison was published in 1911, before many of the papers now in public collections were available. Although it is not the most readable volume on Garrison, it is soundly conceived and well organized. John Jay Chapman's brief, inpressionistic study appeared two years later. Although less scholarly, it is a far more lively book than Swift's. In fact, it contains the most valuable insight into the character of Garrison of any work up to that date. Chapman considered Garrison an aggressive man of feeling and action, whose language was often blatant, whose conduct was exemplary.

More recently, there have been two books, Ralph Korngold's *Two Friends of Man* (1950) and Russel B. Nye's *William Lloyd Garrison and the Humanitarian Reformers* (1955). The former is a journalistic account of Garrison and Phillips in their relationship to Lincoln. Based entirely on secondary sources, it is an unreliable book. At times, for instance, Mr. Korngold misquotes from the four-volume life passages from letters that had already been misquoted from the original manuscript. Nor is Mr. Korngold without his prejudices. In the conflicts between Garrison and Phillips, he accepts unthinkingly Phillips' point of view without even taking into consideration the attitudes of such associates of the two men as Edmund Quincy. Russel Nye's brief study is a scholarly and reliable work, although it is concerned primarily with the abolition movement rather than the man Garrison. Neither Korngold nor Nye, moreover, studies Garrison's later years, which they both mistakenly consider a period of inactivity and retirement.

The emphasis in this book is on Garrison the man as well as on the antislavery cause. In attempting to portray the character and personality of Garrison, I have tried to present him in the context of his family and his closest associates—a side of Garrison neglected by other biographers. I have described the fiery radical, the orator, the politician, the writer of florid editorials as well as the man of family, the kindhearted father and friend, the vain and humorous punster and the writer of bad verse. As a result, the book, based on all available material, is concerned with Garrison's early and late years as well as with the crucial middle period of his life.

In the course of my research I have become convinced that William Lloyd Garrison played a far more important role in the abolition movement than many recent historians have been willing to admit. Although nineteenth and early twentieth-century scholars considered him a central figure, there has been a tendency since 1933 to accept the thesis advanced by Gilbert H. Barnes in *The Antislavery Impulse*. Barnes believed that the antislavery crusade emanated not from Garrison but from Theodore D. Weld—this in spite of the fact that Weld was so modest and self-effacing that had the abolition impulse depended on him for its dissemination Northern opinion could hardly have been aroused to the extent that it was during the decade of the 1830's. The Weld legend has been propagated since Barnes's death by his one-time collaborator, Dwight L. Dumond, most recently in his profusely illustrated, quarto volume, *Antislavery: The Crusade for Freedom in America* (1961). The Barnes-Dumond thesis on American abolition sentiment, including as it does a highly subjective and pejorative appraisal of both the character and the importance of Garrison in the movement, constitutes an antislavery myth which, as C. Vann Woodward has pointed out, is ripe for reinterpretation.[1]

Actually, Garrison was the great publicist of the movement; he deserves primary credit for bringing the problem of slavery to the attention of the nation. His florid indignation and his instinct for publicity would not brook indifference in the North or in the South. As editor and personality, Garrison remains the chief symbol of the abolition crusade.

It is hoped that this study will help restore Garrison to what I believe to be his rightful position in the American antislavery movement.

Just as *Against Wind and Tide* is ready for the press—both galley and page proofs having passed through the author's hands —there appears (unfortunately, too late for consideration in connection with this book) John L. Thomas, *The Liberator, William Lloyd Garrison*.

Walter M. Merrill

Wichita, Kansas
March 1963

AGAINST
WIND
AND TIDE

CHAPTER I

———◆•◆———

Son and Apprentice

I N N E W B U R Y P O R T , Massachusetts, on 10 or 12 December
1805,[1] William Lloyd Garrison was born. His parents, Abijah
and Fanny Garrison, both originally from New Brunswick,[2] had
rented a room or two in a meager colonial house on School Street.
Their quarters were already crowded with two children, James
Holley, four, and Caroline Elizabeth, two, when the baby was
born. But the climate was less severe than in St. John, and they
hoped that the seafaring Abijah would find more lucrative opportunities than he had in the Maritime Provinces.

Newburyport with its population of six thousand was situated
at the mouth of the Merrimack River. As it is today, Newburyport
was a long, narrow town shaped like a sausage, with two main
streets—Merrimack along the river and High running approximately parallel on a ridge of higher ground—and with a series of
streets running between the two, either parallel or at right angles.
School Street was one of the least impressive of the latter. By 1805
the town was already proud of its aristocratic past. Mansions had
been built on High and State Streets by the wealthy merchants
even before the Revolution. The Tracys, the Jacksons, the Dal-
tons, the Parsons, and the Marquands (ancestors of the novelist)
had established the town as a center of taste and fashion. In Massachusetts only Boston and Salem could rival it. Since the town
engaged in both coastal and West Indian trade, the waterfront
bristled with swarming wharves and busy shipyards extended as
far up the river as Deer Island, about two miles from town.[3]

[1]

Even though he came there without friends and without influence, Newburyport seemed an ideal place for a man like Abijah Garrison to find employment. He tramped the town from merchant to merchant—doubtless somewhat awed by the relative splendor of the place—and soon he had plenty of engagements as a sailing-master. He sailed to Virginia with corn and flour; he sailed to the West Indies with rum; and he may have gone on a fishing trip to Labrador. He was sufficiently enthusiastic to write his brother on 3 April 1806, in one of his few letters to be preserved:

I have not much time to write you the Particulars of Business here but Earnestly recommend you to Come here if you Possibly Can without Injuring your Self, for I am Confident you wou'd get a decent living here. There is more than fifty ways you might find Employment . . . and always have the Cash As soon as the work is done. Money is as Plenty here as goods.[4]

But in 1807—only two years after the Garrisons settled in Newburyport—Congress, inspired by President Jefferson, who was trying desperately to avoid war with Great Britain and France, passed the Embargo Act, immobilizing all ships engaged in foreign commerce. Coastal trade alone could not support a thriving seaport. The decks, the shrouds, the masts, the spars which had been Abijah's livelihood collected dust in the harbor. Grass grew on the wharves, and the decaying hulks beat against the docks, while land birds rested on ropes and stays.

In addition to Embargo another cruel blow came to Abijah and Fanny early in the summer of 1808. After eating some poisonous flowers discarded by a neighbor their five-year-old Caroline died. Exactly how Abijah reacted to two such stunning blows, we can only conjecture. It must have been painfully discouraging for so active a man to be unemployed, for a sailor to be landlocked. And his discouragement must have been intensified by the shock of Caroline's death. It was perhaps these twin disasters which drove Abijah to take refuge in alcoholic oblivion. As a result conflict between him and his prohibitionist wife grew. On one occasion, when he and his comrades were drinking in the house, Fanny literally threw them out, closed the door, and—worst of all—broke all the bottles. It was more than a self-respecting man could endure.

Not even the birth of another daughter in July 1808, could prevent Abijah from deserting his family. He left Fanny with three children under seven to support.[5]

Hard times lay ahead for Fanny and her family. She began nursing sick people, leaving the children under the care of a neighbor, Martha Farnham, while she worked. On holidays and elections days, after he was old enough, she sent Lloyd out with molasses candy to sell. She sent him also with a small tin pan to a mansion on State Street for scraps of food. This he found the most ignoble task of all, especially when the boys would demand to know what was in the pail. Garrison's pride, so obvious in the young reformer of the 1830's, was doubtless nurtured on the humiliations of his childhood.

When he did not have more important work to do, Lloyd attended the primary school across from the Farnham house. But he was a left-handed boy forced to use his right hand, and he learned to read and write slowly. Even his sister Maria Elizabeth, two and a half years his junior, surpassed him. Eventually, however, encouraged by many a blow on his knuckles, he learned to write a regular and legible hand, samples of which were displayed for their excellence in the counting-houses and banks of Newburyport.

In 1812, the war having driven much of the active population out of Newburyport and having impoverished most of those who remained, Fanny moved to Lynn, with the hope of finding more regular employment. With her she took the eldest child, her favorite son James, so that he could learn the shoemaking trade. At Newburyport she left the other two—Elizabeth with Mrs. Farnham and Lloyd with Deacon and Mrs. Ezekiel Bartlett, pious members of the Baptist church. Lloyd transferred to the grammar school on the Mall, which he attended for three months, or until it was apparent he must contribute to the slender finances of the Bartlett household. He worked at various odd jobs—sawing wood, sharpening saws, making lasts, selling apples from a stand in front of the house. On one occasion when the proud lad found life too hard to bear, he ran away from home, only to be found twenty miles out of town by the driver of the mail-coach, who brought him back to the deacon.

For young Lloyd, however, life was not all drudgery. Many years later, his mind purged of unhappy memories, he could recall his excitement over winning a ball game; he could live over again his thrill at the click of marbles in the dust. And, some years later as the beleaguered abolitionist, he remembered vividly the bloody and painful contests between his gang, the South-end Boys, and the rival North-enders. No less did he remember his graceful and affectionate cat and the reception she gave him one night. Shortly after he had gone to bed, he was awakened by soft fur tickling his face. The cat had brought the litter of kittens born during his absence and arranged them one by one around his head. "My eyes moistened when I realized what she had done," he admitted, "and we all slept in one bed that night." He remembered, also, as long as he lived, the hymns he learned in the Baptist choir—the 34th Psalm, "Wicklow," "Hebron," "Ward," and others. He used to sing them years later to wake his family on Sunday mornings.

Already the pattern was emerging: the fighter, the sentimentalist. The mounting pressures of a frustrated ego impelled the fatherless School Street boy to work and play hard, to fight for the security denied by his birth. Though she could hardly provide the traditional family hearth where he could indulge his love for simple childlike pleasures, his mother did write from Lynn pious letters, urging him to read the Bible, and reporting James's progress in making thirteen pairs of shoes a week, describing her own hard work and her not infrequent quarrels with her employers.[6] For all their illiteracy these letters were written with the same kind of rhetorical flourish that was later to mitigate her son's frustrations. For it was as journalist, as publicist, that he was to achieve notoriety and distinction.

Hardly aware that her son had any special ability, Mrs. Garrison apprenticed Lloyd to a Quaker shoemaker in Lynn sometime in 1814. The boy was small and frail even for his nine years (little bigger than a last, his fellow laborers thought). He worked at shoemaking for several months and learned to make a fairly good shoe, but his fingers became sore with the sewing, his knees throbbed from holding the heavy lapstone, and his whole body ached with pain. He simply was not strong enough for the work.

In October 1815 a man named Paul Newhall persuaded Fanny and her two boys to accompany him to Baltimore, where he planned to establish a shoe factory. They sailed from Salem on the

9th and reached Baltimore after twelve rough days on the water. In spite of the heavy sea, Fanny spent her time keeping a log— a log that is full of the nautical technicalities she must have learned from Abijah.[7] James was so entranced with the happy sailors and their lot that he resolved to go to sea some day. Lloyd reacted differently; he was so sick that he quickly lost whatever idea he may have had of becoming a sailor. In Baltimore James was again apprenticed in the shoemaking trade, while Lloyd helped out with the light work and did errands. Mrs. Garrison became a kind of counselor to the workers in the Newhall factory, who called her Mother and visited her often for moral and religious advice. The factory, however, failed, and Mr. Newhall and his men returned to Lynn after a few months.

Baltimore in 1816 was a thriving metropolis, with a population of more than fifty thousand.[8] Its prosperity was due in part to its espousal of the War of 1812. While Newburyport had expended all its energy to oppose the war, Baltimore had thrown itself into the fighting with vigor and enthusiasm, providing vessels, men, and money for the defense of the city and the country.

Baltimore had engaged in many activities besides those of war. It had startled the mercantile world with the Baltimore clippers— rakish schooners rigged for speed on any course and for sailing closer into the wind than any other vessel. It—or rather Rembrandt Peale—had founded a museum and lighted it with gas so successfully that by 1816 the city had the first municipal gas light company in the country; soon the streets were aglow even on the darkest night. Moreover, owing to its peculiar location between the industrial North and the agricultural South, Baltimore had developed a special prosperity geared to both sections of the country. It was exporting flour, tobacco, and cotton and also developing local industries.

Baltimore seemed a city of unlimited opportunities—opportunities even for a struggling nurse like Fanny Garrison, who determined to stay there with her two boys in spite of the failure of Mr. Newhall's factory. She specialized in nursing merchants' wives —among them was Mrs. Dorsey, the daughter of Colonel Timothy Pickering, who had married a prominent Baltimorean.[9] She was fascinated by life in high society, especially at Harmony Hall, the country seat of an unnamed patient, a lady of quality who, like others of her class, escaped the numerous yellow fever epidemics and the summer's heat in her retreat in the country. It was an impressive place to Fanny. No one lived in such style at Newburyport or at St. John. It was nearly a quarter of a mile from the gate to the house, the avenue lined with fifty-six Lombardy poplars on the left, all trimmed exactly alike, and with the same number of well-groomed cedars on the right. Best of all, Fanny was treated like a lady, and a large retinue of servants catered to her every wish. And the food was so good that she had grown fat—though she hated to admit it, she weighed 162 pounds. In short, it all gave her a faint idea (in some of her letters the idea hardly seemed faint) of Paradise.[10]

But as Fanny tasted the sweets of Paradise, the boys grew restless. It seemed to them that she spent all of her time nursing and attending church (three meetings each Sunday). As though that were not enough, she spent Saturday afternoons running female prayer meetings of her own—the first ever held in Baltimore. Lloyd became so unhappy that Fanny decided to send him back to Newburyport to live with Aunt and Uncle Bartlett. She confessed in a letter to a friend that he "would leave me tomorrow & go with strangers to N.P. [Newburyport] He can't mention any of you without tears." [11]

James was more of a problem, as can be seen by reading his memoirs.[12] He had started to drink while he was still an apprentice in Lynn and had gotten into many scrapes involving girls, liquor, and convivial companionship. On one occasion he had spent two days and two nights doing the roadhouses between Salem and Danvers with "a lovely little girl about my own age." His behavior did not improve in Baltimore, and Fanny had no idea how to control him. She tended to reward his misconduct with loving sympathy, setting him up in a new job when he lost an old one.

Back in Newburyport Lloyd was happier than he had been in Baltimore. He had escaped the maternal apron strings that entangled James. He did what he could to help Uncle Bartlett and to contribute to the household expenses, and he found time for his final formal education at the grammar school on the Mall. By the spring of the next year (1817), however, Fanny had become concerned that Lloyd had been so long idle. She wanted him to find a definite job, and she talked about putting him in a store or at a trade in Baltimore.[13] But since no opportunity was forthcoming, Lloyd enjoyed about six more months of relative leisure before being apprenticed to another trade.

This time he was to become a cabinet-maker and was sent to Haverhill for training. Although the work was not too onerous and he was treated kindly, he soon became homesick again and determined to escape at the first opportunity. He found his chance one morning when his master was away. Tying all he owned in a handkerchief, he started out on foot for Newburyport—some fifteen miles away. He hitched a ride as the daily stagecoach was passing and jumped off and continued to walk when it stopped. The passengers were amazed that so small a boy could keep up with them. In the meantime, his master returned home, discovered his apprentice was missing, guessed that he had started back toward Newburyport, took a short cut in pursuit, grabbed him before he had gone too far, and brought him back. But when he learned how homesick Lloyd had been, he willingly released him from the terms of his apprenticeship. Once more Lloyd had managed to escape an unpleasant situation.

By the time he entered his final apprenticeship in the fall of 1818 Lloyd was beginning to feel the independence and specious maturity of the adolescent. He strutted about the Newburyport streets with all the pomp and gravity of the middle-aged squire. He felt "as tall and as huge, as any Goliah [*sic*] in the land," and he spoke with as much authority. But, Goliath or not, he was fortunate to be apprenticed on the 18th of October, a few weeks before his thirteenth birthday,[14] to the cautious and frugal Ephraim W. Allen, the diligent, if unimaginative, editor and owner of the Newburyport *Herald*,[15] for the usual term of seven years, in return for room and board and a knowledge of the printing trade.

Garrison remembered years later:

I never shall forget the surprise and amazement which I felt on first being led to the case to see the types set and distributed with such celerity by those who were familiar with the work, and my little heart sank like lead within me. It seemed to me that I never should be able to do anything of the kind. However, I was put to learn the different boxes and to ascertain where the capitals and small capitals were placed, and, in the lower case, how the types were diversified, and

[7]

very soon learned the whole. Then I took the composing stick and began to set types, and from that day to this I have delighted in nothing more, as regards manual work, than the manipulation of types.[16]

At last Lloyd had found a congenial trade. In an astonishingly short time he became a rapid and accurate compositor and an excellent pressman. Soon he was made office foreman and given the responsibility of making up the pages of the paper, of preparing the forms for the press, and of handling the job-work.

As an apprentice who lived with his master, moreover, Lloyd became an integral part of a family that had far more stability in the community than his own. The Allens, it is true, were not among the "upper uppers," as they were called in Newburyport; but they were respectable people, and through the *Herald* and later as owner of several ships, Mr. Allen had a considerable influence.

For the first time, also, Lloyd had an opportunity to make close friends. Most readily available, until he went off to Dartmouth, was his master's son, William. Most admired was Tobias H. Miller, some four years Lloyd's senior and already a journeyman printer. Miller he later eulogized as a person "generous, sympathetic, self-denying, reverent"—qualities not always to be associated with Garrison himself—and he marveled at his calm disposition, which withstood all the petty annoyances of the printer's trade without anger and without complaint. When life became hard, Garrison would often look back to Miller's example.[17] Most stimulating was Thomas H. Bennett, also employed by Allen, who was supposed to have published in the *Herald* office about this time a translation of Cicero's *Orations*.[18] It may have been Bennett who taught Garrison Latin and who started him reading English and American literature.

In the meantime, Fanny had had bad luck in Baltimore. Her system had been weakened by many attacks of fever, several of which promised to be fatal; and by the spring of 1819 she was far from well and happy. The latest fever and cough lingered. In spite of persistent bleeding by the doctor and a blister administered to the forehead, she failed to regain her strength. But more difficult for her than ill health were two things: her anxiety over James, who seemed to have disappeared entirely—she heard from him only at long intervals and through Lloyd—and her concern over finances. For months and months, she had been unable to pay for Maria Elizabeth's room and board at Martha Farnham's, and she was worried that she might never earn enough to pay.

In the spring of 1820 Fanny had an ominous apprehension of her approaching death. She wrote a full letter to Lloyd, telling of her "presentiment that God was agoing to take me to himself—I felt myself Standing on the Confines of the Grave." Then she described her symptoms with a clinical detail that must have horrified fourteen-year-old Lloyd: how her legs were bandaged to prevent swelling, how she had a blister on her breast that relieved the pain, and how with violent spasms she would raise enough blood and matter from her lungs to soak several large handkerchiefs. Her one consolation in her illness was that she was having excellent care, especially from "a Coloured Woman that waits on me, that is so Kind no one can tell how Kind She is and although a Slave, to Man—yet a free Born soul by the grace of God—her name is Henny and should I never see you again—and you should ever Come where she is remember for your poor mothers Sake . . ." [19] Garrison never forgot how kind a slave had been to his mother.

During the last three and a half years of her life Fanny, expecting death at any moment, longed to see her daughter. A former employer paid Maria Elizabeth's fare to Baltimore. Unfortunately, the child arrived with a raging fever—she "puked incessantly for 23 days." Fanny rallied her little remaining strength and nursed her through this illness.[20] Two years later, however, she could not save her from the yellow fever, and Elizabeth died in September 1822.

In Newburyport, a few months earlier, Lloyd had begun his destined career as a writer. He had been working for Mr. Allen and the Newburyport *Herald* for about three and a half years before he had the temerity to write a letter to the editor. But after reading in exchange papers and in the *Herald* itself reports of case after case of successful breach of promise suits, he could not resist writing a letter of complaint to Mr. Allen, signed "An Old Bachelor." [21]

Lloyd was working at the type case when Mr. Allen read the letter. He waited, as anxious as a student whose examination paper is about to be returned. Fortunately, Mr. Allen, who did not recognize Lloyd's disguised hand, liked the letter so much he read it aloud to the office staff. Then he handed it to Lloyd and told him to set it in type. It appeared in the issue printed on the 21st, along with a note from the editor, to the effect that he hoped his readers would not be offended by the querulous tone of the "Old Bachelor's" letter; doubtless the old gentleman had had some sad disappointment in love which set him against the sex. Mr. Allen admitted, however, that he thought breach of promise suits were multiplying with alarming rapidity.

This letter was only the first of a series to appear in the paper. These juvenilia were written with verve and exuberance and with surprising maturity of style for a teenager. The letters showed that, although Garrison's formal education had been abbreviated, he had done a considerable amount of reading on his own.

Lloyd was tremendously pleased to have become an "author" as well as printer. At last, after so many false starts, he had found an occupation to which he could dedicate his life. He might not have the solace of a secure and happy family—a mother and father, a brother and sister who gave him roots in the world. But he did have a center to his life.

During the next year Mr. Allen continued to encourage his anonymous bachelor. In fact, he went so far as to write A.O.B. in care of the post office to urge him to continue his communications to the paper and to request a personal interview. Also, Caleb Cushing, one of the town's leading citizens and later distinguished in national politics, who was editing the paper while Allen was out of town in the spring of 1823, paid this generous tribute to the Old Bachelor: "We invite the attention of our readers to the 'Glance at Europe,' in which we recognize the hand of a correspondent who at different times has favored us with a number of esteemed and valuable communications." [22] Cushing it was who discovered A.O.B.'s identity. Subsequently, he did what he could to encourage the young man, suggested books for him to read, and even gave him free access to his own library.

With such encouragement Lloyd wrote a variety of articles during the remaining years of his apprenticeship. He wrote an imaginary description of a shipwreck, a short story about a fortune hunter, three articles advocating a stronger American policy in regard to South America, and three analyses of the

European situation. No one was more amazed than Lloyd himself at what he could do. He wrote his mother: "I feel absolutely astonished at the different subjects which I have discussed, and the style in which they are written. Indeed, it is altogether a matter of surprise that I have met with such signal success, seeing I do not understand one single rule of grammar, and having a very inferior education." [23]

Ironically enough, Fanny seems to have been the only one who questioned the value of her son's achievement as a journalist. She had earlier suggested that anonymous writers are often lampooned and that he had better send her a copy of one of his pieces so that she could tell him whether he were An Old Bachelor or an Ass, an Oaf, and a Blockhead.[24] Later she had more serious doubts:

Next your turning Author, you have no doubt read and heard the fate of such Characters that they generally starve to death in some garret o[r] place that no one inhabits—so you may see what fortune and luck belongs to you, if you are of them Class of people!—secondly you think your time was wisely spent while you was writing political peices—I Cannot join with you there for had you been searching the scriptures for truth and praying for direction of the holy spirit to lead your mind into the path of holiness your time would have been more wisely spent—and your advance to the heavenly world more rapid—but instead of that you have taken the Hydra by the head and now beware of his mouth—but as it is done I suppose you think you had better go on and seek the Applause of Mortals—but my dear lose not the favour of God—have an eye single to his glory and you will not lose your reward.[25]

By the spring of 1823 it had been seven long years since Fanny had seen her more dependable son. Several times she had urged him to come for a visit, but Mr. Allen needed him at the office. She was all the more anxious to see him now that he seemed fascinated by so impractical a career as writing. Doubtless she had far more to say to him on that subject than she could express in letters. Also, her health was no better; she felt sure she could not live long. She and Lloyd (he perhaps with some misgivings) finally prevailed upon Mr. Allen to spare him long enough for a short visit to Baltimore in July. When Lloyd appeared, she was in tears. He was shocked to find her so emaciated and bent that he could hardly recognize her. Two months later she was dead.

Garrison must have inherited many of his best qualities from his mother—his independence, his determination, his courage, and perhaps his literary talent—but he and his mother were not the best of companions. Like his father before him, he found her difficult to live with; he much preferred to be with the Bartletts or the Allens in Newburyport. He loved her best, as he perhaps later did his wife, when they were separated, when she was in Baltimore and he in Newburyport. After she was dead, she became for him the symbol of the perfect mother. He called her "the masterpiece of womankind" remarkable not only for her personal attractions but also for a mind "of the first order—clear, vigorous, creative, and lustruous, and sanctified by an ever-glowing piety." With forgivable exaggeration, he told how often she had watched over him, wept for him, and prayed over him.[26]

Two years after his mother's death—in December 1825—Lloyd's apprenticeship ended. He had spent seven profitable years under Mr. Allen's direction, for he had learned not only the printer's trade but also much that was to qualify him as an editor in his own right.

All his life Garrison retained indelible traces of his childhood and youth. The work and the fighting, the play and the sentimentalizing—all were ingredients of the reformer and family man of the 1830's and 1840's. He was to be the lion in the arena and the lamb at home, and the pattern had been laid in his earliest years.

CHAPTER II

Young Editor

Sooner than anyone could have anticipated, Lloyd was to have an opportunity to use his knowledge of editorial work because, thanks to a loan from Mr. Allen, he was able to buy the *Essex Courant* in the early spring of 1826. The *Courant* had been founded in Newburyport two years before by Democratic Republicans as the *Northern Chronicler* and had been rechristened by new proprietors in 1825. Garrison promptly changed the name to *The Free Press*.[1] But the new title was a misnomer, for the paper displayed its prejudice in its very first issue (22 March 1826). Prominently placed at the top of page one was the Federalist motto, "Our Country, Our Whole Country, and Nothing but Our Country." Also prominently discussed in this issue—as in many to follow—was the Federalist argument about the Massachusetts Claim for money due its militia for services rendered during the War of 1812. Garrison took the position that it was grossly immoral for the federal government not to settle promptly and generously with Massachusetts.

In addition to political news and editorials, *The Free Press* contained numerous selections from other newspapers and from magazines: Garrison retold the story of the dram-drinking Scottish parson who cheerfully consumed quantities of liquor as he preached against the manifold evils of intemperance. He reprinted the shocking account of the Englishwoman who sold her husband's body for medical dissection. He repeated the inflated claim of William Cobbett that he wielded the most powerful pen in

England. He featured selections from the works of Swift, Pope, Sterne, and Irving. And to raise the literature, as he thought, to the highest possible level, he printed innumerable poems (an average of nearly one per week) by his favorite poet, the saccharine Mrs. Hemans. Ironically enough—a fact which must have caused the crusading moralist of later years to blush for shame—he also printed regularly advertisements for New England rum.

The Free Press, however, was interesting for more than its reprints and its ads for rum. Not infrequently Garrison displayed his sense of humor, as in this bit on "Excessive Heat":

The weather during the present week has been of the most melting kind. . . . Go where you will—hear what you will—say what you will—the weather is the only topic of conversation: it engrosses the attention and occupies the time, till one's patience is exhausted in the conflict. We never penned a paragraph with greater warmth of feeling than the present; it is impossible to write coolly upon any thing. Fat people seem as if they would melt, and lean ones look as if they would dry up. Hot weather is a great consumer of soap and clothes: what comes wet from the back goes wet into the washing-tub; and in forty-eight hours this process is repeated. Steamed on the body, boiled in the kettle, dried in the sun, and made wet again by the very sun as soon as it has been dried—behold the history of a suit of clothes in this season of dripping and drying! You shall see more pocket handker-chiefs in motion, every moment, in the streets, than were ever flitted about in a ball room. One is seen mopping his face as if grief had shed a shower of salt water on his visage; another wipes his hands as if he had been cleansing them from something offensive; and these actions are done with an air of impatience and fretfulness, that plainly be-speaks that the sufferer is tired of these evolutions.[2]

It was while he was editing *The Free Press,* moreover, that Garrison discovered a major poet. One day he found at the door of his office an envelope addressed in a pale and delicate hand. Inside he found another example of "original newspaper poetry," a species he had already learned to loathe. Though his inclination was to tear it into a thousand pieces, he read it first. The piece excelled anything a small-town newspaper editor had any right to expect. He printed "The Exile's Departure" in the issue for the 8th of June. Through the post-rider he identified the abbreviated signature, "W., Haverhill," and found that the poet's sister had copied off the poem and secretly sent it to the paper. Lloyd lost little time in going to visit John Greenleaf Whittier. When he arrived at the homestead in East Haverhill, the young poet is supposed to have been crawling under the barn looking for a hen who had stolen her nest. Whittier's sister called him to the house, and he "came into the room with shrinking diffidence, almost unable to speak, and blushing like a maiden," Garrison later reported.[3] It must have been an awkward meeting, but Lloyd with the poise of the dapper city lad tried to put Greenleaf at his ease and to give advice to his father concerning the education of his gifted son. The elder Whittier resented being told by a complete stranger—and a youngster at that—how to educate his son.

Fortunately, Garrison continued to publish a Whittier poem in almost every issue of *The Free Press*.[4] He rightly deserves credit for discovering and first publishing the new poet's works.

There was little in *The Free Press,* however, to foreshadow the reform impulse which was later to animate both Whittier and Garrison. In the second issue, for example, Garrison printed without comment extracts from what might be considered a proslavery speech by Edward Everett; it was a speech that opposed slave insurrections in the South. A couple of months later, though he did commend the antislavery poem "Africa" he was more interested in the fact that it was written by "a young lady of fine talents" who deserved the reader's support than in the ideas it contained.[5] The last of June, it is true, he seemed more nearly cognizant of the evils of slavery, for he qualified his Fourth of July eulogy of America with a general paragraph on the curse of slavery, a theme he wished orators would emphasize.[6]

Whatever its significance as a paper, *The Free Press* could not continue without an adequate circulation. In the first issue Garrison had admitted that the subscription list was painfully small and that he doubted if there were any other town of 7,000 people in the entire United States where two papers were so poorly supported as at Newburyport. "Our brother of the Herald will perceive," he went on, "that we speak under the rose—i.e. Two words for ourselves, and ONE for him." Unfortunately, Garrison had the talent for reducing even further the small list he began with. After what he said about the Massachusetts Claim in the first issue, ten of his subscribers discontinued their support at once. Garrison commented defensively the following week:

We assure these patriotic gentlemen, that we erase their names from our subscription list with the same pleasure that we insert MORE THAN THE SAME NUMBER in their place. *One* of these persons was conscientious to return his paper; the rest—may have theirs *gratis.* —All that we regret, in the loss of their patronage, is, the probability of the number of BORROWERS being increased; and that they may not vex their neighbors, we shall also *give,* each of them, a paper of this morning.[7]

Garrison antagonized other readers by his virulent invective and his bitter lampoons, but worst of all he got into a controversy with his benefactor, E. W. Allen. Following the deaths of Thomas Jefferson and John Adams on the Fourth of July Garrison wrote a restrained obituary notice for his paper, saying that although he had always disapproved of Jefferson's political ideas, he did admire his great talents. Adams, he said, he preferred as a statesman, in spite of his obvious faults as a man. But now that they were both dead, he suggested that we remember their virtues and forget their faults. He found it increasingly difficult, however, to forget Jefferson's faults when paper after paper eulogized him. He himself was annoyed particularly by Mr. Allen's eulogy in the *Herald,* which he zealously condemned as rhapsodical, impious, and offensive, especially from "a paper, which twenty years ago, viewed Mr. Jefferson as the Great Lama of Infidelity—as the giant who would carry away the gates of Christianity, and open the floodgates of vice! Now a greater prostitution of language than the above [Allen's eulogy] cannot well be made. . . . His [Jefferson's] religious sentiments are notorious; they inculcated a loose morality; they were subtle, indefinite, and unsound." [8]

In his reply to this outburst, Allen touched Garrison to the quick by aspersions on his youth and inexperience. Garrison retaliated with sophomoric arrogance, saying that Allen "flattered himself" to suggest that he would condescend to "breaking a lance with him." He said that he had already bestowed too many favors on "the caterer for the Herald." Garrison's reaction was a comforting way of disclaiming a debt to his benefactor. Although at times he seemed to want things done for him, he always hated to be obligated to anyone. Perhaps his pride made it difficult for him to accept a benefaction gracefully; he often followed the pattern shown here: acceptance of patronage and subsequent rejection of the patron, always on grounds of high principle and with moral indignation. In the present instance, Garrison admitted disingenuously that "every word . . . has come from us with the same reluctance that we should sacrifice so many U.S. Banknotes." [9] Garrison was speaking quite literally about sacrificing banknotes; this attack may well have cost him the paper. At any rate, on 14 September, six months after he had assumed the editorship (conceivably at the time when the notes to Allen were due), he announced that, owing to *"considerations of importance only to himself," The Free Press* was for sale. And the week following he reported that the paper had been transferred to Mr. John H. Harris, a gentleman whose acquaintance with the business was a sure guarantee that the "appearance and ability of the Press will in future be very considerably improved and increased." [10]

But Garrison soon found that his optimism about the future of the paper was unwarranted, for the conservative Federalist bias was immediately shifted toward the more radical Republican position, a point of view, ironically, that would have been far more consistent with the reforms Garrison was later to preach. In his last issue as editor, Garrison had begun a campaign for the reelection to Congress of Federalist John Varnum. The new editor of the paper, however, subtly launched his campaign for the opposing candidate in the very issue in which the transfer of the paper was announced. He began a series of articles signed with the initial C. on the topic "Our Foreign Claims," which discussed at some length the importance of collecting from the federal government money which had, in effect, already been paid into the American treasury by France and other countries for damages to American private property. Then two weeks later the editor mentioned that the excellent series of articles were by Caleb Cushing, the man he hoped would be sent to Congress from North Essex County.[11] In the following issues Harris waged a vigorous campaign for Cushing's election.

Toward the end of October, Garrison read in the Haverhill *Gazette* that *The Free Press* had really been Caleb Cushing's paper all along and that he (Garrison) had been removed because he was unfriendly.[12] Garrison denied this in a letter to the editor of the *Gazette*, insisting that he had been in complete control of the paper during his editorship. But, he alleged, the paper was at present being edited by a Mr. Cross, the new law partner of Caleb Cushing,[13] the implication being that Harris was really only a front for Cushing, that Cushing had bought the paper to assure his victory at the polls.

Garrison was indignant over the article in the *Gazette*. He felt that he had been betrayed by Cushing and that the betrayal neutralized any obligation he may have had to his fellow townsman. Even if Cushing had been a friend and patron, Garrison had no need for his support. He would make Cushing smart just as he had Allen! Without more thought Garrison forced his way into a Cushing political rally and attacked the character of the candidate so viciously and so effectively that Cushing was defeated in the forthcoming election.[14]

The sudden virulence with which Garrison turned against both Allen and Cushing is significant. Frustrated as a child and a failure as a youth, Garrison was painfully on the defensive. Both his father, who had deserted the family, and his mother, who had worked so hard as nurse and leader in the church, had taught him that he could survive only by being independent. When criticized —challenged was the word he would have preferred—he had to assert his independence by repudiating the critic. And the repudiation was the more emphatic if the critic were an older man and former benefactor against whom he could focus the resentment he must have felt against his father.

In December Garrison left Newburyport for Boston. During the following year he migrated from one printing job to another until he finally established himself, in January of 1828, as editor of the *National Philanthropist*, one of the earliest temperance papers. As editor of a reform paper Garrison had to shift his emphasis from politics to morality. He made the transition rather smoothly in the editorial, "Moral Character of Public Men," in the issue for 18 January. "Moral principles," he insisted, "should be inseparably connected with political; and the splendid talents of the dissolute must not be preferred to the competent, though inferior, abilities of the virtuous of our land."

The role of moral legislator, especially in the realm of temperance, appealed to Garrison. In such a capacity he could as editor be independent of the nefarious pressures of the Allens and the Cushings of the world. He set about his new job, moreover, with an enthusiasm born of first-hand knowledge of the evils of alcohol, since both his father and his brother were excessive drinkers. He filled his pages with as many horrible examples of the evils of liquor as he could find. He told about the wife who broke her husband's rum jug and was nearly beaten to death with the jagged pieces. He recounted the tale of the drunkard who was seen late at night stumbling down a dark country road and whose body was found some days later at the foot of a precipice. He reprinted an account of a brandy-drinking contest that ended with the senseless meandering through the night of two of the participants and the death of the third. He also printed reports from temperance societies and urged that more be sent him. In fact, his only real difficulty was that he did not have sufficient material to keep his paper full. He had to advertise for more facts, and he volunteered to write them up if only he were provided with the raw material. In one issue he went so far as to offer to pay postage plus one dollar for every temperance item—a rather desperate device in those days of high postage rates.

In addition to printing items about the deplorable effects of strong drink, Garrison made suggestions about rooting out the evil of intemperance at its source. He felt that it was necessary to attack and even ostracize the manufacturers and vendors of liquor. Grocers (that is, liquor dealers) he thought should be prevented from selling drinks by the glass. And as a special deterrent to drinkers, he advocated publicizing the ingredients of the popular beverages. With the naïveté of the nondrinker, he reasoned that if imbibers knew that brandy is made of "rectified spirits, vinegar, orris root, extract of almond cake, cherry-laurel water, and extract of capsicum," that gin is compounded of "oil of vitriol, sulphuric aether, oil of turpentine," and that sherry is composed of "laurel water, benezoin, lamb's blood, chalk and oyster-shells," they would think twice before drinking. Garrison urged that drinkers should be dismissed from their jobs, and that liquor should be prohibited especially on ships, a reform which could easily be effected if insurance companies would offer premiums to the officers and crews of ships that did not use spirits. He suggested, in addition, that certain customs should be changed, that milk would make an excellent substitute for spirits, that housewives (whose potentially great influence on the temperance cause had never been sufficiently recognized) should stop offering the social glass to all callers, and that treating soldiers to a round of drinks should be abolished. But, above all, he urged that drinkers read his paper, and he was so confident of its beneficial effect that he made a special offer: He would give a free subscription to any moderate drinker who failed to save more on his liquor bills through reading the paper than the paper cost.

Liquor was not the only thing proscribed in the *National Philanthropist*. With considerable vehemence Garrison condemned breaking the Sabbath (a position he was later to reverse with equal vehemence), as well as theater-going, dancing, dueling, gambling, swearing, prostitution, and imprisonment for debt. He also condemned war and promoted peace, commending the lectures of William Ladd, who had founded the American Peace Society in May of 1828. Moreover, Garrison showed his abhorrence of slavery by deploring the law passed in South Carolina prohibiting the teaching of Negroes to read and write: "There is something unspeakably pitiable and alarming in the state of that society where it is deemed necessary, for self-preservation, to seal up the mind and debase the intellect of man to brutal incapacity." [15]

Already in the *National Philanthropist* Garrison's zeal had extended far beyond the alleged intention of the paper. Even as early as 1828, a germinal year in his development, Garrison tended to be a universal reformer. Perhaps the heady atmosphere of Boston, where so many reforms were originating, may have stimulated this tendency. He was interested in temperance, yes, but he was interested in many other worthy causes as well. In fact, his exuberance led him also into the political realm. He could not resist attacking Andrew Jackson, approving Henry Clay and the protective tariff, and advocating the re-election of Governor Lincoln of Massachusetts. For he was a Federalist—as all gentlemen should be! He resented suggestions that he should not meddle in politics, berating a critical correspondent in footnotes three and a half times the length of his letter.[16] In the paper he also had literary comments, for he attacked John Neal, a minor figure who imagined himself a great author. He condemned the immorality in the lives and works of Tom Moore and Lord Byron, although he recognized their talents as poets.[17]

On the Fourth of July Garrison annnounced that he had relinquished his editorship of the *Philanthropist.* Once more he had edited a paper for only six months, and once more he left with a rather ambiguous statement concerning an "adequate and ample inducement to remain" and his inclination "to pursue a different, though perhaps not a more honorable or beneficial employment."

Late in the summer, while he was working with a committee circulating petitions for the abolition of slavery in the District of Columbia, Garrison was offered another position. He was asked to edit in Bennington, Vermont—at that time served only by a Jackson paper—the *Journal of the Times,* a new weekly which was to advocate the re-election of John Quincy Adams. He accepted the job, though he was reluctant to go to "Varamount" and to borrow from the proprietor of the *Journal* the $100 needed for the move.[18] It was agreed that he should be allowed to discuss miscellaneous moral subjects in addition to the political issues involved with the campaign.[19] It looked like an opportunity to combine moral and political interests—to continue the expansive role he had begun to play as editor of the *Philanthropist.*

In his statement "To the Public" in the first issue (3 October), Garrison explained that the paper was to be independent; "it shall be trammelled by no interest, biased by no sect, awed by no power"—a rather extravagant claim in the light of his political commitments. Moreover, the *Journal* was to be preoccupied with three objects, "which we shall pursue through life, whether in this place or elsewhere—namely, the suppression of intemperance and its associate vices, the gradual emancipation of every slave in the republic, and the perpetuity of national peace." [20] Also, he announced his intention of encouraging a popular and practical education and a profitable national industry. Finally, as though it were the least important aim of the paper, he said he intended to advocate the re-election of John Quincy Adams as president.

Garrison's support of Adams in the *Journal* was unenthusiastic and indirect, for he characteristically spent his time attacking Jackson rather than praising Adams. Typical was an editorial which appeared a week before the election. He thanked God that he had been given the opportunity to denounce "a man whose hands are

crimsoned with innocent blood, whose lips are full of profanity
. . . a buyer and seller of human flesh—a military despot, who
has broken the laws of his country." He said that Jackson had to
recommend him only the fact that he had fought countless duels,
failed in all the offices he had filled, and had been victorious at
New Orleans "at the expense of constitutional rights." Perhaps
thinking of himself among the number, he insisted that a hundred
thousand men could be found "better qualified to fill the Presidential chair than Andrew Jackson." [21]

When Jackson was elected, Garrison was convinced that all was
lost. He prayed to God to save the country from "Vandal innovation," for he feared that the federal government would now be
filled with dishonest and unprincipled men who would repudiate
the worthy past. Even after the initial shock of the election had
passed, he considered the general as ridiculous at the head of the
government as Adams would have been at the head of an army.
And Jackson's inaugural address he thought so puerile that an intelligent sixteen-year-old should have been able to do better.

Following the election of Jackson and during his last months as
editor of the *Journal of the Times* Garrison first thought seriously
of becoming a professional reformer. That he should have considered such a career may have been determined much earlier.

As a child in Newburyport he had been painfully insecure. His
family had been poor from the beginning, and there was tension,
perhaps suppressed but surely perceptible to young Lloyd, between his parents. Then following the Embargo of 1807 the father
had disappeared altogether, and there was no longer even a family.
The boy must have longed for what he lacked. There were the
great Federalist houses on High Street, where he went to collect
scraps from gentlemen's tables to furnish his own family's meager
diet. There were other families happy and prosperous in spite of
the Embargo and even the War of 1812. Afterwards there was
banishment to Lynn and Baltimore, where his mother nursed
others but hardly had time for him. Later came the cobbler's
bench in Haverhill and the yearning for Newburyport, the image
of a lost childhood.

Temporarily, he had been able to establish himself in his birth-
place as apprentice printer and even as editor. But no matter how
hard he worked, no matter how meticulously he dressed, no matter

how vehemently he professed Federalist views, no one forgot that he had been born on School Street. High Street seemed forbidden and unattainable.

Gradually, Garrison came to realize that if he could not establish himself the way others did, he could make a profession of being an outcast. If he could not be the successful Federalist editor, he could courageously devote his life to the problems of others. He could be a reformer, denouncing evil and teaching even the Federalists the rights of man.

As editor of the *Journal* Garrison at first wrote against slavery rather conservatively. He considered the emancipation of all the American slaves in one generation impossible. Slavery in the District of Columbia he selected as the first stone to be removed. Americans must be taught, he insisted, to become as excited over the injustices to the slaves in the nation's capital as they had become during the War of 1812 over the impressment of ten white citizens by a foreign country.[22] He wrote and printed petitions and circulated them to New England postmasters; on the 23rd of January he was able to announce that he had sent to the representative of his Congressional district a petition with 2,352 signatures.

In March (by this time he knew that his editorship of the paper would soon end) he wrote an antislavery poem, a striking contrast to his earlier traditional Fourth of July eulogy of America, and evidence of his developing radicalism. It contained these lines:

> . . . Liberty lies prostrate in the dust,
> With hair dishevelled, and with zone unbound;
>
> . . . .
>
> For here, in this her sanctuary and home,
> Hath Slavery boldly raised his iron throne;
> And men, like household goods or servile beasts,
> Are bought and sold, kidnapped and pirated;
> Branded with red hot irons, scourged with whips,
> Laden with chains that pinch their tender flesh,
> Driven in droves e'en by the capitol,
> Imported from afar, then secretly
> Thrown into narrow cells and prisons drear,
> Till bones and sinews in the market rise;—
> And government looks tamely on the while,

Nor drops a tear of sorrowing sympathy,
Nor moves a finger to relieve th' oppressed.

* * *

Then haul our striped and starry banner down—
. . . .
We will no longer multiply our boasts
Of liberty, till all are truly free.[23]

Although this is hardly a poem of conspicuous aesthetic merit, it is characteristic of Garrison, for it shows the way he suffered personally and emotionally over the institution of slavery. Even at this early date in his career, one needed only to say the word, "slave," and his mind flooded with images of human beings treated as property—"household goods or servile beasts," bought and sold, kidnaped and pirated, branded and whipped, driven in chains by that specious symbol of American freedom, the Capitol in Washington. One can imagine him reaching up with expansive gesture for the flag to tear it down "till all are truly free." Already the reforming instinct had been extensively developed.

This time when his six-months term as editor ended, he somewhat disingenuously bade his readers a proud farewell: "I am to occupy a broader field, and to engage in a higher enterprise: that field embraces the whole country—that enterprise is in behalf of the slave population." He announced that slavery was a subject so crucial to the welfare of the republic that it demanded the most minute investigation, that no issue since the Revolution so richly merited the complete attention of Americans. He hoped that under God he "may be the humble instrument of breaking at least one chain and restoring one captive to liberty: it will amply repay a life of severe toil." [24]

Garrison's stint with the *Journal of the Times* completed his editorial training. It is not difficult to observe the steady development of his powers from the precocious apprentice of the Newburyport *Herald* to the young editor of *The Free Press*, the *National Philanthropist*, and the *Journal of the Times*. In *The Free Press* he showed himself to be a fallible and at times irascible young man whose arrogance antagonized subscribers and friends alike, and whose preoccupation with politics excluded any real interest in reform. As editor of the *National Philanthropist*, however, he learned to control his temper, and, with his instinctive abhorrence for the evils of excessive drinking, he was able to conduct a surprisingly interesting temperance paper, though it was difficult for him to concentrate on moral issues alone. In the *Journal of the Times* he was able to capitalize on his wide interests and to edit, as a result, by far the most readable paper yet.[25]

CHAPTER III

———◆·◆———

Higher Enterprises

WHILE he was editing the *National Philanthropist* and the *Journal of the Times,* Garrison read many exchange papers, but the one that finally focused his attention on the cause of the slave was the *Genius of Universal Emancipation,* a monthly which since 1821 Benjamin Lundy had published sporadically in various parts of the country.

Benjamin Lundy, sixteen years Garrison's senior, was a conscientious Quaker from New Jersey who had gone to Wheeling, Virginia, in his youth to learn the saddler's trade. There he had been appalled by the coffles of Negroes passing through town in the interstate slave trade. As early as 1815 he had founded in Ohio an antislavery group called the Union Humane Society. During the next several years he contributed antislavery material to several western papers, and in 1821 he founded in Mount Pleasant, Ohio, the *Genius,* which he later removed to Tennessee and then to Baltimore. Too active a man to be content with merely editing a reform paper, he was determined to do personally all that he could to help the American Negro. Since colonization of freed Negroes appealed to him as a solution of the Negro's problem, he spent much of his time traveling about the world seeking the ideal place for a colony.

When in March of 1828 Lundy came to Boston and stayed in Garrison's boarding-house, the young editor was much impressed with him. He found him in personal appearance no "figure of a

Hercules," but "like the apostle Paul . . . 'weak and contempt-ible,' " [1] but also like Paul strong, courageous, and devout:

He is one of these rare spirits who rise up in the lapse of many cen-turies, to adore and elevate mankind. We have never met with a more extraordinary being; no one, who succeeded so well in grafting his feelings upon our own. . . . No reformer was ever more devoted, zealous, persevering, or sanguine. He has fought singlehanded against a host, without missing a blow, or faltering a moment; but his forces are rapidly gathering, and he will yet free our land.[2]

Soon after he arrived in Boston, Lundy arranged for a meeting of ministers in Mr. Collier's boarding-house.[3] He spoke to them enthusiastically and eloquently about the problems of emancipa-tion, but all the conservative clergy would do was to recommend to the public Lundy's paper. Garrison, like Lundy a man of action, went further. He devoted two and a half columns of the *Philan-thropist* of the 21st of March to an antislavery editorial and a tribute to Lundy and the *Genius*. The paper he esteemed "the bravest and best attempt in the history of newspaper publications," and the editor he lauded as a Quaker who "seemed to inherit a large portion of the heroic and untiring benevolence of William Penn." In fact, Garrison's editorial read as though Lundy's cam-paign to free the slave were on the verge of success. Lundy's voice, he said, rings like a trumpet all over the country, strong prejudices are yielding, "and public opinion is gathering an influence, which in process of time will become irresistible." It sounded as though all Lundy needed to effect emancipation was the full-time services of William Lloyd Garrison!

So Lundy may have hoped, when early in 1829, shortly before Garrison's six-month term as editor of the *Journal of the Times* expired, he walked all the way from Baltimore to Bennington, Vermont, to persuade the younger man to join him as co-editor of the *Genius of Universal Emancipation*. Garrison was greatly flat-tered by Lundy's proposal, especially since it gave him such a convenient excuse to leave Vermont and a job that cost him hard work and left him in debt. He had been unable to repay Henry S. Hull, the proprietor of the *Journal of the Times*, the $100 he had borrowed six months before, and he had gone $70 further in debt for his board. He left Vermont angry and discouraged, blaming Hull for all his trouble. He vowed he "could fellowship the meanest reptile that crawls better than this contemptible puppy!" [4]

News of Garrison's departure from Vermont was not accompanied by universal lamentation. On the 31st of March, an anonymous letter appeared in the *Vermont Gazette* reviewing "the labours of My Lloyd on the eve of his departure." Garrison was described as a young dandy from Massachusetts, an unbearable egotist who wore elegant silver spectacles and who talked with "the pert loquacity of a blue jay." The correspondent felt Garrison considered himself "a pattern of morality and decency" and superior to "nineteen-twentieths of Bennington county," including the "Green Mountain lass [5] he left to wither in the happy expectation of matrimony." Public opinion, the letter said, has been strongly opposed to Garrison because of his "incompetency to the task" undertaken and his presumptions as "the dictator of whatever is correct in morals or orthodox in religion."

One wintry morning in April of 1829, the Boston dandy and moral arbiter took the stage from Bennington for Brattleborough and then down the Connecticut Valley to Worcester and east to Boston. It was an arduous journey, especially that spring, for a late snowfall covered the ground and drifts were several feet thick along the roads. The trip to Brattleborough alone took a full day. The horses slipped, broke through the snow, and fell down repeatedly. Garrison had plenty of time for thought: thought of how hard he had worked as editor of three papers in rapid succession and of how little he had to show for his efforts, little, that is, except debts; thought of frustrating self-sacrifice; thought about joining Lundy as assistant editor of the *Genius* mingled with doubts about the practicality of undertaking such a venture; and, finally, the decision that the security of a journeyman printer's berth in Boston might be preferable to another editorial position.

He arrived in Boston, settled in the Reverend Mr. Collier's boarding-house, trusting that Mr. Collier could early find him a printing job, but he was mistaken. Humiliating months passed while he looked for work. As his debts mounted, Lloyd, to his regret, had to accept the generosity of his friends. He could find no immediate employment, although there were vague promises of a job after the Fourth of July.

In June something happened that took his mind off his bad luck. He was invited by the Congregational Societies in the city to give the Fourth of July address at the Park Street Church. Here was recognition if not security. He forgot about job hunting and set to work on the speech. He expected a good job right after the Fourth anyway, and he could always "take the stage for Newburyport, and *dig on* at the cast for Mr. Allen." [6]

Before he had finished writing the lecture, however, he had a humiliating, if thought-provoking, experience. Two weeks after his arrival in Boston he received a notice to appear for the May muster of the militia. This he ignored on the grounds that he was always excused from training because of his myopia. Unhappily, on the 24th of June he was presented with a bill for $4 for failure to appear at the muster. He explained the circumstances to the "poor worthless scamp" who was clerk of the militia company, and said he would not pay the bill—not mentioning that he did not have that much money to his name. But he was unable to avoid the fine; he was humiliated to have to borrow money from Jacob Horton, husband to Martha Farnham, daughter of the family with whom his sister had lived in Newburyport.[7]

Finally, the Fourth arrived, and Garrison in honor of the occasion dressed all in black and wore a white linen collar that spread well out over his waistcoat. The newspaper reported that his first remarks were almost too faint to be heard. (Garrison had admitted a week before in the letter to Jacob Horton that his knees were shaking in anticipation of the lecture.) But soon he gained confidence and spoke out with an earnest voice: "If any man believes that slavery can be abolished without a struggle with the worst passions of human nature . . . he cherishes a delusion." And the worst passions, he insisted, were in the North, not in the South, for Northern prejudices "bristle, like so many bayonets, around the slaves. . . . Conquer them, and the victory is won." The process of emancipation, he said, must be gradual. "The fabric, which now towers above the Alps, must be taken away brick by brick, and foot by foot, till it is reduced so low that it may be overturned without burying the nation in its ruins." It will take time: "Generations of blacks may go down to the grave, manacled and lacerated, without a hope for their children." But the crusade will continue until the ultimate victory, which is "worth the desperate struggle of a thousand years." Garrison went on to appeal specifically to the clergy, to editors, to women. He urged the formation of abolition societies to free the slaves first in the District of Columbia and then in the country as a whole.[8] It was a memorable speech marked by a new maturity of thought and expression and animated by unmistakable dedication.

Garrison was sufficiently encouraged by the Fourth of July speech to stop looking for a job in Boston and plan definitely to join Lundy as co-editor of the *Genius of Universal Emancipation* in Baltimore. During the five or six weeks before he left Boston, he had time to rethink his position regarding emancipation. He decided that immediate emancipation was more logical than gradual; for, he reasoned, if slavery were considered right for a single moment, then it might be justified for weeks or months or even years. Where Garrison encountered the new idea is uncertain. But immediatism had been enunciated in this country as early as 1815 by three leaders of the Tennessee Manumission Society and in 1816 by George Bourne of Virginia in his *The Book and Slavery Irreconciliable*. And British abolitionists had espoused the idea about six years before Garrison did.

Some time in August he set off by regular packet for Baltimore. He must have been reminded of that first voyage to Baltimore with his mother, more than a decade before. But how everything had changed! He had been a boy homesick for Newburyport; now he was a man committed to "the cause of God's suffering creatures." He was a man strong of purpose and confident of ultimate success. Already he could almost hear "a hundred presses . . . cheering us onward," and "the prayers of good men . . . lifted up in our behalf." The eyes of the country were upon him, and "the grateful benison of the poor slave" could be heard "in many a melting accent." He only hoped "that public expectation, high as it is, will not be disappointed." The voyage to Baltimore could not be too fast to suit him. Unfortunately, however, the wind died down, and the vessel was becalmed "day after day, . . . with sails flapping, and a hot sun blazing" and there was nothing to see "but an illimitable plain of water, as if a second deluge had come over the habitable world." It took the packet fifteen days to complete the trip the new steamboat could do in forty-eight hours. By the end of the voyage Garrison's patience had worn thin.[9]

The first number of the new series of the *Genius of Universal Emancipation* appeared 2 September 1829. It was a handsome sheet, decorated at the top with a stunning eagle and the motto "E PLURIBUS UNUM" and with the line "EDITED AND PUBLISHED BY BENJAMIN LUNDY AND WM. LLOYD GARRISON" beneath the title. On the editorial page Lundy explained the new publishing arrangement, that he had been searching for some time for a competent assistant, but that the cause was so unpopular and the pay so low that he had had difficulty finding one. Now, however, at long last, he had succeeded in discovering a man already known to the public as an advocate of the sacred cause of emancipation. With the joint efforts of his assistant and himself he planned to expand the *Genius* and to publish it regularly once a week. In a second paragraph Lundy commended another new assistant as "an amiable and highly talented female writer" who was to be in charge of "a Ladies' Department, to be devoted, as her motto expressed it, to 'philanthropy and literature.'" Lundy recommended Elizabeth Margaret Chandler to the reader so cordially that one would have forgiven Garrison for being a little piqued at the enthusiasm. This first issue was also adorned with A.O.B.'s poem, "The Slave Trade," its elevated sentiments somewhat demeaned by a rhythm that sounded more like a nursery rhyme than a moralistic appeal.

More important than the poem was Garrison's long editorial, expressing quite explicitly his views on abolition: that the project for colonizing freed Negroes in other countries is at best a temporary expedient; that abolitionists must not rely too heavily on colonization societies to solve their problems; "that the slaves are entitled to immediate and complete emancipation . . . ; that the question of expedience has nothing to do with that of right"; that, moreover, it would be more expedient to set the slaves free today rather than tomorrow; and finally, "that, as a very large proportion of our colored population were born on American soil, they are at liberty to choose their own dwelling place, and we possess no right to use coercive measures in their removal."

Garrison's views were not shared by Lundy, who believed in gradual emancipation and in colonization. But it was agreed that the two editors would avoid conflict in the paper by each signing his own editorials.

Immediate emancipation was not the only one of Garrison's favorite ideas to find expression in the *Genius*. In the issue for

16 September he paid his disrespects to the militia system and began to develop the doctrine of nonresistance, justifying his view by reference to his own personal experience. The system is "a fruitful source of intemperance," and its laws are for the benefit of the rich and a burden to the poor as his own experience testified. It was possible for "a saucy, smooth-faced son of Vulcan" to cause him great hardship for failure to appear at a muster in Boston, even though he had the double plea of nearsightedness and non-resistance principles. He swore he would suffer imprisonment and persecution rather than ever bear arms.

Garrison was happy with his new position. He was an editor of "the bravest and best attempt in the history of newspaper publication." He was praised not only by Lundy but by other local editors. The Winchester (Maryland) *Republican* commended his education and experience and even his prudence and discretion, qualities which Garrison was alleged to possess in greater abundance than his co-editor.[10] He was to enjoy a pleasant equilibrium for several months while he edited the *Genius* with good humor, taking in stride occasional carping criticism. In one issue he even reported the success of the Ladies' Fair for the benefit of the American Colonization Society, although money was raised by such a "fashionable immorality" as the raffle. And when the editor of a local paper said that the fair was worth all of the issues of the *Genius* from now until Doomsday, Garrison rose to the occasion: "Now this we call a *fair* hit, and withal very complimentary. But we don't exactly coalesce in this opinion. We are half afraid that the ladies, by their late exhibition enslaved more (hearts,) than they will emancipate (bodies.)" [11]

But all this was merely happy prelude. In the issue for November 13 under the section labeled "BLACK LIST" appeared the following paragraph:

DOMESTIC SLAVE TRADE

This horrible traffic continues to be pursued with unabated alacrity. Scarcely a vessel, perhaps, leaves this port for New-Orleans, without carrying off in chains large numbers of the unfortunate blacks. The ship Francis, Brown, [Master] which sailed hence a few weeks since, transported *seventy-five*. This vessel hails from my native place, (Newburyport, Mass.) and belongs to *Francis Todd*.—So much for New

England principle!—Next week I shall allude more particularly to this damning affair.

The next week Garrison, resolving "to cover with thick infamy all who were concerned in this nefarious business" devoted a full column of the BLACK LIST section to Francis Todd and his ship. He made generous use of the names of the captain and the owner, dignifying the latter with boldface capitals and plenty of white space. He insisted that men who engage in the slave trade, foreign or coastal, in order to accumulate wealth, should be

☞ SENTENCED TO SOLITARY CONFINEMENT ☜
FOR LIFE:

they are the enemies of their own species—highway robbers and mur-derers; and their final doom will be, unless they speedily repent, *to occupy the lowest depths of perdition.*

There were more personal aspersions on Mr. Todd: People in Newburyport, Garrison said with the malicious satisfaction of the underprivileged Newburyport boy, often wondered how Mr. Todd managed to make more profitable voyages to New Orleans and other ports than his competitors. "The mystery seems to be unravelled. Any man can gather up riches, if he does not care by what means they are obtained." Then followed more details: that the *Francis* carried seventy-five slaves, chained in narrow confine-ment between the decks, and that Captain Brown—and he a Mason!—had wanted to take twice as many, but he was underbid for the other seventy-five by another unconscionable captain. "Where was his charity or brotherly kindness?" Garrison ques-tioned. The editorial ended with a promise to send Mr. Todd a copy of this issue of the *Genius* and with a request to the editor of the Newburyport *Herald* for a maximum of publicity.

There was no immediate response from either Todd or Allen, and Garrison made no further reference to the *Francis* or her un-happy cargo during the remaining weeks of the year. Instead, the sheets of the paper were devoted to more routine matters: tem-perance, colonization to Haiti, slave sales, treatment of the Indians, and Andrew Jackson's fight with the United States Bank. Garrison, by the way, continued to berate Jackson and to urge recharter.

Lloyd even had the leisure to offer in the leading editorial of the issue for 1 January 1830—a custom he was to continue during his career as editor—an effusion concerning his twenty-fifth birthday.[12] His mood was ebullient: "I am now sailing up a mighty bay," he said, "with a fresh breeze and a pleasant hope—the waves are rippling merrily, and the heavens are serenely bright. I have encountered many a storm of adversity—rough, and cruel, and sudden—but not a sail has been lost, nor a single leak sprung."

The next week Garrison reported that a libel suit had been instigated against the editors of the paper by Francis Todd. This suit was followed shortly thereafter by criminal proceedings, Lundy not being named in the indictment because he had been out of town at the time of the alleged libel. And, crowning misfortune, the subscribers were not paying for their subscriptions in advance; in four months not more than $50 had been collected.

Once more Garrison lost his editorship at the end of six months. In March 1830 the weekly publication of the *Genius* terminated. Lundy in a final editorial explained the reasons for the failure and said that, although he disapproved of a few articles Garrison had published, he wished to "commend the young editor for strict integrity, amiable deportment, and virtuous conduct, during the period of our acquaintance." In the future he planned to restrict the paper to the subject of emancipation and to publish it monthly.[13]

Six weeks after the demise of the weekly *Genius*, Garrison was tried by jury and found guilty of criminal libel, and fined $50 plus costs or a total of approximately $100—more money than Garrison could possibly raise. On the 17th of April he was welcomed to Baltimore jail by derisive cries from neighboring cells: "Fresh fish! Fresh fish!"

Garrison's stay in prison was neither unpleasant nor unprofitable. Even the first night he slept long and soundly, and in the morning he inscribed a poetical bulletin to posterity on his wall. The prison routine gave Lloyd time to write a series of poems— most of them sonnets and all of them more or less directly concerned with his immediate predicament. The most famous of these, "Freedom of the Mind," is probably his most effective poem, though it leans rather heavily on Lovelace's "To Althea from

Prison." He had time, also, to stand on the bed and look out on the Baltimore street from a high round window. On one occasion when he saw crowds of churchgoers caught by a sudden Sunday shower, he felt like the criminal who, standing on the scaffold with the rope around his neck enjoyed the safety of his elevated position while down below a maddened bull rushed among the screaming spectators.

He was treated by the warden with courtesy and was allowed to visit other prisoners and occasionally to receive visits in return. He helped some of the prisoners write petitions to the governor. One of these, a huge burly fellow, the proud possessor of a double set of teeth, had been given a life sentence for highway robbery, but his conduct had been so good for years that Garrison's petition brought him a pardon. Lloyd was also allowed to have guests from outside. Benjamin Lundy came to see him almost every day, and his boyhood friend Isaac Knapp, who had come from Newburyport to work on the paper, was a frequent visitor.

An even greater pleasure was permitted. He was allowed to question slaveholders who had come in search of runaway slaves. One day he listened to the conversation between a poor fugitive and his master. The Negro pretended he had never seen the white man before, but his memory was revived by mention of the thirty-nine lashes administered under the apple trees and the flogging in the barn. For a time Lloyd listened to the interrogation in silence. Then, suppressing his anger, as he always seemed able to do on such occasions, he walked up to the Southerner and said calmly: "Sir, what right have you to that poor creature?" The slaveholder looked up innocently and said: "My father left him to me." And Garrison asked him if he would be justified in keeping money his father left if it had been stolen from a bank? The slaveholder seemed utterly amazed to hear such ideas—and in jail at that! The conversation went on at length, with the Southerner trying to ask Garrison questions that would bring out a latent prejudice against the colored people. When Lloyd admitted his willingness to have a Negro even as president of the United States, his opponent asked the final question: "How would you like to have a black man marry your daughter?" But Lloyd had the answer for this one: "Sir, I am not familiar with *your* practices; but allow me to say, that slaveholders generally should be the last persons to affect fastidiousness on that point; for they seem to be enamoured with *amalgamation.*" [14]

Most important as far as his future was concerned, Lloyd was allowed the unrestricted use of his pen. He carried on an extensive correspondence, writing caustic "cards," as they were called, to his principal opponents—to Francis Todd, to Judge Brice, to Richard W. Gill, the state's attorney, and to Henry Thompson, Todd's agent who had arranged the transportation of the slaves.

He also wrote numerous letters to friends—gay, almost neurotically exuberant letters, describing his incarceration and boasting of his righteousness in telling the truth about a fellow townsman's participation in the nefarious slave trade. "How could he freight his noble vessel with the wretched victims of slavery? Is not the horrible traffic offensive to God, and revolting to humanity?" he asked a friend in Newburyport.[15]

Garrison also had the leisure to write and to have printed an eight-page pamphlet about his trial,[16] which he sent to friends and enemies, hoping to extend the publicity about his persecution. He explained that no incident related to the cause of the slave had excited so much attention as his trial and imprisonment, and that, indeed, his greatest concern was that he "was in danger of being lifted up beyond measure, even in prison, by excessive panegyric and extraordinary sympathy." [17] He found time, also, to write three antislavery lectures which he planned to deliver as soon as he was released.

Garrison considered his imprisonment the ultimate justification of his righteous conduct. He had been frustrated as a child and as an editor. But now he had detected a successful Newburyport merchant in a grievous sin, a sin that had to be publicly condemned. For this novel action Garrison was tried, convicted, and confined. What better demonstration could there be of the evil in the world and of the rectitude of his conduct! No longer was he the unsuccessful printer and editor. No longer was he a lonely misfit. His imprisonment proclaimed him a persecuted leader in the noble cause of abolition.

E. W. Allen's reaction to Garrison's current predicament showed considerable insight into his former apprentice's personality. On the 25th of May he printed in the Newburyport *Herald* an editorial which recounted the main events of Garrison's life and gave Allen's estimate of his character. Allen said that in devoting himself to the cause of emancipation Garrison "is prompted by vanity; that a love of display, and eagerness for notoriety, are the main springs of his devotion," although he did credit him with "pure and fixed resolves to contribute all his powers to the cause of humanity and justice."

As for Garrison's attack on Francis Todd, Mr. Allen thought that he had overstepped himself. Allen considered Todd no more guilty of engaging in domestic slave traffic than if he had moved a man and his family, including slaves, from one port to another. In general, Allen's comments seemed restrained for a man who had himself so recently been the recipient of Garrison's vitriolic barbs. But Garrison of course felt that he had been done an injustice—especially by the innuendo concerning his vanity. If it is vanity, he erupted, to plead "for the poor, degraded, miserable Africans, it is at least a harmless, and I hope, will prove a useful vanity. Would to God it were epidemical!" [18] Garrison could rationalize even his least endearing trait. Without such vanity he might never have accomplished all he did—and all he was destined to do.

In the meantime, Garrison's *Sketch of the Trial* had borne fruit in New York. It came into the hands of the benevolent Arthur Tappan, a thirty-four-year-old New England Puritan, now a silk jobber in New York who had grown rich by establishing the revolutionary one-price system and by looking after the morals of his employees. Mr. Tappan took seriously his obligations as a steward of the Lord, spending a large part of his income on philanthropic enterprises, and he recognized Garrison's case at once as worthy of his support. He wrote to Lundy authorizing him to draw $100 to secure Garrison's release and offering an additional $100 toward the re-establishment of the *Genius* on its old basis.[19]

On 5 June, after seven weeks in jail, Garrison was released. Two days later he was on his way north, seeking information needed by his lawyer for the impending civil suit, and urging friends of the cause to help Lundy and himself re-establish the *Genius* on its weekly basis. But a circular letter which he carried with him indicated that Lundy had persuaded Garrison he would have to modify his tone. "In all discussions, however, we shall aim to preserve a proper dignity of style, and extend a becoming liberality towards our opponents. The work will partake somewhat more of a *literary character* than formerly." The letter also said that Lundy planned "hereafter to remain constantly at home, to superintend the publication &c. himself." [20]

It seems apparent that Lundy and Garrison realized that the difficulty with the *Genius* was the result not of their ideas, but of Garrison's personal attacks. Lundy had made it a policy never to attack individuals, a rule which was difficult for Garrison to observe. Moreover, Garrison's attacks were resented more than Lundy's would have been, since Garrison was more distinctly marked as a Northern man.

On his way to Massachusetts Lloyd stopped by in New York to thank Arthur Tappan. Lewis Tappan reported that his brother was impressed with the young man whose face fairly beamed "with conscious rectitude." As a matter of fact, Garrison was so firmly convinced of the morality of his actions that he felt confident he could trust in Providence to sustain him. He was not disappointed. He reached New York penniless, but he was introduced to a gentleman named Samuel Leggett, who said he had read the pamphlet about Garrison's trial and offered him passage to Rhode Island in the luxurious steamboat *President,* of which he was one of the owners. When he reached Boston, Garrison tried to muster support for re-establishing the *Genius.* But he met with nothing but indifference; Northerners seemed to him more prejudiced than Southern slaveholders. They apologized for the slave system, and even his best friends urged him to give up his plans, as "visionary—fanatical—unattainable." "Why should I make myself an exile from home and all that I held dear on earth, and sojourn in a strange land, among enemies whose hearts were dead to every noble sentiment? &c. &c., &c.. I repeat—*all were against my return.*" [21]

Garrison of course throve on opposition and was the more determined to pursue a career as an abolitionist. The immediate problem was how to get back to Baltimore; again his pockets were empty. But he went to the post office and there found a letter from Mr. Lundy, enclosing a draft for $100 from Ebenezer Dole, formerly from Newburyport and, though a stranger to Garrison, an admirer of his work. Garrison's comment: "Here Providence had again signally interfered in my behalf." [22]

HIGHER ENTERPRISES

For several weeks Garrison remained in Baltimore. But since there seemed little chance of reissuing the *Genius* under the old auspices and even less of winning the civil suit scheduled for trial in the fall, he decided to let the case go by default and make his way back to Boston. A few months later he described his frame of mind:

How do I bear up under my adversities? I answer—like the oak—like the Alps—unshaken, storm-proof. Opposition, and abuse, and slander, and prejudice, and judicial tyranny, are like oil to the flame of my zeal. I am not dismayed; but bolder and more confident than ever. I say to my persecutors,—'I bid you defiance.' Let the courts condemn me to fine and imprisonment for denouncing oppression: Am I to be frightened by dungeons and chains? can they humble my spirit? do I not remember that I am an American citizen? and, as a citizen, a freeman, and what is more, a being accountable to God? I will not hold my peace on the subject of African oppression. If need be, who would not die a martyr to such a cause? [23]

CHAPTER IV

———————◆◆———————

The Liberator

THERE were reasons other than personal ones to be a reformer in the 1830's. By that time, although Holmes had not
yet noted the fact, the "one-hoss shay" of Calvinism had collapsed.
As a result, there had been a drastic dislocation of the whole social
and economic structure of American and especially New England
society. On the intellectual level, Emerson's optimistic transcen-
dentalism and Noyes's perfectionism were being substituted for
the more rigid Puritan theology. The pragmatic outgrowth of
the new conception of man as a being capable of almost infinite
improvement was the reform movement. Though Garrison could
not have known it, the men who were destined to lead that movement were those who had been displaced by the changing order.
For generations the leading citizens of the social order, or the
Protestant ministers of the Gospel, had been recruited from prominent New England families. But now a new industrial class had
acquired the pre-eminent position, leaving the men of family "an
elite without a function, a displaced class in American society." [1]

Happily, it was to this class (the very group with whom he
longed to associate) that Garrison appealed when, in the fall of
1830, he came to Boston to preach abolition. He did not reach
them at once. It was difficult even to find a place to speak in
Boston. After two weeks' search he advertised in the *Courier* for a
hall 'in which to vindicate the rights of TWO MILLIONS of
American citizens." To his embarrassment Garrison had a cordial reply from Abner Kneeland, an unfrocked Universalist min-

ister turned rationalist and pantheist and at the same time the leader of the unsavory First Society of Free Enquirers. But since he was more embarrassed for want of a hall than by Kneeland's rationalist theories, Garrison soon accepted the generous offer and spoke three times at Julien Hall, although not without disclaiming the religious views of his host.

Garrison's new lectures reiterated the ideas he had been expressing in the *Genius,* but there was an important new emphasis. He attacked the American Colonization Society and its plan for settling freed Negroes abroad. The Colonization Society had been founded in 1817 under the sponsorship of Henry Clay, Daniel Webster, James Madison, and John Marshall, and its first president had been Judge Bushrod Washington. For a decade or more it had been generally accepted in North and South alike as a noble Christian enterprise, although it had actually resettled only 15,000 Negroes by 1827. As late as June of 1829 Garrison had spoken in Boston under the auspices of the society. While he worked on the *Genius,* in spite of Lundy's enthusiasm for the project, he had become increasingly critical of colonization, characterizing it as no better than a temporary expedient. In the Boston lectures, however, he confessed regret and shame for ever having said a moderate word about colonization. It was merely a scheme, he said, whereby Southern agents were removing free colored because they considered them a disturbing influence in the country.

Three young men who attended the Boston lectures—Samuel J. May and his cousin Samuel E. Sewall and his brother-in-law A. Bronson Alcott—were especially impressed by what they heard. May and Sewall, both descendants of one of America's first abolitionists, Judge Samuel Sewall, were later to become loyal members of Garrison's inner circle; and May became one of Garrison's closest friends.

In many ways May was the antithesis of Garrison. He was both Boston-born and Boston-bred. His father, Colonel Joseph May, was a prosperous merchant, descended from a family that had settled in Roxbury, Massachusetts, as early as 1641, and his mother was a Sewall. He was brought up by devoted parents and given the best possible education at ma'am schools, at Harvard College, and at the Divinity School. In personality he was quiet and gentle; in physique he was frail. By 1830 May had been for five years the

Unitarian minister of Brooklyn, Connecticut. Two men could hardly have been less alike both in background and in personality than Garrison and May, but they both hated vice, corruption, servitude. May had been horrified during a trip in Washington and Virginia to see the coffles of slaves chained painfully together; he had been greatly impressed by Benjamin Lundy, who visited Brooklyn, Connecticut, in 1828; he had become a total abstainer; and he was an enthusiastic advocate of the peace views of William Ladd.

Such was the man who came with his friends to hear Garrison lecture at Julien Hall on Saturday evening, 16 October 1830. May thought Garrison's was the most effective speech he had ever heard. Afterward he and Sewall and Alcott introduced themselves. "Mr. Garrison," May said, "I am not sure that I can endorse all you have said this evening. Much of it requires careful consideration. But I am prepared to embrace you. I am sure you are called to a great work, and I mean to help you." Sewall and Alcott were also enthusiastic, and the four men went off to Alcott's house, where they talked—or listened to Garrison—until midnight. May admitted: "That night my soul was baptized in his spirit, and ever since I have been a disciple and fellow-laborer of William Lloyd Garrison." [2]

The next morning, immediately after breakfast, May went to Garrison's boarding-house. They talked until two in the afternoon. Garrison told the older man (May was eight years his senior) all about himself: that he was poor, entirely dependent upon his own labor for support, and that he planned "to return to the printing business." But before he could concentrate on his own livelihood, he had to inform the world of the evils of slavery and the necessity for emancipation. With evident gusto Garrison read aloud what May called "eloquent, solemn, impressive" letters to many prominent men, including William Ellery Channing, Lyman Beecher, and Daniel Webster. The two young reformers lamented that none of the famous would espouse the cause of abolition.

But Samuel May would espouse the cause—and did. The following Sunday he preached by invitation in the Summer Street Church. His topic was prejudice against the Negro. God, he warned, will not accept prejudice as an "excuse for our indifference to the wrongs and outrages inflicted upon these millions of our countrymen." As he rose to give the benediction, May said:

I have been prompted to speak thus by the words I have heard during the past week from a young man hitherto unknown, but who is, I believe, called of God to do a greater work for the good of our country than has been done by any one since the Revolution. I mean William Lloyd Garrison. He is going to repeat his lectures the coming week. I advise, I exhort, I entreat—would that I could compel!—you to go and hear him.

As soon as the benediction was over, the regular minister of the church upbraided May for violating "the propriety of his pulpit." (He was never invited to preach there again.) The audience gathered in excited clusters after the service. All were startled by the outburst of the visiting minister. Some of them admired his courage, but most of them thought him fanatical and traitorous.[3]

May and Sewall urged Garrison to repeat his first lecture, and they engaged Athenaeum Hall for his use. On this and other occasions, Sewall provided the practical advice so much needed by a zealous reformer. It was he who insisted there must be notices of the forthcoming lecture in the Boston papers and offered to pay for advertisements and even to apply personally to the editors of the *Daily Advertiser* and the *Patriot,* if need be.[4] Without the support—financial as well as moral—of May and Sewall, Garrison might never have launched his career as abolitionist, and he also would probably not have chosen Boston as the place to publish his paper.[5]

It was not difficult for Garrison to convince himself that Boston rather than Washington was the place for his paper. Lundy had decided on Washington, and no city—not even Washington—could support two such papers. Moreover, if a few lectures could bring response from prominent men like May and Sewall, think what a systematic campaign could do! Also, Boston seemed like home to Garrison—more like it even than Newburyport, which had recently spurned him when he wanted to lecture there.

There were other more sophisticated reasons why Boston was a good choice. It was the center of liberal thought. Channing, Emerson, and others were rapidly modifying the rigid Calvinism of their forebearers to make it consistent with the optimistic view implicit in the Declaration of Independence. Not only were all men created free and equal but they were capable, according to Emerson, of virtually infinite perfectibility. If England, where various reforms had been initiated early in the century, could respond to the reformer's zeal, surely New England could be even more liberal. And Boston, the intellectual nerve center, must nurture the new ideas "by the very firmness and narrowness which the Puritan intellect produced." [6]

Garrison realized, however, that much had to be done before he could count on any general support for his paper. First, he had to have a suitable organ to disseminate the truth about abolition and other reforms. He knew that he could count on the complete support of May and Sewall and, to some extent, of Arthur Tappan in New York; and shortly he was to find that he could depend on another aristocratic Boston lawyer, Ellis Gray Loring. He persuaded the printer Isaac Knapp, an old Newburyport friend and fellow roomer at Collier's boarding-house, to become his partner. He prevailed upon his good friend and confidant Stephen Foster, foreman of the *Christian Examiner,* to allow Knapp and him use of the *Examiner*'s type in return for a certain amount of journeyman work on Foster's paper.[7] He enlisted the services of May to find an empty room at 6 Merchants Hall, which was to serve as home and office for the two partners. Finally, he purchased, not without difficulty, the necessary supplies.

But the organizational and physical problems were slight compared to the difficulties of getting subscribers. Garrison must have spent much of his time during the last weeks of the year writing letters to friends and acquaintances asking for help.[8] Some of his letters brought results. James Forten, Negro sailmaker of Philadelphia, sent Garrison on 31 December $54 as payment for twenty-seven subscriptions. Others, though less spectacularly successful, did what they could. Samuel J. May was hard at work in Brooklyn, Connecticut. Simeon S. Jocelyn, engraver and reformer, was helping in New Haven. Charles W. Denison of Stonington, Massachusetts, minister, reformer, and later editor, wrote: "In my own ineffectual way, I will endeavor to prove myself a brother *indeed*." [9] A man named George Cary was seeking subscribers as far away as Pittsburgh and Cincinnati.[10] Gradually during the early months of 1830 the number of subscribers increased, especially among the colored. By February Garrison had ninety subscribers in Philadelphia and thirty in New York, and he expected a hundred from the latter city in a few weeks. By the end of May the paper had a total of five hundred "voluntary" subscribers—a high percentage of them Negroes and only twenty-five in all from Boston.[11]

The first number of *The Liberator* appeared with the new year. On Saturday, 1 January, a handful of subscribers were sent a small, unimpressive-looking sheet, four pages, nine by fourteen and a quarter inches, with four columns to the page. Physically it looked mild and colorless by comparison with the *Genius*. There was no cut at the top of the first page, simply THE LIBERATOR in boldface capitals, beneath which were the names of the two publishers, and then in smaller capitals, the inscription OUR COUNTRY IS THE WORLD—OUR COUNTRYMEN ARE MANKIND.[12] At the head of the first column were Garrison's name as editor and Stephen Foster's as printer, as well as the terms for subscriptions. It was stated that the subcription rate was $2 annually, that agents were to be allowed every sixth copy free, and that all communications with the paper must be postpaid. Following this information was a salutation to the public in verse, probably by Elizabeth Margaret Chandler, who had written so many poems for the *Genius*. More genuinely poetic than the young lady's verse, however, was Garrison's own prose manifesto that began toward the bottom of this same first column:

I am aware, that many object to the severity of my language; but is there not cause for severity? I *will be* as harsh as truth, and as uncompromising as justice. On this subject I do not wish to think, or speak, or write, with moderation. No! no! Tell a man whose house is on fire, to give a moderate alarm; tell him to moderately rescue his wife from the hands of the ravisher; tell the mother to gradually extricate her babe from the fire into which it has fallen;—but urge me not to use moderation in a cause like the present. I am in earnest—I will not equivocate—I will not excuse—I will not retreat a single inch— AND I WILL BE HEARD.[13]

This, the most famous passage in all of Garrison's writings, is of central importance to an understanding of Garrison's personality. As a child he seldom had an audience. His mother was too busy to listen. First, she was preoccupied with trying to reform an alcoholic husband. Later, she was busy nursing to earn a livelihood. And even after she had moved to Baltimore and become sufficiently prosperous to have some leisure time, she preached rather than listened. Back in Newburyport Garrison sought the recognition his mother had failed to give him. He did odd jobs and worked around the house for Deacon Bartlett. He even tried being an apprentice for a shoemaker in Haverhill. But no one appreciated him. No one would listen. It was only when he became apprenticed to Mr. Allen and started publishing anonymous letters in the paper that he found an audience. The knowledge that he had listeners, whether they admired or reviled him, always sustained Garrison, no matter what the misfortune. He did not mind being jailed. He did not mind being persecuted. He did not fear death. Anything, so long as people would listen.

In his struggle to be heard Garrison had learned long before he founded *The Liberator* to supply the reader with a variety of material. In this first issue he stated the credo explicitly: "It will be our endeavor to diversify the contents of the Liberator, so as to give an edge to curiosity, and relieve the eye and mind of the reader. One page will be devoted to foreign and domestic transactions; another, to literary, miscellaneous and moral subjects." The "foreign and domestic transactions" were limited largely to reform of one kind or another as were also the literary—especially Garrison's own flights into verse. Garrison was his own favorite poet, if we may judge by the first number of *The Liberator,* where there were four signed poems by him and one unsigned, though probably his—a total of 113 lines, all of them less than inspired. But the miscellaneous items offered greater variety. There were paragraphs on education, alchemy, weeping (young women "will weep as bitterly for the loss of a new dress as for the loss of an old lover"), brave correspondence, meditation, and brevity; and there was a story about "the grain of mustard seed and the tulip root."

Garrison delineated five groups he was determined to reach: the religious, from whom he expected great encouragement; the philanthropic, from whom he expected pity and also relief; the patriotic, from whom he expected unselfish love of country; and *"the ignorant, the cold-hearted, the base,* THE TYRANNICAL," whom he planned to instruct, to reclaim, and to humanize. Above all others he expected to be heard by the free colored, for "we know that you are now struggling against wind and tide"—like ourselves, he might have added.

Labor, a struggling group that was to become more articulate as the century passed, offered great potentiality as an audience; but Garrison, perhaps owing partly to his reluctance to admit that he himself was a working man, failed to realize its significance. He said in this first issue of *The Liberator* that he regretted that attempts are being made "to enflame the minds of our working classes against the more opulent, and to persuade men that they are contemned and oppressed by a wealthy aristocracy." He admitted there were individual grievances, but he insisted that "they are not confined to any one class of society." He considered it "in the highest degree criminal" to incite laborers "to deeds of violence, or to array them under a party banner. . . . Labour is not dishonorable. The industrious artisan, in a government like ours, will always be held in better estimation than the wealthy idler. . . . We are the friends of reform; but this is not reform which in curing one evil, threatens to inflict a thousand others."

A few weeks later Garrison printed a long letter on the labor problem from Samuel Whitcomb, Jr., in which the parallel between the lot of the slave and the lot of the laborer was emphasized. This letter elicited a full editorial from Garrison, which argued as follows: It is of the nature of things, even in a republic, that there be many social and economic inequalities. The existence of these inequalities does not imply oppression or even a denial of human rights. To say that the wealthy are enemies of the people is pernicious. Indeed, those who would teach such ideas are the true enemies of the people. Although there are undoubtedly some abuses of wealth, there is no evidence whatever "that our wealthy citizens, as a body, are hostile to the interests of the laboring classes." In fact, he concluded, "if our mechanics do not retain their due proportion of power and influence, theirs is the fault." [14]

The argument continued a week later with another letter from Whitcomb and another editorial from Garrison. This time the young editor, somewhat chastened, admitted that he too was a workingman: "It cannot be supposed that we, who perform every day but the Sabbath *fourteen hours* of manual labor on our paper, independent of mental toil; it cannot be supposed that we are inimical to the prosperity or improvement of the working fraternity." But he mustered Burke to support his view that to level society was never to equalize individuals but rather to make a fruitless effort to change "the natural order of things." [15] Like most of his well-born associates among the abolitionists, Garrison remained conservative on the labor question. He had infinite capacity to sympathize with the slave but little to sympathize with the oppressed laborer.

In *The Liberator* as usual, Garrison's favorite subjects were himself, his persecution, and his probable martyrdom. In the first number he discussed his second Baltimore trial at length, quoting from the Baltimore *Gazette* a report of the trial, which included for the benefit of those readers who might not have been up to date on their new editor's activities all the details of his attack on Francis Todd. In spite of the unfavorable outcome of the suit, he insisted: "I will not hold my peace on the subject of African oppression. If need be, who would not die a martyr to such a cause?" This martyrdom theme is central to Garrison's personality. It recurs again and again in his editorials, his speeches, his personal letters, and his verse. It would seem that he felt the closer he approached martyrdom the greater would be the success of his agitation on behalf of the slave.

In the third issue of *The Liberator* (15 January 1831) he printed on the first page a column headed "PANEGYRIC," in which he reprinted attacks on himself from several Southern papers, as though he were setting up a kind of scoreboard of his achievement. Self-righteously he claimed to be almost totally indifferent to the defamation of his enemies. "If I have enemies—I forgive them— I am the enemy of no man. My memory can no more retain the impression of anger, hatred or revenge, than the ocean the track of its monsters." He was grateful, he said the next month, for adverse criticism, though he hated praise: "In print, all encomiums upon me are painful; and I can read with far less emotion, twenty columns of abuse, than twenty lines of panegyric." [16]

Some of the topics Garrison discussed in the early issues of *The Liberator* seemed to have been selected almost because they were controversial and would generate adverse criticism. He expatiated on intermarriage, prostitution, and insurrection. He urged the repeal of the Act of 1786 which fined a minister for joining white and colored in marriage on the grounds that it obstructed a man's pursuit of happiness.[17]

Although he admitted that mixed marriages at the present time were in bad taste, he would not concede that they were unnatural. He was especially amused by the case of Colonel Richard Johnson. Johnson was in many ways a remarkable and energetic man. He had all the courage and dash of the frontiersman combined with the charm of the patrician Southerner. Born in what was later Louisville, Kentucky, he was a lawyer by profession, an Indian fighter by preference. He was a member of Congress for a dozen years, a senator for ten, and an intimate associate of President Jackson's. In 1837 he was to become vice president under Van Buren ("Rumpsey, Dumpsey, Colonel Johnson killed Tecumseh.") But what interested Garrison about Johnson was his persistence in living in sin with a mulatto slave woman he had inherited from his father. Garrison reported that he had read nothing since he started to edit *The Liberator* that had given him greater pleasure than the commentary on one episode in Colonel Johnson's life. The colonel appeared at a gala celebration of the Fourth of July with his colored daughter. The proper Kentucky ladies were much shocked when the good colonel, principal speaker of the day, took his daughter with him under the awning to dance. Johnson was politely but firmly informed that he must "withdraw" his daughter, and so he escorted her to the carriage to wait while he orated about the Declaration of Independence and the equality of man.

Garrison made it clear that he did not wish to defend Colonel Johnson for his libertinism, but that he did want to point out that the disgust shown by the Kentuckians was not due to his immorality but to the color of his daughter's skin. Garrison expressed his views in a long essay on prejudice.[18] A month later Garrison reprinted another item about Colonel Johnson—namely, that when the colonel was remonstrated with by friends for his immorality, he said that if they did not stop bothering him, he would *marry* the girl.[19]

As for prostitution, Garrison gave a good deal of publicity to the First Annual Report of the Executive Committee of the New York Magdalen Society—a report which had brought forth such indignant response from newspaper editors that Garrison, with no factual evidence whatever, questioned whether they might not be "implicated in the disreputable business." The problems raised by the report, Garrison thought, were worth serious consideration since there were in New York in addition to private harlots— the class to which he would probably have consigned Colonel Johnson's poor Julia Chin—at least ten thousand prostitutes. He compared the lot of the ten thousand with that of the half-million adult female slaves in the South whose masters constantly subjected them to enforced prostitution.

In the first number of *The Liberator* Garrison referred to an incendiary pamphlet written by David Walker, whom he considered the best promoter of insurrection ever "sent forth to an oppressed people." A free Negro born in Wilmington, North Carolina, in 1785, Walker had acquired sufficient education to read and write. He had traveled extensively in the South observing the degradation of the slaves, but by 1827 he was settled in Boston running a second-hand clothing business. He would have remained unknown but for the seventy-six page pamphlet, *Walker's Appeal*,[20] which in 1829 and in 1830 went through three editions —each one revised to be more incendiary than the one before. The pamphlet consisted of a closely reasoned and often eloquent argument against slavery, urging the slaves to rise up if necessary and overthrow their oppressors, but also advising them to forgive those masters that could be persuaded to free them voluntarily. Since the pamphlet was not sponsored by Garrison or any other recognized abolitionist, Walker was obliged to circulate it himself. A sufficient number of copies penetrated the South to alarm many slaveholders. In Southern ports incoming ships were searched for the offensive document; in Georgia its circulation was made a capital offense, and rewards were offered for Walker's head. The mayor of Savannah went so far as to complain to Harrison Gray Otis, mayor of Boston, who explained that Walker's offense did not fall within the jurisdiction of Massachusetts laws. Walker died the following spring (March 1830)—poisoned by his enemies, many people said.

Of course, Garrison as a nonresistant deplored bloodshed and violence and could not accept Walker's reasoning, but he condoned the *Appeal*, as he was later to condone the Civil War, by saying that Walker was really only following the creed of the guilty American people who had supplied him with all his arguments and all his methods: "Our guilty countrymen are the ones who put arguments into the mouths, and swords into the hands of the slaves. Every sentence that they write—every word that they speak—every resistance that they make, against foreign oppression, is a call upon their slaves to destroy them." [21]

Garrison gave Walker's pamphlet a maximum of publicity in *The Liberator*. He reprinted a number of articles from other papers on the subject, and he devoted the entire first pages of three issues to an anonymous review of the work.[22]

However, it took a different type of person from Walker to translate the *Appeal* into action. Nat Turner was born on a Virginia plantation in 1800, the son of a primitive slave woman and an unnamed man who ran off while Nat was still a child. Recognizing Nat's ability, one of his master's sons gave him a basic elementary education. Gradually, with the encouragement of his mother and others, the young Negro developed into a religious fanatic who believed himself chosen to lead the slaves out of bondage. As the years passed, visions and voices counseled him. In 1831 an eclipse of the sun foretold an impending insurrection. The Fourth of July and then 21 August were selected for the dire event. At first four and then three more slaves joined with Turner, and on the appointed day they rose up and mutilated thirteen men, eighteen women, and twenty-four children. With the blood of the slain, Nat christened his followers. But the revolt collapsed as soon as it met armed resistance, and on 25 August Nat went into hiding.

On 3 September Garrison, forgetting his nonresistance principles, gloated over the event with the self-righteous satisfaction of an Old Testament prophet. What he had long predicted, he said, was beginning. The first tremor of the earthquake, the first drops of blood, the first flash of lightning had announced the coming catastrophe. Turning his attention more directly on the massacre, he seemed almost to enjoy the images of slaughter that swept before his eyes: "The dead bodies of white and black lying just as they were slain, unburied—the oppressor and the oppressed equal at last in death!"

Who was really responsible for the insurrection? Garrison asked. The whole country was the answer. The guilt of oppressing the slaves was a guilt which no American could evade. And the rioters themselves had no special responsibility. They had done nothing more reprehensible "than the Greeks in destroying the Turks, or the Poles in exterminating the Russians, or our fathers in slaughtering the British." Only the unselfish abolitionist was guiltless of the horrible insurrection in Virginia. Garrison himself had preached the principles of Christ, had appealed to patriot, philanthropist, and Christian "to accomplish the great work of national redemption through the agency of moral power." And how had he been received? He had been threatened, vilified, imprisoned—made "a laughing-stock and a reproach." But falter he would not. "We shall cry, in trumpet tones, night and day,—Wo to this guilty land. . . . The blood of millions of her sons cries aloud for redress! IMMEDIATE EMANCIPATION can alone save her from the vengeance of Heaven, and cancel the debt of ages!"

Garrison had come a long way—at least in his own eyes—since the days of his childhood and youth in Newburyport and indeed since the days of his frustrations as editor. The once lonely poor boy, the debt-ridden editor, the imprisoned martyr were no more. Or rather they were all stages in the glorious incarnation of the righteous reformer of 1831. For Garrison during the first year of *The Liberator* was still alone, but this time he was right and the rest of the country, with the exception of his few followers, was wrong. It was he who could lead misguided, sin-ridden Americans from the degradation of slavery to the rectitude of freedom. Events like the Turner uprising in Virginia would provide him with the ammunition for his crusade.

Garrison reported in *The Liberator* all he could find concerning the remaining six weeks of Nat Turner's life: the lugubrious details of the bloody day of the insurrection, Turner's escape and hiding in a cave only a couple of miles from the scene of the slaughter, his accidental discovery and capture, his lengthy confession (which was published in an edition of 50,000 copies in Baltimore) and his manly bearing at the execution on 18 November.[23]

Garrison's reaction to *Walker's Appeal* and to Turner's insurrection prefigured his later reaction to John Brown and to the Civil War. Like most prophetic men of action, he cared little for consistency. He persisted in his noble goal, emancipation of the

Negro, never compromising that goal but sometimes rationalizing the means. Yes, he was a nonresistant and would not himself fight nor even, later in his career, vote. But he would forgive the sins of those who fought successfully for the goal he longed for. In fact, he could on occasion take an almost sadistic delight in righteous slaughter.

Nat Turner's insurrection gave Garrison infinitely more publicity than he had given it. Although there is no evidence that Garrison in any way influenced the rebel, Southerners insisted that he and his paper were the real culprits. It was true that, even though it had no subscribers below the Potomac, *The Liberator* already had had a surprising influence in the South. The paper was exchanged with approximately a hundred Southern papers, whose editors found Garrison's words so eminently quotable that many Southern readers considered the Boston editor the apotheosis of Northern abolitionism.

After Nat Turner's uprising Garrison's fame was increased a thousandfold. He was attacked by countless Southern papers and even by the important *National Intelligencer* in Washington. This paper had reprinted an article from a North Carolina paper which had asserted that *The Liberator* "is published in Boston or Philadelphia, by a white man, with the avowed purpose of inciting rebellion in the South." The article suggested that the incendiary paper was being circulated by secret agents who posed as peddlers and that such creatures should be barbecued. Garrison wrote a long letter to the editors of the *National Intelligencer* defending himself, his paper, his methods—signing it with his full name, lest there be any further doubt as to the identity of the white man in Boston or Philadelphia. This letter he spread across the entire front page of *The Liberator* for 15 October.[24] The only real purpose of his paper, he exhorted, was "to prevent rebellion."

Southern opposition to Garrison spread like a chain reaction. He received countless anonymous letters threatening all kinds of dire results.[25] In Columbia, South Carolina, the Vigilance Association offered $1,500 for the conviction of any white person found circulating *The Liberator* or *Walker's Appeal* within the state. (Garrison suggested that "the numbers of the Liberator are worth more money.")[26] Georgetown, South Carolina, prepared to fine any free Negro who received *The Liberator*. Raleigh, North Carolina, indicted Garrison and his partner for inciting slave revolts. The Georgia legislature drew up a bill offering a reward to any person who arrested Garrison and brought him to trial within the state. In the original draft of the bill, the amount of the reward was left blank. Garrison offered to save the legislature trouble by inserting the following sum: "$999888777, 666555444, 333222111, 000000000." (The reward was later set at a conservative $5,000.) [27] Governor Hamilton of South Carolina sent a special message to his legislature, asserting that the recent uprising in Virginia "was excited by incendiary newspapers and other publications, put forth in the non-slaveholding States and freely circulated within the limits of Virginia." And Hamilton transmitted with his message several sample copies of *The Liberator,* which were sent him as governor of South Carolina.[28]

Governor Hamilton was not the only South Carolinian who was disturbed. Senator Robert Y. Hayne wrote to Mayor Harrison Gray Otis of Boston, demanding action against the editor of *The Liberator.* Otis, who apparently knew little, if anything, of the new paper, investigated and reported to Hayne that the influence of *The Liberator* had been greatly exaggerated, that the paper was really only supported by a few colored people, and that it was unlikely to have any effect among respectable people. Garrison, delighted by all this attention, inserted the following paragraph in his issue for 29 October:

☞ INFORMATION WANTED. The Hon. Robert Y. Hayne of Columbia S.C., (through the medium of a letter,) wishes to know of the Mayor of Boston who sent a number of the Liberator to him, a few weeks ago? The Mayor of Boston (through the medium of a deputy) wishes to know of Mr. Garrison whether he sent the aforesaid number to the aforesaid individual? Mr. Garrison (through the medium of his paper) wishes to know of the Hon. Robert Y. Hayne of Columbia S.C. and the Mayor of Boston what authority they have to put such questions?

Just as he had thrived on the publicity concerning his imprisonment in Baltimore, so Garrison was delighted with the fame and notoriety brought by Nat Turner's uprising. The more he was attacked and reviled, the more justified he felt. He did not expect, he said, to be appreciated by the present generation; he looked only "to posterity for a good reputation. The unborn offspring of those who are now living will reverse the condemnatory decision of my contemporaries." [29] He even compared himself to Christ and his disciples who had been "buffeted, calumniated and crucified." He announced that his soul was "as steady in its pursuit as the needle to the pole."

As the first year of *The Liberator* approached its end, Garrison realized that the time had come to estimate the achievement of his paper. Considering the fact that it was started without subscribers, that it was dependent on its own resources alone, he felt that it "has succeeded beyond our reasonable expectations." To mark its success, he had decided to enlarge the sheet to royal size with the beginning of the new year. Subscribers would subsequently get a third more reading matter for the same price. The enlargement would practically double the expense of producing the paper, and Garrison called upon the friends of abolition to sustain him. "The cause demands a hundred daily presses; larger dimensions must be given to the Liberator." Garrison expressed his gratitude to his agents, and he urged them to continue and even to increase their support since the insurrection in Virginia has "caused the loss of several valuable subscribers in Washington and Baltimore." [30]

In the first number of *The Liberator* Garrison had asked for an audience of the religious, the philanthropic, the patriotic, the base and tyrannical, and the free colored. Of these groups he seemed to have been heard by the last two. The free colored had subscribed to his paper and approved all he had to say. Tyrannical Southern slaveholders and politicians had also marked his words— horrified at what they heard. The resulting opposition gave Garrison the notorious publicity without which his greatest contributions to the antislavery cause could never have been made. Garrison met Southern indignation in the way that he was always to meet opposition. He remained unshaken, self-righteously confident of the absolute rectitude of his position. Instead of shouting in anger, he smiled and suggested that "a brisk trade in straight jackets might be carried on" in the madhouse of the South.

CHAPTER V

———◆·◆———

Brisk Trade

GARRISON'S "brisk trade" did not involve a coherent and far-reaching plan for abolishing slavery. Instead he improvised. Adopting the idea from Great Britain, where thousands of Britons had abstained from slave-produced colonial sugar for forty years, he advocated in *The Liberator,* as he had earlier in the *Genius,* a boycott of the products of slave labor. He printed articles urging the purchase of free goods. He also printed the advertisement of a free-produce store in Philadelphia specializing in sugars, tea, coffee, chocolate, molasses, tobacco, lamp wick, and cotton goods, saying that orders would be taken at *The Liberator* office.[1] He gave publicity to two free-goods stores in New York and urged the establishment of such a store in Boston, asking prospective purchasers to write *The Liberator.*[2] One can imagine that he may have been slightly discomfited when one of his subscribers asked whether the calicos advertised in the columns of *The Liberator* were "the product of free labor." Garrison's answer: "We presume they are not." [3]

During the same year Garrison realized the urgent need for a more careful organization of the antislavery ranks. He had been in correspondence with leading British abolitionists and had learned what an effective part various societies had played in the development of their antislavery agitation. Boycotting the sale of slave-labor products might be of indirect value, but organizing the antislavery forces was essential, he thought, for effective action.[4]

[56]

In a letter to his future brother-in-law on 12 November, he said an antislavery society would soon be founded in Boston, since there were abolitionists who knew the necessity for having "a concentration of moral strength." [5] On the 13th fifteen men met at the office of Samuel E. Sewall on State Street to talk about organizing an antislavery society. In addition to Garrison's earliest supporters (May, Sewall, Loring, and others), the group included a more recent convert, the printer and editor Oliver Johnson. Johnson was a handsome young man, four years Garrison's junior, who had admired Garrison's work as editor of the *Journal of the Times* and was currently himself editing and printing on Garrison's press the *Christian Soldier*. Garrison was enthusiastic and excited over the meeting at Sewall's office, for he fully expected to find among the fifteen an apostolic dozen ready to found a new society dedicated to his principles. He unfolded "his purposes and plans without reserve," Johnson reported, explaining how successful the British had been with societies consecrated to the basic ideal of immediate emancipation. Before the evening was over, Garrison found that his friends were not all true Garrisonites, for it was impossible to find twelve who would declare for immediate emancipation. The meeting was adjourned until 16 December. Samuel J. May, much disappointed, retraced the eighty long miles to Brooklyn, Connecticut.

On the 16th more was accomplished, though without the help of May, who could not face another trip to Boston with the winter closing in. In his place was David Lee Child, a versatile and able man eleven years older than Garrison. He was a Harvard graduate, had been successively teacher, diplomat, soldier, and lawyer, and was at present editor of the *Massachusetts Journal*. Child was added to the Garrisonian nucleus to form a committee to draft a constitution for the new society. At the next meeting, on the first of January, the committee submitted a constitution, which was accepted, although there were violent differences of opinion about the language of the preamble. These meant a further delay until 6 January while another committee revised the preamble.

On the 6th a nor'easter raged through Boston, dumping snow, rain, and hail into the streets, but the abolitionists felt their way up Nigger Hill, the dark side of Beacon, to the schoolroom beneath the African Baptist Church. There in spite of objections from the three lawyers, Child, Loring, and Sewall, who questioned the expediency of basing the society on the doctrine of immediate emancipation, a preamble was voted by an apostolic dozen. The preamble asserted that all sane, adult persons were entitled "to immediate freedom from personal bondage of whatsoever kind," that man cannot "be the property of man," that all who hold men in bondage are guilty "of grievous wrong," that racial differences provide no basis for depriving men of natural rights. The document also disclaimed the use of violence or insurrection and stated the signers' determination to found a society.[6]

With the constitution and preamble accepted, officers were elected. Arnold Buffum, a Quaker manufacturer of hats, became president. Buffum, a tall and dark gray-haired, bespectacled man of fifty, wore the traditional Quaker garb—a great broad-brimmed hat and a dun-colored, many-buttoned coat. But he had more than the Quaker share of aggressive vigor and independence, and he was promptly disowned by the Society of Friends for his role as an abolitionist. A man named Odiorne, probably a Boston merchant, became first vice president.[7] Second vice president was the "Lynn Bard," Alonzo Lewis, a handsome man in his late thirties who looked more the poet than he was. Lewis was one of the first citizens of Lynn; in addition to being a poet, he was teacher and linguist (said to have known Latin, Greek, Hebrew, Arabic, French, and Spanish), editor and historian. He had also had for years the distinction of being Lynn's only Episcopalian; on Sundays he walked all the way to St. Peter's in Salem.[8] Garrison himself was elected corresponding secretary and Joshua Coffin, recording secretary. Though he was only forty, Coffin was so fat and good-natured that he looked fifteen years older. He was the Falstaff of the abolitionists, full of wit and humor and always talking. By profession he was a teacher (Whittier had been one of his students); by preference he was an antiquarian and historian. Treasurer was Michael H. Simpson, merchant of India Wharf. Also elected was a council of six members, but of this group only Oliver Johnson was to be well known in the cause.

As the antislavery apostles [9] stepped out into the stormy night after the meeting, Garrison turned oracle: "We have met to-night in this obscure schoolhouse; our numbers are few and our influence limited; but, mark my prediction, Faneuil Hall shall ere long echo with the principles we have set forth." Garrison considered the founding of the New-England Anti-Slavery Society a personal achievement; he had proved he did not require the assistance of the aristocratic Child, Loring, and Sewall, though he felt confident that they and many others would soon rally to the cause. With such a start, he reasoned, it would not take more than ten years to free all the slaves.[10] The response of his few associates and the opposition of his many enemies had persuaded Garrison to modify his earlier estimate that emancipation might take a thousand years.

In *The Liberator* for 18 February Garrison published the controversial preamble, the constitution, and an official address of the New-England Anti-Slavery Society. The constitution outlined the rules for the new society: that members must pay $2 annual dues or $15 for life memberships; that twelve officers (including the council) were to be elected at an annual meeting of the membership on the second Wednesday in January; that regular meetings were to be held the last Monday of each month; that the twelve officers were to be the Board of Managers, who were invested with the responsibility for the society's administration; that the board was impowered to appoint agents to further the interests of the society; and that any antislavery society founded on similar principles might become an auxiliary to the New England society by contributing to its funds and sending delegates to its meetings. The constitution also stated the second fundamental principle upon which the society was founded (the first, immediate emancipation, having been delineated in the preamble)—namely, the improvement of the nation's free colored people, improvement of their character and condition as well as their rights and privileges. The address, written for the society by Moses Thacher, member of the council and editor of the *Telegraph* (a Boston reform paper that condemned the use of alcohol and tobacco), assured the reader that "the object of our Society is neither war nor sedition," and expressed in a twofold argument the official Garrisonian condemnation of colonization. Repatriation of the entire slave population of the country, it was said, was statistically impossible and ethically unjust.

Thus, in its organization the new society had three clearly defined aims: immediate emancipation, improvement of the free colored, and opposition to colonization.

As secretary Garrison dominated the meetings, the activities, and the correspondence of the New England society so that by the end of the first year the office of president had become hardly more than honorary. At the first annual meeting an elderly gentleman named John Kendrick was made president, not because he could lead the organization but because he had for so many years been a loyal abolitionist (he had been one of Lundy's earliest supporters), and because he had given so generously to the new society.[11] When Kendrick died a few months later, another patriarch, George Benson, Garrison's future father-in-law, took his place.

The new society became quite essential to Garrison personally, since he found its meetings a regular forum for the discussion and development of ideas. An active and gregarious man like Garrison did not acquire ideas by solitary ratiocination. The society became virtually his alter ego, in whose name he could preach and act without being considered vain.

On behalf of the society Garrison spent a great deal of time during the first half of 1832 accumulating facts for a brief against colonization.[12] In June he published a 238-page pamphlet, *Thoughts on African Colonization,* in which he systematically condemned the American Colonization Society, documenting his attack with countless passages quoted from that society's official publications and from statements of its most distinguished proponents.

The pamphlet was arranged in two sections. The first was argument against the colonization society, and the second testimony from free colored organizations in regard to that society. The argument was carefully divided into ten corollaries, which demonstrated that the society, far from being hostile to slavery, really apologized for it; and that it called slaves property, property which would be more valuable and secure if the free colored and troublesome slaves were transported out of the country. Garrison contended that the society was motivated by fear of insurrection and that it was determined to expel all freed blacks to some such distant land as Liberia. Moreover, the American Colonization Society, unlike the New-England Anti-Slavery Society, disparaged the free colored population as "notoriously ignorant, degraded

and miserable, mentally diseased, broken-spirited," [13] and virtually incapable of instruction or improvement. At this point in the
argument Garrison could hardly contain himself:

'My bowels, my bowels! I am pained at my very heart; my heart
maketh a noise in me.' Are we pagans, are we savages, are we devils?
Can pagans, or savages, or devils, exhibit a more implacable spirit,
than is seen in the foregoing extracts? It is enough to cause the very
stones to cry out, and the beasts of the field to rebuke us.

Of this I am sure: no man, who is truly willing to admit the people
of color to an equality with himself, can see any insuperable difficulty
in effecting their elevation.[14]

Garrison's final and perhaps most effective argument was the
same one that had been used by Thacher in his address, that
colonization of the slave population of the United States was statistically impossible. According to a circular published by the society there were about 2,000,000 slaves and 500,000 free blacks in
the country; and both groups were rapidly increasing. The receipts of the Colonization Society during the last ten years were
$112,841.89, and the expenses, $106,457.72. During that period
1,857 people were transported to Africa. How long and how much
money would it take to transport the entire Negro population? [15]

The second main section of *Thoughts,* occupying the last
seventy-six pages of the pamphlet, documented the free colored
opposition to the American Colonization Society. Garrison reported resolutions from dozens of free colored meetings throughout the country. Since it was apparent that Garrison was counting
on free colored support, one cannot help wondering how many
of the meetings reported in this second section were inspired directly by him.

Although *Thoughts on African Colonization* was the most objective of Garrison's writing, it is interesting to observe how often
even it is personally oriented. To the ten divisions of the basic
argument, for example, he gave personal rather than logical titles.
When he was discussing the motivation of the society, he used the
heading, "The American Colonization Society is Nourished by
Fear and Selfishness"; when he was arguing statistically, it was
"The American Colonization Society Deceives and Misleads the
Nation." One of the arguments he considered most conclusive was

that it opposed immediate emancipation—*his* doctrine. And the pamphlet opened with thirty-eight pages of "Introductory Remarks," which were almost entirely personal. He explained therein that he started serious study of the Colonization Society nearly two years before, as readers of *The Liberator* knew. He reveled in the wisdom of his foresight and the strength of his opposition. "The whole nation," he said "is against me. . . . This malignity of opposition and proximity of danger, however, are like oil to the fire of my zeal. . . . I had rather die a thousand deaths, than witness the horrible oppression under which more than two millions of my countrymen groan, *and be silent.*" On the final page of his introduction Garrison commended his *Thoughts* "to the candid attention of the two most powerful classes in this country—editors of newspapers and the clergy."

Garrison did everything he could to assure a wide distribution of his pamphlet. He wrote friends and associates asking them to sell and to distribute copies free, especially among the clergy, because converting a clergyman was equivalent to converting a whole congregation.[16] As early as 12 May, he began publicizing *Thoughts* in *The Liberator,* announcing on 2 June that it was ready for sale, and subsequently publishing various reviews and testimonials.[17]

Garrison had reason to be pleased by the response to his pamphlet; for it was reviewed throughout this country and abroad, and few abolitionists had anything but the most favorable comments. Arthur Tappan ordered a hundred copies. J. Miller McKim, later to be the father of Garrison's daughter-in-law, was converted to lifelong abolitionism. Theodore D. Weld, ablest and most eloquent of the New York abolitionists, N. P. Rogers of New Hampshire, Amos A. Phelps, destined to be one of the most ardent of abolitionists, and many others dropped the Colonization Society.[18] Garrison said in a letter to Henry E. Benson on 21 July: "Conversions from colonization to abolition principles are rapidly multiplying in every quarter; and we have reason greatly to rejoice—for I look upon the overthrow of the Colonization Society as the overthrow of slavery itself—they must both stand or fall together." [19] Two years later his high opinion of the pamphlet and its effect had not lessened; for he compared himself as publicist to Milton (quoting the sonnet, "I did but prompt the age") [20] and admitted that the authority of his *Thoughts* "remains unshaken."

Although the publication of Garrison's *Thoughts on African Colonization* gave the dragon a stinging wound, the monster, far from dead, was destined to receive many another blow from the slave's champion during the next several years. Garrison was also determined to do what he could to realize another of the New-England Anti-Slavery Society's aims—the improvement of the free colored population. In *The Liberator* for 4 March 1831 he quoted a colonizationist as saying: "If the free colored people were generally taught to read, . . . it might be an inducement to them to remain in this country. ☞ *We would offer them no such inducement.*" "Here," Garrison exhorted, "is the cloven foot of colonization." Garrison, of course, would offer the Negro every inducement to remain in this country. He would not only teach him to read but also offer him the advantages of a higher education.

In June Garrison was in New Haven, where he talked at length with the Reverend Simeon S. Jocelyn, minister in a colored church there, and with Arthur Tappan about plans to found a colored college. Jocelyn was eager to have the college in New Haven—"no place in the Union, is their [the Negroes'] situation so comfortable, or the prejudice of the community weaker against them." Garrison thought that the site selected for the college was the best in New Haven and one of the most beautiful he had ever seen. From New Haven Garrison went on to Philadelphia, where he attended a so-called convention of free colored people—fifteen delegates from five states attended. Prominent on the agenda was a discussion of the projected college. The plan was to raise $10,000 from the colored, which was to be matched by an equal amount from the whites. Tappan had already offered $1,000. Garrison was enthusiastic: "Depend upon it, great things are in embryo. The colored people begin to feel their strength and to use it." [21]

But on 10 September, a city meeting in New Haven, attended by the mayor, alderman, common council, and seven hundred *freemen,* adopted resolutions asserting that they would oppose the founding of a colored college on the grounds that it would be "an unwarrantable and dangerous interference with the internal concerns of other states," and that it would be "incompatible with the prosperity" of Yale and other educational institutions now operating in the city. Though he withheld his full comments until he could pronounce the editorial condemnation of "this anti-intellectual crusade" in more universal terms, Garrison was horrified by this turn of events and said at once that he had "rods in pickle for more backs than one." He confessed that he would have expected such action from the South but not from New Haven, Connecticut. Ironically enough, the categorical language of the city's resolutions especially offended him; those who planned the new college would have accepted, he said, even the slightest hint of disapproval as sufficient reason not to establish the college in New Haven.[22]

New Haven was not the only town in Connecticut to object to Negro education. Canterbury, six miles from Brooklyn where the Mays and Bensons lived, was far more violent in its reaction to a school for young ladies of color proposed by Prudence Crandall, mannish-looking, thirty-year-old, fanatical spinster, who was an abolitionist as well as a schoolmarm. Garrison and his group became intimately involved in the controversy, but legal action ultimately prevented the founding of the school.

This was not the end of the antislavery society's efforts to improve colored education, however. Garrison was shortly to make a trip to England to solicit funds for a colored school.

In the meantime, he could look back on the two years since the founding of *The Liberator* with some satisfaction. He had established a lively and controversial reform paper, which had far more influence, especially in the South, than could have been anticipated from its small circulation. He had also founded the New-England Anti-Slavery Society, which established beyond dispute his leadership among New England abolitionists. Although the society's actual contribution to the cause was limited as yet, the organization, completely dominated by Garrison himself, had great therapeutic value for its leader: it gave his personality the basic support which he craved. Indirectly, the Colonization Society itself had helped to develop Garrison's leadership, for without that organization to combat he might never have developed such momentum in favor of immediate emancipation.

CHAPTER VI

To England and Beyond

D URING the first two years of the publication of *The Liberator* Garrison had been greatly influenced by the British abolitionists. One of the agents of the *Genius,* an English Quaker merchant named James Cropper, had been corresponding with him for several years and had supplied him with antislavery circulars, tracts, and pamphlets [1] that preached immediate emancipation with all the vituperation of the most extreme British advocates for abolition. It was a policy of the last resort instituted only after more moderate methods had failed to persuade Parliament to free the West Indian slaves. But Garrison responded with all the exuberance of his ardent nature, accepting the new British position with unabashed and absolute conviction.[2] Having been so greatly impressed by the British campaign for emancipation, Garrison was naturally eager to secure closer personal rapport with the British leaders.

The opportunity to do so occurred in the spring of 1833. The New-England Anti-Slavery Society had for some months been trying to raise money for Negro education. Partly as a result of efforts of the Tappan brothers in New York, who in July 1831, had founded the Society for Promoting Manual Labor in Literary Institutions,[3] Garrison and his society had decided that a manual-labor school would be more feasible than a college. Such a school would make it possible for indigent colored students to be educated at a minimum of expense by working part-time. It was thought that a Negro school would not only attract many free

[65]

colored students but would also offer an inducement for emancipation, because many white fathers of colored offspring would gladly free their children if they could place them in such an institution.[4]

On 9 March *The Liberator* announced that Garrison as agent for the Anti-Slavery Society was planning a mission to England "for the purpose of procuring funds to aid in the establishment of the proposed MANUAL LABOR SCHOOL FOR COLORED YOUTH, and of disseminating in that country the truth in relation to American Slavery, and its ally, the American Colonization Society." In the same issue the society also announced that it was soliciting funds for Garrison's mission, listing those who would collect funds in various towns and cities. The total collected eventually was $517,[5] which was enough to pay his passage to England and most of his expenses there, though he had to borrow money for the return trip.

Leaving *The Liberator* in the capable hands of Oliver Johnson, Garrison left Boston on 5 April, allowing plenty of time for a ceremonial farewell tour. He planned fund-raising addresses to various groups before sailing from New York on 1 May.[6] In both Boston and Providence, Garrison admitted that "the highest interest and most intense feeling were felt and exhibited by the audience." He reported how the colored people had wept freely and how they had clustered around him to shake hands. He himself was also much affected when he realized that "it might be the last time I should behold them together on earth."

In Brooklyn, Connecticut, which was seething with excitement over the Prudence Crandall affair, he spoke to a white audience. Though he was not received with the exciting gratitude bestowed by the colored, he was "happy to learn that the effects of the address are most salutary." From Brooklyn he went to Hartford and thence to New Haven, where he stayed for several days while Nathaniel Jocelyn, brother of Simeon, painted his portrait, the plan being to have it engraved and sold to his friends. Garrison commented with Shakespearean allusion: "This sticking up one's face in print-shops, to be the 'observed of all observers,' is hardly consistent with genuine modesty, but I can in no other way get rid of the importunities of those who would pluck out their eyes to give me." [7]

Then he went to Philadelphia and from there to New York, where his enemies were conspiring to have him kidnaped and sent to Georgia. Garrison was no less flattered than he had been by the tribute from his friends. So long as he was the center of attention, it made little difference whether he were surrounded by friends or enemies. He returned to Philadelphia, meaning to baffle his enemies by taking a packet from that port rather than from New York; but the ship had sailed before he arrived. He spent the several remaining days of April shuttling back and forth from one town to another, at one time traveling through rain in an open wagon. He was successful in eluding his pursuers and even managed to pose for the Jocelyn portrait and to give a final farewell address to a large and appreciative audience at the African Methodist Church in New York.

During the weeks before his sailing Garrison speculated on his achievements and his career. The magnitude of the cause he had undertaken filled him with awe, and his impressionable imagination conjured up an apocalyptic vision. He seemed to be standing on a great height overlooking the continent of Africa, where he could watch a thousand flaming villages and hear the agonized groans and screams of the dying. And there was a voice from Heaven calling, *"Plead for the oppressed!"* It was a vast and theatrical panorama which Garrison described with all the gusto of his inflated nineteenth-century rhetoric. He envisioned the African Golgotha, the churning passage of the slave ships, their wakes littered with the bodies of men, women, and children; and the waves chanting their requiem. There were "the cries of the suffocating victims in the holds of ships." And in America thronging around Garrison were "the two millions of slaves in this guilty land,—debased, weary, famishing, bleeding and bound"—appealing to their champion. "And I see unborn generations of victims stalking like apparitions before me; and once more I hear that voice from Heaven, saying in a tone awful and loud, and with increasing earnestness,—*'Plead for the oppressed!'* " *"I must,"* Garrison concluded, *"obey the voice from Heaven,* whether men will hear or whether they will forbear." [8]

Garrison also speculated about the mission immediately ahead. It would take six months, maybe a year. He would be well received by the people. In the presence of the great antislavery leaders

(Clarkson, Wilberforce, Brougham, Buxton, O'Connell) his "spirit will be elevated and strengthened." He would tell them the heartrending story of the Negro in America, and hearts "will melt with pity, and devise liberally for his rescue." Already Garrison had found a place for himself among the immortals: the great British reformers would welcome him to their fraternity.

On 1 May Garrison was safe aboard the *Hibernia,* lying at anchor ten miles below New York, waiting for a favorable breeze. It was a perfect May Day—bright and sparkling—and Garrison rhapsodized over birds singing in trees and glowed as he remembered the eventful history of the last several weeks. He could hardly have had a more exciting send-off. Friends and enemies conspired to give him stimulation and satisfaction which he would not forget. Garrison's exuberance, however, was short-lived; for he was seasick before the *Hibernia* lost sight of land, and he remained so sick during the first week of the twenty-one-day passage that he could hardly eat anything. It was humiliating.

Garrison landed in Liverpool on 22 May. He found the city an unattractive commercial emporium about the size of New York. But something happened there that greatly impressed him. Going to Dr. Raffles' church for a service, he was ushered to an empty pew. In a few minutes the usher, with no indication that he recognized Garrison as an abolitionist, brought a colored man to the pew, treating him with the utmost politeness. Shortly thereafter, as if to prove conclusively the absence of prejudice, he introduced to the pew several handsomely dressed ladies. Garrison could not help speculating on what would have happened if a colored man had been seated with white people in an American church.[9]

Soon after landing in England Garrison went up to London, where James Cropper introduced him to the leading abolitionists. Thomas Powell Buxton, who had inherited the mantle of Wilberforce as leading abolitionist, invited him to breakfast, but when Garrison appeared at the appointed time and place, Buxton was slow in coming up to greet the American. Instead, he stood still for a moment, staring at Garrison, a puzzled expression on his face. "Have I the pleasure of addressing Mr. Garrison, of Boston, in the United States?" "Yes, sir," was the reply, "I am he; and I am here in accordance with your invitation." Buxton lifted up his hands and exclaimed, "Why, my dear sir, I thought you were a black man! And I have consequently invited this company of ladies and gentlemen to be present to welcome Mr. Garrison, the black advocate of emancipation from the United States of America!" Garrison thought it was the greatest compliment ever paid him.[10]

Garrison felt happy and at home with the English abolitionists, who were everywhere and always discussing his favorite topic— immediate emancipation. It was expected that Parliament at the current session would pass the bill freeing all British slaves, though many details remained to be discussed and determined— notably, whether the owners were to be compensated for their freed slaves and whether the freedmen must serve an apprenticeship before being entirely liberated. The year 1833 was an exciting and satisfying time for Garrison to be in England, but hardly the time, Garrison reasoned, to solicit funds for a colored school in America. Such a project must have seemed picayune and insignificant to the British abolitionists, who were currently so preoccupied with their own problems. Also, Garrison felt embarrassed—even humiliated—to ask the English for money to support an American charity when there was obviously so much poverty in England. Perhaps, he thought, the manual-labor school ought to be supported entirely by Americans, although the British agreed to help later after their own emancipation was complete. And so Garrison was confronted with a problem. He had come to England primarily to collect money for a manual-labor school. That being impossible, what should he do—return promptly to the United States where he had many duties and responsibilities? Such was his first inclination, though he was sorely tempted to see some of the sights of England first. "But," his conscience dictated, "neither time nor duty, will allow me to act the mere tourist. I cannot travel for amusement, nor even for relaxation: of course, you [readers of *The Liberator*] may expect little from my pen that is foreign to the subject of emancipation." [11]

Soon Garrison solved his problem to his entire satisfaction. He decided that he was needed, at present, in England rather than America. He was needed for the alternate purpose mentioned in the official announcement of his English mission—to disseminate the truth about American slavery and colonization. It was fortunate for Garrison's peace of mind that England was currently besieged by an agent for the American Colonization Society, one Elliott Cresson, a distinguished Quaker philanthropist from Philadelphia. Colonization had always been a monster for him to conquer, but now the monstrosity was clearly personified in one man. Certainly annihilation of colonization would help his colored friends more than a school possibly could. He would dispose of Elliott Cresson. The school could wait.

In chivalrous fashion, Garrison first issued a formal challenge to debate, which his associates on several occasions tried to deliver to Cresson. When Cresson was finally induced to accept the document, he replied that he was in the hands of his friends. Garrison promptly applied to the friends, who suggested a conference between the opponents. But Garrison wanted an audience and publicity, and so he wrote to the *Times,* repeating the challenge and attacking colonization. When this had no more effect than the personal challenge, he decided to arraign the Colonization Society at a public meeting of his own. The Wesleyan Chapel in Devonshire Square was made ready for him.[12]

On 10 June the audience, including Elliott Cresson and several of his friends, assembled. Garrison began to attack the Colonization Society on the grounds that it was not abolitionist as it professed to be, but that it was instead the deadly enemy of immediate emancipation. As the argument progressed—and he was developing it along the same lines as in *Thoughts on African Colonization*—Cresson was called upon to deny Garrison's allegations. It was an excited and one-sided meeting. On several occasions during the meeting George Thompson, a British abolitionist whose personality in so many ways resembled Garrison's, taunted Cresson, daring him to reply. Finally, Cresson said a few words, to the effect that he was being persecuted, that "under existing circumstances, and with such a chairman [James Cropper], and such a lecturer, and such a meeting, I should hold it unworthy of myself to enter upon any discussion." The audience hissed and cried "Hear! Hear!"[13] Since, owing to the many interruptions, Garrison's lecture was far from finished at ten o'clock, the meeting was adjourned until the next evening. At that time he finished his analysis of colonization, and several others expressed their abhorrence of the society.[14]

No matter what Garrison did, Cresson would not debate with

him. And so a second time Garrison aimed through the *Times,* inserting on 28 June an advertisement that cost him £6/6/5, repeating the challenge and offering to pay to the mayor of New York twenty guineas if Cresson would prove a statement he had published about Garrison. This statement, which had been published in the *Baptist Magazine* in June, accused Garrison of being "a violent pamphleteer, who often sacrifices truth to the support of his mistaken views, and whose very quotations are so garbled as entirely to pervert the real meaning of the speaker." [15]

The most dramatic occasion on the trip abroad was the Great Anti-Colonization Meeting in Exeter Hall on 13 July. There James Cropper again presided, and Garrison again spoke at length. He paid his disrespects to Cresson, ironically sympathizing with the ill health now given as excuse for not debating and pointing out that his health was quite good enough for several meetings of his own. He said that Cresson "is constantly discanting, in the most lugubrious and pathetic manner," about how much he was being persecuted. But who, Garrison questioned, were his persecutors? They were none other than James Cropper, Zachary Macaulay, Thomas Powell Buxton, and even William Wilberforce; Garrison again associated himself with the most distinguished of British abolitionists. To this group should be added the venerable Thomas Clarkson, now a blind old man, for he had been enlisted on the side of colonization only through a shocking fraud; and Garrison quoted Clarkson's neutral statement in regard to colonization and the garbled version released by the American Colonization Society.

Having disposed, as he thought, of Elliott Cresson, Garrison told his audience he wanted to describe American slavery. In his enthusiasm to paint as black a picture as possible, he made a tactical blunder. He condemned his own country with words that, quoted out of context, gave his enemies—and especially Elliott Cresson—an opportunity to brand him as unpatriotic. First, he told of his great love for his country and of his pride in its institutions and in its arts and sciences. Then, admitting that he had "solemn accusations to bring against her," he began an indictment of his country. He accused her of the hypocrisy of "professing to be the land of the free and the asylum of the oppressed," while she espoused the cruel system of slavery. He accused her of disen-

franchising about half a million free colored people; of starving
and plundering a large part of the population; of participating
extensively in the domestic slave trade; of kidnaping annually
100,000 slave babies; of stealing the labor of two millions of people annually; "of ruthlessly invading the holiest relations of life,
and cruelly separating the dearest ties of nature"; and, finally, "of
being callously indifferent to the accumulated and accumulating
wrongs and sufferings of her black population." [16]

At the end of his long speech Garrison exhorted Britain to help
him storm "that great BASTILLE OF OPPRESSION, the American
Colonization Society. . . . Let the British nation assail it with the
battle-axe of justice; let their artillery of truth, charged to the
muzzle, blaze against it." With such help it would soon be blown
into fragments, and all those unjustly imprisoned within freed.

The audience cheered, but Garrison's enemies snickered, remembering not his attack on Elliott Cresson or his attack on the
Colonization Society but his attack on the United States. They
lost no time in sending word of Garrison's betrayal across the
ocean.

Garrison remained abroad a month after the meeting at Exeter
Hall. During that period he continued his controversy with Cresson in the public press,[17] he visited Clarkson, although without
persuading him to abandon his neutral position in regard to the
Colonization Society, and he attended the funeral of Wilberforce.
In addition, he received an important testimonial against colonization signed by all the leading abolitionists except Clarkson (Wilberforce had signed it only a few days before his death).[18]

In order to sail from England, Garrison needed more than the
desire to do so, because by August he was again without funds.
Happily, he was spared the humiliation of appealing to his new
English friends by the generosity of Nathaniel Paul, an American
colored minister in England seeking aid for a group of Negro refu-
gees in Canada. He and Garrison had several times shared plat-
forms in England, Paul giving the colored man's testimonial on
behalf of Garrison and his work in America, even comparing him
on occasion to Jesus Christ.[19] With such an opinion of Garrison,
Paul was not hesitant to lend him the £40 necessary for the return
passage.[20]

Garrison sailed from Portsmouth on the *Hannibal* on 26 August. During the month-long voyage—the ship did not reach New York until 29 September—Garrison had plenty of time to think about his mission to England. He was satisfied that, although he had not raised any money for the manual-labor school, his trip had been a professional and personal success. Colonization had been discredited; the English leaders were now friends of American abolition; and he himself had grown in stature and reputation. Never before had he known what it was to be generally respected. In America he was admired by personal friends and by radical abolitionists, but he was abhorred by Southerners and even by many respectable Northerners. In his adopted city of Boston—as the events of the next several years were to demonstrate—he was hated far more than he was loved. But in London no one even disliked him—no one, that is, except American colonizationists. In England he had been accepted—in a way he was never to be in his own country—as *the* leader of American abolitionists. And as such he had often been the center of attention, for he represented to the British a hope for universal, world-wide emancipation.

The importance of Garrison's contacts with the British abolitionists has never been sufficiently emphasized. With his flamboyant journalistic skill and his earnest forcefulness Garrison made a considerable impression in 1833. He made friends at that time for himself and for American abolition, friends who were to render great service to the cause, both morally and financially, in the years to come.

In New York he was to receive a striking reception. Thousands of people, it is said, were on hand to greet him, for his trip to England and his return to the states had not been neglected by the press. It was reported in the New York *Courier and Enquirer* that a meeting was being called at the time of Garrison's return for the purpose of establishing an antislavery society in the city. With heavy sarcasm it was suggested that Garrison had displayed "such *patriotic ardor* abroad" that all New Yorkers must listen to "the solicitations of the *pacific* Garrison." They must pass resolutions freeing the slaves, paying his salary, and denouncing colonization.[21] Other papers agreed, urging all who disapproved of abolitionists and their methods to attend the meeting at Clinton Hall to give Tappan, Garrison, and the others a fitting reception.

By the time Garrison landed on 2 October,[22] the town was filled with thousands of excited, shouting people, who pushed on towards Clinton Hall like a great flow of lava. Garrison joined the mob and was carried along to the hall, which was found to be locked and empty: the trustees had denied the reformers use of the building.

In the meantime, at the Old Chapel in Chatham Street, Tappan and his associates were busy organizing the new city antislavery society. By the time the mob discovered their whereabouts, the meeting was practically over. The great gates at the front of the building kept them at bay long enough to cover the abolitionists' retreat. When the mob broke into the chapel, they found sitting calmly in one of the pews a solitary Quaker who looked up in surprise. The mob held a mock meeting, elected an ignorant Negro chairman and forced him to speak, and the day ended on a raucous note. All this Garrison witnessed, "standing by . . . undisguisedly, as calm in my feelings as if those who were seeking my life were my warmest supporters." [23]

Garrison's reception in Boston a few days later, though less spectacular, was equally hostile. He was greeted by a handbill, which in part read as follows:

BOSTONIANS AWAKE!!

The true American has returned, *alias* William Lloyd Garrison, the "Negro Champion," from his disgraceful mission to the British metropolis, whither he went to obtain pecuniary aid, and the countenance of Englishmen to wrest the American citizen's property which he has fought and labored for, from out of their hands, and thereby deprive the southern section of our happy union of the only means of obtaining livelihood. He had held meetings in the city of London, and slandered the Americans to the utmost of his power. . . . Americans! will you brook this conduct? I think not. He is now in your power— do not let him escape you, but go this evening, armed with plenty of *tar and feathers,* and administer him justice at his abode at No. 9, Merchants' Hall, Congress-st.

A NORTH ENDER

Boston, Oct. 7, 1833 [24]

The *Evening Transcript* reported the next day that "the Liberator office was surrounded last night by a dense mob, breathing threatenings which foreboded a storm." [25]

Although Garrison officially labeled the riots as, next to the persecution of Prudence Crandall, "the blackest page in the history of party fury in this country" and called his detractors cowards, ruffians, hypocrites, and liars, he was, as usual, not displeased by all the attention. If he was not revered in New York and Boston as he was in London, at least he was not unknown. It was a satisfaction to record the facts in *The Liberator,* where he published several pages of reprints from New York and Boston papers, describing the mobs and commenting on his return home.

But there was one thing that troubled him—the accusation that he had slandered his country abroad:

I did not hesitate there—I have not hesitated here—I shall hesitate nowhere to brand this country as hypocritical and tyrannical in its treatment of the people of color, whether bond or free. If this be calumny, I dealt freely in it, as I *shall* deal, as long as slavery exists among us. . . . Still—*slavery aside*—I did not fail to eulogize my country, before a British audience, in terms of affection, admiration and respect.[26]

Garrison was troubled also by the financial condition of *The Liberator.* He tried to keep up a bold front to his subscribers, hoping to laugh them into paying for the paper with duns like this:

Kind Patrons! behold our situation! We must *dun,* or be *undone.* Send us our dues, that you may receive in return the plaudit of *well done.*[27]

In the final issue of the year he discussed the problem seriously in a statement "To the Patrons and Agents of the Liberator." He thanked his patrons for support but carefully distinguished between those who paid for their subscriptions and those who did not. He admitted that, owing to his long absence in England and the interruptions of the editorial routine since his return, "perhaps our paper has not exhibited that energy and spirit which formerly characterized it"—not that this was any excuse for not paying for a paper received. He also thanked his agents—naming two specifically—for their efforts in securing new subscribers, though he characterized the list of agents as large and showy rather than productive. The same issue contained a special announcement that since the editor would be absent next week making arrangements in regard to the next volume of the paper, the next number would not be published for two weeks.[28]

Actually *The Liberator* was seriously embarrassed financially for two reasons in addition to those given in Garrison's statement. It was feeling the competition with another abolitionist paper, the *Emancipator* in New York; and Garrison and his partner, Isaac Knapp, had impoverished the firm by printing "quantities of circulars, addresses, tracts, books, etc., for gratuitous distribution," the most expensive of them being *Thoughts on African Colonization.* The situation was so serious that even Garrison, usually such an optimist, said in a letter to a friend: "Whether we shall be able to continue the Liberator much longer is certainly doubtful; although its extinction would be a heavy blow to our great and glorious cause, and would deeply afflict my own heart, and greatly rejoice our enemies all over the land." But Garrison was not entirely discouraged, for in the same letter he referred to the great success of his English mission and insisted rather naïvely that the protest against the Colonization Society signed by Wilberforce was in itself worth thousands of dollars to the cause. In spite of the clamor against his person, the defiant tone was as clear as ever: "My health is perfectly good, my spirit lofty as the Alps, my zeal unabated, my faith unshaken, my courage unsubdued. My enemies will find out, by and by, that I am stormproof." [29]

At this time Garrison's mind was full of thoughts not only about himself and *The Liberator* but also about the best way to extend the organization of the antislavery movement. As early as the spring of 1831 he had been advocating the formation of a national antislavery society.[30] More recently he had been advocating it with increasing enthusiasm. Before he sailed for England, he had felt that such a society should be formed immediately.[31] His experience in England and the success of the British emancipation bill had confirmed him in that opinion. The Tappans and other New York abolitionists had also wanted to form a national organization, and they had conceived the formation of the city antislavery society early in October as a step in that direction. But they had decided to postpone the national society after the riots in New York and Boston. Garrison had argued vehemently against such a delay on the grounds that they must capitalize on the success of British emancipation while it was still fresh in everyone's mind. He succeeded in having the convention to organize the national society set for 4 December in Philadelphia, and the call went out on 29 October. Garrison wrote to the Bensons, to Whittier, and to many of his personal friends, enclosing the call to the convention.

Later in November Garrison set off for Philadelphia by way of Providence. On the steamer between New York and Philadelphia he traveled with May and several other friends. A stranger on board asked May what the abolitionists were going to do in Philadelphia. When he explained that they were going to found a national organization, the stranger expressed all the usual objections to abolitionism. At this juncture Garrison approached, and May gladly "shifted my part of the discussion into his hands" and marveled at Garrison's dialectical skill, as he described the abilities and potentialities of the Negro race. As the conversation —or monologue—progressed, a crowd of people gathered to listen.

Finally, the unknown gentleman testified, "I have been much interested, sir, in what you have said, and in the exceedingly frank and temperate manner in which you have treated the subject. If all Abolitionists were like you, there would be much less opposition to your enterprise. But sir, depend upon it, that hair-brained, reckless, violent fanatic, Garrison, will damage, if he does not shipwreck, any cause."

May stepped forward and said, "Allow me, sir, to introduce you to Mr. Garrison, of whom you entertain so bad an opinion. The gentleman you have been talking with is he." [32]

In Philadelphia, the abolitionists did not find everyone so good-natured and understanding as the gentleman on the boat; for they were insulted on the streets, and found the entrance to their hall heavily guarded by police sent by order of the mayor. Approximately sixty delegates from ten states attended the convention on 4 December. Buffum, Coffin, May, and Whittier, along with Garrison, led the Massachusetts group. There was a small group from Maine and another from Connecticut. Most powerful was the group from New York, led by Lewis Tappan and Elizur Wright. There were about a dozen Presbyterian and Congregational ministers, a small group of Unitarians and of Quakers, including the famous Lucretia Mott, well-born Philadelphia

Quaker whose antislavery convictions had already attracted considerable attention. There were, also, a few Negroes.

The New Yorkers were determined that the radical Garrison not control the meeting, and Arthur Tappan (not present) was nominated for president, Lewis Tappan for membership on the Executive Committee, Elizur Wright for secretary, and William Green, another New York abolitionist, for treasurer, whereas Garrison was relegated to the minor position of secretary of foreign correspondence. But Lewis Tappan himself did present a somewhat niggardly resolution honoring Garrison for having "the confidence of the people of England."

General discussion continued through the morning and into the afternoon, with only crackers and cold water to dispel growing appetites. In the afternoon a constitution was adopted, condemning slavery as a sin, urging immediate emancipation without colonization, the abolition by Congress of slavery in the District of Columbia, the abrogation of interstate slave trade, and the government's discontinuance of the use of force. Although the views expressed in the constitution were acceptable to the whole convention, some wanted a more imposing and glamorous instrument, and so a committee of ten was chosen to prepare a Declaration of Sentiments.

About half of the committee met early in the evening at the house of a colored gentleman with whom Garrison was staying. After an hour of general discussion of the nature of the document in question, specific suggestions were called for from each person present. But when another hour had passed without any specific progress, it was decided "to entrust the matter to a sub-committee," [33] consisting of Garrison, May, and Whittier. The subcommittee retired to the home of Garrison's colored host, where after a brief discussion, "it was of course determined"—to quote May—that Garrison should be the one to write the important paper. May and Whittier left about ten, promising to return at eight in the morning. At eight o'clock they found Garrison, with shutters still closed and lamp still burning, at work on the final paragraph. An hour later, after a few minor revisions, the Declaration of Sentiments was presented to the committee as a whole, which examined it painstakingly for three hours, resisting urgent demands from the convention for the committee's report. Many suggestions and criticisms were made as Garrison sat calmly by, evincing, according to May, "the most unruffled patience." There were objections to the harshness of the language, to the extent to which both North and South should be indicted for the sin of slavery. But in the end the only significant change was the deletion of most of a long section in condemnation of the Colonization Society, which the group thought so nearly dead that it should not be immortalized in "this Declaration of the Rights of Man." When Garrison found that the vast majority approved of this revision, he said, magnanimously, "Brethren, it is your report, not mine." [34]

The declaration was read to the convention shortly after noon. There followed a profound silence lasting several minutes until the spirit moved one of the Quaker delegates who called for its immediate adoption. But the majority of the group felt that the convention should act in such an important matter more deliberately, and so the entire afternoon, from one to five, was spent analyzing the paper sentence by sentence. "And just as the darkness of night had shut down upon us we resolved unanimously to adopt it." [35]

The next morning Samuel J. May, his voice faltering with intense emotion, read to the convention: "We have met together for the achievement of an enterprise, without which, that of our fathers is incomplete, and which, for its magnitude, solemnity, and probable results upon the destiny of the world, as far transcends theirs, as moral truth does physical force." The new declaration affirmed the rights stated in the Declaration of Independence, asserting that all men have rights to their own bodies as well as to their labor. It labeled that American citizen "who retains a human being in involuntary bondage . . . a MAN-STEALER." It proclaimed that all slaves should be freed, that all laws protecting slavery are null and void. It insisted that all colored persons should enjoy the same prerogatives and privileges as white persons. It denounced slavery as a crime, so that planters freeing their slaves should not be compensated. Further, it outlined procedures by which the society should function: that local societies should be organized throughout the country; that agents should be sent forth to warn and rebuke; that tracts and periodicals should be circulated; that help of the pulpit and press should be enlisted;

that preference should be given to the products of free labor. "We may be personally defeated, but our principles never. TRUTH, JUSTICE, and HUMANITY, must and will gloriously triumph."

In the silence that followed May's reading of the Declaration of Sentiments sixty-three persons (the Declaration of Independence had been signed by fifty-six) filed up to the platform one by one to sign the document. Garrison rejoiced that the number at the convention was small, insisting that "sixty are better than five thousand." Had they wanted the larger number, he said, they could easily have been "rallied together" earlier in the winter.[36]

The Declaration of Sentiments represents Garrison's rhetorical style at its best. His language here is more restrained than usual not only because other members of the committee and the convention exerted a moderating influence but also because he is following so closely the Declaration of Independence, which he hoped his statement would excel as much as the cause of abolition excelled the cause of revolution. The other great influence on the style and content of Garrison's declaration, as on so many of his writings, was the Bible. How could anyone, Garrison may have questioned, object to a document that merely urged men to follow the Declaration of Independence and the Bible? The most objectionable part of the Declaration of Sentiments was the specific program recommended: the organization of many antislavery societies throughout the country, the institution of a systematic schedule of abolition lectures, the circulation of appropriate tracts, the conversion to antislavery principles of all newspaper editors and clergymen, and the boycott of the products of slave labor. These were the familiar Garrisonian objectives.

Although the fact cannot be definitely documented, it would seem that there had been a great deal of maneuvering behind the scenes at this founding convention. Certainly, the New York reformers distrusted Garrison's radical ideas. They may also have been suspicious of the motives for his trip abroad and of his urgent desire to found a national society immediately following that trip. Conceivably, they permitted him to write the Declaration of Sentiments, thinking that a vain man like Garrison might prefer such an honor to the more extensive responsibilities he might have undertaken later as an officer of the society. They may have reasoned that in this way his influence could be limited.

At any rate, Garrison did not work closely with the American Anti-Slavery Society after its founding. He was granted the subordinate post of secretary of foreign correspondence, its few responsibilities further restricted by the Executive Committee's requirement that he clear all his correspondence with them. Within a month he was sufficiently restive under such restrictions to resign the office altogether.

Nevertheless, the new society did enhance Garrison's prestige, if not his power. It also helped him to solve financial problems by purchasing part of his large stock of pamphlets, and indirectly it helped him solve his crucial personal problem—whether an impoverished editor of an antislavery paper could afford to marry.

CHAPTER VII

———◆◆●———

A Passionate Attachment[1]

G ARRISON had not always planned to marry. In fact, he
was a determined bachelor by the time he was sixteen, as
can be seen by his letters to the Newburyport *Herald* during the
years of his apprenticeship. His first testimonial to the single life
had appeared over the signature "An Old Bachelor" in the issue
for 21 May 1822. He had warned against the snares set by design-
ing women, women who would sue an unsuspecting man for the
breach of a promise he may never have made. Three weeks after
his twentieth birthday, in his last article for the *Herald*, Garrison
wrote an "Essay on Marriage," his most complete statement of
the bachelor point of view. Marriage, he believed,

may be likened to a mill-pond, in which a person, heated and sweltering
unthinkingly plunges headlong, and is quickly taken with shivering
fits. . . . Marriage was instituted to please the commonalty—not to
shackle the scholar, the philosopher, the statesman, the warrior. . . .
Families are so many cares, which distract the plans, weaken the
strength, and tame the fire of genius.[2]

That women were a temptation to him one might suspect from
the vigor of his protest, even if there were no further evidence.
But any reader of the *Herald* can see that Garrison was a susceptible, though cautious, young man. On 28 May 1824, for example, a poem was printed over Garrison's pseudonym, A.O.B.,
which hardly sounded like the words of an old bachelor. It
lamented the conventional predicament of unrequited love, suggesting that suicide was the only satisfactory solution.

A PASSIONATE ATTACHMENT

In the papers he edited between 1826 and 1831, Garrison continued to play the dual role of the woeful lover and the disillusioned bachelor. In *The Free Press* (1826) and the *National Philanthropist* (1828), he was predominantly the bachelor, condemning suits for breach of promise and delighting in maxims about the vanity and unpredictability of women.

But by 1828, when he became the editor of the *Journal of the Times,* he had renounced his bachelorhood. In the first issue on October 3 he told his reader in rather sentimental verse that he was "a new and altered man," quite ready to bow humbly to a girl named Mary, his would-be bride.

In the same paper seven weeks later, Lloyd explained that his attachment for the young lady had not diminished, for he was "up to the eyes in love," though for want of money to pay the parson he was "compelled to live in single blessedness—or wretchedness—from sheer necessity." His friends noticed what had happened. Whittier said of him: "He goes to see his Dulcinea every other night almost, but is fearful of being 'shipped off,' after all, by her. Lord help the poor fellow, if it happens so." [3] And Stephen Foster, the printer from Maine, joshed him about Mary's use of cosmetics. Garrison replied in kind, resolving he would make it part of the articles of marriage that she must buy her own brushes. In fact, he said, if she persisted he'd be the painter, and he imagines the scene:

Hold your head steadily, dearest—so—very still—you shall look in the glass presently—a little more vermilion, a denser flame of health on this cheek—I like to see the *blood,* Mary, mounting up to the very temple, commingling with that lily whiteness—your eyebrows are hardly coal black—a little darker, in order to give a deeper brilliance to your starry eyes, or rather to their light—shut your mouth, and draw back that little saucy tongue, you pretty witch, for I'm going to put a ruby blush upon your twin (not thin) lips, after I've kissed them —there—softly—softly—smack goes the brush. . . . *Cetera desunt.*[4]

Unfortunately the rest really is missing. We do not know whether the young lady shipped him off, or whether the affair died a natural death during the long Vermont winter. There is no further trace of Mary Cunningham in extant Garrison papers.

Although necessity kept young Garrison single for several more years, he never again ridiculed women and marriage.

The next year, on the evening of 5 April, Garrison was in Providence, Rhode Island, lecturing to the free colored people at the African Church. The occasion had a special importance both to Garrison and to the audience because Garrison was about to embark on his mission to England. But the real importance of the evening no one could have known. Among the most prominent white members of the audience were the George Bensons. Mr. Benson, a venerable gentleman of more than eighty, had been deeply interested in the cause of abolition for half a century. In 1790 he had helped to found an antislavery society in Providence; in 1792 he had been made an honorary member of the Pennsylvania Society for Promoting the Abolition of Slavery, which Benjamin Franklin had founded. In the early years of the century he had been a successful merchant, a director of the Providence Bank, and a trustee of Brown University. But he had resigned from business because he did not approve of what he considered sharp business practices, and for some time the cause of emancipation had been his chief interest.

On this evening he had brought with him to hear Garrison his attractive, twenty-two-year-old daughter, Helen. Helen had doubtless been eager to hear Mr. Garrison for months, because she had heard her father and her two brothers praise him again and again for his courage and strength, for his fearless attack on the American Colonization Society, and for his uncompromising support of the Negroes. After the lecture she was convinced that her family had not exaggerated his virtues. The next morning she did not need to be urged to go to her brother's store to see Garrison again. She lingered at the store for a long time to hear him talk, and she left convinced that "I should ever take a deep interest in your welfare."

Always susceptible to feminine beauty, Garrison must have noticed Helen's oval face, regular features, large lively eyes, and dark brown hair. Years later he explained how strongly he had been attracted: "If it was not 'love at first sight,' on my part it was something very like it—a magnetic influence being exerted which became irresistible on further acquaintance." [5]

It is curious that if Lloyd fell in love with Helen at once, he should wait ten months before writing her a letter. His "first offence, in an epistolary shape," as he called it, was a rapturous effusion to the beauties of spring, a testimonial to his "great repugnance to quill driving," and a suggestion that she organize a female antislavery society in Providence. It is strange, also, that he "mislaid" the letter for several weeks before mailing it.

In her reply Helen said that she would answer his letter with great eagerness if she did not feel that her talents were so inferior to his. As for the formation of a female antislavery society, she assured him that she had too little influence to be of service. This first letter was characteristic of Helen. It showed her modesty and humility, her adulation of Garrison, and her reluctance to engage directly in the public controversy. All her life, though she was deeply interested in the abolition movement, she remained in the background, leaving to her energetic husband all the activity and the resulting fame.

The first week in March 1834, Garrison visited Providence and Brooklyn, Connecticut, at that time the home of the Bensons. In Brooklyn, he stayed at Friendship's Vale, the Benson's eighty-acre farm,[6] and saw a good deal of Helen. On a drive with her to the adjoining town of Canterbury, he wanted to declare his love, but "my tongue was tied, and my heart timorous, and so I was dumb." But on 8 March, as soon as he had returned home and even though he was tired and busy, he wrote, somewhat circuitously,

to embody my whole heart, that you may divide it among all the members of that most estimable family residing in "Friendship's Vale." Nay, I forget myself—how can I send to you that which I left in Brooklyn? All of you have got possession of my heart, and I doubt whether I should be able to recover it by making another trip to B. You kindly presented to me a pretty little gift, bearing on one side the inscription, "Liberty is the Watchword," and on the other my name, which I estimate very highly; but—gracious—you will remember, doubtless, that it was in a circular shape. Have you anything to give me *in the shape of a heart*, Helen? Just examine carefully, if agreeable, and let me know hereafter.

Understandably, Helen was puzzled to know how to interpret this cryptic paragraph. He was apparently trying to compliment the whole Benson clan. Perhaps she felt a little disappointed that he should be so reticent in expressing any special love for her. At any rate, she wrote a provocatively guarded reply, saying that he did not know her well enough to realize how inferior she was to him, that he would be terribly disappointed if she were "to accept of as much friendship, as you have so condescendingly offered." She added that the whole family would gladly share in his affections, though she coyly admitted that her sister Anna expected little would remain after he had "bestowed the greater part upon a certain person, who shall be nameless."

Helen's letter brought a melancholy response from Garrison on March 19, attesting to his loneliness. Even during the trip to England, he said, while cheered by the thought of his thousands of friends, he was unhappy "that among them all there was not one who cherished toward me aught beyond 'friendship's affection.'" Then followed a sentimental outburst: "And therefore I wept in sadness and in solitude. Is it ever thus to be? Alas! all may be mated but me—I have no attractions to enkindle or secure love—there is none in this wide world whose heart I am authorized to claim—none, into whose bosom I can pour the wealth of my affections."

Although he soon had one whose heart he could rightfully claim, the antithesis between the thousands of friends and associates and the lonely lover became a significant emotional pattern in Garrison's life. On the many absences from Helen after their marriage, he was to write home melancholy letters professing love for her and sadness at the separation. The profession was sometimes so excessive that it seemed in part the repression of feelings of guilt at the separation.

If the letter of 8 March confused Helen by its vague indirections, the one of the 19th spoke to her plainly. Now she was certain he wanted to marry her, and she wrote at once, wishing he could receive the letter immediately. Answering his complaint that he had "no attractions to enkindle or secure love," she confessed, *"I never saw one that possessed more*—for they have completely entwined themselves around my heart, and the connecting link, I trust, death can only dissolve." Then she specifically accepted the proposal which he had never specifically made.

After he received this letter, Garrison was still concerned, concerned that their love for each other might supplant their love for God. In his otherwise joyous letter of 26 March, replying to Helen's acceptance of his proposal, he cautioned: "I trust there is One whom we love and admire more than we do each other—

and only one. Oh! he is infinitely lovely!" In a later letter he applied the same basic idea to the problem of happiness. If we first give our homage to God and then our complete devotion to each other, he reasoned, we cannot fail to be happy, though we must not expect perfect happiness on earth since heaven is our true home. On earth it is only right, he said rather significantly, that we should possess a certain restlessness of mind which cannot be entirely satisfied.[7]

Just as Garrison feared that his love for Helen might diminish his love for God, so he was afraid—gratuitously, it would seem—that his affection for her might overstep the bounds of propriety. He asked her to forgive him if he ever said or did anything unworthy of himself and to attribute it to his "passionate attachment." "But," he assured her, "I remember nothing with which to upbraid myself; for I love you with a pure heart, and would not for worlds behave unseemly in your sight." "The consummation of our wishes, according to the forms of law," he pompously stated, was what he desired.

The conjunction of Garrison's concern about love of God and his concern for propriety perhaps bespeaks a sexual hesitancy or self-doubt not uncommon to some affianced couples. As usual, Garrison was voicing "good reasons" to conceal his real reasons.

Garrison also wrote much to Helen about the temptation to excessive self-love: "We should meekly bend like the reed to the breath of eulogy, but be lofty and unyielding as the oak when the tempest of an unrighteous persecution is raging around us. How contemptible, how foolish, how disgusting is personal egotism!" Perhaps he was seeking thus to suggest to his future wife that after the joining of their two lives all thought of self must be merged in their mutual interest. It was as though he were dramatizing himself as a kind of object lesson to her.

But personal egotism he could not escape. When the engagement was only a month old, he reported to Helen that at his recent lecture the audience "gave me *four* tremendous rounds of applause before I opened my lips, and applauded me excessively throughout my extempore speech!" Even when he tried to compliment Helen, his vanity obtruded: "Your solitary love for me is dearer to me than the multitudinous friendships of all my admirers." Persecution by his enemies he rationalized into a tribute, confessing that he feared future panegyric rather than present defamation. "I shall be honored and applauded, long after the defenders of slavery are cast into oblivion. This is the fruit of benevolence." When he attended a party "as the lion of the occasion," he was presented with an acrostic poem celebrating his ability and his achievements with what he termed "excessive panegyric." Excessive or not, he could not resist sending Helen a copy of the poem. When he visited Philadelphia, he complained to Helen that he had so many friends it was difficult for him to get any rest: "Hundreds are grieved because it is out of my power to visit them." In the same letter he confessed that he was "getting to be quite in demand among artists," and he resented Jocelyn's giving him "a face as broad as that of a Dutch burger," a forehead that was too low and eyes, nose, and mouth that barely resembled his own. He regretted the failure on account of his friends, who would be greatly disappointed.

Garrison's self-interest could reach almost passionate heights—over the split which he observed in his own personality, he wrote: "Dear Helen, am I not a strange compound? In battling with a whole nation, I am as impetuous, as daring, and as unconquerable as a lion; but in your presence, I am as timid, and gentle, and submissive as a dove." Abroad, he claimed an Indian fortitude in the face of a hostile world; at home, he was as tender and as sympathetic as a child, weeping spontaneously at kind words or fine thoughts or beautiful music—or over a letter from Helen.[8]

Four times during his courtship Garrison channeled his feelings into verse—three sonnets and one acrostic. The poems involved Garrison's love for Helen, his unhappiness at separation from her, and the ways in which his devotion to his fiancée had sharpened his perception of the ills of slavery. The two best sonnets he communicated to Helen by way of publication in *The Liberator*, doubtless surprising her since the engagement was still supposed to be a secret.

If such curious egotism as Lloyd had displayed could not dampen Helen's love, it was indeed a raging fire. And poor Helen's only rival, as the poems clearly indicated, was not any other woman but the cause. Ultimately, even his love for her had to be evaluated in terms of abolition. He said, a month following the appearance of the two sonnets: "I ought to plead for the slave more earnestly and more eloquently now than ever, because I can realize how dreadful a thing it is for lover to be torn away from lover, and husband from wife, and parents from children."

It would seem that Garrison was trying to translate his abolition phrases into the language of personal love—perhaps to help him feel more at home in the latter area: after all, he had long been comfortable in abolition, but he seems to have had some pre-marital anxiety about the strange world of love.

Toward the end of April 1834, while Garrison was in Connecticut on his way to the first annual meeting of the American Anti-Slavery Society—it may have been at the very moment when he was with Helen in Brooklyn—a letter addressed to him in a feminine hand arrived at his Boston office. This letter was to give Garrison a further chance to show how indivisible were his personal life and the reform movement. The letter confessed: "I have latterly thought that my peace of mind, and usefulness in society, will depend on a union with thee. I have had a slight fancy for many . . . , but one only has captured my heart—my hand and heart are thine." The writer said that she expected to be disowned by her Quaker meeting, but that she still wanted only to be married to him.

Garrison wrote at once to the young lady telling of his engagement. He also reported the incident to Helen, regretting that the young Quaker was doomed to disappointment. Helen was incredulous. She could not believe that any "young lady with the least delicacy of feeling, and in her right senses would have written such a letter," and she asked her name. By 2 June, the date of another letter to Helen, Garrison seemed a little piqued by his fiancée's unwillingness to believe him. He assured her that the proposal was genuine and that the girl's name was Leah Fell. Then he expatiated seriously on the topic of woman's rights. Was there really any reason why women should not as freely tell their love as men? "Will it be said that delicacy ought to deter a woman from first avowing her love? Is not this tantamount to saying that there is something indelicate in a marriage proposal?" Many women, he thought, had died broken-hearted simply because they were too proud or too conventional to reveal their love. Even Helen herself, he suggested, should have revealed her developing love for him if he had not declared himself first.

Cogent as Garrison's argument was, Helen was not convinced immediately, though she admitted in the next letter "that if a woman was allowed to choose a husband for herself, her choice would generally be the most judicious one." A week later, after a bit more coaxing from Garrison, she capitulated: "I have half a mind to think with you there is nothing so improper in a woman's proposing." All during their long life together Helen was never seriously to differ with her husband.

Garrison gave the impression that Leah was a young girl who really did not know any better than to propose to a man who had attracted her. "A pretty, artless, simple-minded girl," he called her. Actually, Leah was at the time of her proposal to Garrison a mature woman of thirty-six—seven years her would-be fiancé's senior—who had been a successful teacher for some years.[9]

Garrison said in his first letter about Leah that her proposal was not a matter for any levity, yet in other matters not so entwined with his self-esteem, he could display a lively sense of humor—if, to modern ears, a questionable taste in puns. In one of her letters Helen relayed a message from Mrs. May:[10] "Tell Mr. G. I like to make appropriate presents, and I know a little *nigger cat* in this town, I could procure and send to him; and I must hear from him by a sonnet in the *Liberator.*" Garrison rose to the occasion:

I return my thanks to my lively friend Mrs. May in *black and white,* for the feline gift she is disposed to send me. As I am opposed to colonization, let the little sable animal remain until I visit B. I may possibly volunteer a sonnet upon it, by and by—especially if a *cat*-astrophe overtake it, so that I may say of it, "Requies-*cat* in pace!" in conveying its mortal remains to the *cat*-acombs.[11]

In his letters during the late summer there were many puns, as though Garrison were relaxing or as though he had a case of nervous epistolary giggles. He was both fascinated and amused by the balloon ascensions of Charles Ferson Durant, the first professional aeronaut in the United States. He described to Helen on 4 August one of Durant's ascents, telling her that he was going to make another one soon. "Shall I beseech him to wait until after our wedding, that you may get a view of his ascension? Perhaps if you will consent to go up with him, . . . he will consent to postpone his flight." In a letter to George Benson, written at midnight, 21 August, two weeks before the wedding,[12] Garrison talked humorously about Durant, suggesting that since in the old days they used to hang witches for riding on broomsticks, they ought to hang Durant. In the next paragraph Garrison discussed the Reverend Mr. Frost of Oneida Institute, through whose "influence many colonizations have been sadly *Frost* bitten, and nothing but an abolition poultice could cure them." Then he returned to the wedding theme: "In a fortnight from to-day, comes the consummation of my desires. I shall no longer herd with bachelors. A single life is indisputably an odd life; and, therefore, by taking one unto myself, I make things even."

But Garrison had more to do during the summer of 1834 than make puns. He had to decide where he and Helen would live. Roxbury appealed to him as an attractive location—it was near the city (only fifty minutes by foot and a few minutes by omnibus) and it was almost like the country in its beauty. Unfortunately, he found that in Roxbury cottages "are as much in demand, as the madman Garrison is in the southern States." Of the few available, he liked best the one where he had been boarding— the whole house was then for rent. It had "recently been enlarged and materially improved" and it was located in a secluded setting. In short, it seemed to him an ideal cottage for a honeymooning couple, although hardly what we would call such. It had seven bedrooms—six of them commodious, one small; it had "two fine parlors and a sitting room"; and both a cellar kitchen and an upper one. In fact, it had all the modern conveniences; there was a splendid well in the back cellar, the water being "conducted into the kitchen, so that it is not necessary to go out of the house for it." All of this Garrison hoped to rent for $150 per year, though the owner wanted $200.

After deciding on the house Garrison characteristically took upon himself the arrangement of every domestic detail. He had to find some furniture. Helen had suggested that they would need nine or ten chairs and a sofa. In addition to these, he bought "three common tables, one toilet table, wash-stands, looking glasses, clock, &c. &c. &c., besides all the paraphernalia of the kitchen." He also had the bedrooms and entries carpeted for 23 cents per square yard. For a time he was stopped by the problem of beds—both how many and whether double or single. Three double and two single seemed about right. Then there must be feather beds, even though feathers cost 30 cents to 50 cents per pound, a double bed requiring about thirty-five pounds.

As though he feared being alone with his bride, Garrison persuaded Isaac Knapp, his partner, and Eliza Chace, a good friend of Helen's, to board with them. He also hoped Knapp's sister, Abigail, would spend part of her time with them, as a companion for Helen. "When George Thompson arrives [he added], I have no doubt that he will gladly hire a part of our cottage for his lady, whom you will find to be an excellent young lady, of amiable manners and good intelligence. In this manner we shall get a social little circle."

There was another problem—who would do the housework? He hired as servant a woman who "is very highly recommended —indeed, as the best among the best—is modest in her deportment and genteel in her appearance—is an excellent cook who needs no instruction, is a professor of religion and a member of the Baptist church in Boston—in short, she is just such a person as we need. . . . Your mind will now be relieved of much anxiety." For the cook, moreover, he provided some supplies: "one barrel of molasses, half a barrel of rice, half a barrel brown sugar, and half a barrel loaf and lump." And all these were free from the taint of slave labor, since they came from a free-goods store. "House-keeping," he admitted, "is a much more formidable enterprise than I had anticipated."

To every arrangement the selfless Helen gave her unqualified approval:

I shall be extremly [sic] happy to see Miss Knapp at our house; I should think her brother would like to have her with him very much, and it would add to our happiness in contributing to his; I shall consider it a privillage [sic] to claim her as a companion.

I presume the tables are exactly such as I should like; so make no hesitancy in purchasing them. Do not fear but what everything will suit me. I can assure you I am not difficult.

In regard to finances, she responded in the same way. Garrison wrote to say that he must have a regular salary for editing *The Liberator*. He was hoping that the New-England Anti-Slavery

Society would take over the financial responsibility of the paper and pay him a salary. One thousand dollars seemed to him a fair amount, since he said he could get that much by abandoning *The Liberator* and lecturing as general agent for the national society.

Helen agreed that he must have a regular income, though she urged him to feel no anxiety on her account. "I know I am not extravigant [*sic*] and shall always wish to live exactly as you see proper."

Already Garrison had put Helen to the test, and she had proved herself quite the opposite of his aggressive and domineering mother. In Helen, as he himself observed in a letter to his brother-in-law on the first anniversary of the marriage, he sought a refuge from the vicissitudes of the cause. "It was undoubtedly wise in me to select as a partner one who, while her benevolent feelings were in unison with mine, was less immediately and entirely connected with" the cause. "By her unwearied attentions to my wants, her sympathetic regards, her perfect equanimity of mind, and her sweet and endearing manners, she is no trifling support to abolitionism, inasmuch as she lightens my labors, and enables me to find exquisite delight in the family circle, as an off-set to public adversity." [13]

There seem to have been two strains in Garrison's nature, one passive, the other active. He longed to have things done for him. He needed a mother or a wife who would unselfishly minister to his needs, but at the same moment he felt almost guilty about his passivity. He felt that he must venture out into the world to demonstrate his vigorous masculinity. As Fanny Garrison's son he had felt a similar tension. For, although he professed deep love and admiration for her, he preferred to worship at a distance, surrounded by friends.

Helen had, also, the quality of simplicity which was important for the wife of an abolitionist. In many of his letters Garrison stressed the importance of this trait: Helen must be simple both in her tastes and in her manners, so that she could set a good example for the free colored people, whose love of extravagant dress and gaudy ornaments needed to be discouraged. When he found that she again agreed with him, Garrison said: "Your humility charms me, and your good sense and wise judgment greatly redound to your credit. Our views, on this point, are perfectly in unison. I love simplicity of dress, of manners, and of mind—of course, I love you." In short, Garrison was saying that he loved her because she agreed so perfectly with him.

As the wedding date approached—it had been set for 4 September—Garrison's letters to Helen made it clear that he thought the same standard of simplicity should be applied to the wedding celebration as to their life in general. The ceremony must not be marred by the presence of wine nor even, he hoped, though he did not insist on this, by a wedding cake—at least it must not be of "that rich and showy kind which is commonly resorted to on similar occasions." Also, he thought the ceremony should be early in the morning, so that they would be able to make the forty miles to Worcester before dark—leaving them forty miles more to Boston on the second day. As usual, Helen was all agreement. Wine she would not think of serving, the wedding cake she would gladly banish as a useless and foolish custom, and the hour for the ceremony she thought he should decide.

Thursday, 4 September, arrived, a dull New England morning, with sky overcast and just a suggestion of fog. But the lights within the Benson house defied the gloom without, as the family made last-minute preparations. The Reverend Samuel J. May, who had arrived early, seemed more nervous than the bride and groom; it was difficult for him to speak clearly during the service. Garrison's wishes were followed precisely—at eight o'clock the guests began to appear; and by nine o'clock—and, according to Garrison, without bustle or confusion—all the guests had assembled, the ceremony had been performed, the company had departed, and Lloyd and Helen were in their spacious carry-all, setting off as man and wife—accompanied by Aunt Charlotte, Garrison's mother's youngest sister, and Eliza Chace. Soon the clouds blew away, and the brightest of autumn days allowed them to enjoy the northern Connecticut countryside, which, Garrison said, "for wildness, beauty and opulence of scenery, was rapturous and romantic in the extreme." [14]

But the wedding trip could hardly be described as completely rapturous and romantic. They had no sooner reached Worcester (about six-thirty that evening) than Aunt Charlotte was taken violently ill. She vomited at intervals during the night. Eliza became even sicker and had not recovered when they set off for Boston in the morning. It rained steadily the second day. Everyone was soaked through, and Garrison worried about his new clothes. In fact, somewhere between Oxford and Worcester he lost a package containing coat, trousers, vest, and various manuscripts. At Worcester he lost the whip given him by Henry Benson. Even the horses had their difficulties, losing shoes and injuring hooves. But despite everything they reached a gloomy Roxbury early in the evening.[15]

Undaunted by the vicissitudes of the wedding trip, Garrison was still not ready for a conventional honeymoon alone with his bride. He wrote Anna the second day after their arrival at the cottage, asking her to visit them. A week later he wrote to George assuring him that we—that is, Helen, Eliza Chace, Abigail Knapp, Isaac Knapp, and I—"are now prepared to see our abolition friends, especially those from Providence and Brooklyn." He reported that they were looking forward to a visit from Mr. and Mrs. May the next week, and he urged the Bensons to join them as soon as their baby was born.

Garrison had already found that his wishes were Helen's law, and she did not protest his latest plans for acquiring "a social little circle." But she well might have wondered at her husband's restlessness. How could a man want to begin a marriage with so many people in the house? Was he for some reason afraid to be alone with her? He had never been close to any woman before except his mother, whom he greatly loved and admired, although for years before her death they had seen little of each other. Helen resolved to give him all her love, to honor and obey him. Whatever he wanted, she wanted too.

CHAPTER VIII

Magnets of Attraction

GARRISON had married Helen Benson to acquire the security and equilibrium of a family—not only their own immediate family but the whole Benson clan. He desired a family partly because he had never really had one of his own. His father he could hardly remember. His independent mother had neither the time nor the inclination to give him the tenderness and care he needed; he had preferred to live in Newburyport while she worked in Baltimore. His elder sister he could not remember, and the younger one had died the year before their mother, while he was still an apprentice. Only his brother had survived; and James Holley Garrison was little comfort, for he had spent his time drinking and sailing about the world as merchant and naval seaman. But to desire a family is not equivalent to adjusting to it. Since Garrison had had so little experience living with a family, he must at times have found the adjustment to Helen's difficult. Consequently, his feelings toward Helen, like his feelings toward his mother, may have been somewhat ambivalent. He may even have feared that the intimacy of the marital relationship would reveal some deep-seated inferiority, a hidden weakness in his character. He may have sensed that Helen might see that he was not always the bold and independent man he wished to appear. Perhaps, therefore, he longed for a large family partly as a protective device—to prevent too close an intimacy even with Helen.

During the first years of his marriage Garrison felt strongly "the all-powerful magnet of attraction" [1] of Helen and the family, but he also felt strongly the pull of the active life of an abolitionist. He and Helen lived on in Roxbury, while he edited *The Liberator*, lectured, and attended meetings.

In the early spring of 1835 Garrison made a trip to New York and Philadelphia on antislavery business, and Helen visited her family in Brooklyn. Garrison's letters from "Babylon the great" described the vacancy in his heart at his separation from his bride and family and implied that he was slightly jealous that she would see without him all the friends and relatives in Brooklyn and Providence (the city where George Benson now lived). From Philadelphia, his favorite city next to Boston, he wrote more letters to Helen, telling of the "hundreds in this city who long to see and embrace you," but assuming that she "would shrink from the thronged assemblies in which I mix." Among the friends he singled out for special praise the energetic Quaker abolitionist Lucretia Mott, "a bold and fearless thinker . . . of most amiable manners, and truly instructive in her conversation."

By the end of March Lloyd was back in Brooklyn with Helen. He had arrived in time for a driving spring snowstorm, and the two of them planned—perhaps as they sat before a roaring fire— to move from the so-called cottage in Roxbury to a boarding-house, where Helen would have less work to do during her pregnancy. Early in May Helen was still with her family, and they had decided to move into a house at 23 Brighton Street (ominously close to the Leverett Street Jail), helping George Thompson out of some of his difficulties by assuming his lease.[2] Garrison was making all the arrangements for the move.

Settling into the new house was interrupted by another trip to New York—this one for the annual meeting of the American Anti-Slavery Society. Again Garrison wrote his wife, feeling a little guilty this time, for he protested the separation rather too emphatically, trying to console Helen with the suggestion that at least "we can hope to be eternally together in bliss hereafter."

The next summer the young couple were again separated when Garrison set off with Aunt Charlotte, Fanny Garrison's sister, on what seemed an unlikely mission to claim the Lloyd inheritance in New Brunswick. Although it made him feel important to seek an inheritance and to discover a large family connection in New

Brunswick, the trip proved frustrating. He could not recover the property he should have inherited without a lawsuit that would have cost more than the value of the property. Again Garrison reminded himself how much his young wife meant to him. He resolved to return as fast as possible. But the trip back was a nightmare. Nothing but fog, fog, fog! At least the experience brought forth a sally into rollicking verse:

> *Misty*-cal Lines
> Or mud or mire, or marsh or bog,
> Is better than this drizzling fog.
> The *Boundary* cannot sail—a clog
> Embargoes her—it is the fog.
> It gripes and binds like any cog
> In miller's wheel—tenacious fog!
> O [, de] liver me from a mad-dog,
> And next—from this drear eastern fog!
> I like not to be flogg'd, or flog—
> As little do I like a fog.
> Hail, murrain, lice, and many a frog,
> Did Egypt plague—but not this fog!
> It blears and stupifies like grog—
> O, vile narcotic, muddling fog!
> In vain our eyes are all agog
> To see—we look in vain through fog.
> 'Tis obstinate as any hog—
> It will not budge an inch, this fog.
> Poor patience keeps her easy job
> No longer—how she scolds the fog!
> Better to have king Stork, or Log,
> Reign over us than spectre Fog!—
> Call this not *East*-port more—transmog-
> Rify it thus—the *port* of Fog! [3]

A month later, with Eastport only a memory, Lloyd and Helen were in Brooklyn with the Bensons. Garrison wrote to his brother-in-law Henry Benson, who had gone to Boston to help Isaac Knapp with *The Liberator,* his mood reflecting the sylvan atmosphere of the country as well as his impatience for the stimulus of the city. He was a man between two worlds, feeling the magnetic pull of each: "The quietude of Brooklyn is refreshing to my spirit. It seems as if the moral elements had suddenly become hushed, and that violence, oppression and sin no longer abounded in our land. Would it were so indeed!" And then—almost in the same breath: "Unless you and friend K. supply me pretty freely and very regularly with letters and papers, I shall not be able to content myself here long, away from the field of strife." [4]

Lloyd and Helen stayed on in Brooklyn, probably because of Helen's advancing pregnancy. His letters, although expressing his joy at being with his wife and her family, showed an increasing restlessness and a desire to return to the city and active agitation. He became almost pathetically eager for the bundle of newspapers sent him regularly and surreptitiously by Henry Benson, the bundle being addressed to George Benson lest Garrison's enemies find him out.

Lloyd and Helen were still in Brooklyn on their first wedding anniversary. Lloyd celebrated in part by writing a letter to George, praising bride and marriage. All that he had hoped for he had found. He had nothing to regret "but my own unworthiness." Helen was "a loving attentive and obedient wife—a pleasant and desirable companion—and a most disinterested and pure-minded creature." Garrison congratulated himself on the choice of a wife —admiration for the efficient and eloquent Lucretia Mott notwithstanding. He had found someone who was loving and attentive in a way that his mother had never been. Not only that but, as he had said before, she helped him understand the ultimate horrors of slavery. He could imagine now how a slave husband must feel to have his bride torn from his arms, how a slave wife must feel to have her beloved sold at auction. In the mirror of his own domestic happiness Garrison saw "the terrific image of the monster Slavery reflected" more clearly than ever before.[5]

Garrison was content to remain in Brooklyn for only a few more weeks after his wedding anniversary. When, toward the end of September, he heard it rumored that he was staying in Brooklyn because he did not dare return to Boston, he and Helen moved into the new house.[6]

Garrison's conscience may have bothered him that he had remained in Brooklyn so much of the time during the year of George Thompson's lecture mission to the United States. Thompson, who had been Garrison's best friend among the British abolitionists, had landed in New York in September of 1834, about two weeks after the honeymooners had arrived in Roxbury. For several months before this time Garrison had been briefing readers of his paper about Thompson, characterizing him as an electrifying orator and the greatest living British abolitionist, a man whose current mission to this country was comparable in importance to Lafayette's during the Revolution.[7]

But Garrison's propaganda was insufficient to endear Thompson to America. Nor were his own performances on the lecture platform—impressive as they were—calculated for popular approval. Thompson was a massive frame of a man, five feet ten inches tall, with large head, prominent slightly aquiline nose, deeply set eyes, determined mouth. His voice, though at times calm and conversational, was resonant and full-bodied. And the action of body, hands, and arms was wonderfully varied and expressive, echoing effectively the vehemence and passion of the man.[8] But he was also an aggressive and sometimes sarcastic foreigner who tried to dominate every meeting he attended, antagonizing the more moderate abolitionists, and challenging the uninitiated. As a result he stirred up much resentment—not all of it polite. At Concord, New Hampshire, there were broken windows. At Lowell, Massachusetts, on 1 December, a heavy brickbat narrowly missed Thompson's head. This "deadly missile" Garrison was delighted to have displayed in the Anti-Slavery Office with a label describing how "the Citizens of low(h)ell" had brutally attacked the visiting abolitionist.[9]

Garrison was angry at Lowell for its reception of Thompson, and his anger—ironically for one who claimed all mankind as his countrymen—brought out his latent suspicion of foreigners. He said there was always ample material for such a mob in a city like Lowell: "Manufacturing towns always contain suitable materials for a mob . . ." Indeed, "many of the rabble were foreigners of the *lowest* grade, who assembled to put down a foreigner of the *highest!* It shows what sort of animals are opposed to abolitionists, and furnishes good proof of the excellency of the anti-slavery cause." [10]

Thompson was not easily discouraged. Though the opposition became more pronounced as he lectured throughout the Northern states and as far west as Ohio, he continued on his mission until

November 1835. He ignored denunciation in Northern as well as Southern papers, where he was ridiculed as the apostle of "Caledonian Damsels" and "pussy cats of Glasgow" (benevolent ladies had contributed toward his trip) and where he was attacked as an emissary of the British government bent on the overthrow of the United States. It was not until the end of September, about the time Garrison returned to Boston from Brooklyn, when lynching was threatened and he was hit on the side of the face with a stone, that he stopped lecturing and sought refuge with friends. He went from one hideout to another during October and November.[11] Toward the end of November he sailed secretly from Boston to St. John, New Brunswick, and from there home, rejoicing that he would be able once more to "breathe the air of a country where the divine right of Kings to govern wrong is acknowledged and respected." [12]

A few months before Thompson returned to England, conservative elements in Boston were sufficiently disturbed to call for a meeting at Faneuil Hall to protest against the tactics used by the abolitionists. On the afternoon of 21 August the elite of Boston filed into the sacred hall, where a series of speakers reprimanded the radical abolitionists for their unseemly agitation and incidentally reassured Southerners—a considerable number of whom were supposed to have attended the meeting themselves—by telling how respectable Northerners felt. Garrison was horrified that the "Cradle of Liberty" should be used for such a vile meeting. He reported in *The Liberator* the next day that Faneuil Hall had been "turned into a worse than Augean stable. . . . If a modern Hercules could draw the vast Atlantic through it, he would fail in his attempt to purify it." Henceforth, he proclaimed, it must be called "the REFUGE OF SLAVERY," or, as he called it the next week, "the COFFIN OF LIBERTY."

By this time Garrison had become so greatly concerned by the violence of feeling about the abolitionists that he urged Thompson and others to discontinue their public speeches. "There is yet too much fever, and too little rationality in the public mind, either for him or any of us to make addresses to the patient without having him attempt to knock us down. Write—print —distribute—this we may do with profit to our cause. . . . By and by . . . we shall raise a blush of shame upon" the cheeks of Bostonians who really do "have a strong patriotic attachment for Faneuil Hall." [13]

During the night of Thursday, 10 September,[14] a substantial gallows, constructed of maple beams five inches in diameter, standing some eight or nine feet high and large enough to accommodate two persons, was raised in front of Garrison's house in Boston. The gallows attracted the interest of a good many people; by nine o'clock quite a crowd had gathered to inspect it. About ten-thirty the city authorities took it down and sawed it up. Garrison regretted that he had not been in town to preserve the gallows for the antislavery museum, and he suggested that the two nooses might well be intended for the execution of "those twin-monsters, SLAVERY AND COLONIZATION," instead of for Thompson and himself.[15]

Others had to endure what Whittier called "suffering by proxy." In Concord, New Hampshire, in spite of his Quaker garb Whittier was mistaken for Thompson and his coat was so thoroughly splattered with rotten eggs that he had to discard it, although it made an appropriate gift for a Southern freedman after the war.[16] Such, Thompson said, was "the fruit of keeping bad company." [17] But Garrison himself was yet to undergo his most exciting and most dangerous experience.

CHAPTER IX

———◆◆◆———

Hurricane Excitement

THE Boston Female Anti-Slavery Society had announced from various pulpits and in various papers their anniversary meeting for 14 October. It was, they said, to take place at the Anti-Slavery Hall, 46 Washington Street, and George Thompson would deliver the principal lecture. The Boston *Commercial Gazette*, indignant over this announcement, accused Thompson of hiding behind petticoats, but assured him that the ladies would not be able to protect him this time. There would be, they said, violence "from men of property and standing, who would have a large interest at stake in this community." There was soon such general excitement about the projected meeting that the ladies announced its postponement until 21 October, when there would be speeches by leading friends of the cause. It was rumored that Thompson would still be the chief speaker, and the excitement seemed as intense as ever. It must have been about this time that Garrison received the following undated threat:

You are hereby notified to remove your office and not to issue the paper any more. If it is issued again beware of yourself you will have a coat of tar and feathers and you will do well if you get your life saved. We shall have no mercy on you after this Notification *Beware*

Thirty Truckmen
pr C. Adams, secty.

Please show Mr. Garrison & Thompson this [1]

The day before the meeting Federalist Mayor Theodore Lyman, a wealthy merchant turned politician, received petitions from storekeepers in the vicinity of the antislavery rooms at 46 Washington Street who anticipated damage to their property during the meeting the next day. On the morning of the 21st the Boston papers featured the meeting in such a way as to add to the general excitement. Anxious to be prepared for any emergency, the mayor sent to the Anti-Slavery Office to inquire whether Thompson were going to speak that afternoon. He was assured that the Englishman was not even in town.[2] In the course of the morning two merchants from Central Wharf, both of whom had participated in the conservative Faneuil Hall meeting in August, came to the editor of the *Commercial Gazette* to require him to write, print, and post about the town handbills which would wake up the populace and prevent the meeting. By one o'clock five hundred copies of the following had been distributed in hotels, barrooms, readingrooms, offices, and among the workers of the North End:

THOMPSON
THE ABOLITIONIST

The infamous foreign scoundrel *Thompson* will hold forth *this afternoon,* at the Liberator Office, No. 48, Washington Street. The present is a fair opportunity for the friends of the Union to *snake Thompson out!* It will be a contest between the Abolitionists and the friends of the union. A purse of $100 has been raised by a number of patriotic citizens to reward the individual who shall first lay violent hands on Thompson, so that he may be brought to the tar kettle before dark. Friends of the Union, be vigilant!

Boston, Wednesday, 12 o'clock.[3]

When Garrison arrived at the Anti-Slavery Hall sometime between two and three o'clock,[4] about a hundred men were milling around the entrance to the building. On climbing the stairs to the meeting room on the third floor, he found fifteen or twenty women surrounded by a crowd of noisy young men. As he pushed his way into the room, he could hear the ominous whisper, "That's Garrison!" But he took his seat and waited. The crowd remained. In a few minutes he stood up and said calmly:

Gentlemen, perhaps you are not aware that this is a meeting of the Boston *Female* Anti-Slavery Society, called and intended exclusively for *ladies,* and those only who have been invited to address them. Understanding this fact you will not be so rude or indecorous as to thrust your presence upon this meeting. If, gentlemen, . . . some of you are *ladies*—in disguise—why only apprise me of the fact, give me your names and I will introduce you to the rest of your sex, and you can take seats among them accordingly.[5]

Garrison's words had an hypnotic effect—for the moment at least. Miss Mary Parker, boarding-house keeper as well as president of the society, persuaded him to take advantage of the lull to leave the room. He locked himself, along with another abolitionist named C. C. Burleigh, in the Anti-Slavery Office next door—to protect the publications stored there, he said. Meantime, the mayor was shouting to the mob, telling them to go home, that Thompson would not speak, that he was not even in town.

The meeting began. Miss Parker read the Bible and offered up a prayer for forgiveness "of enemies and revilers," but the onlookers became more interested in the Anti-Slavery Office than in the meeting. Garrison heard a crashing thump as someone kicked in the lower panel of the door. Eyes glared up at him. He continued at the desk, writing a description of the events of the day. What a wonderful opportunity for a nonresistant! Maybe he should give himself up to the mob? A vision flickered through his mind. He saw his body quivering at the end of a rope attached to a tree on the Common. What a potent symbol for the abolitionists his martyrdom would be! But Burleigh persuaded Garrison to stay there in the office, while he himself went out to distract the mob's attention. Burleigh opened the door, stepped into the hall, closed the door and, locking it again, walked off. The stratagem worked.

Meanwhile, Mayor Lyman, in the wake of two or three constables, forced his way into the meeting room. He urged the women: "Go home, ladies, go home."

"What renders it necessary we should go home?" Miss Parker questioned.

"I am the mayor of the city, and I cannot now explain; but will call upon you this evening."

As Mr. Lyman spoke, several women rose. "If the ladies will be seated, we will take the sense of the meeting," Miss Parker replied.

"Don't stop, ladies, go home."

Miss Parker again: "Will the ladies listen to a letter addressed to the Society by Francis Jackson, Esq.?" (Francis Jackson was a wealthy Boston merchant and abolitionist who had offered the society the use of his home.)

Mr. Lyman almost shouted: "Ladies, do you wish to see a scene of bloodshed and confusion? If you do not, go home."

Mrs. Maria W. Chapman, a charming and handsome woman, one of the most effective of female abolitionists, said, "Mr. Lyman, your personal friends are the instigators of this mob; have you ever used your personal influence with them?"

Mr. Lyman replied, "I know no personal friends; I am merely an official. Indeed, ladies, you must retire. It is dangerous to remain."

Mrs. Chapman: "If this is the last bulwark of freedom, we may as well die here as anywhere."

Mr. Lyman: "Do you wish to prolong the scene of confusion?"

The president broke in: "Can we pass out safely?"

Again the mayor: "If you will go *now*, I will protect you, but cannot unless you do."

Still not to be hurried, the ladies would not leave until they had duly voted a motion to adjourn.[6] Then, two by two, colored mixed with white, they trailed down the steep stairs, into the hall, and out into the street. But such a procession hardly calmed the excited mob. White and colored marching together! What would be next?

As the ladies, surrounded by taunts, hisses, and cheers, disappeared into the crowd, attention focused on the sign, "Anti-Slavery Rooms," which hung outside the building. Here was another symbol of the fanatical cause! The mob lunged toward the sign. Mayor Lyman ordered it removed. When it fell to the ground, the mob pounced on it and like wild animals with a chunk of meat tore it to pieces.[7]

About this time, Garrison was being urged to escape out the back of the building. The Anti-Slavery Office was located on Washington Street, less than a block from the City Hall (now called the Old State House) on State Street. It was possible to reach the City Hall down Wilson's Lane, which ran back of the building into State Street. Garrison crawled out a back window, dropping onto the roof of a shed. He could hear the mob in front of the building: "*Garrison* is there! Garrison! Garrison! We must have Garrison! Out with him! Lynch him!" In a flash he rushed into a carpenter's shop on Wilson's Lane and hid on the second floor behind a pile of boards. Almost at once the mob was there too, winding a rope around his body and forcing him to climb down a ladder to the ground, though some were for throwing him out the window.

Then the unexpected happened. Two or three powerful men seized Garrison, shouting: "He shan't be hurt! You shan't hurt him! Don't hurt him! He is an American!" With the momentum of the pressing throng of arms and heads and legs they moved down the lane toward the City Hall.[8]

Then followed a quick consultation between the mayor and his advisers, while Garrison borrowed coat, hat, and pantaloons—his own new suit had been reduced to rags. It was decided that Leverett Street Jail, more than a mile away, was the only safe place for him. Garrison agreed to a technical charge of disturbing the peace, provided he not be subjected to any expense for board and lodging. A carriage appeared, and the prisoner-to-be was pushed through the crowd into the coach.

In heroic simile Garrison later compared the mob to an ocean "lashed into fury" by a storm. It bore down on the frail coach. Men hung onto the wheels, forced open the doors, grabbed the horses, and tried to overturn the carriage. But the police rushed in, pushed back the mob, closed the doors, and, with the crack of a whip, the coach rolled off at high speed for the jail. Again in Leverett Street the crowd rushed the carriage, but Garrison was lodged safely in a cell, "accompanied," as he said, "by two delightful associates, a good conscience and a cheerful mind." [9]

In the evening he was visited by a number of friends, including Whittier and May, who found him in high spirits, enjoying this confinement even more than the one in Baltimore. He wished that he could receive them more hospitably and that he could put them up for the night.

The next morning, after a sound sleep, he inscribed on the walls of his cell the memorial that William Lloyd Garrison had been confined there "to save him from the violence of a 'respectable and influential' mob, who sought to destroy him for preaching the abominable and dangerous doctrine, that all men are created equal . . ." He hoped that the inscription would remain until all the slaves had been freed. On the wall he also wrote a poem, testifying to the peace and freedom of his mind. The poem ended this way:

Confine me as a prisoner—but bind me not as a slave.
Punish me as a criminal—but hold me not as a chattel.
Torture me as a man—but drive me not like a beast.
Doubt my sanity—but acknowledge my immortality.[10]

That same morning he went through the form of a trial and was released, though he was advised to leave town for the present.

All those who saw Garrison on the 21st agreed that he acted with courage and dignity, although Samuel E. Sewall admitted that he was not so supernaturally calm as he had been reported.[11]

While Garrison was showing his courage to the mob, Helen had a less ostentatious way of demonstrating hers. Although she was then more than six months pregnant with her first child, she tried to attend the meeting of the Female Anti-Slavery Society. She got within sight of 46 Washington Street but turned back because of the crowds. She stayed for a time at a nearby house and then returned home where she expected to find her husband, but there was only the colored servant, who reported that a gentleman, much agitated and anxious to see her, had called. A few moments later Samuel E. Sewall returned. The expression on his face announced that something was wrong; she imagined the worst. When he told her what had happened and that Garrison was at that moment in the mayor's office, she determined to go to her husband at once. En route to the City Hall, she met some friends who persuaded her not to expose herself in her condition to the mob in the streets. She went to a friend's house to wait in agonizing suspense until five o'clock when she heard that her husband was safe in the Leverett Street Jail. When she saw him there, she wondered at his calmness and composure and was proud that he had been "willing to sacrifice his life, rather than compromise principles." [12]

Garrison's composure in the face of the Boston mob was nothing new. As we know, he had schooled himself to the martyr's philosophy since the days of his earliest adversity. After his imprisonment in Baltimore, he had expressed his willingness to die a martyr to the cause. He had explained on many occasions that he did not fear death and persecution, because Jesus had shown him the way: "I do not forget that Christ and his apostles,—harmless undefiled and prudent as they were,—were buffeted, calumniated and crucified; and therefore my soul is as steady to its pursuit as the needle to the pole . . ." [13] To his brother-in-law he had written, about five weeks before being mobbed in Boston: "If we perish, our loss will but hasten the destruction of slavery more certainly. My mind is full of peace—I know what it is to rejoice in tribulation." [14] And a few days after being mobbed, he said: "I speak the express language of my soul when I say, that I would rather have the peril and outrage through which I have passed, than such a reception as Lafayette received, comparing the motives and objects of those who engaged in the general excitement. Give me brickbats in the cause of God, to wedges of gold in the cause of sin." [15]

Indeed, the real suffering in Garrison's life had been not on 21 October but earlier. As a boy he had been ignored by his family and humiliated by poverty. More recently, his several failures as editor had brought renewed frustration. Now, however, he was no longer alone and no longer frustrated. Surrounded by family and friends, he was the editor of his own abolitionist paper and the founder and leader of the New-England Anti-Slavery Society. Why should he be unduly alarmed over the incidents of the 21st? Perhaps the obscure misfit of a few years before would have fled before the mob, but the man of family, the distinguished leader of 1835, could survive—in fact, enjoy—the attentions of any mob.

Garrison's response on the 21st followed one of the most persistent emotional patterns to be observed in his life. He gloried in the hostility of the mob, but he was also quite willing to submit to a technical police charge which would lodge him in the safety of the jail.

When Garrison came to describe the Boston mob for *The Liberator* (7 November), he wrote at considerable length, though he had promised only a simple statement, since he approved of Burleigh's eye-witness account printed shortly after the event. He expressed not only his ideas about martyrdom but also his views of basic human rights. He translated the personal experience of the near-martyr into universal terms, and the event of the day became something more than a conflict between a particular mob and an individual man. It became "the most disgraceful event that has ever marred the character of Bostonians." His argument, which shows little understanding of mob psychology, runs thus: Had the mob merely sought to tar and feather or lynch the foreigner, George Thompson, they would have dispersed when the mayor told them that Thompson was not in town. Since they did not disperse, it was evident that they opposed the Female Society and even the whole antislavery cause. From this argument it was but one step to assert that the conflict was really between despotism and freedom:

No. Their grand design, then, is not simply to drive an English philanthropist from our shores, but to mal-treat, gag and enslave AMERICAN, NATIVE-BORN CITIZENS! The struggle is between Right and Wrong—Liberty and Slavery—Christianity and Atheism—Northern Freemen and Southern Taskmasters. The great question to be settled is not whether 2,500,000 slaves in our land shall be either immediately or gradually emancipated—or whether they shall be colonized abroad or retained in our midst—for that is now a subordinate point; but whether freedom is with us—THE PEOPLE OF THE UNITED STATES—a reality or a mockery; whether the liberty of speech and of the press, purchased with the toils and sufferings and *precious blood* of our fathers, is still to be enjoyed, unquestioned and complete—or whether padlocks are to be put upon our lips, gags into our mouths, and shackles upon that great palladium of human rights, the press. . . .

With editorial exuberance Garrison was identifying the cause of abolition with the cause of universal freedom in order to demonstrate that slavery itself represented a contradiction of natural rights. To him the basic conflict on 21 October was clearly between freedom and tyranny. The Female Anti-Slavery Society and the abolitionists at bay were the forces of freedom; the ravenous mob and the mayor too, though perhaps not so absolutely,[16] represented tyranny. And (startling irony to Garrison!) the mob, unlike the rabble at Lowell, were "gentlemen of property and standing." Garrison seemed to have forgotten the threat from the "Thirty Truckmen," as he rationalized his frustration into righteous indignation in defense of the cause. Probably, Garrison also emphasized the gentility of the mob in order to link it to the conservative meeting in Faneuil Hall the preceding August. That meeting, he thought, had provided the theory of despotism; the Boston mob, the practice.

And so Garrison was able to use his experiences with the mob as a powerful weapon to further the cause of emancipation—just as he had used, in a minor way, the brickbat which narrowly missed Thompson at Lowell. That the notoriety which he had achieved was an effective weapon is attested by the fact that the circulation of *The Liberator* increased noticeably and, more important, that several able new abolitionists were recruited at this time. Among them was Dr. Henry I. Bowditch. Recently returned from studying medicine in Europe, Bowditch saw the mob in Washington Street and asked what the matter was. Upon being told that the crowd was trying to snake out Garrison and Thompson in order to tar and feather them, he said: "Then it has come to this, that a man cannot speak on slavery within sight of Faneuil Hall and almost at the foot of Bunker Hill? If this is so, it is time for me to become an Abolitionist." The next day he subscribed to *The Liberator*.[17] Another of the recruits, Wendell Phillips, then a young lawyer just starting to practice, had a more violent reaction. He wanted to fight and wondered why his regiment had not been called out. (He later argued that several of the rioters should have been shot to break up the mob.) Charles Sumner wrote to Dr. Francis Lieber, 9 January 1835: "We are becoming abolitionists at the North fast; the riots, the attempts to abridge the freedom of discussion,—and the conduct of the South generally have caused many to think favorably of immediate emancipation who never before inclined to it." [18] Edmund Quincy, though he did not become an active abolitionist until after Lovejoy's death in 1837, recorded his shock over the Boston mob in his journal; he was amazed that such an event could happen in a democracy.[19]

Two days after the riot Lloyd and Helen rushed back to Brooklyn, which Garrison welcomed as a retreat. Having been somewhat intimidated by the Boston mob, he no longer complained about the quiet routine of Friendship's Valley. Rather, the problem was "whether it is necessary for me to abide in the city." Garrison rationalized that if he remained in Brooklyn he would be relieved of many household cares and would have more time to write for *The Liberator*. Also, boarding at the Bensons' would be much less expensive than keeping house in Boston.[20]

Before the end of the month they had decided to remain in Brooklyn, and by 4 November Garrison was in Boston to make arrangements to break up housekeeping. He had returned to the city rather cautiously, having the driver of the coach let him off not at 23 Brighton Street but at a friend's house; he had promised his wife to take "all proper precautions" and "not needlessly [to] run into danger." [21] Three days later he wrote from the house "that we fondly expected to call our home": "The carpets—tables —chairs—sofa—looking-glasses—&c. seem almost to have found a tongue, to welcome my return, and to congratulate me upon my escape out of the jaws of the lion. The clock ticks an emphatical and sonorous welcome. As for puss, she finds it a difficult matter, even with all her purring and playing, to express her joy." His friends also were kind and sympathetic and eager to welcome him back; in fact, one of them presented him with $45, "which comes most seasonably." One might well wish to be mobbed to get such attention! The second night in Boston he spent at home—along with *The Liberator* staff, Isaac Knapp, Henry Benson, and Charles C. Burleigh, for moral support. Knapp rose early in the morning to get breakfast, "as if he were hired 'help.' " In the morning the maid appeared; she was soon busy cooking, cleaning, and packing.

When Garrison first "sallied out in the street, to see and be seen," he was rather disappointed that almost no one seemed to recognize or pay any attention to him. He had imagined that the whole city would know him after the famous riot. However, before the day was over he saw an excited group parading through the streets, carrying a billboard with a picture of George Thompson and a Negro woman who was represented as saying, "When are we going to have another meeting, brother Thompson?" This Garrison interpreted as a signal for caution. The next two nights he slept at a friend's house.[22]

Making plans to dispose of his furniture and to break his lease, along with the regular work of editing *The Liberator*, occupied Garrison's time during succeeding days. But he also ran inadvertently for the state legislature, since a friend had put up his name; without any electioneering, he received some seventy or eighty votes.[23] The furniture Garrison decided not to sell at auction both because it would not bring a satisfactory price and because such a sale would give him and the cause bad publicity,[24] and so he persuaded friends to use or store most of it. The rest, including his prized portrait of Clarkson and a clock, he put in the Anti-Slavery Office. The lease offered more problems; he feared he would have to pay the rent until the landlord found another tenant. "Was ever married man more unfortunate with houses?

Four times within sixteen months have I removed my furniture, and we have the authority of Benjamin Franklin for saying that three removals are as bad as a fire; so that I have had one fire and a third!" [25]

As for *The Liberator,* Garrison was, as we know, busy making the best possible publicity out of the events of October 21. In the issue for 7 November he printed an inconspicuous little paragraph under the heading, "THINGS WHICH ARE NOT TRUE": "It is not true that I left either the building or the city because I was intimidated—but I left both at the earnest entreaty of the city authorities, and of several friends, and particularly on account of the delicate state of Mrs. Garrison's health." This paragraph caught Helen's eye, and she at once wrote scolding him for referring to her pregnancy in the paper. Garrison replied that she was certainly much more sensitive on this subject than the Queen of England, who had no compunction about announcing forthcoming events. But he asked her pardon and confessed that it was the only way "to exculpate myself from the base charge of cowardice, preferred against me by the newspaper press." [26]

Although the "social little circle" in Boston was diverting, Garrison became increasingly eager to be with his family. By Thanksgiving he was back in Brooklyn eating a bountiful dinner with them. He reported to his brother-in-law George Benson the "immense slaughter among the turkeys, geese and chickens . . . destroyed by the jaw-bones of the people without the slightest remorse" and described how in retribution "the conglomerated fragments of fowls and puddings and pies . . . soon united in getting up an insurrection in the stomach, and peace was not restored until good digestion waited on appetite." [27]

No matter how much he may have enjoyed the Thanksgiving celebration, Garrison could not resist moralizing over the absurdity of appointing one day a year to be thankful for the blessings of God. We should be thankful every day. He resented, also, the proclamation of Thanksgiving by a civil officer, which smacked of union of church and state.

Winter came early in Brooklyn that year. Garrison especially enjoyed sleighing with the Bensons; one day they drove all the way to Canterbury. Doubtless he liked even more sitting by the family hearth, "surrounded by such kind parents and sisters." Being a part of a congenial family and knowing that he and Helen would soon be responsible for enlarging the circle made Garrison glow with contentment. He grew increasingly attached, also, to the quiet village of Brooklyn. If one may judge by his letters, he showed no signs of homesickness for Boston.

But in his retirement with the family in Brooklyn, Garrison never forgot the cause. Through letters, newspapers, pamphlets, and books he was in constant touch with friends and associates. He followed every new development, offered advice, and issued instructions. Connecticut, "the Georgia of New England," was about to be abolitionized by Amos A. Phelps, radical abolitionist and pastor of the Pine Street (Trinitarian) Church in Boston. Garrison advised him to avoid at first New Haven, Hartford, and the other large towns. "Begin at the outskirts, and work your way as quietly as possible into the centre. It is in this manner that Rhode Island has been almost entirely conquered by bro. Stanton." [28] George Benson he urged to keep the mill going by sending in all possible petitions to Congress for the abolition of slavery in the District of Columbia.[29] Isaac Knapp he instructed to give precedence over everything else in *The Liberator* to reports concerning the Congressional debates on the abolition petitions.[30] Henry Benson he asked to reprint from the Lynn *Record* an amusing anonymous poem, headed, "There were some little souls." The poem was written on the occasion of the Boston riot—probably by Garrison himself. Here is the first stanza:

> There were some little souls, with the optics of moles;
> And they said to one another, let us try, try, try,
> If we cannot get Judge *Lynch* to serve at a pinch,
> The ends of little you and little I, I, I.[31]

As the time for the annual meeting of the Massachusetts Anti-Slavery Society (successor to the New-England Anti-Slavery Society) approached, Garrison's letters were full of advice—advice that he would have preferred to give personally had not the baby's imminent arrival prevented his being in Boston. (Births of subsequent babies were not to cause such interference with his anti-slavery activities.) He told Henry: "I entreat, that the *new* Board of Managers may be elected from among *old* and sound materials. Let there be no electioneering after *respectable* and influential persons." [32] He advocated that Henry C. Wright, good friend and nonresistant abolitionist, be elected a vice president of the society.[33] He advised resolutions at the meeting honoring George Thompson, Charles Stuart, and Harriet Martineau.[34]

Interested though Garrison was in all that was happening in the outer world, Helen and her "delicate condition" were his constant preoccupation. Wife and family were *the* magnet of attraction in January 1836. News of the birth of a child to the Samuel J. Mays brought this sympathetic response in a letter to Henry Benson:

What an enviable couple they must be who are able to produce a beautiful *bud of May* in freezing January! Give my congratulations to bro. M. and his wife, and tell them there is a pair in Brooklyn who are resolved to present a greater phenomenon in the course of a week or two—we expect that *a whole Garrison* will then be born at a single birth! . . . When will the age of wonders cease? [35]

Two and a half weeks later, at twelve noon, 13 February, after more than twelve hours of labor Helen was delivered of George Thompson Garrison. (Some of Garrison's critics suggested that he name his next child Benedict Arnold.) [36] It was "a fine plump boy," according to the grandfather.[37] The father promptly celebrated the event by writing five sonnets, which he had printed in *The Liberator* a week later. As one might have foreseen, the theme of all five was the same: the birth of a son makes the abolitionist feel more keenly than ever the horrors of slavery. Everything was grist for the antislavery mill.

CHAPTER X

---•◆•---

Central Luminary of Ohio

WHILE Garrison had been busy establishing *The Libera-tor*, founding the New England and the national anti-slavery societies, traveling to England, getting married, and pro-ducing a son—and publicizing all that happened—a very different kind of man had been laboring for the cause of abolition in Ohio and New York.

Theodore D. Weld had been born two years before Garrison in Hampton, Connecticut. He was the son of a Harvard graduate who was minister of the Congregational Church at Hampton. Whereas Garrison was dapper and meticulous in dress and man-ner, Weld was slovenly, never blacking his boots or brushing his coat—his hair, either, for that matter. He had a thin high-bridged nose that twisted to the right, and even as a young man his face was lined by the severity of his expression.[1]

Weld's early years had been spent very differently from Garri-son's. He was sufficiently mature at fourteen to take complete charge of a farm of a hundred acres, and by the time he was sixteen he had earned enough money to go to Phillips Academy at Ando-ver. But, determined to complete the two years in one, he worked so hard that he seriously strained his eyes and had to stop his schooling. At seventeen he took up lecturing, going about the countryside to give courses of lectures in several places. By 1825, five years later, his eyes were well enough for him to enter Hamil-ton College, where he came under the influence of Charles Grand-ison Finney.

Finney, trained as a lawyer, had become the most successful Presbyterian evangelist of his day, the Billy Graham of the nineteenth century. He would descend upon a town, preach two or three hours night after night, warning in the most graphic and theatrical manner of the terrors of hellfire and damnation and welcoming the saved to the glories of eternal bliss. After he had been preaching for several nights, the whole countryside for miles around would be alive with excitement, and converts would pour into the fold—more to escape hell than to reach heaven, some thought. When Finney came to the vicinity of Hamilton College, Weld was determined not to respond to his appeal. He warned his fellow students against the evangelist. But subsequently when he was visiting an aunt in Utica, he was tricked into hearing Finney. The effect on the young man was instantaneous. Finney preached on the text, "One sinner destroyeth much good," and Weld imagined that the whole sermon was directed at him. He was soon under Finney's spell and became a minister of the "Holy Band," preaching along with the master throughout New York State.

Weld became very friendly—the friendship reminds one of Garrison's for Henry C. Wright—with another member of Finney's band, British army officer Captain Charles Stuart, a bachelor who spent much of his time preaching against intemperance and slavery. It was through Stuart's influence that Weld became interested in temperance, manual-labor education, and, eventually, in Negro emancipation. Stuart persuaded him to transfer from Hamilton to Oneida Institute in Whitesboro, New York. There he became monitor of the milking class and earned his board and room with farm labor. He also taught Sunday school, preached, lectured on temperance, and became an ardent Sabbatarian.

In the meantime, Finney had located himself in New York City and interested Garrison's early benefactors, Arthur and Lewis Tappan, in manual-labor education. In July 1831, the Tappans founded the Society for Promoting Manual Labor in Literary Institutions, of which Weld became the general agent. Weld lectured extensively on temperance and manual-labor education and also occasionally on abolition. He worked so hard that he could report to Lewis Tappan in a letter on 28 July 1832 that in twenty-five days he had given—not to count lectures almost every evening—

thirty-two public speeches. It was an average, all told, of more than two appearances a day, each lecture running about an hour and a half. "And yet you and brother Finney . . . think I should *settle in a city!* Nay—nay—brother—God has marked out for me a station of another sort. The highways & hedges of the west." [2]

In October Weld was in Hudson, Ohio, where Western Reserve College was located. The president of the college, Charles B. Storrs, a professor of mathematics named Elizur Wright, and another professor called Beriah Green heard him preach, for he gave five lectures on temperance and four on manual-labor education in the town. But since they had already been influenced by Garrison's more aggressive doctrines (Storrs had been receiving *The Liberator* since February 1831),[3] they had more impact on Weld than he on them.

By the time Weld enrolled in Lane Seminary in Cincinnati to finish his education for the ministry, he had become a radical abolitionist. However, the general student body, containing as it did many Southern students, was conservative on the issue of slavery. There was even a large and active colonization society on the campus. Determined to convert all the students to his views, Weld first persuaded several key Southerners. With their help he attacked the colonizationists. There resulted the famous "Lane Debates," an eighteen-night revival meeting in February 1834, during which problems concerned with slavery and colonization were discussed at length. Weld introduced the first problem, whether the slaveholding states ought to free the slaves immediately, which consumed two evenings. There followed testimonials from several of the eighteen Southern students participating, who described the conditions of slavery in their respective states. One of them, a colored man, brought the audience to tears as he told how he had been transported to Charleston as a child and sold as a slave. After nine nights of discussion the majority voted for immediate emancipation. Then followed nine more nights during which the students discussed the American Colonization Society, reaching almost unanimously the conclusion that the society did not deserve to be supported by Christian people.

In the antislavery society formed at the end of the revival Weld remained in the background, all of the officers and many of the places on the board going to Southerners. But Weld found plenty to do in helping the free colored in Cincinnati, for he taught elementary subjects to school children in a lyceum organized for that purpose. He also made a statistical study of the Negro problem in the city. More important, he spent every free moment of his time with the colored people, discussing their problems and becoming their friend.

The president of Lane Seminary was Lyman Beecher. He was a man sometimes considered wiser in the loins than the head, for he was the father of both Henry Ward Beecher and Harriet Beecher (who was to marry in 1836 Lane professor Calvin Stowe). Beecher had the reputation of being the foremost preacher of the day, and the trustees, with prodding from the Tappan brothers in New York, had counted themselves most fortunate to persuade him to leave his church in Boston to run the seminary. Beecher was himself a proponent of colonization, believing there was no basic conflict between colonization and abolition, and he was a relatively conservative man. In Boston, for instance, he had spent much of his tremendous energy fighting Unitarianism. He was disturbed over the students' dedication to principles of immediate emancipation and especially over their social intercourse with Negroes in Cincinnati. After all, except for the explosively large free colored population, Cincinnati was virtually a Southern city.

Beecher called Weld into his office to discuss the problem. He insisted that the students would defeat their purpose of helping the colored people by treating them as equals. The city was seething, he said, with the prejudice that would extinguish all the students' best efforts if they persisted in fraternizing with the colored. Weld was adamant. He insisted that the students had to live closely with the colored people in order to win their confidence and that prejudice against the Negro was odious and sinful and not to be tolerated.

In May, three months later, the Cincinnati press began to attack the Lane students, rebuking their "sophomoric declarations" and their social radicalism. Weld replied that thelogical students had to educate heart as well as mind and that it was the duty of seminaries to familiarize their students with the most pressing moral problems of the day. During the summer President Beecher, as well as most of the faculty, was out of town, and the students had the freedom to continue their work with the Negroes in

Cincinnati. Weld also had the opportunity to discuss abolition with James G. Birney, whom he had met some two years before.

Birney had been born in Danville, Kentucky, the son of a man of wealth and standing in the community. He had been educated by tutors and at private schools and had graduated from Princeton in 1810 and studied law in Philadelphia. Subsequently, he had settled in Huntsville, Alabama, where he build up a profitable law practice. Shortly after he met Weld in 1832, he had sold his plantation, freeing all his field hands, and returned to Danville to become an agent of the American Colonization Society. By the summer of 1834, having some doubts as to the effectiveness of colonization as a solution for the slavery problem, he came to Cincinnati to consult with Weld. As a result of their talks together he forswore colonization in an article that was printed with money raised by the students at Lane. Weld had reason to be delighted with his convert, because he became an enthusiastic abolitionist and helped Weld distribute antislavery tracts to sympathetic people in Alabama, Mississippi, and Louisiana.

But Weld did not find the trustees of Lane Seminary so co-operative as he had Birney. At a special meeting they stated the policy that theological seminaries should not take sides in any issue over which Christians differed. They went further than this. They prohibited at Lane all student societies except those concerned with academic matters. Weld advised the students to ignore the rules since they could not be enforced until ratified by the whole board in October. The student abolitionists worked on through the summer, but in October the board ratified the action of the special meeting. The abolitionist students, by a standing vote, resolved to remain no longer at the seminary. Fifty-two of them signed a full statement of their position. Virtually all of the student body removed itself from Lane, a group of the dissidents enrolling in various other theological schools, others going into the field as antislavery lecturers, and a third group, with encouragement from the Tappans in New York, setting up a school of their own in the vicinity so that they could continue their social work with Cincinnati Negroes.

In the meantime, Beecher, Stowe, and another professor signed a statement justifying the action of the trustees and blaming Weld for all the trouble. Weld promptly left school to become a full-time agent of the American Anti-Slavery Society.

Garrison was aware of the antislavery activities of Weld late in 1832, for at that time he invited him to speak at the anniversary meeting of the New-England Anti-Slavery Society.[4] He knew of Birney's entering the cause in the summer of 1834, because on 16 August he reprinted from the Lexington (Kentucky) *Intelligencer* a letter from Birney which renounced his connection with the Colonization Society, and he pronounced Birney's letter "one of the most important documents that the anti-slavery cause has yet produced in this country." It is a letter, he said, that "drives the last nail in the coffin of the monster Colonization." And the following spring he called Birney "the emancipated and emancipator."[5] In *The Liberator* for 3 January 1835 he wrote an editorial about the statement signed by the fifty-two Lane rebels, expressing his great admiration for their action in leaving that "Bastile of Oppression." He said that he had read the statement with "moistened eyes and thrilling heart," and he considered the Lane students abundantly "worthy to preach the truth as it is in Jesus." He hailed especially the writer of the pamphlet, whoever he might be, for his "pen of extraordinary power," for his discriminating mind, for his clear and conclusive argument, and for his style that was both simple and sublime. The following week Garrison reprinted on the first and second pages of his paper the full Lane statement. By November Garrison knew the writer's identity, for he spoke in a letter to George Benson of "the lion-hearted, invincible Weld at the West."[6]

Weld continued to propagandize the West as an agent of the American Anti-Slavery Society, and he was instrumental in persuading the Lane rebels who had remained near Cincinnati to found their own school to transfer to a manual-labor college at Oberlin, of which Finney was president and which Arthur Tappan promised to support to the full extent of his income if necessary. In the spring Weld organized the Ohio State Abolition Society. He also attended the General Assembly of the Presbyterian Church at Pittsburgh, working hard behind the scenes, buttonholing key delegates so that when the issue of abolition came to the floor forty-eight (there had been only two the year before) were favorably disposed. Twenty-seven of these were clergymen, six from slave states.

Weld's skill as an organizer was matched by his extraordinary forensic ability. He followed the evangelical method of Finney. He would settle down in a community, speaking for a couple of hours night after night until he was certain that his listeners had been convinced by his arguments and his eloquence. His voice was full and resonant, and he spoke without notes and with the greatest fluency, precision, imagination, and humor. Birney prophesied that he would abolitionize all of Ohio in a year. His first meeting in a new town would usually be in the Presbyterian church with the blessing of the minister. But since a riot often followed the first meeting, he would speak subsequently in any available place—store, barn, warehouse, or private house. If leading local citizens heckled him, he would challenge them to a debate, which often ended in public admission of error on the part of his opponent. He followed Finney's practice of sending converts into the audience to urge further repentance. After a meeting at Oberlin, for instance, he acquired six more agents for the national antislavery society.

Some of Weld's converts at this time became men of real distinction. At Steubenville Edwin M. Stanton, then a young lawyer but destined to become Lincoln's secretary of war, sat on the front row and soon rose to appeal to the audience on Weld's behalf. At another small town two future United States senators, Joshua R. Giddings and Ben Wade, became abolitionists and helped to organize a local antislavery society. Near Cincinnati William Henry Harrison defended Weld, though he was later as candidate for President rather noncommittal on the slavery issue.

The effectiveness of Weld's campaign in Ohio was reflected in the annual reports of the American Anti-Slavery Society for 1835 and 1836. In 1835 a total of 220 local societies were listed as affiliated with the national society. Of this number only 38 were in Ohio. The following year the number of local societies had risen to 526, of which Ohio had 133.

Weld's skill and effectiveness as organizer and evangelical lecturer cannot be questioned, but his modesty made him somewhat deficient as a publicist. Elizur Wright wrote to him repeatedly from headquarters in New York, urging that he furnish the national society with publishable materials, but Weld insisted that his reports remain confidential. He resisted, also, Wright's entreaties that he speak at anniversary meetings of the American Anti-Slavery Society in New York, refusing even to attend those meetings, for he loathed "the stateliness and pomp and circumstance of anniversary" as mere ostentation and make-believe. "I am a Backwoodsman," he said, "who can grub up stumps and roll logs and burn brush heaps and break green sward." What the cause needed was *"work, work,* boneing down to it." As it was, too many abolitionists spent their time attending meetings.[7] All his life Weld was obsessed with the fear that he might seem vain or egotistical—a defect not shared by Garrison, who loved nothing more than attending and speaking at anniversary meetings, and who would gladly publish in *The Liberator* even his personal letters to Helen.

Weld did such a brilliant job abolitionizing Ohio that the Tappans and Wright were eager to have him work in New York State. He might not want to operate in the great city, but here was a vast country area awaiting his efforts. After giving a few lectures in Pennsylvania, he went to the Empire State, heading directly for the chief trouble spot, Utica. There after a stand of many nights he had made a tremendous impact on the populace and especially on one of the state's wealthiest philanthropists, Gerrit Smith, who had previously been a colonizationist. Additional successes followed the same patterns in New York as in Ohio: riot the first night and then after successive presentations the converts flowed down the aisles. It was only at Troy that he met with humiliating defeat, for the throngs who came to hear him speak there would not respond. Challenged by the problem, he stayed on in the town until he had been wounded by several missiles and threatened by the mayor with forcible ejection. He continued to evangelize New York, but his vocal cords were showing the strain of two years of uninterrupted effort, and he was forced to stop public speaking lest he lose his voice altogether.

About this time the national society decided to increase to the Biblical seventy the number of agents in the field. Weld was prevailed upon to enlist and train the new men. Late in the summer of 1836 he went to New England to recruit. He visited a series of colleges, finding many able men willing to volunteer.

From New England he went to New York to consult with the national executive committee before returning to Ohio. At Oberlin he added twelve more to the group of agents. Finally, all of the recruits were called to New York for indoctrination.[8] Garrison himself came down from Boston for the occasion, which he considered, next to the organizational meetings of the New-England and the American Anti-Slavery Societies, the most important in the history of the cause. The meeting lasted from 8 to 27 November. Such topics as immediate emancipation, colonization, compensated emancipation, prejudice, and the treatment of the free colored were discussed. "Weld," Garrison said, "was the central luminary, around which they all revolved." Beriah Green and Charles Stuart as well as Garrison also spoke—the latter briefly but often. Garrison thought it especially fortunate for the agents to meet and talk with himself, lest they believe the propaganda spread everywhere against him. The only differences of opinion apparent at the meeting were on religious questions. On these Lewis Tappan and Garrison, so he reported, "harmoniously agreed to differ." [9]

After the indoctrination was over, Weld resigned as agent in order to give his throat a long rest. He stayed on in New York working at the Anti-Slavery Office, where he edited tracts and gave advice regarding the deployment of the agents. He worked with Wright, who as executive secretary was in charge of the office, with Henry B. Stanton, formerly his fellow student at Lane Seminary now back in New York after demonstrating in New England his ability in the lecture field, and with Joshua Leavitt, Yale graduate, former minister, and journalist, currently editing the national society's paper, *The Emancipator*. Whittier was also in the office, already at thirty well known as poet and editor, and perhaps, with his wit and his occasional temper, the liveliest person there. Weld and Whittier worked hard on several projects together and became congenial friends.

Weld remained in New York for several years. In 1837 James G. Birney joined the staff as executive secretary, occupying himself with problems related to auxiliary societies and agents, while Wright took charge of foreign correspondence and some of the editorial work. Stanton was given responsibility for the finances, and Weld became editor of special publications. Gradually, Weld was becoming convinced that speaking was not his only possible contribution to the cause.

Although Weld had sworn not to marry until the slave was free, Garrison had, during the agents' meeting, introduced him to a young woman reformer whose attractions he could not resist. Angelina Grimké, born the same year as Garrison, and her sister Sarah, nearly thirteen years her senior, were daughters of a wealthy and prominent South Carolina lawyer and judge. Neither of these had been contented in Charleston, although they had both tried for a time to live the life of the conventional aristocracy. Angelina had fallen in love with a man who died before their marriage and Sarah seemed in love with the law and regretted that her sex prevented her entering her father's profession. Both sisters had been influenced by their brother Thomas, who before his death in 1834 had graduated from Yale, become an eminent lawyer and state senator, and—more important as far as the girls were concerned—an effective reformer. During the nullification controversy he had stood firmly for union principles. He had pioneered, also, in the causes of temperance, world peace, and manual-labor education.

Even as children the girls had felt sorry for the slaves, suffering personally when they were punished. Sarah had tutored some of the more intelligent among them and resented the fact that it was illegal to teach them to read. She later told Garrison that she had talked with hundreds of well-treated slaves, but had never found one who did not long for freedom.[10] Angelina had prevailed upon her mother to give her a slave girl who was especially difficult to handle and had found her a place in another family, refusing to accept wages for her work.

One of the crucial events in Sarah's life was her visit with Quaker friends in Philadelphia when she was twenty-seven. Eventually she moved to Philadelphia, and her sister later joined her there. It was natural that they should absorb antislavery views from the Quakers, but the Grimké girls eventually proved too liberal even for the Friends. They disputed openly about slavery, they refused to use some of the archaic forms of Quaker speech, they wore their own types of bonnets, and they prayed aloud during the silent Friends Meeting.

In the later summer of 1835, about seven weeks before the

Boston mob seized him, Angelina shocked even her sister by writing an encouraging letter to William Lloyd Garrison. She apologized for disturbing such a busy man, but said she could not resist writing to one "standing in the forefront of the battle." Each week, she said, she had opened her *Liberator* with fear that he would in some small way compromise or retreat. But this he never did, and she had grown confident that even the most terrible physical violence could not shake him. "The ground upon which you stand," she said, "is holy ground." She knew that he would suffer the martyr's death rather than forsake it. She said that she used to think slavery would end in civil war, but now she had a hope "that *our* blood will be spilt, instead of the slaveholders; our lives will be taken, and theirs spared—I say a *hope,* for of all things I desire to be spared the anguish of seeing our beloved country desolated with the horrors of a servile war." [11]

"Thrilled—subdued—strengthened—soul-animated," in *The Liberator* for 19 September, Garrison published the letter along with an editorial of nearly equal length, apologizing for giving publicity to a young lady (he had recognized her as the sister of the late Thomas S. Grimké). He had to publish her letter, he said, "that our cruel assailants may perceive how heavenly is that temper, and how pure that principle, which they are branding as fanaticism and madness [and] . . . that female abolitionist[s] may derive support and comfort from its perusal, in the midst of danger and distress." Welcoming her as one of the disciples—one of *his* disciples—he said of the letter: "Its spirit, dignity, endurance, faith, devotion, are such as have never been excelled by the noblest exhibition of Christian martyrdom even since the days of the apostles." In short, he considered Angelina Grimké's letter worth more to the cause than all the resolutions and speeches of a thousand meetings.[12]

When, a few months later, Miss Grimké published for the American Anti-Slavery Society an *Appeal to Christian Women at the South,* Garrison was more moderate in his enthusiasm, though he announced its publication in the issue for 24 September 1836 and printed, two weeks later, excerpts and his own comment on the "noble and truly eloquent" document. Perhaps he felt that he had been too exuberant about the earlier letter, or his enthusiasm might have been mitigated by the fact that this was an official tract released by the national society, whereas the letter was a personal tribute to himself. At any rate, Miss Grimké's *Appeal* was a valuable contribution to the cause. In it she urged Southern ladies to read, to pray, to speak, to act. They should free their slaves and try to educate them, even though they might have to break the law to do so. In South Carolina the pamphlet caused an uproar. Postmasters burned it publicly, and it was vowed that Miss Grimké would be imprisoned if she ever returned to South Carolina.

In the meantime, the Grimké sisters began to speak in public meetings—at first to small groups of women and then, as interest spread, to mixed gatherings. They resolved to dedicate their lives to abolition and to become skillful lecturers. But they needed further training—hence their appearance at the agents' meeting in November of 1836, and their meeting with Theodore Weld. Under Weld's guidance Angelina, who was more fluent and articulate than Sarah, soon excelled. She lectured in the city and branched out to include many small communities near New York.

Weld was frequently in the company of the two sisters; often politeness demanded that he be their escort, though he was resolved to avoid entanglements. Even after he had fallen in love with Angelina, he held back, avoiding even taking her arm as they walked down the street. Poor Angelina hardly dared to hope.

In the summer of 1837 Angelina and Sarah were invited by Garrison to lecture in New England. They and he were to become involved in distressing clerical disputes before there could be time for Angelina and Theodore Weld to confess their mutual love.

CHAPTER XI

---◆◆◆---

The Clergy Militant

GARRISON and Weld represented the two basic areas of antislavery activity that had developed during the thirties. Garrison's New England was dominated by the New-England Anti-Slavery Society (called after 1835 the Massachusetts Anti-Slavery Society); Weld's New York and Ohio by the American Anti-Slavery Society. Both parent societies adopted the doctrine of immediate emancipation, although they interpreted the meaning of the term differently. The national society, using the definition that had been developed at Lane Seminary and in New York City, meant that gradual emancipation should be immediately begun, whereas the New England society, taking the definition which Garrison had found in Great Britain, usually meant by the term exactly what Garrison's audiences or readers thought he intended, that the slave must be freed immediately and treated like any other citizen.[1]

Garrison's immediatism was certainly more radical, less reasonable than Weld's, and it tended to antagonize conservative and even intellectual people. Whereas Weld's view was one that the more liberal elements in the Protestant churches could accept, Garrison's soon proved anathema. The clergy whom Garrison had counted on for support were slow to recognize in his flamboyant assertions and his harsh invective the words of the true Christian Garrison felt himself to be. Although he spoke with dedication and quoted the Bible frequently, he often seemed impatient and even militant. For all his words to the contrary, he seemed more

[128]

the leader of a mass movement than the Christian martyr. Weld, on the other hand, seemed more patient, more reasonable. He followed Finney's revivalist tactics, allowing his audiences time to absorb his message before expecting their support. By comparison Garrison seemed independent and hurried. He lectured on a definite schedule, moving from town to town, from convention to convention, often not giving his auditors time to digest his radical views. Also, he seemed so self-righteous, so sure of himself; he lacked Weld's self-effacing humility, which appealed more readily to the well-educated clergy. Garrison's analysis had the strength and weakness of simplicity. He viewed the world as a clear dichotomy between good and evil. Everything was the work of God or of the Devil, and he was the one to choose between them. It was his duty to carry on "the strife of Christ against the empire of Satan," [2] even though the strife might involve famous ministers of the gospel.

The mild, middle-aged, highly respected William Ellery Channing of the Federal Street Church in Boston was the first of those ministers to feel the sting of Garrison's invective. Descendant of two of New England's most distinguished families, Channing was one of the leading ministers and theologians of the day. He was a man tremendously influential in theology and literature, for he had done much to shape both the Unitarian and the Transcendental movements. Unlike most Northern ministers and most abolitionists, he had lived in the South; as a young man he had spent a year and a half as tutor to David Meade Randolph in Richmond, Virginia. As early as January 1834, Garrison had sent Channing an assortment of antislavery tracts, and a letter requesting a public statement regarding slavery and reminding him of the "fearful responsibility [that] *rests upon him who withholds his influence.*" [3]

The only answer to Garrison's letter appears to have been Channing's small book, *Slavery,* which was published late in 1835. In this work Channing for the first time expressed himself publicly on the crucial issue, explaining that "people, in proportion as they have felt vehemently, have thought superficially, or hardly thought at all; and we see the results in a singular want of well defined principles, in a strange vagueness and inconsistency of opinion, and in the proneness to excess which belongs to unsettled minds." [4] Calmly and reasonably Channing considered various aspects of the slavery issue. He demonstrated that man cannot justly be considered property. He analyzed the infallible human rights, showing how they were inconsistent with slavery. Drawing on his own experience in the South, he said: "Sympathy with the slave has often degenerated into injustice towards the master. I wish it, then, to be understood, that, in ranking slavery among the greatest wrongs, I speak of the injury endured by the slave, and not of the character of the master." [5] He discussed the evils of slavery from a philosophical point of view, demonstrating eloquently the fallacies of Scriptural arguments for the institution.

He also discussed intelligently and fairly the abolition movement and its leaders. He believed, in short, that the removal of slavery was essentially the duty of the slaveholder and that Northerners had no right to interfere, that emancipation should undoubtedly be gradual, that the slave needed a guardian although not a master. Priority should be given to the improvement of the slave's domestic relations. In short, he asked "for no precipitate measures, no violent changes." [6] Thinking chiefly of Garrison and his followers, he defended the abolitionists as "men blameless in life, and holding to the doctrine of nonresistance." [7] He exonerated them from the charge of having instigated insurrection and deplored their persecution by mobs in Boston and elsewhere. It was true that they had erred as enthusiasts often err by "exaggerating their object, of feeling as if no evil existed but that which they opposed." [8] They had erred, also, by adopting as their motto "Immediate Emancipation" and by using the system of agitation through abolition societies, and by appealing so extensively to the free colored. It was Channing's conviction (and herein is his most significant difference with the abolitionists) "that if a good work cannot be carried on by the calm, self-controlled, benevolent spirit of Christianity, then the time for doing it has not come. God asks not the aid of our vices." [9]

Garrison's immediate reaction to the book was that "it abounds with useful truisms expressed in polished terms, but, as a whole, is an inflated, insistent and slanderous production." [10] Its only real value, he said, lies in its plagiarisms from abolitionist writings; "the rest is a farrago of impertinence, contradition and defamation." He was especially resentful that after the abolitionists had "macadamized the road . . . the big folks are riding upon it in their coaches as proudly as if they had made it all." [11]

During the several months following the publication of Channing's book, many columns of *The Liberator* were devoted to it. On 27 February, following the publication of a revised edition of Channing's work, Garrison's own review appeared. It was an ill-natured diatribe discussing point by point twenty-five objections to Channing's ideas, but the review revealed far more of Garrison's personality than it did of Channing's views of slavery.

Garrison was shocked that some of his "abolitionist brethren" thought the work "worthy of extensive circulation, and even of panegyric." Whatever of value the work possessed "is entirely neutralized by a strong admixture of error." In essence, Channing's *Slavery* is "utterly destitute of any redeeming, reforming power— . . . it is calumnious, contradictory and unsound—and . . . it ought not to be approbated by any genuine abolitionist. 'He that is not with us is against us.' "

Garrison's whole attitude, though it may appear today merely irrational and ill-natured, is understandable. Channing with his aristocratic background, his Harvard education, and his adulation from the intelligensia was a real threat to Garrison. He had so much that Garrison lacked and envied. Now as a latecomer to the cause and one still reluctant to be called an abolitionist he had written a book that was being accepted as a distinguished commentary on slavery, even by some of Garrison's most faithful followers. It behooved Garrison to protect his own pre-eminence in the cause by pronouncing judgment on Channing, by demonstrating how he had strayed from the Garrison party line.[12]

Another famous minister who disagreed with Garrison and was therefore suspect was Lyman Beecher. Beecher had not been neglected by *The Liberator*. Garrison had reprimanded him for a prayer before a military assembly, had printed one of his sermons, had condemned another, had quoted his opinion on Indian rights, had approved his view of temperance, and had reported his trial for unorthodox ideas. But, most significant, Garrison had condemned him for his failure to support the abolitionist students at Lane Seminary.[13]

In July 1836, Beecher's moderate abolitionism was in Garrison's mind as he read the famous preacher's Pittsburgh speech on the

Sabbath question. The reforming instinct welled up within him. Here was another sinner who must be shown the light! The demonstration took the form of a gratuitous reply to Beecher in nearly five columns of fine print in *The Liberator,* condemning Beecher's Sabbatarianism and airing his own radical views on the subject, although he had formerly been quite conservative about the Sabbath.[14] The Sabbath, he insisted, far from being, as Beecher alleged, *"the great sun of the moral world . . .* the cord by which heaven holds up nations from the yawning gulf of corruption and ruin" is but one day in seven, with no gospel authority for its holiness. Surely the true source of morality is in the life and teachings of Christ, not in the observance of any form or ceremony.[15]

Following the attack on Beecher, Garrison received several letters remonstrating with him for engaging in sectarian controversy in *The Liberator.* Although he continued to insist that the Sabbath question was not sectarian, he admitted in a letter to Henry Benson that "the discussion of it is not exactly proper in the Lib^r." He resolved not to permit the paper to become the arena of such controversy.[16] Seldom did Garrison come this close to admitting that he had made a mistake.

No matter how fervently Garrison may have resolved not to become involved with sects, his temperament was such that he could not resist comment when church questions were debated. Soon he had insulted virtually all the Protestant denominations. The Methodist church he called " 'a cage of unclean birds, and synagogue of Satan.' "[17] The clergy of the Congregational church he considered foes of man and of God. The Baptists he thought blackhearted and conniving. Eventually, owing to the efforts of Channing, Beecher, and others, the Protestant churches of Massachusetts and Connecticut closed their doors to Garrison and other abolitionists.[18]

Although Garrison was constitutionally incapable of a different course of action, especially since he had been so offended by church and clergy on numerous occasions, it was most unfortunate that he so thoroughly alienated many of the most conscientious men in New England.

In March of 1837, at the Anti-Slavery Office in Boston, in the midst of a heated argument between Stanton, Whittier, and Garrison, a vigorous, redheaded, gray-eyed man in his mid-twenties came to the door. John Humphrey Noyes sat down quietly and listened to the exchange. Noyes, recently a divinity student at Andover and then at more austere Yale, had developed in the last few years increasingly liberal views. Extensive reading of the Bible convinced him that Christ having returned to earth in 70 A.D., the millennium was at hand, that man was, therefore, perfectible, and that Noyes himself was living in a state of perfect holiness. He was at present preaching his new theology, as well as more radical theories about multiple marriages, to family and friends and editing a paper, *The Perfectionist,* in Putney, Vermont.

When the discussion between Garrison and his more conservative colleagues ended, Noyes introduced himself. He and Garrison seemed congenial at once. Here was a reformer as radical as he was. Garrison expressed interest in Noyes's paper, which he apparently had been reading for some months, if not from its inception in 1834.[19] He said he had been ruminating on the subject of holiness and perfection for some time and that he planned to devote more of his energies to it when he had abolitionism in the clear light of day. Noyes reported later: "I spoke to him especially on the subject of government, and found him, as I expected, ripe for the loyalty of heaven." [20]

A few days later Noyes wrote his new friend a long letter developing his perfectionist ideas in some detail and telling him how much he rejoiced "to find in you a fellowship of views and feelings on this subject which has long been a rarity to me." Confiding in Garrison as a fellow sufferer, he admitted that he himself was accounted "a crazy man or a fool" and that in the eyes of the world he had become an outlaw. Then with a vigor of language which Garrison must have envied, he described the government of the United States as "a bloated, swaggering libertine, trampling on the Bible—its own Constitution, its treaties with the Indians—the petitions of its citizens: with one hand whipping a negro, tied to a liberty-pole, and with the other dashing an emaciated Indian to the ground." Present governments, he was convinced, stood in the way of abolition. Governments therefore—the federal government in particular—must be overthrown before the reign of Christ could begin.

Colorful, eccentric John Humphrey Noyes appeared, like Lazarus come back from the dead to tell him all, at a critical time in Garrison's career. Garrison was beginning to lose the initial impulse that had sustained *The Liberator* and the Massachusetts Anti-Slavery Society for some six years, and he was susceptible to new influences. For a time, Noyes's personality and some of his theories had a recognizable impact on him.

In the early summer of 1837, about three months after the meeting between Garrison and Noyes, another event occurred that was to have a more crucial influence on Garrison's future course. The Grimké sisters came to New England to lecture under the auspices of the Massachusetts society. They naturally became involved in his controversy with the clergy. They lectured first to various female and juvenile societies in the Boston area. Their speeches at the Boston Female Anti-Slavery Society brought the society thirty-five new members. About the middle of June they talked to the Boston Juvenile Anti-Slavery Society. Sarah told how as a child she had been given a slave girl who was afraid to eat for fear she would grow fat and be eaten by the family. Angelina reported seeing twenty children in chains driven through the streets of Charleston en route to New Orleans where they would be sold. And Henry C. Wright, who had been assigned to the sisters as a kind of press agent and business manager, displayed on the platform a whip and chains such as might have been used on children in South Carolina.[21]

Gradually they branched out to speak, wherever possible in churches, at surrounding towns—at Lynn, Salem, Danvers, Rowley, Newburyport. They spoke, Wright said in one of his many accounts of their activities published in *The Liberator,* as though they were a part of the slave system—"a penitent part," giving first-hand evidence of the cruelties and inequities of slavery. They discussed slavery in the District of Columbia, the corruption of churches in the South, the guilt of Northern participation. At Amesbury in a crowded church they debated two men on the subject "Does the Bible Sanction Slavery?" Henry Wright thought that the slave had never had more efficient advocates than they: "The Lord has opened a wide door of usefulness to these sisters. Wherever they go they awaken a deep and powerful interest for the suffering slave." [22]

For several weeks the Grimkés lectured with little opposition. But by the middle of July latent objection against them and against Garrisonian perfectionism, of which woman's rights seemed a corollary, found expression in a *Pastoral Letter* from the orthodox Congregational clergy to their churches; this was followed in subsequent weeks by three *Clerical Appeals*. The *Pastoral Letter* deplored the loss of deference lately suffered by the clergy and urged that church doors be closed to itinerant moralists, insisting that ministers must have control over the topics to be discussed in their churches. The letter also warned against the pernicious effect of allowing women to participate in public meetings: "If the vine, whose strength and beauty is to lean upon the trellis work and half conceal its clusters, thinks to assume the independence and overshading nature of the elm, it will not only cease to bear fruit, but fall in shame and dishonor to the dust." [23] The first *Clerical Appeal* (*The Appeal of the Clerical Abolitionists on Anti-Slavery Measures* was the full title), which appeared a few days after the letter, was a more damaging document, since it was signed by five ministers claiming to be sincere abolitionists. The *Appeal*, moreover, attacked Garrison and *The Liberator* directly for aspersions on individual clergymen, who, though sincere Christians, were not yet abolitionists. Early in August, a *Second Clerical Appeal*, issued by the faculty of Andover Theological Seminary, confirmed the findings of the earlier documents. It also condemned "public lectures of females" as a "departure from propriety" and highly disapproved of "representations to which *children* have listened." [24]

Garrison was pleased with the Grimké lectures and stimulated by the opposition which they had evoked. As usual, opposition gave him confidence, and this time that confidence was reinforced by the strength he felt in his new allies, Angelina and Sarah Grimké and John Humphrey Noyes. He reveled in his new opportunity to declare war against so impressive an antagonist as the entire New England clergy. He wrote to his publisher: "Only think of a public 'clerical' admonition! . . . Have you done penance, and obtained absolution? For my part, I am growing more and more irreverent. . . . Surely you must be a pugnacious man to employ such an Ishmaelitish editor. 'Wo is me, my mother! for I was born a man of strife.' " [25]

The strife took the form of an eight-column reply in *The Liberator* of 18 August. Garrison spread it across the front page and part of the second. He attacked all of the signers of the *Appeal* for their crass egotism and Charles Fitch, minister of the Free Church of Boston, for his habitually harsh language. After listening to him on a number of occasions, he said, "it has seemed to me that I have not yet begun to give meat for men, but only milk for new-born babes." Garrison resented particularly the *Appeal*'s appearance at a time when he was out of the state, implying that Oliver Johnson, the substitute editor, was really the one who had offended the clergy. He also felt that the *Appeal* should have been offered for publication directly in *The Liberator*. (Garrison was always proud of the fact that he printed in his paper all available attacks against himself.)

The gravamen of Garrison's complaint was that the clergy "belong to a class which has been wont to speak in oracular tones, as it were immediately from heaven, and men have not dared to doubt its inspiration; but the fallibility of the clergy is beginning to be stoutly denied and profanely ridiculed along with that of his Holiness the Pope." One of the great virtues of abolitionism, from Garrison's point of view, was that it "brings ministers and laymen upon the same dead level of equality, and repudiates all 'clerical' assumption, all spiritual supremacy. Nothing can be more offensive to it, than this attempt to enforce opinions in an oracular tone, as *clergymen*." Abolitionism was good because it put Garrison himself on a level with the great minister, traditionally the leading citizen in the Puritan theocracy. As abolitionist leader he had as much right to pontificate as Channing or Beecher.

Just as abolitionism leveled society, so it ought to be concerned with all good causes, Garrison thought. True, the abolitionist regarded the cause of emancipation as worthy of special devotion, "inasmuch as it is struggling against wind and tide, against the combined powers of Church and State." But it did not follow that he loved other noble causes less because he loved abolition more. Indeed, upon the success of abolition all other causes and even "the very existence of our Republic" depended. As a group, Garrison insisted, abolitionists were remarkably active in all good causes—peace, temperance, home and foreign missionary work. In fact, "they take a more than ordinary interest in every object which is calculated to advance the interests of the Redeemer's kingdom." [26]

These were dangerous ideas. How could the abolitionists retain a unity of opinion sufficient to accomplish their main purpose if they must support every current reform? Garrison's friends and associates were deeply concerned. John Greenleaf Whittier wrote lamenting the controversy. This was no time, he insisted, for sectarian controversy and division in the antislavery ranks. Unified effort was essential to defeat the enemies of liberty, who were threatening the right of petition on the floor of Congress and trying to annex a great slave territory. "The poor slave, sighing from the prison-house of his bondage, implores us to lay aside our feuds, and unitedly seek his deliverance." [27] Elizur Wright wrote Garrison cordial letters of advice, rebuking him for sectarianism. He said that if he were editor of the *Emancipator,* he

would riddle your leading editorial of Oct. 6 till your friends would hardly be willing to own it. I would show up its sectarian spite as plainly as ever a dissenter showed a skeleton. . . . I fear the deceitful spirit of *sect* has stolen upon you unawares, and that you are uncon- sciously becoming, no new thing in the world, a *close-communion anti-sectarianist!* Much as I love this cause, so much more do I *hate sect,* that Heaven helping, I will back out of it, if our strongest men are to stand eternally at the door, key in hand, to shut out every luck- less wight who cannot give all the passes, grips, and watchwords! . . . Bah! I am sick of these outrages on God's *common sense.* Human nature must have room to play. . . .

I have said all this hypothetically. I live in hope that you will shake off the delusion and will nobly refuse to build an anti-slavery *sect* in the ruins of the theological. . . . In my own heart I believe that your zeal in this controversy arises from your having so completely identified yourself with the slave. You seem to yourself to be pleading wholly for him, but *I know you do not seem so to the lookers on*—especially to those who know little of your history. I would to God you could only look at your late Liberators through *my eyes.* If you did not see your "blunder" [I] would shut my mouth forever. But enough.

Yours in love,
E. Wright Jr.[28]

Benjamin Lundy, now the editor of the *National Enquirer,* berated Garrison for his arrogance and his "erratic and dogmatical course" in *The Liberator*.[29] Amos A. Phelps and Samuel J. May questioned the wisdom of his conduct. Isaac Knapp told Tappan that if his partner turned *The Liberator* into a radical religious and political organ, he himself would publish an abolitionist paper.

Even antislavery societies went on record in opposition to Garrison. The national society urged the public not to confuse their own doctrines with those advanced occasionally by individual abolitionists; and it sent James G. Birney, later the most prominent of political abolitionists, to New England to study the situation. His report was so pessimistic that Lewis Tappan concluded that Garrison's influence was waning and that his war with the clergy might divert him entirely from the cause. Indeed, the board of Garrison's own Massachusetts society announced that they were not controlled by any one person.[30]

But the controversy had started, and like an atomic reaction it continued despite anything societies and friends could do. In September the clergy issued a fourth document, generously annotated with quotations from letters of indignant ministers.[31] At the quarterly meeting of the Massachusetts Anti-Slavery Society the clerical enemy breached Garrison's inner defenses, when John Gulliver, deacon of the Reverend Mr. Fitch's church, laid the dispute before the entire convention. He spoke calmly, forcefully, commending Garrison as the friend who had revealed the truth about colonization and had pioneered the entire antislavery movement. Garrison was a man, Gulliver said, of talent, of courage, and—at least until the present controversy—of unquestioned integrity. He had "led us right so often, we have appeared to think he can never lead us wrong." But we "have done him an incalculable injury" by such adulation.

Garrison could hardly have missed the innuendo in Gulliver's words: we have greatly injured him because we have "exalted him above measure" until, like a king, he can do no wrong. Gulliver was convinced that Garrison had done wrong. He had run his paper with tactics that reminded one more of the slaveholder than the abolitionist. *The Liberator*'s language had often been cruel, its influence mobocratic. "What did the opponents of Garrison do just before the great mob in Boston, that he is not doing now in regard to Messrs. Fitch and Towne [the chief signers of the clerical appeals]?" The great sin of Fitch and Towne had been that they "had the audacity to find fault with Garrison. . . . And for this they must be crushed." Indeed, the clergy generally—at least twenty-four of whom were attending the very convention Gulliver was addressing—were to be condemned for the same fault. They were to be condemned in spite of the fact that without their cooperation the cause of abolition could not possibly succeed. "Is it not time," Gulliver concluded, "to lift up our voice against its [*The Liberator*'s] faults, and labor to have it reformed? Shall it be sustained by the funds of the society, and may we not rebuke it for its sins?"

Gulliver had struck what seems to the modern reader a staggering blow against Garrison and his paternalistic leadership, and the effect of his speech spread far beyond the portals of the hall at Worcester where he spoke, because Gulliver insisted that Garrison publish it in *The Liberator*. It was difficult for Garrison to refuse, since he had made such a virtue of publishing critical as well as laudatory material. He apologized to his readers "for inflicting upon them such an unprofitable gallimaufry. But I will pardon the deacon, if they will pardon me for excessive editorial liberality. I append a few notes." The "few notes" were about fifty percent longer than Gulliver's speech.[32] Despite the length of his footnotes, Garrison could not disparage Gulliver's basic charge: that it was unfair for the Massachusetts society to support *The Liberator*—as it had been doing since the first of the year [33]— when it had no control whatever over the paper.

When toward the end of the year the society was not willing to continue its financial responsibility for the paper, Garrison was not disposed to object. He had not the slightest intention of altering the course of his paper to suit his critics, especially if those critics were clergymen. *"The cause must be kept in the hands of laymen,* or it will not be maintained." [34] In the prospectus for the new volume of the paper [35] he announced the termination, "by our own choice," of the society's financial responsibility for *The Liberator*. It was no new experience for him to run "a journal contending against wind and tide." He would edit the most compelling paper possible and trust to Providence—ultimate financial arbiter of all his ventures—for continued support, though he was willing to assist by raising the subscription price from $2 to $2.50. He served notice of his intention to broaden the area of reform sponsored by *The Liberator*. Henceforth with John Humphrey Noyes he would seek "the emancipation of our whole race from the dominion of man, from the thraldom of self, from the government of brute force, from the bondage of sin." He would show that man was an infinitely perfectible being. He would demonstrate that the clergy, who were tainted with the Puritan doctrine of original sin and refused to admit man's perfectibility in this life, had to be reproved, lest they avow, among other abhorrent contradictions, that a man can be both a Christian and a slaveholder.[36]

CHAPTER XII

---◆·◆---

Toward Crashing Unanimity

ALTHOUGH there was much to divide the ranks of the abolitionists during the turbulent thirties, one dramatic and tragic event brought them together. On 7 November 1837 the Reverend Elijah P. Lovejoy died at the hands of an angry mob in Alton, Illinois.

New England born and educated, Lovejoy had earlier been run out of St. Louis for antislavery activity. Moving twenty-five miles up the Mississippi River to Alton, he tried to found an abolition press. Three times a mob broke up his equipment and threw it into the river. The only way to save the fourth press was to match force with force. He arranged to have the press delivered late at night so that it would attract a minimum of attention, and he managed to assemble about fifty men who succeeded in lodging it in a nearby store. The next day—the fatal 7th of November—threats were whispered along the streets, and even the attorney general predicted that Lovejoy would be dead within the fortnight. By ten in the evening a raucous mob, its courage whetted by liquor, attacked the store and its defenders, first with a volley of stones and then with scattered shots. The defenders returned the fire, killing one of the crowd. At this point, the mayor appeared but with insufficient force to quell the riot. The crowd surged toward the building, with ladders poised and torches ready. Flames were licking at the eaves of the wooden roof when Lovejoy and the others came outside to defend themselves; they could see a ladder and one of the incendiaries mounted on it silhouetted in the moonlight against the bright flame. Lovejoy and his men fired and the mobster fell with a scream of agony. The defenders ran back into the building to reload. When they came out again, the mob was ready. As the door opened there was a withering fire. Lovejoy fell to the ground with five bullets in his body. Writhing, he pulled himself to his feet, worked his way inside and up to the second floor, shouting all the time: "I am shot! I am shot! I am shot!" [1]

Garrison's reaction to the death of Lovejoy in the pages of *The Liberator* was restrained and effective—perhaps he had been subdued by opposition from clerics and moderate abolitionists. Instead of unleashing his famous invective to slay Lovejoy's murderers, he supplied a simple comment, to the effect that Lovejoy's loss would be an invaluable gain to the cause, although he wished that he had died as a Christian without resisting the mob. Then, in a series of quotations, he let newspaper editors throughout the country—many of whom had been wholly unsympathetic towards his own near-martyrdom two years before—speak for him. Almost without exception they denounced the terrible murder and on much the same ground that Garrison had used to condemn the Boston mob—freedom of speech and press had been violated. Garrison must have smiled with satisfaction, but he had the wisdom to remain silent.

About the time the excitement over Lovejoy's death had waned, Garrison had further cause to smile. On 20 January 1838 his second son was born. Although he was not named Benedict Arnold as Garrison's enemies had advised, Helen was "so reckless of consequences,—so anxious to show her contempt of public opinion,—so determined that he shall bear an odious name,—that she says it is her wish to call him—William Lloyd Garrison." Their two babies, Garrison said, were as alike "as two twin-cherries upon one stem." [2]

It may have been in part the violent death of Lovejoy and the happy birth of his son that reminded Garrison of another reform that must be advocated.

Men must be liberated from all use of force. "Next to the overthrow of slavery, the cause of PEACE will command our attention," Garrison proclaimed in *The Liberator* for 5 January. By peace he meant the total abrogation of force as a sanction and consequently the denial of any organization or any government dependent to any extent on the use of force. Ultimately the only kingdom on earth was to be the kingdom of Christ; all traditional governments were labeled as "Anti-Christ." These were ideas which Garrison felt that the abolitionist should understand, for they were "vitally connected with the bloodless overthrow of slavery." Garrison intended to advocate still another emancipation in the new *Liberator*—the liberation of women. The Grimké sisters had reminded him that women's rights must be established as equal to those of men. All of their recent speeches had demonstrated that far from being inferior to the male clergy of New England they were superior.[3] He would do all that he could to vindicate their rights, to justify Angelina's confidence that he was the Moses of his day.[4] He would lead Americans of both sexes to the promised land!

When, after being seriously ill during most of the winter, Angelina returned to New York on 23 April 1838,[5] she must have felt as though she had already reached the promised land. She must have been certain of it when shortly thereafter Theodore Weld proposed marriage. (The courtship had probably been accelerated by Weld's fear that his fiancée was being unduly influenced by the ultra views of Garrison.) They were married in Philadelphia on 14 May. The ceremony was as unorthodox as the couple themselves, who felt that they could not subscribe to any of the traditional services. In Pennsylvania it was legal to be married without the participation of minister or magistrate, provided the marriage certificate was attested by twelve witnesses.[6] Garrison was among the signers, although he feared that Weld's sectarianism would corrupt Angelina unless she could emancipate him.[7]

Garrison did not fail to implement the doctrine of universal emancipation proclaimed in the prospectus for the new *Liberator*. He established two new departments in the paper—one called "non-Resistance," the other "Equal Rights." And he attended the usual run of conventions, losing no opportunity to discuss his radical notions. Early in 1838 he went to the conventions of the American Anti-Slavery Society in New York and of the American Anti-Slavery Women in Philadelphia. In May he figured prominently in a convention of local New England antislavery societies in Boston. While the delegates were in town, there was a meeting of the "friends of peace," who called a convention for the following September. This was precisely the occasion that Garrison desired to organize his nonresistance principles into a consistent society. The existing peace societies he considered altogether unsatisfactory; in fact he fully expected to have to give them the same kind of rough treatment that he had meted out to the colonization societies.[8]

About two hundred delegates assembled for the Peace Convention on the 18th of September. More than half of them came from Massachusetts, and a large proportion of the whole were known to be Garrisonians. After protem. officers had been elected and the convention was in the process of making up a roll of members, Garrison rose to speak. He suggested "that, as mistakes often occur in procuring signatures, each individual should write his or *her* name on a slip of paper." Many good friends smiled; others looked grave. But Garrison had raised the controversial woman question so adroitly that no one formally objected to his suggestion. As a result women became members of the convention and were qualified both to speak and to vote. When Abby Kelley, a noble but rather masculine-looking woman,[9] a school teacher turned abolitionist, was appointed to the business committee, several of the more conservative members of the convention— both clergy and laymen, according to Garrison—asked that their names be stricken from the roll. The convention went on for three days, with resolutions and counterresolutions and speeches pro and con. With nice understatement Garrison reported in *The Liberator* that "the discussion was continued with great animation."

Garrison was made the chairman of a committee to draw up a constitution and a declaration of sentiments for the new organization (The New-England Non-Resistant Society). The resulting document he declared one of the most " 'fanatical' and 'disorganizing' instrument[s] penned by man. It swept the whole surface of society, and upturned almost every existing institution on earth." Garrison thoroughly enjoyed the "deep and lively sensation" caused by the presentation of his document to the convention, and he was astonished that after "a very long and critical debate," it was accepted by a majority of better than five to one. The minority, however, included many of the most able members of the convention—notably Edmund Quincy, Wendell Phillips, William Ladd, and Samuel J. May.[10]

In *The Liberator* for 28 September, Garrison, excited as a small boy displaying a new toy, presented his new declaration in a double-column spread. He proclaimed allegiance to no ruler but God and Christ, loyalty to no country but the kingdom of Christ. He pledged opposition not only to all wars but to "all preparations for war." He testified against naval ships, arsenals, fortifications, militia systems, standing armies, officers, soldiers, military monuments, trophies, celebrations, appropriations, and edicts of war. He adopted the nonresistance principle wholeheartedly, promising not to bear arms, not to hold any military or civil office, not to vote for any such office, not to sue at law, not to use any physical coercion whatever. "We cordially adopt the non-resistance principle; being confident that it provides for all possible consequences, will ensure all things needful to us, is armed with omnipotent power, and must ultimately triumph over every assailing force."

Once he had adopted such submissive and inclusive principles of nonresistance, one wonders how Garrison expected to reform the world. With so many prohibitions how could he *do* anything? But Garrison had the solution for this problem. He would be, in effect, a belligerent nonresistant. Consistency be damned!

But, while we shall adhere to the doctrine of non-resistance and passive submission to enemies, we purpose, in a moral and spiritual sense, to speak and act boldly in the cause of GOD; to assail iniquity, in high places and in low places; to apply our principles to all existing civil, political, legal, and ecclesiastical institutions; and to hasten the time, when the kingdoms of the world will have become the kingdoms of our LORD and of his CHRIST, and he shall reign for ever.

To speak more specifically, the newly organized nonresistants expected to publicize their views in newspapers, to employ lecturers, to circulate tracts, to form societies, and to petition state and local governments. They did not bother to question how one could petition a government without accepting its existence.

Garrisonians, though they may have been critical of parts of the Declaration, were convinced that the Peace Convention was a great historical event and that the Declaration of Sentiments would be remembered by succeeding generations. Edmund Quincy gives us a glimpse in his journal [11] of the nonresistants—Johnson, St. Clair, Alcott, Wright, and Garrison—"assembled together in an upper chamber" of Miss Parker's boarding-house in Hayward Place, discussing "that immortal instrument." Garrison himself explained in a letter to May [12] that he heartily approved of the new society, "because it destroys at a blow all the unnatural and artificial distinctions that obtain in society, and sunders, as by the touch of fire, all human cords by which the intellect and souls of men are bound." Even more important as far as Garrison personally was concerned,

Our association places every man upon the dead level of equality. He that would be greatest, must be the servant of all. It gives no power but that of love, and allows of nothing but suffering for Christ's sake. It has no ranks, no titles, no honors, no emoluments, to hold out to man as an inducement to support it. On the contrary, it requires of every man a cheerful willingness to sacrifice all these, and count them as dung and dross.

Nonresistance, perfectionism, anticlericalism, woman's rights! Had he been a more practical or more reflective man, Garrison would never have added so many extraneous reforms to his basic abolitionism; but if he had been practical, he would never have accepted abolitionism as a profession. It took an emotional, impulsive, egocentric, active person to launch a campaign for immediate emancipation in 1831; and it took the same kind of person to become a universal reformer in 1838. A less expansive, more thoughtful man would have paused to take stock of his problems at that time: *The Liberator,* always in the red, had lost the financial support of the state society; the clergy had been thoroughly alienated; national, state, and local antislavery societies had become increasingly critical; friends were growing skeptical; and associates were becoming enemies. A timid, a logical man would have been discouraged, would have retrenched, compromised. But not William Lloyd Garrison. He praised God that his paper was all his own once more, and he raised the subscription price although the paper had not sold at the old rate. He attacked the clergy as pusillanimous and un-Christian. He upbraided critical antislavery societies. And he rejoiced that his enemies had come into the open. Now that the dross had been removed the true metal would be hard and bright.

As a matter of fact, the true metal was extraordinarily resilient in 1839 and 1840. Even before the annual meeting of the Massachusetts society in January 1839, there was danger that Garrison and his paper might become bankrupt. Creditors were dunning him; Knapp, his recently married partner, was demanding a dependable salary, and yet Garrison was planning to publish a new paper, the *Non-Resistant,* for the new society. But a committee of true Garrisonians, including the merchant Francis Jackson, Edmund Quincy, and William Bassett, promised to assume some of *The Liberator*'s debts and to supervise its financial affairs; and Oliver Johnson agreed to remain as an assistant to the editor, whereas Isaac Knapp seemed content to have a few columns to sell for his own advertising profit. Providence had intervened again.

During the last weeks of 1838 and the early days of the new year, there were rumors of clandestine plots to overthrow the board of the state society as well as Garrison and *The Liberator.* At first, Garrison seemed little troubled; he even used the promise of a stormy session at the annual meeting as bait to lure his sister-in-law to Boston for a visit.[13] But when he analyzed the plot further, he grew more concerned. It was the work of clerical abolitionists, the leaders being Amos A. Phelps, dissident Garrisonian, and Charles L. Torrey, Congregational minister turned abolitionist. He wrote May on 4 January that the conspiracy is "deplorable and alarming. It is the old leaven of sectarianism working afresh, and determined" to overthrow *The Liberator* by founding an official organ of the Massachusetts society.[14] Fortunately, the Board of Managers of that society, realizing the danger, had decided to publish their own official monthly, *The Abolitionist,* to be edited by Phillips, Quincy, and Garrison, and to be distributed free by the auxiliary societies.

In spite of his concern over the plotting, Garrison remained unruffled. To George Benson he said: "Besides getting up a new paper, the design is to settle the 'woman question' against us. Thus we have all the materials for a warm and earnest collision." When the plotters tried to convert some of the free colored to their views, Garrison congratulated himself that they were so loyal to him that if he went to hell, they would follow.[15]

In *The Liberator* for 11 January he issued a call to action that sounded more like a general girding his troops for battle than a nonresistant urging the use of moral suasion:

Strong foes are without, insidious plotters are within the camp. A conflict is at hand,—if the signs of the times do not deceive us—which is to be more hotly contested, and which will require more firmness of nerve and greater singleness of purpose, . . . than any through which we have passed to victory. Once more, therefore, we would speak trumpet-tongued—sound an alarm-bell—light up a beacon-fire—give out a new watchword—so that there may be a general rallying of our early, intrepid, storm-proof, scarred and veteran coadjutors, at the coming anniversary—all panoplied as of yore, and prepared to give battle to internal contrivers of mischief, as readily as to external and avowed enemies.

The response to Garrison's call to action can be measured by the attendance at the annual meeting of the Massachusetts Anti-Slavery Society on the 23rd, which was the largest to date. After the routine business had been disposed of and before the annual report had been read, Wendell Phillips presented two resolutions that had been submitted to the Business Committee, disclaiming responsibility for their contents. The first, disregarding the monthly *Abolitionist,* proposed that the cause demanded the establishment of an official, weekly organ of the state society, devoted exclusively to antislavery topics and advocating political as well as moral and religious action. The second resolution recommended that the Board of Managers, if practicable, arrange with Garrison to make *The Liberator* that organ.[16]

These two resolutions set off the first day's conflict.[17] Alanson St. Clair, a minister who had been associated with Garrison for some years and whom Garrison was later to describe as "tugging for a subsistence at the dry teat of 'evangelical' abolitionism," [18] led off with an hour's speech in favor of the first resolution. Charles L. Torrey, pastor of the Richmond Street Congregational Church in Providence, Rhode Island, and an abolitionist of several years' standing, pre-empted the rest of the afternoon. He denied the existence of any plot but said that the circulation of *The*

Liberator was so small that another inexpensive and official paper was needed. He suggested the employment of a first-rate editor for the new paper, a man of the caliber of Elizur Wright or John Greenleaf Whittier. He listed as sponsors of the resolution for the new paper four men—Phelps [19] and Stanton in addition to St. Clair and himself. Apparently taken off guard at being linked with the other three, Stanton spoke up: "I warn the gentlemen to be careful. . . . I defy any one to show a letter or a fragment of a letter, to prove that I have been implicated in the plan." [20] Torrey condemned Garrison especially for his nonresistance principles which led him to ignore in his paper essential political matters, and even led to his refusing to vote. He recommended, therefore, that a new paper be established. [21]

Garrison was indignant: "Am I recreant to the cause? who believes it?" The answer "No! No!" burst from the floor and from the crowded galleries.

"Let me ask him a question," Stanton said. "Mr. Garrison! do you or do you not believe it a sin to go to the polls?"

The audience was breathless, as Garrison considered his answer. "Sin for *me!*" he said.

Stanton pressed: "I ask you again, do you or do you not believe it is a sin to go to the polls?"

Garrison's answer was the same: "Sin for me."

Mrs. Chapman reported that the abolitionists were stirred "as if they had seen the slave-driver stand suddenly forth with his scourge and manacles, in visible embodiment of the spiritual tyranny they now felt."

Garrison's friends rose to his defense. May said: "We have never wanted means of communication with the public . . . ; when the Massachusetts Society wants an *organ,* she sounds a trumpet." Loring replied that he had no intention of speaking on the question of whether a new paper were needed. "I only say that to make such a paper the organ of the Society, and to sustain it at the expense of the Society, over the head of the Liberator would have a tendency to injure the latter." Phillips argued earnestly and at length against the first resolution.

When it became apparent that Garrison had the votes, his four opponents tried to delay the proceedings. They attempted to divide the resolutions; they endeavored to refer them to a committee; they tried to adjourn the meeting. There were calls, "Vote it down!" "Vote it down!" Then Loring moved for "an indefinite postponement," which passed at once.

Before this conclusion had been reached, Phelps and St. Clair had raised another issue—" the right of women to a voice in the decision." This matter was referred to the president, Francis Jackson, for a ruling. When he said, *"The Chair rules that it is in order for women to vote,"* no one questioned his judgment.

When, on the third day, the annual report of the Board of Managers, written by Garrison, came up for action, St. Clair presented a qualifying resolution, asserting that it was "the imperious duty of every abolitionist who could consciously do so, to go to the polls." Although the resolution might have seemed innocuous in another context, the "four" had been so thoroughly beaten by this time that any of their recommendations were suspect. The resolution was not voted, but Garrison's substitute—hardly a model of clarity and directness—was adopted almost unanimously:

Resolved, That those abolitionists, who feel themselves called upon, by a sense of duty, to go to the polls, and yet purposely absent themselves from the polls whenever an opportunity is presented to vote for a friend of the slave—or who, when there, follow their party predilections to the abandonment of their abolition principles—are recreant to their high professions, and unworthy of the name they assume.

Then the annual report was adopted by a vote of at least 180 to 24.[22]

It was the end of a three-day battle. Tempers had been lost; but Garrison had won: *The Liberator* had been sustained, women had been allowed to participate in the meeting, and the old Board of Managers had been re-elected. Garrison's ranks, however, did not emerge unscathed. At least two dozen dissidents separated themselves from the society. Garrison announced editorially that the good ship *Abolition* had survived a white squall, "the most violent gale yet recorded in her log-book, to the imminent peril of her existence, and not without injury to her spars and rigging, and the loss of some of her crew." Professed abolitionists, he said, have exhibited a shameful spirit of insubordination. "The anti-slavery house in this Commonwealth is now divided against itself—and how can it stand?—What its most powerful enemies could not do, is now to be effected by the treachery of its former friends." [23]

The division in the antislavery house was gradually separating Garrison from one of his oldest and closest friends—John Greenleaf Whittier. When Garrison first quarreled with the clerical abolitionists, Whittier had urged moderation and advised against internal feuds and sectarian controversy. Since Garrison ignored his friend's advice, Whittier publicized the moderate point of view more widely in a series of letters to the *Pennsylvania Freeman*. Never one to take advice graciously, Garrison was offended at Whittier's temerity. What right had the young poet to question Garrison's wisdom? After all, he owed everything to Garrison; without him Whittier might still have been an unknown Essex County farmer! And so Garrison turned against Whittier. He called him a compromiser like Henry Clay, who would do almost anything in the name of peace.[24] Whittier was not pleased with the analogy. He wrote to Garrison admitting that perhaps he was defective in moral judgment, but saying he could not view the world as a dark cavern haunted by ghastly shapes of treacherous abolitionists. "No shadows and omens of thick-coming disaster throng before me: no ghosts of treason wearing the similitude of loved and familiar friends, scowl on me from the Shadow World of the Future. My sphere of vision is mainly limited to the Actual and the Present." Many of the shapes that were haunting Garrison, Whittier suggested, were really perfectly respectable reformers. Amos A. Phelps, for example, no matter what his religious or political views, was still an uncompromising abolitionist, who believed in immediate emancipation just as firmly as Garrison himself did.

This was harsh criticism from an old friend, but Whittier was also affectionate: "I shall not quarrel with the friend of twelve years standing, whom I have known and loved in prosperity and adversity—who first stimulated me to active exertion in the cause of the slave. . . . I have no idea of gratifying the enemy by the spectacle of a 'passage at arms' between a Quaker and a Non-Resistant." [25]

As the months following the stormy annual meeting of the Massachusetts society passed, Whittier continued his friendly advice, while Garrison grew increasingly impatient. By July—when ill health forced Whittier's retirement as editor of the *Pennsylvania Freeman*—Garrison said of him: "Had his advice (honestly expressed) been followed, mischievous consequences would have ensued. Especially at the present crisis does he 'stumble at noonday as in the night'—and through his blindness, others are led astray." [26] Whittier's appraisal of Garrison at this time was more specific and more searching. He said that he did not question his sincerity, but that Garrison had the kind of intellectual temperament to which doubt was inadmissible. For him belief was equivalent to knowledge. "He believes in the sincerity of his heart that his new religious doctrines are *destined to pour new life-blood into the veins of Abolition, and preserve it from corruption,* hence *as an abolitionist* even, he feels bound to advocate them in his paper, as he has done for the last three years." [27] Whittier thought that Garrison's expressing his religious views extensively in *The Liberator* was as bad policy as if he had himself filled the columns of the *Pennsylvania Freeman* with Quaker doctrine.

Others were less patient with Garrison. Lewis Tappan, leader among moderate New Yorker abolitionists, wrote in his diary on 6 June: "Garrison and others have grown lukewarm on the antislavery subject & have loaded the cause with their no-government—woman's rights—non-resistant &c until we have got among breakers. Garrison told me 2½ years ago that there were subjects he considered paramount to the antislavery cause, to which he meant to devote his attention chiefly. It is a sad mistake to make it instrumental in carrying on other matters." [28]

No matter what Whittier and others might say, Garrison would not retreat a single inch. He controlled the Massachusetts society and *The Liberator,* and he intended to reinforce that control and to extend it, if possible, to the national society. In March he availed himself of another opportunity to assert his leadership when Henry B. Stanton, Lewis Tappan, and James G. Birney came from New York to meet with the state society. The New Yorkers departed without the slightest hope of persuading Garrison to compromise, the vote going 142 to 23 in favor of Garrison and his supporters. The next chance for a test of the strength of opposing forces came in May in New York at the annual meeting of the national society. Here the outcome was inconclusive, Garrison winning on the issue of admitting with full rights the female delegates and losing over the desirability of political action, though a compromise motion sponsored by Whittier cushioned the blow.

Then in July came the national convention in Albany, where delegates assembled from national and state societies to discuss the advisability of forming an abolitionist political party. Since there were only sixty Garrisonians in a total delegation of five hundred, the meeting was what Garrison thought a tame affair, accomplishing nothing—only three resolutions approving political action after three days of discussion! There should have been, Garrison insisted, scorching resolutions against Henry Clay and the American church and clergy as well as laudatory ones on West Indian emancipation to be celebrated on the glorious First of August.[29] Actually, Garrison had had little chance to make the meeting memorable, because the committee on arrangements at the very beginning of the convention excluded all "extraneous matters" from the discussion.

Garrison had suffered a setback at Albany, but he was determined that it be temporary. He laid careful plans for the more important struggle scheduled for the following May (1840) at the annual meeting in New York. He determined to indoctrinate his constituents in pamphlets, speeches, and editorials. "The message I have received from the Lord must be delivered, without the omission of a single word, whether this impudent hard-hearted, stiff-necked generation will hear or forbear." [30]

During 1839 differences between Garrison and the New Yorkers became increasingly apparent. There was a basic difference in their use of the term immediate emancipation, although the general public tended to understand the slogan according to the radical Garrisonian rather than the conservative New York interpretation. They differed in regard to political action, the New Yorkers recommending and Garrison abhorring its use. Also, Garrison's religious digressions were so controversial that the moderate abolitionists sided with the clerics against Garrison. Whether women should participate actively in the agitation was rapidly becoming an issue. There was an essential difference, moreover, regarding the nature of abolition societies. Garrison had such radical, anarchical tendencies that societies under his aegis tended to become mere autonomous forums for discussion rather than bodies to organize systematically and practically the areas over which they had jurisdiction.

In addition to the differences between the two groups of abolitionists, there was the more basic fact that the nature of the movement for emancipation had changed. As a result of abolitionist agitation, Southerners who had early in the 1830's considered slavery a regrettable evil were now defending the institution as a positive good. They were barring abolitionist propaganda from Southern mail. Since the Southern opposition had thus stiffened and Northern agitators were quarreling among themselves, real progress toward emancipation in the later thirties was being made in a new way. Petitions to Congress were becoming more effective than abolitionist agitation. John Quincy Adams had demonstrated intelligent and skillful leadership in this new campaign.[31] Early in 1839 Adams offered his own plan for gradually abolishing slavery by constitutional amendment, a plan which Garrison opposed as inconsistent with Adams' vow to his constituents not to compromise with slavery.[32] In April Adams wrote a long letter "to the Citizens of the United States, Whose Petitions, Memorials and Remonstrances have been entrusted to him . . . ," attacking the doctrine of immediatism as impractical: "Have you converted many to the true faith of immediate emancipation without indemnity? Is the temper with which your arguments are *received;* nay, is the temper with which they are *urged,* of that character which conciliates acquiescence and ripens hesitancy into conviction?" In short, he declared immediate emancipation "a moral and physical impossibility," concluding that as long as the current type of antislavery organization is in control of the abolition movement, the freedom of the slaves "is as far beyond the regions of possibility as any project of the philosophers of [Swift's] Laputa."

Although Garrison did not like Adams' letter, his reaction showed surprising restraint. He merely published an extended reply by William Goodell in *The Liberator* for 22 July, limiting his own remarks to a few sentences about the effectiveness of Goodell's reply to Adams' unfortunate letter.

There was another source of friction for the abolitionists. It was difficult to conceive how the American Anti-Slavery Society could be sustained financially. That society had agreed not to solicit funds in areas organized by state societies. As the state societies—

especially those in New York, Ohio, and Massachusetts, the most densely populated areas in the North—grew more powerful and more effective, the area over which the American society had direct jurisdiction became smaller and smaller. Consequently, the national society became increasingly dependent for support on the state societies. During the fiscal year 1837–38 Massachusetts, for example, paid to the parent society $10,643.18.[33] It was decided that the next year the state society should pledge $10,000 to the national. By the first of February 1839, however, the local society was in arrears $3,680, there being an additional payment of $2,500 due the first of May. Both societies were concerned, and the managers of the Massachusetts group requested the Executive Committee of the American society to send agents into the Commonwealth to collect funds which were to be turned over to the local treasurer with the promise that he would remit them to New York.

The national society, however, not content with this arrangement, virtually abrogated all agreements between the two societies and appointed special agents to collect money from the state without any control or advice from the local society. Garrison and his followers were mortified; they considered this action unfair, discourteous, and hostile. But still they were willing to make all efforts to fulfill the original pledge to the American society. On 5 April Francis Jackson as president and Garrison as corresponding secretary of the Massachusetts society published in *The Liberator* an appeal addressed to all the auxiliary societies and all individual abolitionists throughout the state asking for funds to redeem the pledge of $10,000 to the national society. Since only five weeks remained before the end of the fiscal year, prompt action, the appeal urged, was essential. "Every man ought to be his own lecturer, every society its own collector, and every town its own agent."

At the end of the fiscal year Garrison's society indicated its willingness to pledge $5,000 toward the support of the parent society for the coming year, the cut in the amount being due, Garrison said, to an anticipation of greater local expense.[34] By the following February, however, Garrison had lost patience with the New York Executive Committee, and he announced that the Massachusetts Anti-Slavery Society would no longer continue any financial support of the national society, even though that society was in dire financial need. The real reason, he alleged, why the Massachusetts and other state societies were refusing support was not that the country as a whole was in a depressed financial condition—three years before when there was a far more serious depression, funds were forthcoming. Nor was it that the local societies were inefficient and unconscionable. Rather the entire blame was to be attributed to the Executive Committee of the American Anti-Slavery Society; for there was "a growing distrust in their clear-sightedness, sound judgment, rigid impartiality, and anti-sectarian spirit." [35]

In the meantime, personal friction between abolitionists continued. Like Whittier, Gerrit Smith, the wealthy philanthropist of New York State, found it difficult to understand Garrison's attitude toward other abolitionists. He said in a letter to Amos A. Phelps, 5 March 1840: "Mr. G's immeasurable abuse of brethren who differ from him, has long been a great trial to me. But I have hoped, that he would come to be governed by a kinder & more patient & more reasonable spirit. But the coarse, unprovoked, wanton attack, which he makes in the above address [on behalf of the board of the Massachusetts Anti-Slavery Society] on the motives of his brethren, makes me almost despair that he will ever meet differences of opinion with the temper of a christian gentleman." [36]

Shortly after he had written this letter Smith heard from Lewis Tappan, who regretted that "the Massachusetts madman" had virtually ruined the antislavery society. "We are now a sad spectacle to the nation. The predictions of opponents seems to be about to be verified. They said we were a fanatical set of men, that we could not stick together, that the concern would soon be blown up." He regretted that public confidence seemed to have been "withdrawn from us." He advised coming out promptly and explicitly "against Garrison, H. C. Wright, etc. I do not like to have you term them 'pure minded brethren,' for it looks like identifying yourself with them in some degree." [37]

Conflict between abolitionists had become so extensive that the New York executive committee anticipated the end of the national society at the May meeting in New York. Anti-slavery journals, moreover, discussed the issue frankly. Whittier said in the *Pennsylvania Freeman:* "It cannot be denied . . . there is a jealousy and fear with respect to the powers lodged in the hands of the Executive Committee and an unwillingness to sanction its proceedings, which will be likely to increase instead of diminish." But, he pointed out, the committee was in a quandary which made it impossible for them to adopt any course of action that would be generally acceptable. He therefore recommended that the committee's debts be paid and the society be dissolved.[38] The *Philanthropist* also concluded that the national society was no longer of sufficient use to warrant its continuancy, and that it should unobtrusively dissolve itself in May.[39]

The tension within the ranks was being felt in Philadelphia as well as in New York. Garrison had many followers in that city, as even his enemies would admit. And in the spring Wright was in town, apparently urging them to support his friend. At a meeting of the executive committee of the Pennsylvania society, when some of Garrison's opponents were absent hearing a sermon, the committee appointed several women to represent the society at the international antislavery convention in London, scheduled shortly after the annual meeting of the national society.[40]

Garrison, unwilling to admit that the American Anti-Slavery Society had outlived its usefulness to the cause, said in April: "That society must and will be sustained, under the guidance of a trustworthy committee, let who will plot to destroy it, whether treacherous friend or open foe." [41] A month later in a letter to his wife Garrison admitted how serious he considered the situation: "There is to be a desperate struggle this week at New-York. I anticipate a breaking up of our whole organization. But my mind is calm and peaceful. The Lord of hosts is my rock and refuge." [42]

Garrison's mind was calm and peaceful not merely because he was trusting to the Lord as rock and refuge, but also because he had taken every precaution (proving himself more politician than nonresistant) to assure the success of his faction in New York. He had publicized his views of the New York committee and urged a large attendance at the annual meeting in a pamphlet, lectures, editorials, and letters. He had sent three or four men to New York and one to Philadelphia to lobby for his cause.[43] He had made arrangements with railroad and steamship companies for extra trains and boats at special rates so that it was possible for loyal

Garrisonians to make the round trip from Boston to New York, including board in New York at fifty cents per day, for a total fee of $5.

"The earliest, the truest, the most untiring and zealous friends of our old anti-slavery organization," as Garrison described them, rallied at the depot in Boston. They came from down east, from the thick-ribbed hills of Vermont, and especially from the Massachusetts counties of Essex, Middlesex, Norfolk, Plymouth, and Suffolk. They came prompt and numerous at the call of humanity in spite of business duties and hard times "to save our heaven-approved association from dissolution, and our broad platform from being destroyed." An extra train loaded to the windows with Garrisonians was dispatched from Providence, but still the faithful poured into the station until a second special train had been loaded—"our numbers continually augmenting at every stopping-place between the two cities." "O, it was a heart-stirring and rare spectacle—such as has never before been witnessed in the progress of our all-conquering enterprise; and many were the spectators, who were looking on with wonder and surprise at such a gathering of fanaticism, and such a 'dying away' of abolitionism." At Providence Garrison's horde—numbering by then 450 men and women, 400 of them from Massachusetts and the majority women—was transferred to the chartered steamboat *Rhode Island,* which sailed for New York, the American flag crackling in the breeze (true Liberty's flag not having been designed! Garrison suggested).

There never has been such a mass of 'ultraism' afloat, in one boat, since the first victim was stolen from the fire-smitten and blood-red soil of Africa. There were persons of all ages, complexions, and conditions —from our time-honored and veteran *Seth Sprague,* through ripened manhood down to rosy youth. There were, indeed, the moral and religious *elite* of New-England abolitionism, who have buckled on the anti-slavery armor to wear to the end of the conflict, or to the close of life. It was truly a great and joyful meeting, united together by a common bond, and partaking of *the one spirit of humanity.* Such greetings and shaking of hands! such interchanges of thoughts and opinions! such zeal, and disinterestedness, and faith! Verily, it was good to be there! [44]

Such was the enthusiasm that Garrison was able to muster at the prospect of a civil war among abolitionists. It would seem as though he could contemplate with pleasure the forthcoming schism in antislavery ranks—provided, that is, he was to be the leader of the victorious faction.

On the afternoon of 12 May the convention opened in the Fourth Free Church of New York. Garrison had a chance to show his strength on the first issue to come before the meeting. In the absence of the president, Arthur Tappan, the vice president and Garrison's close associate, Francis Jackson, presided. He appointed a representative business committee, its membership being fairly divided between New York and Massachusetts, although with Garrison as chairman and with Abby Kelley as a member. At once there were objections to the appointment of Miss Kelley. A vote being called for on this issue, the division stood 557 in her favor to 451 opposed.[45] At once three of Garrison's leading opponents asked to be excused from serving on the committee on the official grounds "that the innovation seemed to them repugnant to the constitution of the Society—that it was throwing a firebrand into anti-slavery meetings—that it was contrary to the usages of the civilised world—and that it tended to destroy the efficiency of the female anti-slavery action."[46] Still recalcitrant the following day, the leaders of the minority held a preliminary meeting in the evening to consider forming a new association. "After prayerful consideration" it was decided to organize a new society, and a call was issued for a general meeting the next day—the 14th. On the 15th about three hundred members of the minority group of the old society officially formed the American and Foreign Anti-Slavery Society. They adopted a constitution, urging among other projects "the formation of Women's Auxiliary Anti-Slavery Societies." And they elected officers: Arthur Tappan as president, James G. Birney and Henry B. Stanton as secretaries, and Lewis Tappan as treasurer.

Meanwhile, the old society continued its meetings through Friday, the 15th, with Garrison and his followers in control. Three ladies, Lucretia Mott, Lydia Child, and Maria Chapman, were put on the executive committee. It was resolved that the election of neither Martin Van Buren nor William Henry Harrison could be countenanced by conscientious abolitionists. A rather mild (understandably so after Garrison's recent political maneuvering) resolution condemning political action was adopted. The old executive committee's transfer of the *Emancipator* to the city society was protested. The American church was condemned: "Resolved, That the Church ought not to be regarded and treated as the Church of Christ, but as the foe of freedom, humanity and pure religion, so long as it occupies its present position." And Garrison's current pet project, the forthcoming World's Anti-Slavery Convention in London, was heartily approved, with N. P. Rogers, Charles L. Remond, and Lucretia Mott being selected as Garrison's fellow delegates. Garrison's exhilaration was reflected in a letter to his wife: "We have made clean work of every thing— adopted the most thorough-going resolutions—and taken the strongest ground—with *crashing* unanimity." [47]

CHAPTER XIII

---•◆•---

Abroad Again

As late as April Garrison had been uncertain whether his plans to attend the international antislavery convention in London, which was scheduled to begin a few days after the New York meeting ended, would materialize. It depended on what happened in New York.[1] But early in May he read in the *Emancipator,* official organ of the national society, a letter from prominent English Quaker and abolitionist Joseph Sturge that filled him with apprehension. Sturge said:

It is reported that several of our female friends to the cause, are likely to be appointed from America. . . . I fear such a step would be any thing rather than a help to our cause. . . . In all our labors in this country, they held their meetings and committees perfectly distinct from ours, and the idea of appointing any female delegates to the coming Convention, will never, I believe, occur to one of the Committee in this country. So that if any do come from America, they will have to encounter the strong feeling against it, which exists here. . . . I am sure the kindest thing to *them,* as well as best for the cause, would be for you to do all you can to discourage it.[2]

Garrison rationalized that the letter had been "extorted by 'a member of the Executive Committee' at New York." But he was sufficiently concerned to decide that he definitely must go to London, no matter what happened in New York.[3] Victory on the woman issue here would be incomplete without a further victory abroad. The war was international!

[161]

Before he could undertake the trip, however, Garrison had to make arrangements for the care of his brother James. In the fall of 1839 James's ship had put into Boston, where he was confined to the Navy Yard, incapacitated after years of excessive drinking and suffering from what Lloyd called a "fistulous abscess, of a cancerous nature, situated at the base of the back bone." Garrison had gone to see him and had persuaded the commodore to give him leave to recuperate at the Garrison house. Three months had passed with few signs that James's health was improving, and so Lloyd applied for his brother's discharge from the Navy on the grounds that he was no longer capable of performing any useful function as a seaman. But the discharge was no routine matter, because James, his leave granted by the commodore having expired, had been marked on the purser's book as a deserter. The resulting negotiations were a humiliating task for Lloyd, since he had to intercede with the Secretary of the Navy, proslavery James K. Paulding, as well as with Congressman Caleb Cushing, with whom he had quarreled some years before. But Garrison performed his duty to his brother without complaint. Finally, an honorable discharge was obtained, although with financial penalties to both brothers; and James officially took up residence with Lloyd and Helen.[4]

During the winter and early spring of 1840 Lloyd and his family had watched over the wayward brother. Though James never fully regained his health, he conquered his passion for drink long enough to write a fascinating account of his misspent life. It was the perfect penitence for the imaginative sailor, for he could savor in retrospect every salacious and lugubrious detail he recorded.[5]

As the time for Lloyd's departure for England approached, it was apparent that James would need special care which Helen, since she was pregnant, could not be expected to give him. The choice seemed to be between hospitalization and a sojourn with the Bensons at Brooklyn. Since it was hoped that the quiet of the country and the regular chores on the farm would be of therapeutic value, James was sent to Connecticut.

On 19 May Garrison sailed from New York,[6] his departure delayed by the recent anniversary meeting. His mind pulsed with thoughts of his great victory in New York, of his hatred of that city and of Wall Street in particular, of his separation from Helen, of the baby she would bear during his absence, of the brother who was trying hard to be a farmer in Connecticut, and of the fight to be anticipated in London. But, withal, he felt content to be going abroad again. Although he loved his wife, he felt periodically the need to escape the family circle, as he had earlier felt the need to live apart from his mother. In a sense Helen was a mother to Garrison; she brought him the loving attention and care his own mother had not bestowed. Now once more—coincidentally, at the trying period of an accouchement—he needed to sally forth into the world in order to re-establish his manly independence and effectiveness.

It was a long and tedious voyage, especially since he feared the ship would be late for the convention, but Garrison passed the time, when he was not seasick, exploring the ship and writing letters to family and friends. He had little use for the passengers. The women were devoid of "cultivated minds," and the men were "a prayerless, . . . low-minded set, . . . and disposed to make light of every thing serious and sacred." [7] As he told Edmund Quincy, there were two kinds of animals aboard, the wild and the tame, but the wild ones were in the cabins, and the "cows, sheep, pigs, turkeys, geese, ducks" were in the long boat.[8]

On 4 June, the very day that Helen was giving birth to Wendell Phillips Garrison, Lloyd wrote both to his wife and to James. He was feeling guilty at having left her once more when she needed him, and the letter was a characteristic rationalization. He told her that she would never know the strength of his love, since he was "not accustomed to the use of fond terms," and that he would never wilfully be separated from her. And then with a curious turn of thought that made him feel virtuous again: "Sometimes you have hinted that I was too ready to go away from home." But, he insisted, he had always forgiven her such a reproach "on the ground of your affection for me, which I know to be pure and intense." [9]

To James he wrote of the clear weather, the strong breeze, the sturdy ship—one of the fastest on the Atlantic—whose 660 tons at times shot ahead at thirteen and even fourteen knots. He told of the cabin with its thirty passengers, which seemed "the Cave of Forty Thieves." "Card-playing, gambling, drinking, swearing, and boisterous merriment, constitute the order of the day." The description was enough to make the ex-sailor drool, as he hoed and harrowed corn and potatoes and drank cold water. The letter became increasingly moralistic. Lloyd told his brother how much he had thought of him since he left, how anxious he was to hear how he was "in body and in mind," how much he hoped that he liked "Brooklyn, and farming, and the quietude of nature," how tremendously he hoped that he would be restored to health and "reconciled to God," so that they could sing praises together "through all eternity, in company with dear mother, and our departed sisters, and with an innumerable host of the wise and good in all ages." [10] It was enough to drive a man to drink even if he had no inclination in that direction.

Although he tried hard to help his wayward brother, Garrison totally failed to understand the nature of James's ailment. He would have been amazed could he have realized how much he and James were really alike. Both had been frustrated and ignored as children and young men. As the success of Alcoholics Anonymous today has indicated, dedication to a mission—whether it be temperance or abolition—can absorb the feelings of inadequacy and frustration which lead to various emotional excesses. For James the anodyne was alcohol; for Lloyd it was the antislavery cause.

The ship docked at Liverpool on 16 June, after some special excitement for Garrison when a copy of a Liverpool paper came to hand, reporting the attempted assassination of Queen Victoria and Prince Albert by an octoroon. Doubtless anticipating a violent reaction, Garrison read the story aloud to a group of passengers. When they heard that the would-be assassin was partly Negro, their response did not disappoint him. They yelled like fiends and called for the criminal's immediate execution by hanging and quartering. Garrison calmly reminded them that an Englishman was presumed innocent until proved guilty and volunteered his opinion "that it was possible, nay probable, that the lad was deranged"; so the court subsequently found.

Shortly after this episode Garrison stepped ashore, praising the solid earth, thanking God for His mercies, and announcing that "there is not a man upon the surface of the globe, whom I am not willing to recognize as 'a man and a brother' " [11]—not a man, that is, except those who disagreed with him, such as his enemies in

New York, the passengers on the ship, and perhaps Joseph Sturge in England.

Then came the trip to London. Garrison arrived before the end of the convention, although James G. Birney had been praying that unfavorable winds would delay Garrison and "his troop of males and females" until the convention had adjourned.[12] Garrison was shocked to discover that the American female delegates had been excluded from participation. Unheard-of effrontery! How could any Briton, Garrison wondered, so discriminate against women when his country was ruled over by a woman? [13] But the London committee stood with the old New York Executive Committee on such matters.[14] They had no intention of being run by women delegates, and especially liberal Hicksite Quakers like Lucretia Mott. Many English reformers were Quakers but of the orthodox type, since there had been no split in their group as there had in the United States.[15]

It was all reported to Garrison. Lucretia Mott and the other American delegates who had arrived in time for the opening session had known that they were in for trouble even before the first day's meeting, since Mrs. Mott had been officially informed of the intended rejection three days earlier.[16] The women delegates had prepared a protest and waited for the meeting.

The convention had opened auspiciously at Freemason Hall with the appearance of the venerable and venerated Thomas Clarkson and his young grandson. Garrison heard how the five hundred in the audience stood in respectful silence as the old abolitionist, with the aid of two younger men, found his way into the hall and was unanimously elected chairman of the convention. The business of the meeting began, though the question burning in everyone's mind—whether the American women should be seated as delegates—had been postponed out of deference to the frailty of the aged Clarkson. A paper had been read on the objects of the convention which reviewed the fundamental principles of the British and Foreign Anti-Slavery Society, implying that the convention was basically an activity of that society rather than a world's convention in any strict sense.

Following the paper, Joseph Sturge, real leader of the convention, had suggested that Chairman Clarkson, lest he become exhausted by the activity of the meeting, might want to leave. Again the audience stood as the old man tottered out of the crowded hall. As soon as Clarkson was safely out of earshot, Wendell Phillips had risen with the crucial resolution—that a committee of five be appointed to prepare a correct list of the members of the convention, including the ladies from Massachusetts and Pennsylvania, who were understandably aggrieved to have been refused admission. They had traveled, he said, four thousand miles to the meeting fully expecting to be accorded the same rights as in their own country.

A long argument had ensued, the English leaders insisting that they had never intended to invite ladies to the convention, that certainly there were no British women delegates. Although they appreciated all the wonderful things done for the cause by women both in England and America, they considered it highly improper for them to participate directly in a convention, and they pointed out that even many American groups excluded ladies from the business of their abolition societies. Supporters of Phillips' resolution argued that on the grounds of both common courtesy and abstract justice the women delegates must not be excluded. Who was to say that their credentials were in any way inferior to those of the male delegates? Would the British exclude half of the human race from a "world's convention"? After many speeches pro and con, George Thompson, assuming the role of moderator, summarized the argument for both sides. He insisted that the fate of the whole convention hinged on the present question, which he sincerely wished had never been introduced. He admitted that he felt personally responsible to some extent for the current predicament since he had written a number of the American women inviting them to come to London for the occasion of the convention; "but he confessed he did not then anticipate they would come as delegates." [17] In short, "he earnestly requested his American friends to withdraw their motion"—which they steadfastly refused to do.

Thompson's efforts at conciliation had proved ineffectual, and the exchange grew more heated. One eloquent spokesman, William H. Ashurst, London solicitor and warm-hearted philanthropist, came to the support of the ladies. He said it was not a question of what had been the intention of the London Committee but of what it ought to have been. He pointed out that the convention was meeting on the principles of universal benevolence, and "they ought to welcome all who came there for the purpose of carrying those principles into effect." How could they, acting on those principles, consider excluding the women from America? It might be said that the convention should follow the customs of the place where it was meeting, but such a premise could easily be reduced to absurdity. Suppose they were meeting in the state of Virginia?

Gradually the basis of the argument shifted away from the legalistic point of view. The opponents of the Phillips resolution began to point out that the convention was being asked to make a decision on an issue only remotely concerned with the selection of delegates to the convention and the slavery issue. They were being asked for a pronouncement on woman's rights. Since this was an issue, another speaker pointed out, that had never been adjudicated or even discussed in England, the convention could not be prepared for a wise decision. James G. Birney, currently the abolitionist candidate for the American presidency, said that the woman question—contrary to the implication of several of the speakers—had not been settled even in the United States. Moreover, it was suggested that those in America who favored equal rights for women also favored the nefarious, nonresistant doctrine of no-government. This suggestion brought Phillips to the floor to insist that there was no necessary identification between the two doctrines, that he for one could not accept for a moment the no-government idea. Further, he volunteered his opinion that the recent schism in the antislavery ranks in America was fundamentally concerned not with woman's rights as had been alleged but with political action.

When a vote was finally taken on the resolution, it was defeated by a large majority. Thompson urged that since the question had been decided, good feelings be resumed. Phillips was magnanimous: "He did not doubt but that the supporters of his motion would co-operate with the Convention with just the same cordiality as if it had been carried. All they asked was an expression of opinion on the subject, and having obtained that, they would go on with them with a perfect feeling of cordiality." [18]

By the time Garrison appeared in London, pleasant relations between the two factions seemed to have been restored, but Garrison was not slow to stir up the old feelings of animosity. Regretting that his inability to arrive a few days earlier had prevented his carrying the point triumphantly, since he could no longer participate directly in the debate on the woman question, he did what he could to keep the issue alive. He insisted that this was no world's convention but merely a conference of the British and Foreign Anti-Slavery Society and such delegates as they chose to receive. He refused to present his credentials and swept up to the balcony to glare down on the inferior throng like a bound but potent Prometheus. He was convinced that as a result of his action the woman question "will be canvassed from Land's End to John o' Groat's house." He noted that "many excellent and noble minds are highly displeased at the decision of the Convention, and denounce it strongly. The new organizers have done what they could to injure us, and have succeeded in creating some prejudice against us, especially on the part of the clergy; but the effect will be temporary." [19] Even though his precious issue had been defeated, Garrison felt that his timely action had virtually turned that defeat into victory. It may have been true that such a self-righteous and theatrical gesture gave the issue of woman's rights a maximum of publicity, but one might question Garrison's willingness to sabotage the whole convention because of its rejection of the women delegates.

At any rate, Garrison thrived on the personal adulation that followed his refusal to participate in the convention.[20] He sat in the balcony, as though holding court, surrounded by American associates like Lucretia Mott, Negro Charles L. Remond, and Nathaniel P. Rogers, in addition to English admirers, including Lady Byron, philanthropist widow of the late poet. Even those on the floor courted him, passing resolutions pleading with him to join the meeting and applauding when his name was mentioned, "as if they could *clap* him down." [21] He remained impervious, certain that an ideological defeat had been translated into a personal victory.

Garrison's opportunity to express his views about the proceedings came at a farewell party for the foreign representatives. According to Elizabeth Cady Stanton, wife of moderate abolitionist Henry B. Stanton, he spoke so foolishly that the cheers which greeted him rapidly changed to expressions of disapproval; and the chairman of the meeting eventually had to ask him to take his seat.[22]

Although Garrison's action at the convention doubtless antagonized many of his former British friends, there were plenty of others who made the trip worthwhile. He dined with Lady Byron and saw her often. He met writers like Amelia Opie, William and Mary Howitt, and James Montgomery. He was entertained by the wealthy Quaker banker, Samuel Gurney, who sent seven barouches to the city to convey Garrison and his friends to his magnificent home in the country. "A great sensation did we produce as we paraded through the streets of London." At Gurney's he met the Duchess of Sutherland (ranked next to the queen, according to Garrison) and her brother Lord Morpeth. The duchess arrived in a glittering barouche drawn by four prancing horses and attended by six servants. She was most gracious, Garrison thought, when she told him that she had given £20 to help the fugitive slaves in Upper Canada, and when she shook him cordially by the hand in parting. "She has since expressed a wish to have an interview with me; but I think it doubtful whether I shall find time to call." [23] He did find time to call—apparently the very next day—and was delighted with the great lady, though "Household and Duchess bewildered his republican faculties." [24] He also visited Wentworth House, seat of Earl Fitzwilliam, where he found a room one hundred and forty feet long and lined with art treasures, the cost of which, according to Rogers, "would defer for a twelve month the starvation of all Britain and Ireland." [25] Almost always Garrison was accompanied by friend Charles Remond, "a great favorite in every circle. Surely, if dukes, lords, duchesses, and the like are not ashamed to eat, sit, walk and talk with colored Americans, the *democrats* of our country need not deem it a vulgar or odious thing to do likewise. . . . You see how abolitionism is rising in the world!" [26]

But Garrison's special friend on this trip was Nathaniel Peabody Rogers. A native of New Hampshire and a New Englander of ancient lineage, Rogers was a successful lawyer-turned-editor of Concord's lively *Herald of Freedom,* an abolitionist paper to Garrison's liking. Like other reformers he was conscientious and stout-hearted, but unlike many of them he was also a person of considerable personal charm. George Thompson said that he hardly knew anyone superior to him as a companion. He had "a full mind; ready, polished wit, and a comprehensive and glowing heart." [27] Physically he was a man of slight build with a head that looked almost too big for his body. His features were regular, the intensity of his expression emphasized by deep furrows in the forehead and lines around the mouth. His eyes were bright and seemed to penetrate and smile at the same time. Since Rogers' favorite ideas coincided with Garrison's—he was both a nonresistant abolitionist and religious liberal—and since he had a natural diffidence, a perfect complement to Garrison's arrogance, the two men were most congenial friends.[28]

About the middle of July Garrison and Rogers, accompanied during part of the trip by Remond and Thompson, set off to Scotland and Ireland. They left the "magnificent" Victoria Hotel, taking passage on the Northern Railway. "We shot out of London," Rogers reported,[29] "with the lightning speed of the British Locomotive, and were, in a twinkling, deep in the country." Church spires loomed ahead; a forest of staunch British oaks—"in shape like a mass of clouds"—surrounded them. They thundered, with the roar of a cannonade, through a dark tunnel. They passed, meadow, brook, and moorland, in sight of "crumbling old Towers and kingly Castles," arriving at sunset in Sheffield, cutlery shop of the world.

On 20 July, after having visited York, they took coach—mounting to the top for economy and view—from the Turf Hotel in Newcastle upon Tyne for Scotland. The macadamized road, smooth as pulverized rock could make it, stretched white into the distance. It was less than a day's ride to the border; they spent the evening at Melrose, exploring the ruins of the old abbey. Rogers remembered Garrison "enthusiastically as parcel of the scene" as they clambered through the ruins. His presence reminded Rogers "to look *future*, as that old ruin caused us to look *past*." As the twilight deepened, they groped their way through vast galleries and under Gothic arches. They "climbed the ruined stair, to the top of one of the old towers, and sat there among the ivy, and heard the *primeval* ticking of the Abbey clock, that had seemed to outlast the massive walls in which it hung. *Time's keeper*, surviving *Time's ravages* upon the chiseled stone."

But the whole trip was not to be dedicated to sightseeing and mellow speculations on the past. In Edinburgh the next day, as they walked through the ancient streets, they were advised by placard after placard announcing that Garrison, Remond, and Thompson would speak that evening at a temperance meeting. Although Garrison had not previously been informed of the event, he could hardly refuse "to lift up my voice in favor of the first great moral enterprise which I ever publicly espoused." [30] And what more appropriate place could there be for temperance reform than Scotland, where so much alcohol was consumed! Garrison had been busy reprimanding his British friends for their drinking habits—even many ardent abolitionists imbibed regularly. Now he was to have a chance to express himself publicly on the subject.

As the three men entered Dun Edin Hall, which was jammed with about two thousand persons, they were met with deafening cheers and applause. When Garrison introduced Remond "as the representative to Scotland of the colored people of New England," the multitude responded "with clapping, and waving of hats, caps, and kerchiefs, and with Scottish *hurrahs,* till the rafters of Dun Edin hall fairly trembled." [31] Although infants and children fell quietly asleep in their mothers' arms, most of the audience remained attentive to Garrison and the other speakers from seven o'clock until the meeting adjourned after two in the morning. Garrison was impressed. He wrote to his wife that he was "satisfied that the cause of humanity on both sides of the Atlantic, and throughout the world, will be greatly aided by our present mission. . . . I feel, I have long felt, that my feet are planted upon the eternal Rock. . . . How happy I am to be accounted worthy to assist in filling up the measure of the sufferings of Jesus!" [32]

On the morning of 24 July a public breakfast was given at the Royal Hotel to honor Garrison and his friends. Garrison was delighted to find gathered there "some of the most respectable and eminent friends of humanity, literature and science, in that enlightened and magnificent city." [33]

From Edinburgh the abolitionists proceeded to Glasgow, where, as the American delegates who refused to associate themselves with the London antislavery convention, they were honored at a public reception. George Thompson, who was well known to the audience, introduced Garrison with an embarrassingly flattering eulogy. When Garrison rose, he was greeted with wild cheering, applause, and waving of handkerchiefs. He admitted that he felt quite unqualified to speak after such an eulogy. "He thought he could receive unshrinkingly, the rotten eggs and brickbats of a mob, but he could not receive such a eulogium as he had been compelled to listen to."

Garrison went on to deliver a long, rambling, but rhetorically effective speech. He flattered his audience by saying that the hall where they were meeting, Dr. Wardlow's Chapel, was more significant to him than Melrose Abbey, York Minster, Abbottsford, St. Paul's, or any of the buildings he had seen on his trip. It was important because it had been the arena for the great battles between freedom and slavery. He talked about the World's Convention, from which half the world had been excluded. He reviewed the course of American slavery, condemning the church as the most deadly enemy of abolition. He urged that an abundance of antislavery documents be sent to the United States, even though they could not be circulated directly to the Southern states. He assured his audience that the dome of Heaven was "one great whispering gallery"; only whisper "immediate emancipation" and the phrase was thundered around the country. He said that "the slaveholding states threatened disunion, but that they could not live twenty-four hours without the free States. (Cheers.) As an anti-slavery woman remarked, it was like the threat of the town poor to leave the town. (Laughter.)" [34]

When Garrison had entered the chapel, he had found at the door a man passing out handbills, and he had taken one. It was a Chartist appeal for impoverished labor, signed "A White Slave." After reading it over, Garrison resolved to read it aloud to the audience within.[35] Toward the end of his speech he took the handbill out of his pocket and presented it to the assembly. The parallel between abolition and labor reform had never been a meaningful one to Garrison [36] and he took this occasion to make his position clear. Although he expressed sympathy for oppressed labor, he insisted that there was a basic and essential difference between a so-called white slave and a real black slave—the difference between oppression and slavery. Whereas the white laborer may be impoverished and exploited, he nevertheless had freedom to work for his employer or to seek work elsewhere. The slave had to do his master's bidding or suffer the consequences—perhaps even death itself.[37]

Garrison's reluctance to sympathize with labor problems reminds one that, in spite of his many radical ideas, he was never a consistent liberal in regard to labor. It is as though he had to retain some conservative characteristics in order to qualify as a gentleman reformer. Although part of Garrison's personality demanded expression, another part sought respectability, and he wanted to be associated with reformers of good family like Quincy, May, Sewall, Rogers. He was a gentleman also in manner. People who had known him only by reputation were always surprised when they met socially to find him moderate, even-tempered, and gracious.

The good impression he made in Britain was partly due to his genteel appearance. Audiences were often more pleased with his manner and the way he spoke than with what he had to say. The editor of the Edinburgh *Witness,* for example, said that he had expected to find Garrison bold and boisterous, but was pleasantly surprised that "his appearance as a speaker is exceedingly becoming—his manner is calm, gentlemanlike, and impressive—and his utterance polished and agreeable." [38]

On 28 July Garrison and Rogers sailed to Dublin to visit Richard D. Webb. Webb was a Quaker printer, an Irishman with all the reform impulses that Garrison desired in a friend—he was an abolitionist, teetotaler, and nonresistant. He was also a jolly, round-faced son of Erin, a man with humor, intelligence, and judgment. Although he and Garrison were to meet only at infrequent intervals during the coming years, they remained close and congenial friends. The voyage to Ireland took only one night. In the morning Garrison and his traveling companions joined in Dublin Richard and Hannah Webb and the Motts, whose visit was just ending. It was a quiet, "Eden-like," three-day visit *en famille,* which gave Garrison stimulating companionship and much-needed rest.[39]

Garrison recrossed the channel in time for the sailing of the steam packet *Acadia* on 4 August. Webb could not resist coming along to see his friends off. The bon-voyage party also included Elizabeth Pease of Darlington, England, another Quaker who had found Garrison and his doctrines irresistible. A tiny steamer took the group alongside the *Acadia;* Rogers and Garrison climbed aboard. As soon as they had seen to their luggage and found their quarters, they came back on deck to wave their friends good-by. But, alas, the small boat was out of sight. Garrison felt cheated. Richard Webb had come all the way from Dublin for such an unceremonious farewell. There should have been a long last wave of hat and handkerchief "till distance should hide you from our sight." [40]

To save money, Garrison and Rogers had booked passage in the forward cabin—the third class of a century ago. Although the accommodations were unpleasant and uncomfortable and they were tempted to transfer to the after cabin, they "resolved, *as a matter of anti-slavery self-denial and economy,* not to change." Luckily, the voyage was a short one. In spite of a dense fog that closed in for several days and a tempestuous head wind of gale proportions that lasted two more days, the *Acadia* made a record crossing of twelve and a half days.[41] Even the mammoth steamer *President,* which had sailed three days earlier, arrived in New York after the *Acadia* had docked in Boston. The vessel touched first at Halifax, which reminded Garrison of his native Newburyport. The town turned out in force and made "the welkin ring" with their cheers for the record-breaking ship. Although taken by surprise, Boston gave the ship a stunning welcome. Thousands crowded the wharves to shout and cheer. Garrison admitted: "It was one of the most thrilling scenes I ever witnessed; and as it was the termination of my voyage, I could not help weeping like a child for joy." On the dock was "a deputation of our white and colored anti-slavery friends" who welcomed him enthusiastically and gave him the good news that his wife and children were all well. Soon Helen was in his arms, and the trip over.

Since he had officially gone to London to attend an antislavery convention which he boycotted, Garrison felt called upon to defend his mission in letters and in *The Liberator.* He reassured friends and readers that his mission had been "one of the most important movements of my life," and that the cause of abolition would soon be entirely successful. "There are causes in operation, which, in the course of a very few years, will assuredly emancipate every American slave." He said that his refusal to participate in the convention was perhaps the act of which, during his whole life, he was most proud, for it had "done more to bring up for the consideration of Europe the rights of woman, than could have been accomplished in any other manner." He reported, in addition, striking progress in the cause of temperance and of non-resistance, for he spoke and distributed tracts on those reforms throughout England, Scotland, and Ireland. "In short," he admitted, "I did what I could for the redemption of the human race." [42]

Garrison and his followers now set about running the American Anti-Slavery Society. They elected a new executive committee, which founded, as official weekly organ of the society, the *National Anti-Slavery Standard,* and they planned annual conventions. The old activities of the national society—the maintaining of an anti-slavery library, the arrangement of a program for lecture agents in the field, the continuance of a petition campaign, and the carrying on of systematic correspondence—all these were discarded.[43]

Money was needed, however, to launch the new paper. Since most of the state societies had withdrawn from Garrison's national society, a nation-wide appeal was unsuccessful. And so John A. Collins, a former student at Andover Theological Seminary, who had apparently been helpful to Garrison during the controversy with the clergy, was dispatched to England to raise funds. There he had some success in the provinces, even though the Executive Committee of the British and Foreign Anti-Slavery Society, probably owing to the recent events at the international convention, refused to contribute.[44]

During the next several years there was a gradual diminution of the effectiveness of the American Anti-Slavery Society. The newly organized American and Foreign Anti-Slavery Society suffered a similar fate. The latter did succeed in acquiring as members many county and some state societies, though the major state societies and some of the leading abolitionists, like Weld, did not respond to its appeal.[45]

Although the schism in the national antislavery organization marked the end of a significant phase in the abolition movement, after which it was no longer possible for individual abolitionists to wield the power they had formerly, Garrison had certainly shown strength in maintaining the American Anti-Slavery Society against fearful odds. He had also won a moral victory and new friends in Great Britain.

CHAPTER XIV

Smiling at Satan's Rage

JUST as his mission abroad in 1833 had helped establish Garrison as a national leader among American abolitionists, so the mission of 1840, with its emphasis on woman's rights, temperance, and nonresistance, had confirmed the new direction of his career. Since as nonresistant he could not subscribe to emancipation through political action, which was the method becoming increasingly popular with abolitionists and indeed with the whole Northern section of the country, he was obliged to supplement his plea for emancipation with agitation for other reforms. Far from realizing that his abolitionist methods had become outdated, he rationalized that what the world needed in 1840 was a truly universal reformer, a righteous, unselfish man who would dedicate his life to the abolition of all sin from the world. Many were now working to free the slave, but he alone was striving to obliterate all sin from an evil world.

Garrison still needed to be a reformer in 1840. His "private ail," to use Thoreau's phrase, would not let him relax and enjoy life. This ail had not yet been righted, the spring had not come to him, the morning had not risen over his couch. He was not ready to "forsake his generous companions without apology." [1] And so Garrison's great problem after 1840 was to adjust himself to the changing world of reform. His solution was to insist that he was the universal reformer, that since so many were now working for abolition—and he took credit for recruiting a large proportion of them—he was wise to distribute much of his energy elsewhere.

[176]

During 1841–1842 a portion of this energy had to be expended on his brother James. James had remained with the Bensons until their Brooklyn house was sold in the spring of 1841, and then had gone to New Brunswick determined to be more successful at recovering the Lloyd inheritance than his brother had been in 1835. Far from being successful, the trip disturbed the equilibrium established in Connecticut, and poor James went on his last half-hearted spree. When he returned to Boston, he was so ashamed that he wrote Lloyd a long confession of guilt, explaining in detail exactly what had happened, how he had tried to commit suicide, and how he was determined to spare his brother further humiliation by changing his name and flying from Boston forever.

But James was deprived even of the pathetic satisfaction of disappearing. He spent the year of life remaining to him with the Garrisons. Oblique references in Lloyd's letters give brief glimpses of the pain and frustration of that final year. It was about three o'clock on the morning of 14 October 1842, as Lloyd watched by his side, that James's suffering seemed to pass into sleep. Half an hour passed before Lloyd realized what had happened. He reported that James "retained his senses to the last, and died with all possible fortitude and resignation, being perfectly aware that his end was approaching." [2]

During the summer of 1840, while Garrison was still abroad, events had been developing that were to give Garrison an opportunity to extend his reforming activities. A meeting was held in Groton, Massachusetts, to investigate whether "the outward organization of the Church [were] a human or a divine institution." Toward the end of September a Non-Resistance Convention was held at Chardon Street Chapel in Boston. At the close of this meeting it was decided to call another convention to consider basic religious questions like the divinity of the Sabbath and the nature and authority of the ministry and the church. The call for this, the famous Chardon Street Convention, was published in *The Liberator* for 16 October over such names as Edmund Quincy, Maria W. Chapman, Oliver Johnson, Abby Kelley, William H. Channing (nephew of the famous Dr. William Ellery Channing), and A. Bronson Alcott. Although Garrison's name was conspicuously absent from the call, he was generally given credit for sponsoring the whole project. Many newspapers again attacked Garrison and his paper. Garrison was pleased with all the publicity, and he quoted the belligerent words of half a dozen papers in *The Liberator* for 6 November. "But, truly, none of these things disturb me," he said. "I can 'smile at Satan's rage, and face a frowning world,' for my trust is in the Lord, and Christ is my Redeemer. . . . These are solemn, glorious, stirring times to live in!" [3]

The Sabbath Convention was a picturesque spectacle. Abolitionists and political reformers joined with Transcendentalists. Even timid clergymen—some fifty in all—appeared at one time or another during the three-day meeting. There were arguments in favor of the conservative view of the Sabbath—many of them vulgar and malicious, Garrison thought, though he credited Amos A. Phelps with "tact and spirit" in his four-hour speech.[4] Not so Father Taylor—the sailor preacher to be immortalized in *Moby Dick* as Father Mapple. Garrison said he "behaved in a most outrageous manner, and exhibited a dreadfully malignant spirit." Some of the Transcendentalists—notably A. Bronson Alcott, who was enough of an anarchist to oppose violently having any organization at all at the meeting, objecting even to the election of Quincy as chairman—joined the Garrisonian abolitionists in attacking the Sabbath as a sacred day. But the three-day discussion ended without any definite vote or action. Quincy reported in his journal: "No vote was taken & the Conv^n adj^d to March. Snow Storm." [5]

Emerson's was the most colorful account of the convention:

A great variety of dialect and of costume was noticed; a great deal of confusion, eccentricity, and freak appeared, as well as of zeal and enthusiasm. If the assembly was disorderly, it was picturesque. Madmen, madwomen, men with beards, Dunkers, Muggletonians, Come-outers, Groaners, Agrarians, Seventh-day-Baptists, Quakers, Abolitionists, Calvinists, Unitarians and Philosophers—all came successively to the top, and seized their moment, if not their hour, wherein to chide, or pray, or preach, or protest. The faces were a study. The most daring innovators and the champions-until-death of the old causes sat side by side. The still-living merit of the oldest New England families encountered the founders of families, fresh merit energizing and expanding the brows, and lighting a clownish face with sacred fire. If there was not parliamentary order, there was life, and the assurance of that constitutional love for religion and religious liberty which, in all periods, characterizes the inhabitants of this part of America.[6]

Although Emerson may have been amused and exhilarated by the convention, Garrison, perhaps remembering his experience with the clergy in 1836–1837, was surprisingly restrained. Instead of reporting the meeting in detail himself, he reprinted accounts of it from various exchange papers, some of which he characterized as tolerably accurate and some as prejudiced. After subscribers had repeatedly requested a full report of the convention, he explained that Mrs. Chapman, the secretary, had not had sufficient time to translate her voluminous notes before she went abroad and that, moreover, funds were not available to finance a report that would surely run to three or four hundred pages.[7]

But the Reverend Nathaniel Colver, a "new organizationist," as Garrison called those who broke away from his national society, and a conservative participant in the convention, put an end to Garrison's restraint. Colver wrote to leading British abolitionists that Garrison had been heading *"an infidel convention,"* and that his abolitionist influence was certainly on the wane because he was identifying himself with Transcendentalists as well as "the wildest of the no-marriage Perfectionists." When word of Colver's attack reached Garrison through his English friend, Elizabeth Pease,[8] Garrison was irate. One of his proudest achievements had been the reputation and popularity which he had enjoyed in Britain. Now his bitter enemy, a corrupt and morally deformed priest, was attacking him "assassin-like in the dark," trying to destroy that reputation. He could hardly imagine a more wicked, a more malignant action! He had arguments for Colver: he denied allegations of infidelity; he insisted that there was no correlation between a man's religion and his abolitionism; he described the multiplicity of religious sects among British abolitionists as a basic strength. But no matter how much he reasoned, the basic fact was that he had been challenged in an area where he had felt confident and secure, in spite of the fiasco at the World's Convention. To the English he had been *the* leader of American abolitionism. Now, he feared, "in consequence of the innumerable slanders that have been busily circulated by the lying spirit of 'new organization,' my reputation and popularity are at a low ebb in England."

But, as we know, Garrison could rationalize himself out of any criticism. Far from being infidel, he insisted that his "religious sentiments," except for certain forms and ceremonies, were "as rigid and uncompromising as those promulgated by Christ himself." No one, he said, had greater respect for the Scriptures. "They are my text-book, and worth all other books in the universe." The Chardon Street Convention had been held in an attempt to determine certain truths about religion and especially about the Sabbath. How could such an intention be construed as an aid to infidelity? As a matter of fact, Garrison said that he had "just as much to do with" the convention as Colver and no more. They had both attended the convention and both had participated in the discussion, but neither had arranged nor run the meeting.

As for Colver's innuendo that Garrison's influence was waning, a subject on which Garrison well might have been sensitive, he argued illogically: "This cannot be true—else this restless accuser and the great mass of a corrupt priesthood would not be seeking to move heaven and earth for my downfall. My influence in the world will be in exact proportion to my fidelity to God and his cause; and it will not be in the power of men or devils to destroy it." And the Transcendentalists whom he was condemned for consorting with—"they may be right or wrong in their distinctive peculiarities; but why this sneer against them, because they chose to give their views on the question before the meeting?" " 'The wildest of the no-marriage Perfectionists.' What this means, or to whom it applies, I do not know."

Garrison's statement that he is ignorant of the "no-marriage Perfectionists" is disingenuous, since we know that he and John Humphrey Noyes had met in 1837. Indeed, there is abundant evidence that he was still much influenced by Noyes, who seemed sufficiently radical even for Garrison. In his Fourth of July (1841) speech at Providence Garrison quoted a sentence "from a letter in his possession from an esteemed friend": *"My hope of the millennium begins where Dr. Beecher's expires—*viz. at the overthrow of this nation." [9] The friend, of course, is Noyes and the letter the one he wrote to Garrison in March of 1837. The entire letter, moreover, he printed, anonymously and without any comment of his own, under the heading "Declaration of Sentiments," in *The Liberator* for 13 October 1841.[10] Whittier was so annoyed by the publication of the anonymous letter—he did not recognize the author, although he must have heard him talk when Noyes called on Garrison in the spring—that he berated Garrison for printing so "decidedly sectarian" a letter.[11]

During 1841–1842 Garrison was subjected to more than the usual financial pressure. His brother's long illness, with the doctor's fees, the expense of medication, and the cost of the funeral had added greatly to his already high household expenses. The same year the receipts from *The Liberator* fell short of expenses by approximately $200, and Garrison had had the bad judgment to lend $55 to friends. Now Garrison urgently applied to other friends for loans. Loring was unable to help; Philbrick advanced $50 to pay the papermaker; Francis Jackson loaned another $50; and $40 came from his brother-in-law George.[12]

There had been further aggravation that year over a financial agreement signed with Lewis Tappan, on which Garrison reneged supposedly because Tappan had taken advantage of him. On this matter Garrison appealed to Weld for help. He apparently talked with him about the possibilities of bankruptcy. He told Weld that a distinguished New York judge had said that the agreement had been designed to produce a certain impression on Garrison, whereas it had an entirely different legal meaning. Weld wrote to Tappan, urging a charitable interpretation of Garrison's actions, saying that he thought it not certain Garrison had been dishonest, although "if I believed him fully in his *right mind* I could not but feel toward him an abiding indignation." [13] Garrison was certainly not "in his right mind" when it came to financial matters, though it seems unlikely that he was consciously dishonest.

In the spring of 1843 Garrison paid Noyes and his philosophy of Perfectionism high tribute in a review of Noyes's pamphlet, *The Doctrine of Salvation from Sin*. The pamphlet, he said, "treats of a subject that is second to none that can engage the attention of mankind. . . . There is no doctrine which is more opposed, dreaded, hated, misrepresented, by the existing priesthood and the nominal church . . . than the rational, scriptural, glorious, and only truly reformatory doctrine of salvation from sin in this life!" Garrison went on to commend Noyes for his effective and lucid defense of the idea and insisted that every Christian "is under sacred obligations to bear witness to its truth, and to exemplify that truth in his life." He even suggested that the basic doctrine

[181]

of Perfectionism, that man can become entirely free from sin in this life, is the philosophical basis for both total abstinence from liquor and immediate emancipation. The priesthood and the church opposed Perfectionism so violently "because they profit by human iniquity." In their judgment, "to sell human beings by the pound at auction, like bales of cotton, is a meritorious act compared to the promulgation of the doctrine, that, in this life, men are bound to be perfect in holiness." [14]

The rapport between Garrison and Noyes, however, was of short duration. Toward the end of 1843 Noyes published in *The Perfectionist* an editorial which Garrison reprinted in the "Refuge of Oppression," that first-page, first-column section of *The Liberator* dedicated to the most nefarious of proslavery propaganda. The crux of the editorial was that though Noyes had considered himself an abolitionist for ten years, he wished to "protest against exaggerating the relative importance of abolitionism, making it the centre of all reform, holding it separate from, and independent of religion, exalting it into rivalry with, and of course hostility to, the system of the Bible, making adherence and non-adherence to it, instead of belief and unbelief in the gospel of Christ, the supreme tests of character." [15] In its very nature, Noyes insisted, abolition is "a subordinate reform"; it can never rightfully be anything more than a branch of the great religious reform God is effecting in the world. To consider it a more basic reform is both seditious to God and treasonable to abolitionism.

He objected also to the way in which abolitionists and other reformers had forced their interpretation of the Bible to support their peculiar ultra doctrines. He reprimanded the abolitionists, Garrison especially, for exaggerating the merits of the Negro race. Moreover, he protested against "the general semi-infidelity of the Garrison party." The national antislavery society formerly depended, he said, on the conservatism of individual members to prevent its religious corruption. But in the schism of 1839–1840 those conservative members were ousted, leaving "it entirely in the hands of Unitarians, Universalists, and other free-thinkers. The equilibrium which had been maintained by the counteracting forces of liberalism and conservatism, was destroyed, and the Society passed from its negative character into positive hostility to the more orthodox churches." But in spite of the corruptions of the abolition societies, Noyes avowed his devotion to immediate emancipation and his determination either to alter the Constitution or to secede from the Union in order to extirpate the national crime of slavery. Finally, he commended to Perfectionists the Liberty party, urging that they support it in the coming election.

One can readily imagine Garrison's reaction to Noyes's editorial. To be accused of disproportionately emphasizing abolition when he himself had of late done so much to be a universal reformer! To think that a man he had called in print "an esteemed friend," a man whose basic idea had appealed to him as elemental in its implications, a man who was himself branded as an infidel and an adulterer should attack Garrison and his party for their radical doctrines of abolition and of religion! It was incomprehensible. Instead of dignifying Noyes's attack with a careful rebuttal, Garrison decided to treat it like any other insidious proslavery document and let it pass with no more than a paragraph of condemnation. And although Garrison's religious views retained their Perfectionist tinge—John Humphrey Noyes was conspicuously absent from subsequent issues of *The Liberator*.[16]

Within the next two years a better-known "infidel" found approbation in the pages of *The Liberator*. In the 1830's Garrison's references to Tom Paine reflected the prejudices of the period. He considered him the arch infidel, the immoral atheist, and was indignant when an opposition paper compared him with Paine: "In associating us with Thomas Paine, Rousseau, and the atheistical Jacobins of France, he [the editor of the Boston *Recorder*] maligns every principle that we cherish and assassinates our reputation." [17]

But toward the end of 1845 he read a recently published edition of Paine's religious works. It was his first direct experience with Paine's writings, and he was so much impressed that he wrote a long editorial review of the book, reversing his previous opinion of Paine. He explained that he had been educated "to regard him as a monster of iniquity" and was consequently "intimidated in early life from seeking an acquaintance with his opinions and doctrines as expressed by himself, without priestly distortion or caricatures." Now that he had read Paine's own words he felt obliged to be so impolitic as to state publicly his impressions. He considered Paine a remarkable intellect, "a close reasoner," "a powerful writer," an intrepidly honest man. Paine was to be commended for making "all his appeals to the reason of men, and not to their fears or selfishness." He expressed eloquently what Garrison had long felt—at least as it applied to himself—that reason was the most effective weapon against error, that freedom of the mind was an essential human ingredient, and that every man was entitled to his own opinion.

Garrison agreed, also, that even the Bible must be interpreted rationally, though he would not follow Paine in denying all that was miraculous.[18] Surely, he thought, the divine content of the Bible would withstand unscathed reason's deepest probes; and "what is clearly monstrous, or absurd, or impossible, cannot be endorsed by reason, and can never properly be made a test of religious faith, or an evidence of moral character." Only the priests, Garrison said—delighted to have found in Paine an anticlerical ally—insist on the ridiculous belief that the entire Bible is divinely inspired and absolutely true. It is the priests and their nefarious allies in the South who prove "on the strength of a text . . . it is lawful to go to war, to sustain governments of brute force, to strangle criminals on the gallows or shut them up in prisons, to enslave human beings! What can be more monstrous than this?" But, according to Garrison, Paine and his followers had gone too far: they had treated the Bible "as profanely as the priesthood do idolatrously" by denying much of its most efficacious moral teaching.[19]

Exerting a far greater influence on Garrison than either Noyes or Paine was another "infidel," Henry C. Wright.[20] Wright, some eight years Garrison's senior, was like Garrison a Calvinist by inheritance. Although he was descended on both sides from families that had been in New England since the 1630's, his people were of the same lower middle-class category as Garrison's, his father being a small farmer and house-joiner in Litchfield County, Connecticut. After his mother's death while Henry Wright was still a young boy, his father married again and young Henry was given the responsibility of looking after the younger children. He acquired in the process an almost neurotic tenderness and affection for children.[21] When the time came for him to learn a trade, he was apprenticed to a hatter. He became so efficient that he could complete his required work by noon and read the rest of the day.

Soon his father was convinced that he should become a minister. He entered Andover Theological Seminary, where he worked very hard, rejoicing when a vacation came because it gave him time for continuous application. "I . . . busied myself in study from sixteen to eighteen hours every day during the vacation. . . . I scarcely spoke to any one during the whole time, except to the family where I snatched my hasty meals." [22] As his study of theology continued, he became increasingly impatient with the traditional forms and ceremonies of religion and with the pious pretensions of ministers.

Shortly after graduation he married a Newburyport widow some years older than he who had four young children; and he was called to a church in West Newbury. Though he had earlier been aware of the problem of slavery and colonization, it was during his seven-year ministry (1826–1833) at West Newbury that Wright first heard of William Lloyd Garrison and his antislavery crusade. He sympathized with Garrison's work, but was unwilling to be identified with him. As late as the spring of 1833 he wrote: "I am not prepared to identify myself with abolitionists. They seem to me too vituperative, too sweeping in their denunciations. Especially does Garrison. Yet in my conscience, I am certain he is right in his principles, and probably should approve his spirit and measures, if I were the victim for whom he is pleading." [23] Early in the summer of the same year he resigned his ministry because he believed that even under the most favorable circumstances "the position of a minister is adverse to freedom of thought and speech." [24] Two years later he joined the Massachusetts Anti-Slavery Society, feeling somewhat guilty that prejudice had prevented his joining earlier. "Henceforth," he announced, "my voice shall be heard among abolitionists, come what may to reputation or life. . . . I have swallowed down, and digested Garrison, Thompson, Liberator and all, and henceforth Anti-Slavery is to be an element of my existence. In it I mean to live, and move, and have my being." [25]

Soon Wright was showing all the zeal of the convert in his devotion to Garrison and his principles. Following an interview in November, he reported that Garrison had "a warm heart and a clear head. He is doing work for our race; more to extend the empire of Christianity than all the ministers and churches, as such." [26] Wright accepted all of Garrison's ultra doctrines; immediate emancipation (even at the expense of dissolving the Union), nonresistance, temperance, woman's rights, and the corruption of the clergy and traditional religion. In Wright Garrison found a completely congenial colleague, a conscientious, frugal, self-sacrificing man, a man who had more education than he himself, but whose similar social background made the younger man feel completely at home. One suspects that there was always a social barrier between Garrison and Phillips and even between Garrison and Quincy; but Garrison and Wright met and associated on the same level.[27]

Wright rose rapidly in the hierarchy of reform. Within a few months after his antislavery conversion Garrison was urging that he be placed on the Board of Managers of the Massachusetts Anti-Slavery Society.[28] In 1838 he was active in the founding of the New-England Non-Resistance Society, of which he became an agent and, two years later, a vice president. In September 1842, at Garrison's suggestion and partly with money raised by him, the Society sent Wright on a reform mission to Great Britain.[29]

Wright found Great Britain most congenial. He had escaped his nagging wife, who had by that time lost whatever appeal she may have had; and he was glad to live apart from her troublesome children.[30] He could lead the life of the reformer unmolested. He journeyed energetically from town to town, speaking calmly and bluntly against war and slavery and selling his own radical tracts and especially his children's book, *A Kiss for a Blow*. Everywhere he preached on the nobility of man and child and the ultimate value of human brotherhood.[31] And he practiced what he preached, for he made many friends, especially in Ireland and Scotland.

While Wright was in Britain two events occurred which caused great consternation in abolitionist circles. In the spring of 1843 the Free Church of Scotland, insisting on the right of individual congregations to appoint their own ministers, broke away from the established church. Since in making the break the Scottish church forfeited state support, there was need to raise a considerable sum of money. It was arranged that contributions should be sought from the entire Presbyterian organization, including the church in America. The appeal for funds met with a fertile reception in Charleston, South Carolina, where sermons were preached and where collection trays were promptly filled with what the abolitionists considered blood-stained money—money, they urged, that should be at once returned to South Carolina.

Another incident excited the wrath of Garrison and Wright. A white man named John L. Brown, deciding to make an honest woman of his slave mistress, helped her to escape. But in South Carolina where fornication without benefit of clergy was preferable to intermarriage or to aiding a fugitive slave, Brown found that his good intentions and his white skin were insufficient proof against the exigencies of Southern justice. He was dragged into court, prosecuted for helping a slave to escape, and sentenced with pious Christian exhortation "to be hanged by the neck till your body be dead. And may God have mercy on your soul!" [32]

The sentencing of Brown heated abolitionist tempers, especially in Britain, to the incandescent point. Garrison announced that no event since the beginning of antislavery agitation in this country —not even the mobbing of Garrison or the murdering of Lovejoy —"has so powerfully affected the public mind in Great Britain, as the act of sentencing this young American to the gallows, for performing one of the most humane and Christian deeds which can be done among men." Meetings were held throughout England and Scotland. In London a memorial signed by 1,300 ministers and officers of local churches demanded that Brown be saved. The agitation even reached the heights of the House of Lords, where two peers of the realm (Brougham and Denham) indulged in pious and pathetic allusion. [33]

It was exactly the kind of excitement that Garrison dearly loved. He gave the case of John L. Brown and the Free Church of Scotland full coverage in *The Liberator*. On the day set for Brown's execution, 26 April 1844, he devoted most of the issue to it, even though Brown's sentence had by that time been commuted to whipping—a fact which he announced inconspicuously toward the end of an editorial following some two pages of propaganda based on the assumption that Brown was about to be executed. Three weeks later he reprinted quantities of material fresh from England, even though by this time, as Garrison again announced in an inconspicuous editorial, Brown was not even to be whipped. He explained that he had reprinted the spirited proceedings above out of deference to British philanthropists.[34]

The best known of British reformers, the elderly Thomas Clarkson, whom Garrison so much admired, was becoming uncertain about Garrison's reputation. In the summer of 1844 Mrs. Chapman asked him to write an article for *The Liberty Bell,* the annual publication associated with the antislavery bazaar. Near the end of July Clarkson wrote to ask Lewis Tappan's advice about writing for a Garrisonian publication. Tappan said that he was grateful to Garrison for his early support of the cause, "but I should not like, since he has of late years mixed up the subject with eccentric and visionary notions, to be thought to be of the same School." [35] Tappan replied that he saw no objection to Clarkson's publishing there, though he advised disclaiming affinity with the publishers of the volume.[36] Clarkson's little article duly appeared in the 1845 *Liberty Bell,* and in a foreword he commended Garrison for having kept the flame of abolition alive during the difficult early days.

Wright, in the meantime, continued his British mission at a furious pace. Rising regularly at two or three in the morning, he wrote his autobiography, lectured on peace, on abolition, and on the Free Church of Scotland; and he contributed an average of nearly two letters a week to *The Liberator.*[37] But no matter what Wright might say or publish, the Free Church was not inclined to return any of its ill-gotten gold to Charleston. Leaders of the church retaliated with diversionary attacks on the fidelity of Wright and Garrison, emphasizing their radical views of the Sabbath, the church, and the ministry. And they succeeded in immobilizing indefatigable Wright at least one day a week, for Scottish custom forbade reformatory lectures on Sunday.[38]

By the spring of 1846, the war with the Free Church having reached a stalemate, it was apparent that something drastic would have to be done. A great public meeting of members and friends of the Glasgow Emancipation Society was held. Wright, Douglass, Thompson—all of the seasoned generals available—were there. Speech followed speech. Thompson stormed the hall with all his rhetorical power, reiterating the theme that had already been placarded about the cities, "Send back the money!" Then in a great peroration he eulogized William Lloyd Garrison—"there breathes not a man more worthy the love, the trust, and the esteem of the friends of God and man!" And he introduced a resolution that was adopted by acclamation, "that we extend to Mr. Garrison an invitation to visit this kingdom, to cheer us by his presence, and encourage us by his counsels." Wright added his plea to Thompson's: "What can I add to the motives urged on the other side, save that I long to see you, and will do all in my power to make your visit both agreeable and useful? Come, come, come!" If he would come, Wright agreed to return—doubtless in triumph —to America with him.

When the full report of the meeting reached Garrison, he was moved to devote practically an entire issue of his paper to it. He did not exclude even Thompson's eulogy, "though there are . . . reasons why I should wish to withhold it." He also printed— for the advancement of the cause—a goodly overrun of the issue.[39]

Seldom, if ever, had Garrison been more pleased. He would like nothing better than another trip abroad. And to go this time with a special invitation from the British! But he did not want to appear impulsive. It was a matter, he concluded, that must be carefully considered. "I do not see how I can go—I do not know how to refrain from going." Soon the executive committee of the Massachusetts society had made up his mind for him. A sub-scription drive for funds to pay for his trip was launched.[40]

On the eve of his departure a great meeting of free colored friends paid their respects, while Garrison reminisced about his early days fighting for the cause. He reviewed for them his earlier trips abroad. He remembered 1833 and his arrival in England at the crucial moment of West Indian emancipation. He remembered exposing the colonizationist Elliott Cresson during that mission— not mentioning the major objective of the trip, to raise money for colored education. He remembered being ushered into the presence of Wilberforce, he an unknown young man as though on trial; and he recalled with a thrill of pleasure how Wilberforce as a result of the interview had reversed himself on colonization, condemning Cresson and the American Colonization Society. He remembered 1840, his second trip abroad, and how since the female co-delegates were not admitted to the convention, he had refused to participate. He could still feel the righteous satisfaction of 1840. The culprits on that occasion, he said, had been the London Quakers; but today the case was altered, for he sailed not as a delegate from America but at the express invitation of British abolitionists. Not that he lacked an antagonist in the Free Church of Scotland, which Garrison resolved would "disgorge its ill-gotten gains." [41]

At noon on 16 July, too late to bid his close associates good-by at the Anti-Slavery Office as planned, Garrison could be seen bustling through the crowd at the *Britannia*'s pier, waving a vigorous farewell to Edmund Quincy and other friends gathered to see him off.[42] Since Quincy had agreed to be substitute editor of *The Liberator*,[43] it may have been he who was most affected by Garrison's departure. As he watched the *Britannia* steam off, Quincy wished, with an adulation difficult to understand in one so intelligent and sophisticated, that "the foremost of the reapers" were divisible into many parts so that all who needed him could have a share. Garrison had an impressive catalogue of virtues, Quincy thought: "the native logic, the keen sagacity, and the earnest eloquence which mark his public speeches," "the assurance which waits upon his personal presence, . . . the amiableness of his disposition, the purity of his life, the disinterestedness and sincerity of his nature." [44] When he wrote to Richard Davis Webb about Garrison, Quincy could only think of "one swingeing fault. It is a horrid trick he has of being right." Quincy admitted that it is generally thought that he rules his associates "with a rod of iron & that we can't call our souls our own," but that actually he is "more often overruled on points of difference." [45] (One might question whether Garrison were ever overruled on a major issue without a schism resulting!)

It was a tedious, fog-infested voyage for Garrison. He was soon sick of the sea if not seasick. But there was time in abundance for sentimentalizing over wife and family. His feelings toward his wife always seemed most tender when she was at home and he journeying abroad. Helen's image, he wrote, was "constantly before me," and one by one he recalled incidents of their life together: their first meeting, happy days with the Benson family, and deaths of close friends and relatives, the births of children (five of them now—four sons and precious Fanny). He could hardly restrain himself when he found a pair of Fanny's socks in his pocket. "You should have seen me when I made the discovery

—how I smiled, how I exulted, how I kissed and pressed to my heart the tiny little things! It was next to having her in my arms, and seeing her sweet face, and hearing her pleasant voice." [46]

The *Britannia* docked at Liverpool fifteen days after leaving Boston. Garrison was especially looking forward to seeing his two best friends, Wright and Thompson. He did not have long to wait to see Wright, for he and Richard D. Webb of Dublin, who had been in town four days awaiting Garrison's arrival, were at the pier to meet him. The three friends went up to London, where they found George Thompson at the station. Although Garrison had not seen Thompson in eleven years, the two men seemed as congenial as ever. Thompson insisted that Garrison make his house London headquarters. To his wife Garrison wrote: "To be once more with George, is a revival of days gone by. He is still the same loving, faithful friend—the same playful, mirthful, entertaining companion—the same modest, unpretending man." [47] But he had acquired one bad habit in the last decade. Continuously and almost unconsciously he used snuff. Garrison was not slow to reprimand; Thompson smiled goodnaturedly at the preaching.[48]

The size and the splendor of Thompson's city astonished Garrison even more than it had previously. Here was "the central point of human existence," with its thronging masses of people, its "multitude of vessels from various parts of the globe." Garrison stood on a bridge over the Thames and studied the traffic; the boats and steamers of every conceivable size and description stretched off toward the horizon in both directions. Here in London were quantity and variety and uncanny mechanical precision. "Huge as is the city, and complicated as are its arrangements and mysterious as are its modes of existence[,] every thing goes on with a regularity and precision truly marvelous. There is no violent collision—scarcely any jostle—the mechanism is perfect, 'like clock-work'—and no one is allowed or expected to interfere with another." [49]

Like Thompson the city also had its vices. The one that appalled Garrison was prostitution. He described to Helen the immense number of prostitutes that swarmed the brightly lighted London streets, telling her that they were of all grades, some ragged, some fashionably dressed. They would accost all passersby, take them familiarly by the arm, so that all young men, even the married, were subject to "a perpetual temptation." One experience he remembered vividly. He was waiting for an omnibus in front of the Lord Mayor's house when a voluptuous-looking, handsomely dressed young woman passed by. She stopped, turned around, and "in the most insinuating manner acted as though she expected me to go with her." But in a moment the bus carried him safely out of reach. As he pondered over the shocking experience, Garrison successfully avoided temptation, even in thought, by imagining her first as his sister and then as his daughter: "I thought of her as a sister—as *my* sister—seduced, it may be, by some villain. . . . I thought of her as a daughter—as *my* daughter—once the hope, the pride, the ornament of the family circle—now a castaway, and forever shut out from virtuous society." [50]

Almost at once upon reaching London Garrison became immersed in reforming activities. On 4 August he attended a session of the World's Temperance Convention. Although the meeting was held in a relatively small room and was not open to the public, Garrison had been given a ticket for admission and appeared the first day, full of enthusiasm. But an incident occurred that was not calculated to enhance Garrison's reputation abroad. When the Reverend Edward Norris Kirk, distinguished Congregational minister from Boston, gave what Garrison considered a proslavery speech, he rose to reply. As soon as the audience realized that Garrison intended to rebuke Kirk, the initial applause turned into angry objections. "Sundry individuals raised the cry of personality, and protested against the discussion of extraneous topics! Great excitement followed." [51] Kirk disclaimed proslavery sentiments, and Garrison, deciding that the convention was too closely regulated to allow freedom of speech, did not attend another session. The whole thing, Quincy concluded from across the Atlantic, "appears to have been almost as great a humbug as the Anti-Slavery World's Convention." [52]

But at the next meeting on 10 August at the Crown and Anchor Tavern, Garrison found all the freedom that he could have desired. In fact, the meeting resulted in the formation of a new British society, the Anti-Slavery League. A few days later there was a large public meeting in the same hall, where all was arranged to Garrison's liking. George Thompson was in the chair. Henry

C. Wright gave the first speech, a real "scorcher," and Garrison himself followed the hatchetman. There was "a tempest of applause," when he began to speak. The audience rose from their seats and cheered ecstatically. "I made a long speech," Garrison said, "which elicited the strongest marks of approbation." Then came Frederick Douglass with "one of his very best efforts." Finally Henry Vincent, moral-suasion Chartist (or moderate labor leader) whom Garrison was eager to cultivate, spoke with enthusiastic response. When the meeting adjourned at midnight after nearly six hours of speech-making, the Reverend Mr. Kirk was one of the few to have left the room. "Everything was encouraging in the highest degree," Garrison confided to his wife.[53]

Garrison was proud that a new society, dedicated to the principle that slavery was an unqualified evil to be abrogated at once, had been launched and endorsed. It was the object of the new league to overthrow slavery throughout the world, especially in the United States. Moreover, since it was Garrison's league it was dedicated to bringing about the extinction of slavery in cooperation with the American Anti-Slavery Society—not the American and Foreign Anti-Slavery Society.

To save time and expense, Garrison resolved "to hold as few public meetings as possible" during his current mission. Rather, it was his intention to become personally acquainted with those who controlled the press and public opinion. Soon after his arrival he called on Douglas Jerrold, to whom he had a letter of introduction from a friend in Liverpool. Jerrold was a writer who had suddenly become prominent as "the principal editor of the inimitable 'Punch.' " *Punch* at this time had a large circulation and was especially receptive to humanitarian reform. Jerrold seemed to be much interested in Garrison's ideas on American slavery and the evil influence which it exerted on Britain and the world. He promised to be helpful, and he promptly reprinted in *Punch* some articles from *The Liberator*. Garrison also saw the editor of the *Daily News*, a paper founded by Charles Dickens, who promised to cover the American antislavery movement. Garrison made an arrangement with Richard D. Webb to cull periodically from both the *Standard* and *The Liberator* appropriate articles for the *News*. Garrison cultivated the friendship with William and Mary Howitt begun in 1840. The Howitts were poets and reformers who had for several years been connected with the *People's Journal,* first as contributors and then as part proprietors. Mrs. Howitt, who had admired Garrison extravagantly since the first day she saw him, soon was at work on a short sketch of his life. It appeared in the *People's Journal* in September. Garrison much enjoyed the attendant publicity—for not only was the journal with the article and a portrait of the reformer displayed in every corner of London but also placards were set up in other leading English cities.[54]

He planned to get acquainted with the editor of the *Nonconformist,* the Reverend Edward Miall, a vigorous writer who exerted a strong influence over certain radical religious groups. He took breakfast with John Bowring, reformer and wealthy member of Parliament. He spent one Sunday with William Lovett and Henry Vincent, both moral-suasion Chartists bent on a series of basic political and economic reforms, and another Sunday with William H. Ashurst, his friend, and, under the pseudonym Edward Search, loyal contributor to *The Liberator.* At Ashurst's he met the eloquent Unitarian minister, William J. Fox, and the whole group bowled on the green, even though it was Sunday. He also revisited Mrs. Rawson at impressive Wincobank Hall. And he met for the first time Joseph Barker, once a beggar but now, according to Garrison, one of the world's great men, a printer who had a new press destined to revolutionize the cultural world by making books available at an astonishingly low price. Occasionally he spent his time more frivolously, singing antislavery songs, while Douglass contributed Negro melodies and Wright sang an Indian war song.

Garrison dedicated his present mission to making useful friends [55] rather than holding meetings (the temperance meetings had not gone well). He did his best to arrange news coverage and editorial support for his own brand of abolitionism and other reforms. He praised the American Anti-Slavery Society and *The Liberator,* depreciated the American and Foreign Anti-Slavery Society, the Evangelical Alliance, and the Free Church of Scotland. However, he found it impossible to resist meetings altogether. He held a massive one—about 6,000 people—at Exeter Hall in London, and organized smaller gatherings in Bristol, Birmingham, and Sheffield as well as later in Edinburgh, Glasgow, Manchester, Liverpool, and many other towns.

When Edmund Quincy wrote a goodnatured letter scolding Garrison for not writing more for *The Liberator,* Garrison replied that he had undergone an amount of labor he would have thought physically impossible. He had been hurried from place to place and from meeting to meeting, turning "day into night and night into day." He had spoken repeatedly in public and incessantly in private. And he had carried on an extensive local correspondence —the cheap penny post in England encouraging everyone to write. "Now talk of writing, to a man who has as yet found no time to sleep! 'It be very easy to cry, *blow louder!*' said an indignant French trumpeter, who had expended his last breath, 'but vere is de vind?'—So it is to cry, 'Write! write! write!'—but where is the time and place? Under the most favorable circumstances, I am a bad correspondent; under the worst, what can you expect?" [56]

From England Garrison went for short visits to both Scotland and Ireland. In Scotland he delivered many a broadside against the Free Church and its tainted money. The ladies of Edinburgh— about 250 contributors in all—presented him with an elegant silver tea and coffee service, the value of the gift somewhat mitigated by a duty of $60 imposed by the Custom House in Boston. [57] In Glasgow a public breakfast was given in his honor. "As a testimonial of affectionate regard to myself, it was overpowering to my feelings." [58] In Ireland he continued the strenuous pace of activities, his speeches creating "no small stir" in Belfast.

Lewis Tappan, who had been following Garrison's mission from across the Atlantic, wrote Joseph Sturge in October: "Garrison and his party utter a great deal of truth although they seem to do it in a bad spirit, reminding one of the zealot of whom it was said 'he serves God as if the devil were in him.'" [59]

The whole trip, Garrison thought, was much too hectic and hurried. In order to accomplish all that was necessary, he should have come over two or three months earlier. He vowed never to undertake another foreign trip unless there could be "some time for essential repose." But in spite of the bustle Garrison seemed to thrive on the trip. His health steadily improved, and he was able to throw off an attack of what he called influenza. Again it seemed that he needed a respite from family responsibilities. Once more he had been able to demonstrate his effectiveness in a foreign context, and he felt rejuvenated as a result. He went home with fresh zest for life and for labor in the cause.

On 11 December, the day following or preceding Garrison's

forty-first birthday, Helen presented her husband with their second daughter and sixth child—"the finest babe ever yet born in Boston!" [60] Garrison confessed in a letter to his old friend, Samuel J. May, the minister who had married them twelve years before, that he felt venerable and patriarchal, and that he found—though his activities belied the fact—"such a family to be a considerable drawback on my public usefulness, especially in regard to lecturing and travelling in furtherance of the anti-slavery cause; and it is also a heavy burden on Helen, who has no additional help to that of Ellen." [61]

By the time of the antislavery bazaar, the week before Christmas, Garrison had sufficiently recovered from English mission, transatlantic voyage, birthday celebration, and the acquisition of a new daughter to be an active participant.

Ever since the first antislavery fair was given by the New England Anti-Slavery Society in 1834, the public sale of articles donated by friends of the slave here and abroad had been an important source of revenue for the cause.[62] The success of the fairs was owing more to the efforts of Maria W. Chapman than to anyone else. Mrs. Chapman, a handsome and determined woman a year younger than Garrison, had been active in the cause since her marriage to the Boston merchant, Henry G. Chapman, in 1830. She was a woman of both editorial and executive capacities, for she had been one of the leaders of the Boston Female Anti-Slavery Society as well as editor of that society's reports, published annually under the title *Right and Wrong in Massachusetts*. She had also on occasion helped Garrison in editing *The Liberator*.

The fair of 1846, pretentiously called the National Anti-Slavery Bazaar, promised to be an especially exciting one, since Garrison had been busy on his trip abroad collecting articles, including among the more unusual a manuscript letter from the poet James Montgomery written to one of Garrison's hostesses in England.[63]

The doors of Faneuil Hall opened at ten in the morning on Tuesday, 22 December. Mrs. Chapman and the other ladies of the cause had turned the great hall into a stunning emporium,[64] with evergreen decorations hanging gracefully from every possible appendage and with table after table of the most enticing articles. In the center of the hall was the Toy Table, where could be bought an international assortment—from Scotland, Ireland, England, Wales, and France. Near the top were needle-books, bags, purses, cushions. For boys there were Chinese kites—a brilliant assortment—miniature horsemen and animals, lap dogs as big as life, games, puzzles, maps, railway handkerchiefs, models of mahogany furniture, kaleidoscopes.

Raised on a platform to the right of the speaker's rostrum was the Book Table. Here were the most elegant writing materials, ordered by Richard D. Webb from France, "the cream-laid, wire-wove, highest finished, hand-edged, embossed, flower-painted, emblematic, gilt-edged" stationery, as well as all kinds of pens and wafers and wax. On this table also were silver-mounted jewel boxes made from the ancient "oak of the tower of Carlisle Castle, where Mary of Scotland was imprisoned in 1568," paper knives shaped as sabers and daggers, mammoth shells, flowers pressed in books, "books of ferns from Castle Howard woods," "mosses in baskets, papier mache blotting books, card receivers, and fine bronze medallions." On the Book Table also was a new collection of English water colors—some of them given by Lady Byron—and oil paintings as well as lithographs, mezzotints, and engravings. There were even "a few English books and tracts" mixed in with Sheffield cutlery and linen writing cases. Prominently displayed was *The Liberty Bell,* the eighth annual antislavery yearbook, with its miscellaneous articles by leading reformers. Featured among the imports "were leaves of richly watered silk and satin," on which were printed the following words:

TRANSATLANTIC WHISPER
Our hearts are with you, encouraged by the
lovely and the patient spirit of
THE UNDAUNTED GARRISON [65]

Not only could the visitor to the National Bazaar of 1846 spend the day—or days—shopping for Christmas and New Year presents, but he could stay on for the evening and hear stalwart abolitionists preach the dogmas of the cause. On successive nights Wendell Phillips, Parker Pillsbury, James N. Buffum, Abby Kelley Foster, Samuel May, James Freeman Clarke, William H. Channing, Edmund Quincy, Addison David, and Garrison himself lectured on slavery, emancipation, and other reforms. Mrs. Foster thrilled the crowd by reading an "Address of the Women of Edinburgh to the Women of the United States," which had been signed by ten thousand devotees.[66]

The Bazaar of 1846 inspired James Russell Lowell to write for the *Pennsylvania Freeman* "Letter from Boston," the first section of which runs as follows:

> By way of saving time,
> I'll do this letter up in rhyme,
> Whose slim stream through four pages flows,
> Ere one is packed with tight-screwed prose,
> Threading the tube of an epistle,
> Smooth as a child's breath through a whistle.
>
> The great attraction now of all
> Is the "Bazaar" at Faneuil Hall,
> Where swarm the anti-slavery folks
> As thick, dear Miller,[67] as your jokes.
> There's GARRISON, his features very
> Benign for an incendiary,
> Beaming forth sunshine through his glasses
> On the surrounding lads and lasses
> (No bee could blither be, or brisker),—
> A pickwick somehow turned John Ziska,
> His bump of firmness swelling up
> Like a rye cupcake from its cup.
> And there, too, was his English tea-set,
> Which in his ear a kind of flea set,
> His Uncle Samuel for its beauty
> Demanding sixty dollars duty
> ('T was natural Sam should serve his trunk ill,
> for G., you know, has cut his uncle)
> Whereas, had he but once made tea in 't,
> His uncle's ear had had the flea in 't,
> There being not a cent of duty
> On any pot that ever drew tea.[68]

The resplendent bazaar, with its choice assortment of foreign items, was a fitting close to a year in which Garrison had extended his social and professional contacts abroad.

In many ways the years between 1840 and 1845 were for Garrison eclectic, meandering, anticlimactic. There was none of the violent excitement of the riotous thirties, with the mobs and schisms. It was a period of gradual adjustment to elemental changes in the climate of abolition, and of unconscious reorientation to diminishing personal power at home and abroad. The early forties were years of personal attack and personal adulation, years of special pleading for liberal Christianity, for nonresistance, for temperance, and for woman's rights. They were years of prelude and preparation for the shattering political and military events of the decades to come.

CHAPTER XV

The National Scene

O N T H E national scene the 1840's were replete with crucial political events. They were the years of Harrison's brief and Tyler's longer administration and of various attempts at social reorganization—Brook Farm, Fruitlands, Northampton Association, and Oneida Community, to name a few. They were the years of Polk's administration, the annexation of Texas, and the Mexican War. They were the years of changing political parties: the emergence of the abolitionist Liberty party, then the splintering of the Whigs and the Democrats, and later the combination of liberal Democrats and Whigs to form the Free-Soil party. Of all these shifts and changes Garrison was an eager observer and critic.

Though he preferred to talk in moral terms, Garrison was never immune to the fascination of politics. In his farewell speech to the free colored of Boston on the eve of his departure for England in 1846, he confessed that "political temptation has cost me, too, many a struggle." He recollected how excited he used to become over a town election when he was a young man in Newburyport, how he was sometimes unable to sleep at night for fear the opposition might prevail at a forthcoming town meeting.[1] He had, as we know, electioneered for Harrison Gray Otis for governor and opposed the candidacy of Caleb Cushing for congressman before his editorial career had even begun. Then he had edited two political papers—one of them, the *Journal of the*

Times, supposed to be devoted primarily to the re-election of John Quincy Adams for president.

In the early years of *The Liberator,* though he avowed his intention of keeping out of politics, he found it difficult to resist comment on political issues. In general, he expressed a conservative point of view. For instance, he was enthusiastic about the innumerable factories that towered over his head as he walked through Rhode Island, and he expressed his "strong interest in the perpetuity of that system which fosters and protects the industry of the American people." [2] But abolitionist principles always superseded conservative political ones. Toward the end of 1834, he urged the free colored of Boston to scatter their votes, selecting candidates for their antislavery views rather than for their party. He asked them to elect Amasa Walker to Congress rather than his Whig opponent.[3]

The pages of *The Liberator* during the thirties contained appeals and sample petitions to Congress on various issues, especially the abolition of slavery in the District of Columbia. But when it came to implementing political action through parties, Garrison objected. As early as 1834 he announced: "I belong to no party in particular, but to all parties in general—in other words, I am not deceived or influenced by *names,* but governed by *principles.*" [4]

Toward the end of 1839, stimulated by abolitionist talk of the advisability of forming a third political party in the forthcoming national election, Garrison had editorialized at some length against the proposed party. He was struggling to be not only a consistent moralist who abhorred political parties and political action, but also an expedient adviser to abolitionists who did not share his rejection of political action. He said that forming such a party would be suicidal, that great changes in public opinion were brought by the truth of Jesus, not by powerful political bodies. "Why should we alter our course? If God be with us, who can be against us? . . . Who will be so impious as to contend that he will forsake us, frown upon us . . . if we refuse to organize ourselves into a political party?" [5] Actually, he said, the Whigs and Democrats cannot be considered more hostile to abolition than Methodists, Calvinists, or Unitarians. If we must have another political party, we should logically have another religious sect as well.[6] Abolitionists whose conscience will tolerate political action must not despair of converting Whigs and Democrats to their principles as long as those parties profess the truths of the Declaration of Independence. In the end, Garrison was still confident, truth will through moral suasion prevail over all sects and all parties. It is crass infidelity to claim "that genuine abolitionism can be manufactured only in a political machine-shop." [7]

In spite of all Garrison could do, the Liberty party—so named by Gerrit Smith—was formed in April of 1840. James G. Birney, successful Kentucky lawyer who had freed his slaves and turned abolitionist—a man until recently greatly admired by Garrison [8]—was nominated for the presidency at an antislavery convention in Albany.

Garrison's opposition to the third-party movement became all the more bitter when he realized that the new party had been organized by his old enemies of 1840, those who withdrew from the American Anti-Slavery Society to found a new national organization.[9] Now they had done it all over again—this time in the political arena. The convention he dismissed as the most ridiculous farce in the history of presidential nominations. Less than one hundred and thirty people (100 of them from New York) [10] had nominated a president for the whole country. "A National Convention, forsooth! Why it was not as large as a common village meeting!" [11]

Since the Liberty party was without any systematic organization, without any experienced politicians in its membership, and without any clearly defined platform, it was not surprising that Birney polled only 7,069 votes in the national election. The results of the election were to Garrison evidence that the Liberty party could never be effective. If Whigs and Democrats, he said, "cannot be converted by moral-suasion, it is perfectly plain that the third party will forever constitute a most insignificant minority and thus fail to accomplish its object. If they can be, then this new party is as needless as a fifth wheel to a coach." [12]

During the next several years Garrison had few good words to say for any of the political parties. He seemed instinctively to prefer the Whig to the Democratic, though he considered them both "a terrible curse to the land" and the sooner overthrown the better.[13] In 1845, the Democrat Polk being in the White House, Garrison said that the Whig party was being ground to death between the antislavery group and the Democrats, whereas the Democratic party impressed him as "the incarnation of total depravity." If only the Whigs would forget about compromising to gain Southern votes and support the cause of liberty! [14] Five months later he was convinced that the country was being ruled by neither party but by slave power.[15] He agreed with Birney that both major parties were profligate, but such, he insisted, was the natural result of a party's governing by majority rule and might-makes-right. Even the Liberty party, once it had been in power for a period, would be as bad as they.[16]

"The only reason," he said, "why the two great political parties are not anti-slavery is because the people of the land are pro-slavery." What is needed to effect abolition "is simply a moral change in the people. . . . Truth no more relies for success on ballot boxes than it does on cartridge boxes. . . . Political action is not moral action, any more than a box on the ear is an argument." In fact, the Liberty party in absorbing the moral and financial energies of its members actually retards the essential "moral revolution." [17]

Garrison also took the Liberty party to task for what he considered its equivocal interpretation of the Constitution. Some of the members of the party seemed to say, he said, that the Constitution does not support slavery and is really, therefore, an antislavery instrument. If this is true—that the Constitution prohibits slavery—then the Liberty party should say so directly and officially. And the first thing that the party would then be committed to do if it came into power would be to declare the slaves all legally free. The results of such a declaration seemed to Garrison perfectly clear—"a civil and servile war, blood flowing like water, the Union dashed into fragments." [18]

Garrison's description of the Liberty party's interpretation of the Constitution was characteristically superficial and revealed more of his own incapacity for legal argument than of the new party's point of view. The basis of the party's argument appeared as follows in the platform for 1843: "The fundamental truth of the Declaration of Independence, that all men are endowed by their Creator with certain unalienable rights, among which are life, liberty, and pursuit of happiness, was made the fundamental law of our National Government by the amendment of the Constitution which declares that no person shall be deprived of life, liberty, or property without due process of law." Thus, the Liberty party sought to incorporate the principles of the Declaration of Independence into the Constitution under the due-process clause of the Fifth Amendment, according to which Congress "is forbidden to deprive men of their inalienable rights." [19]

Garrison's own interpretation of the Constitution in regard to the slavery issue was direct and unequivocal. Soon after founding *The Liberator,* he decided—and the decision was to make an indelible impression on his thinking about politics and reform— that the Constitution was a proslavery document, that it protected and legalized slavery. There had been much talk, he said, about the sacred compact established between the North and the South when the Constitution was adopted. "A sacred compact, forsooth! We pronounce it the most bloody and heaven-daring arrangement ever made for the continuance and protection of a system of the most atrocious villainy ever exhibited on earth." [20] Moreover, the Constitution was adopted deliberately and after much thought. Everyone knows, Garrison said, that the South would never have entered into the compact without guarantees for the perpetuation of slavery. It was therefore provided that masters should exercise all the political rights of their slaves, that the Northern states were obliged to return runaway slaves, and, further, that troops were to be raised and apportioned according to the free white population of the several states. In short, all possible was done to reduce the slaves to nonentities. "When," Garrison lamented, "has a nation sinned so perversely, against so much light, so deliberately, so understandingly, as our own?" [21]

Although in his own thinking Garrison had been analyzing the Constitution as a nefarious document since the early thirties, and had openly advocated disunion in *The Liberator* since the spring of 1842,[22] his disunionism did not receive official cognizance until the eleventh annual meeting of the Massachusetts Anti-Slavery Society in January of 1843. There was a considerable amount of discussion of the compact between the North and the South during the three-day session. A number of resolutions were introduced, mildly condemning the Constitution and suggesting dissolution of the Union. But on the third day, Garrison introduced a resolution that supplanted the earlier ones. It declared

"That the compact which exists between the North and the South is 'a covenant with death, and an agreement with hell'—involving both parties in atrocious criminality; and should be immediately annulled." [23] The resolution was officially adopted. Beginning on 17 March Garrison printed it as superscription to the editorial column of *The Liberator.* As the gap between Garrison and the political abolitionists widened, the Liberty party formally condemned Garrison's new ideas.

In May of 1844 the constitutional issue was introduced at the annual meeting of the American Anti-Slavery Society. Again three days of discussion produced a series of resolutions condemning the Constitution and urging dissolution. This time specific duties and obligations were enjoined upon all loyal abolitionists: "to withdraw from this compact . . . , and by a moral and peaceful revolution to effect its overthrow" as provided in the Declaration of Independence; to support no political party dedicated to the preservation of the Union (Garrison no longer proposed the halfway measure of reforming the existing parties) and, ideally, to refrain from all voting. "Henceforth, therefore, until slavery be abolished, the watchword, the rallying cry, the motto on the banner of the American Anti-Slavery Society shall be, 'NO UNION WITH SLAVEHOLDERS!' " The crucial vote on these radical resolutions stood at 59 to 21. Protests were read into the minutes. One of them, sputtering with such words as "impracticable," "intolerant," "presumptuous," was signed by eight men, including the lawyers David Lee Child and Ellis Gray Loring, formerly among Garrison's most prominent supporters.[24]

In an editorial Garrison told how pleased he was with the result of the meeting, indicating that such a bold and revolutionary step could not be taken without a certain amount of opposition. That there had not been more was evidence, he thought, that it was time to make his views "known to the country in an official form." Some of those who objected to the new resolution, he pointed out, were the very ones who had objected to the adoption of the slogan "immediate emancipation," a doctrine now generally accepted. Moreover, the ideas just adopted were in no sense a creed necessarily to be accepted by all members of the society. There must be unanimous agreement as to the basic principle of the utter sinfulness of slavery; but unanimity could hardly be expected in the application of that principle "to existing and political institutions." Garrison went on to defend the action of the majority from every conceivable point of view, answering in the process seventeen different objections that had been raised by the minority.[25]

In a full-fledged "Address to the Friends of Freedom and Emancipation in the United States," signed for the Executive Committee of the American Anti-Slavery Society by Mrs. Chapman, Wendell Phillips, and himself, Garrison announced his views to the world. The American Union was formed, he said, "by a guilty compromise between the free and slave-holding States," a compromise which sacrificed the Negro on the altar of slavery, which deprived the North of "equal rights and privileges," and which incorporated the system of slavery into the federal government.

In this address is to be found the crux of Garrison's constitutional argument. He seemed to recognize that whether the Constitution were to be considered pro- or antislavery depended on one's original premise. If the slave were to be described as a person, the Constitution would protect his rights as a person. If he were described as property, it would protect his owner's property rights.[26] "But," Garrison said, ". . . slaves are recognized not merely as property, but also as persons—as having a mixed character—as combining the human with the brutal. This is paradoxical, we admit; but slavery is a paradox—the American Constitution is a paradox—the American Union is a paradox—the American government is a paradox; and if any one of these is to be repudiated on that ground, they all are." [27]

In effect, Garrison was accepting the Southern argument, that the Constitution established and protected the institution of slavery, and then insisting that the North must break with the South in order to avoid constitutional responsibility for slavery. That he should do this was consistent with his long-held nonresistance doctrine and with his more recent opposition to the new organizationists, who thought that they could discredit slavery and yet honor the Constitution.

For the Executive Committee Garrison wrote a rhetorical peroration, commending "bloodless strife" or death for the cause and urging secession:

Secede, then, from the government. Submit to its exactions, but pay it no allegiance, and give it no voluntary aid. Fill no offices under it. Send no Senators or Representatives to the national or State Legislature; for what you cannot conscientiously perform yourself, you cannot ask another to perform as your agent. Circulate a declaration of DISUNION FROM SLAVEHOLDERS, throughout the country. Hold mass meetings—assemble in Conventions—nail your banners to the mast! 28

Now once more Garrison had a battle cry comparable to the old "Immediate Emancipation!" And, holding out the stimulating prospect of renewed persecution, it gave him new vigor. NO UNION WITH SLAVEHOLDERS! NO UNION WITH SLAVEHOLDERS! The words were to be choric commentary for years to come.

Characteristically, Garrison was satisfied to agitate for disunion, and he did not bother with any specific program to follow the act of secession. "The form of government that shall succeed the present government of the United States, let time determine." There is a need, he said, "to argue that question, until the people are regenerated and turned from their iniquity. . . . In ceasing from oppression, we establish liberty. What is now fragmentary, shall in due time be crystallized, and shine like a gem set in the heavens, for a light to all coming ages." 29

Two weeks after the publication of his "Address to the Friends of Freedom," Garrison scornfully denounced the Democratic party for nominating for president James K. Polk, a slaveholder who favored annexation of Texas. He said that Polk had been nominated "by one of the most barefaced cases of political gambling and jugglery ever witnessed." And he had been chosen, Garrison thought, because of the opposition to Van Buren of South Carolina, which considered "the general government to be a mere sattellite [sic] to that State." But at least Garrison was gratified that Van Buren, whom he probably hated because in his Inaugural Address of 1837 he had promised to veto any bill abolishing slavery in the District of Columbia, had been repudiated. He had been dropped, Garrison said, in spite of "his sycophancy and self-prostitution—his volunteer support of the accursed system of slavery." Garrison was shocked, also, at the popular approval of Polk's nomination in New York, where 25,000 people were sup-

posed to have gathered in the park to demonstrate for the Democratic candidate. He said: "They would have shouted just as
vociferously if 'Beelzebub, the prince of devils,' had been nominated, instead of his servant Polk." [30]

Polk and Van Buren were not the only ones condemned by
Garrison on this occasion. He also upbraided the delegates—especially those from Massachusetts—for voting as they did. One
of the first to turn to Polk, George Bancroft, the famous historian,
Garrison likened to Benedict Arnold, calling him "an ambitious
unprincipled, time-serving demagogue, who would sell his country
as Judas sold his Lord." [31]

Henceforth, Garrison was convinced that "the pirate flag of
slavery" was the banner of the Democratic party, and men who
support it "are the enemies of God and the human race. . . . A
more profligate and desperate party never existed on earth." Garrison was more convinced than ever that righteous men must
secede from all political parties and from a union supported by
them.

In August (1844) Garrison attended a meeting of the Eastern
Pennsylvania Anti-Slavery Society,[32] where there was an important
discussion of the disunion issue. The question was debated quietly
but effectively for three days. Leader among the pro-Union
speakers was Thomas Earle, the lawyer-editor who four years
earlier had been nominated as the vice-presidential candidate for
the Liberty party. Even Garrison was impressed by his dignity and
decorum and said that the only reason his argument was not more
convincing was that it was founded on expedience rather than
principle. By the end of the convention it was apparent that the
consensus favored disunion, though no resolution was voted.

In September Garrison was delighted to be able to report to
his readers that the rallying cry, NO UNION WITH SLAVE-
HOLDERS, had swept across the Atlantic. At the tenth annual
meeting of the Glasgow Emancipation Society, a resolution was
passed congratulating the American Anti-Slavery Society for its
boldness in the campaign against slavery and urging that an increasing number in the United States should adopt the position of
disunion. Also Garrison reported that leading British abolitionists
—notably James Haughton and Richard D. Webb of Dublin and

John Murray of Glasgow—were sending their "Huzzas!" across the ocean.[33]

Although he never makes entirely clear his definition of the terms Union and disunion, Garrison's meaning is somewhat clarified by the ways in which he answered objections to his theory. Gerrit Smith, in withdrawing from the American Anti-Slavery Society after it had officially accepted the new position, claimed that disunion was strictly a nonresistance point of view. Garrison was indignant and insisted rather disingenuously in three long editorials [34] that the constitutional argument was not based on nonresistance and that indeed there was a great variety of religious and political positions represented in the membership of the American society. When Elihu Burritt, the learned blacksmith, wrote of the Union in glowing, magical terms, as though it were of divine origin and antedated the Constitution (a cardinal element in political abolitionist creed), Garrison asserted that the Union was strictly man-made. "The American Union is but another name for the American Constitution. There was no such Union until the adoption of that Constitution; and the repeal or abrogation of the latter will be the dissolution of the former." [35] When Amasa Walker accused the American Anti-Slavery Society of making a false issue out of the Constitution, since that instrument could be amended by political action without any necessity of disunion, Garrison insisted that it could never be amended since the slave states were in the majority. (At this time they were really equal in number to the free states.) Whereas the Constitution provided for its amendment, it did not provide for its overthrow, which, Garrison thought, would be the only realistic solution.[36]

The question of the number of slave states was to Garrison a matter of great importance. As early as the spring of 1842 he had shown his concern over the possible annexation of Texas as a slave state: "Unless the administration of our national government pass out of the hands of the slaveholding power within the next four years, a war with Mexico will be waged on various pretexts, but either with a design to aid the Texians [sic] in their conflict with that country, or to bring Texas into the Union by conquest from Mexico, and by agreement with the Texian authorities." It was time, Garrison urged, for the people of the North to "act with all the energy and decision that becomes freemen." [37] Toward the end of 1843, Garrison reasoned this way: Texas is either a rebellious province of Mexico or an independent state; but in either case it cannot morally be annexed to the United States. For if it were annexed, those who voted against annexation would be justified in seceding since they had been, according to Garrison's view, released from their constitutional obligation to remain in the Union.[38] Garrison urged his readers to petition Congress for disunion, and he printed sample petitions in *The Liberator*.[39] By the spring of 1844 Garrison feared that annexation was imminent and that it would probably take place during the current session of Congress. New England would have only one choice, he said—secession.[40] When in May of that year a treaty of annexation was signed by Calhoun and others, Garrison—shifting the grounds of his argument from oral to practical—insisted that the result of its adoption would be the ruin of American agriculture, commerce, and manufacturing; then war with England; and, finally, civil war. "Speechless horror," he warned, was the appropriate reaction. President Tyler's message accompanying the treaty Garrison described as "easily and summarily . . . impudent, hypocritical, mendacious, and infernal." [41]

The Texas question proved a rallying issue for many conscientious New Englanders—abolitionists and nonabolitionists, Garrisonians and non-Garrisonians. Near the end of 1845, when annexation seemed inevitable, a great meeting was held at Faneuil Hall to protest.[42] By the end of the year annexation was a fact. In March Garrison exploded in *The Liberator*, calling annexation a "deed of perfidy, black as that Egyptian darkness which could be felt," a "crime unsurpassed in the annals of human depravity!" "The Slave Power," he lamented, "now holds a mastery over this nation, seemingly omnipotent." He said that the Constitution had been overthrown and that the Union no longer existed. He urged the people of Massachusetts "to recall their Senators and Representatives from the hall of Congress—to treat the General Government as a nullity. . . . NO UNION WITH SLAVEHOLDERS. Freemen, to the rescue! and God defend the right!" [43]

By the spring of 1846 the United States was at war with Mexico. At the New-England Anti-Slavery Convention, a few weeks after the outbreak of hostilities, the war was a principal topic of discussion. Pejorative epithets were bandied about, branding the war as "iniquitous" and "horrible" and blaming Governor Briggs of Massachusetts for his "treacherous and unprincipled" conduct in summoning citizens to arms.[44] Garrison later called the war "the most atheistical and impious . . . ever recorded on the gory pages of History," [45] and he belittled the Massachusetts volunteers as impoverished ne'er-do-wells comparable to Falstaff's ragged followers.[46] He sympathized with slave-free Mexico, hoping that she "may be victorious in every conflict, until not an invading foot treads upon her soil." With insight foreshadowing his attitude toward the Civil War, he distinguished between defensive and offensive war. "This is [for] Mexico strictly a war in self-defence, and retaliatory only to the extent of driving back the invading myrmidons from this country; and she deserves to be crowned with success, and the United States to be covered with defeat, as a matter of justice, and for the preservation of liberty." [47]

For the most part, however, annexation and war ceased to excite Garrison by the time Texas had been added to the Union. Since the fact of annexation had not had the results he anticipated, he turned his energies elsewhere. Even in the very issue of *The Liberator* in which he reported on the New-England Anti-Slavery Convention mentioned above, he gave far more space and emphasis to the Free Church controversy in Scotland than to the Mexican War. In the meantime, he continued to press for disunion, and he watched with interest the organization of the Free-Soil party.

Garrison was pleased when, early in 1848, a petition was presented to the state legislature requesting the call of a convention to discuss the means by which Massachusetts could peacefully secede from the Union. In an editorial he praised all those who spoke in favor of the petition and blamed those who opposed it.[48] A year later Garrison attended a session of the legislature when a similar disunion petition was presented. He was much offended that many of those present considered the whole matter "a capital joke." He reminded the readers of his paper that some six years before, certain congressmen, including John Quincy Adams and George N. Briggs, the current governor of Massachusetts, had signed an address to the free states that annexation of Texas by the federal government "WOULD BE IDENTICAL WITH DIS-

SOLUTION." "But where is George N. Briggs now" that the contingency described in the address was fact? Garrison closed his editorial: "Again we cry—'No Union With Slaveholders!' " [49]

By 1847 the Liberty party had been embalmed and Garrison had written its obituary in *The Liberator*. Complete failure, he called it. True, it had drawn 70,000 votes at the last election, but these were mostly birds that had been flushed out of the bushes by faithful abolitionist beaters. Still unwilling to admit that the hope for emancipation lay with the political abolitionists, Garrison said that the party had done much harm in opposing the old-line abolitionists and in distracting attention from that bulwark of American slavery, the church. "Religiously, it has swallowed a camel—politically, it has strained at a gnat." [50]

In the meantime, a new political movement was gathering momentum.[51] In both Democratic and Whig parties liberal elements were becoming increasingly disaffected over the slavery issue. Because their views on slavery were congenial, the Barnburners in the Democratic party might be considered comparable to the Conscience Whigs, and the Hunkers parallel to the Cotton Whigs. Thus the issue of abolition was achieving a liberal-conservative split within each of the major parties.

Of such a development Garrison as a dedicated abolitionist was fully aware. When the Barnburners in 1847 walked out of a New York State convention dominated by the conservative Hunkers, Garrison reported the facts in *The Liberator*. And when at approximately the same time in Worcester, Massachusetts, Whigs of the Conscience variety sought to oppose the candidacy of Zachary Taylor, Garrison again reported in *The Liberator* on this defiance of the proslavery forces.[52]

But it was a subsequent meeting of the Free-Soil party, the coalition of Barnburners and Conscience Whigs which resulted from these maneuvers, that elicited his editorial comments. In an editorial in *The Liberator*, which characteristically followed the leading one about his own health and the planned treatment thereof, Garrison recorded his gratification "to see the old parties dissolving," although he regretted that the seceders limited themselves to "the non-extension of slavery." Such an issue he considered "destitute of principle, and inferior to that which was made in opposition to the admission of Texas." Trying to found a party merely on the nonextension of slavery "is attempting to make brick without straw—to live without food—to walk without legs—to scotch the snake, instead of killing it. . . . It is an absurdity in morals to talk of defining the boundaries of sin—of limiting the indulgence of crime—of driving slavery back to its constitutional covert." The only true ground is that slavery is the greatest of sins, slaveholders the greatest of sinners. "Talk not of uniting freemen and tyrants, abolitionists and slaveholders, under one government, any more than of reconciling Christ and Belial together. . . . NO UNION WITH SLAVEHOLDERS." [53]

A month later Garrison was in Northampton taking the water cure, and Edmund Quincy, substituting as editor, wrote an editorial enthusiastically praising the Free-Soil party. "The day of prophecy is passed; that of fulfillment is come. For long years the abolitionists have been looking forward to the state of things which is now beginning to develop itself." He gave the abolitionists credit for instigating the new political movement, pointing out that for nearly twenty years the abolitionists had been laboring, with the knowledge that eventually there would be a "reconstruction of the political parties." The bread they had cast upon the waters was "returning unto them, after many days." It remained for the abolitionists to lead to yet loftier heights—and not to fall back upon their imperfect stage of progress. "While the Abolitionists who accept the morality and the method of the American Anti-Slavery Society," he admitted, "cannot act with the Free-Soil party in its organization and at the pools, they must watch its progress with lively interest, and cannot help giving it incidental assistance. Their relation to it is of a totally different character from that they bore to the late 'Liberty party.'" The Liberty party, Quincy explained, had been organized by deserters from the American Anti-Slavery Society, but the Free-Soil party was activated by honest hatred of slavery, and was "led by men whose purity of purpose and personal honor are above suspicion." [54]

In the election of 1848, in which many political factions offered candidates, the Democratic candidate, Zachary Taylor, was elected and the Free-Soil candidate, Van Buren, received a relatively small vote.

Garrison returned to town about a week before the election and resumed editorial duties on 17 November with an emotional outburst that was as much a reprimand of Quincy for his enthusiasm as it was an attack on political action. He praised God that the election was over, for he considered such a political struggle as the country had survived infinitely worse than an epidemic of the Asiatic cholera. Doubtless thinking of Quincy's editorial, he said: "Under the excitement legitimately growing out of it, men lose their reason, and 'play such fantastic tricks before high heaven as make the angels weep.' . . . The people must be cured of this madness of politics, or their damnation is sure. . . . Men, claiming to be moral and upright . . . must be driven from the polls as they are from the grog-shop and the house of ill-fame, by conviction of sin, by the power of conscience, by the potency of truth." "The Constitution," he asserted vehemently, "making ample provision as it does for a navy and an army, and giving Congress authority at any moment to declare war . . . is an evil instrument, to be regarded with abhorrence by all good men. The Union, erected as it is on the prostrated bodies of three millions of the people, deserves to be held in eternal execration, and dashed to pieces like a potter's vessel." [55]

Garrison was amazed at what he considered Quincy's bad judgment about the Free-Soil party. That a man in whom he had such confidence should, left to his own devices, stray so dangerously was to Garrison further evidence of how much the cause still needed him. He must never leave his editorial chair again. If you could not trust Quincy, whom could you trust?

For months Garrison brooded over the evil influence of the free-soil movement. To think that men who claimed to be God-fearing abolitionists could support a party "disposed to maintain all the pro-slavery compromises of the Constitution"! "For abolitionists to go down to it, and to merge their principles and object in it—what is it but to exhibit the greatest infatuation, or the basest treachery? No compromise, no partnership with slavery!" [56]

CHAPTER XVI

———◆•◆———

Communities, Friends, and Enemies

S INCE he was so critical of politics, parties, and government, one might have expected Garrison to have been much interested in the attempts at social reorganization so prevalent in his day. But he remained a conservative in this area as he did in labor reform. Brook Farm, and the less-famous utopian communities at Oneida, Hopedale, Fruitlands, Skaneateles, and Northampton attracted only an occasional notice in letters and editorials. This was the case even though George W. Benson, Garrison's brother-in-law and one of his best friends, was a founder of the Northampton Association of Education and Industry in 1842. The two men must have discussed communal living many times, but Garrison's letters to Benson in 1842 showed only a cursory interest in the new project. He said on 22 March: "I trust all your hopes will be realized, in regard to your undertaking. Look well to the present, and the future will take care of itself." [1] From time to time Garrison helped his brother-in-law recruit members for the community.[2] He referred to articles about the community in various newspapers.[3] And in the summer of 1843 he became sufficiently curious to visit Northampton for three months, where he lived within a mile of the association. Even his letters from Northampton, however, showed more concern over his own and his wife's health (Helen's arm had been badly hurt in a carriage accident apparently caused by his carelessness), the beauty of the scenery, the coldness of his neighbors, and an occasional antislavery meeting than over problems of social reorganization and of the welfare of the community.[4]

The last week of the year a convention for the reorganization of society was held at Tremont Hall in Boston. The various communities were ably represented, according to Garrison. George Benson was there from Northampton; Adin Ballou, magazine publisher and author of several little-read books, from Hopedale; George S. Ripley, philosopher and Boston Unitarian minister, from Brook Farm. In addition, Socialists Albert Brisbane and William H. Channing were there to philosophize. Garrison was impressed by the four-day meeting. "This question of social reorganization is evidently destined to produce a great sensation in the country, if nothing more," he said. "The chief obstacles to the success of these communities or associations will lie in the breasts of their members, and not in the present state of society. If they will dwell together in love, having the same mind that was in Christ Jesus, they will surely prosper. If they attempt to walk by sight, and not by faith they will perish."[5]

Some three months later he wrote an editorial "To the Friends of Human Progress," indicating that he was interested in the various experiments in social reorganization, though he knew firsthand only the one at Northampton, which he considered beautiful in location and catholic in spirit (no politics or sectarianism). He thought that it had good chances of success since there were 125 members and more new applications for membership than could be accommodated. He recommended this community especially for its enlightened school.[6]

Garrison referred a number of times to two of the leading theorists of the associationist movement, the English and French socialists Robert Owen and Charles Fourier. Owen he called that "celebrated atheistical philanthropist,"[7] a man chiefly suspect because of his absurd and dangerous theory of property. For, according to Garrison's interpretation, Owen held that it was as wrong for a man to claim absolute ownership of a hat or coat as to claim property rights to another human being, "that everybody should help himself, according to his necessities; (he being the sole judge,) wherever the means of subsistence and comfort exist."[8] Fourier he admitted was known to him only vaguely, though he planned to study his theory.[9] He did know that Fourier's admirers celebrated his birthday on a Tuesday when it fell on Sunday—conduct unbecoming radical reformers.[10] But Albert Brisbane, the American publicizer of Fourier, he knew more intimately; for Brisbane wrote Garrison a series of letters on social reorganization which were published in *The Liberator*, though with no further comment from Garrison than a general recommendation for his readers' perusal.[11]

One of the reasons Garrison was little interested in the community movement was that he did not understand the theorizing of the utopian socialists. "Much of their language is to us, and we are very certain to the laboring classes generally, quite unintelligible, and altogether too sublimated for common use and acceptation." [12] Social reorganization, he had no doubt, was needed, but he questioned whether it would come about "in any other way than by individual enfranchisement and special reform." [13]

For disagreeing with him, Garrison criticized two men, formerly his close associates. John A. Collins, one-time general agent for the Massachusetts Anti-Slavery Society and fund-raiser for the American Anti-Slavery Society, was by 1844 devoting himself to the community at Skaneateles, where he was publishing a new paper, *The Communist*.[14] After the failure of the community he suffered the further degradation of publishing a Whig paper and then of becoming the Whig candidate for the California legislature—making every effort, Garrison feared, to live down his reputation as an abolitionist.[15] Also Nathaniel P. Rogers, after he and Garrison had disagreed over other matters, was condemned as an atheist and devotee of Owen's theory of no private property.[16]

Temperamentally, Garrison was not the kind of person who could have thrived within the confines of any community. He was too much of an individualist to live in communal amity with other individuals. For him there could be no union with slaveholders and indeed no union with abolitionists. North must secede from South and moral abolitionist from political. In the final extremity friend must renounce friend, since man must be governed by moral right alone. This, Garrison felt instinctively, was the true philosophy for living.

For years, Garrison had felt obliged to sacrifice friendship for moral rectitude. Friends and associates, no matter how close, he had, as he thought, unselfishly relinquished whenever they were wrong—that is, whenever they differed from him on essential issues. We have already observed the pattern. We have seen him turn against his former master, E. W. Allen, and his early patron, Caleb Cushing.[17] We have also seen a mounting coldness in his relations with Whittier over politics. With the Tappans there was a complete break in spite of all the two brothers had done for reform in general and for Garrison in particular. Of Lewis Tappan, whose fortune proved more durable than his older brother's, Garrison said in 1851 that he had "long ago lost the respect and confidence of the true abolitionists of the country." [18] Both Amos A. Phelps and Henry B. Stanton had been banished from the Garrison clique in 1839–1840 over the issues of woman's rights and political action, even though both were members of the board and general agents of the Massachusetts Anti-Slavery Society and Garrison had said that Phelps's lectures—referring to a published version of them—were worth their weight in gold and had designated Stanton as the Napoleon of the cause.[19] The two chief lawyers among the Garrisonians, Samuel E. Sewall and Ellis Gray Loring, lost caste in Garrison's eyes when they refused to support the radical policy of disunion. Lydia and David Child were replaced as editors of the *National Anti-Slavery Standard,* official organ of the American Anti-Slavery Society after the schism of 1840, when they did not follow precisely the Garrison party line.[20]

During a period of many years Garrison's relationship with Gerrit Smith, wealthy New York State landowner who dedicated his wealth to reform, vacillated from critical distrust to cordial admiration. At first Smith was suspect as a colonizationist, but then he came into greater favor by giving money for a manual-labor school. In the middle thirties Garrison found him "not so good a man as you have the reputation to be," because he attempted to combine abolition and colonization and because he used hard language.[21] But when early in 1836 Smith gave $1,000 to the American Anti-Slavery Society, Garrison could not disguise his approbation. The following summer, in a letter to Garrison, Smith acknowledged "that I am more indebted to your writings than to those of any other man for my abhorrence of slavery. Nor is the pupil in this case any the less grateful, because the master has occasionally boxed his ears." [22] Smith's generous tribute was followed from time to time with financial contributions to *The Liberator*,[23] and the two men remained on excellent terms until Smith began to urge that antislavery societies needed to be reorganized politically and that a third party might be the solution to the slavery issue. Garrison was shocked and branded his views as "palpably absurd and fallacious." [24] Then when Smith refused to interpret the Constitution as a proslavery document and denied that the slavery issue should divide the North and the South, Garrison lost patience and wrote a series of four long editorials answering Smith's argument.[25] Garrison did not feel any more friendly when in 1847 Smith accepted the nomination for the presidency from a fourth party, the Liberty League. In the years following the Civil War, however, the two became cordial friends again.[26]

Garrison also sacrificed several friends closer than Gerrit Smith. There was Isaac Knapp, close associate since the early days in Newburyport. The two men had known each other well, had taken excursions together, one time in 1826 tramping from Newburyport to Boston; and Knapp, as we know, had been sufficiently loyal to visit Garrison in the Baltimore jail in 1830. It was Knapp who had the courage to become Garrison's partner in 1831 and make it possible for him to begin publishing *The Liberator*. The two men struggled together through years of poverty and persecution. In the summer of the first year of *The Liberator* Garrison wrote of his partner: "He is willing, for love of the cause, to go through evil as well as good report; to endure privation, and abuse, and the loss of friends, so that he can put tyrants to shame and break the fetters of the slaves. He has been of essential service to me; and his loss would not easily be made up." [27] As we know, when Garrison was married in 1834, Knapp shared the house with the newlyweds. The following year Garrison was mobbed in Boston and the full burden of the paper fell temporarily on Knapp, who managed to print *The Liberator* in spite of troubles with everyone from landlord to city authorities.

At the end of 1835 the partnership was dissolved, Garrison becoming editor and Knapp publisher.[28] Soon Knapp was overwhelmed with his various duties. Not only did he have to make all the financial arrangements but with Garrison out of town a large part of the year in Brooklyn, Connecticut, and elsewhere, he also had editorial responsibility, which worried him as his readers might have guessed from the following notice in the issue for 21 May:

The publisher is without advice from the editor since the reception of his letter of the 11th inst. from New York. He regrets, with the readers of the Liberator, the necessity of the editor's frequent absence, and at the same time is happy to inform them that arrangements have recently been made which will enable him to remain more constantly in the city.

By the summer of 1837 Knapp was sufficiently pressed financially to appeal for a personal loan in *The Liberator*.[29]

It is not possible to say precisely what had happened. Garrison said that although Knapp had always lacked energy and good business judgment, he developed a passion for becoming a large-scale businessman.[30] He printed at his own expense numerous antislavery tracts—propaganda, according to Garrison, that could much more easily be given away than sold. He established an abolitionist depository—a kind of bookstore. Although for a time he had a surprisingly large sale, he kept such muddled accounts that half the time he could not tell what he owed or was owed. He found it increasingly difficult to meet necessary payments. The sight of his creditors and their constant duns "drove him to despondency." "He neglected his business, and in an evil hour secretly resorted to the intoxicating bowl; his temper became soured, his vision obscured, his moral sense injured; and he made himself a burden to our cause, and a prey to self-inflicted misery." (It was Garrison's third experience with alcoholism: first his father, then his brother, and now his partner.) Then to multiply his troubles Knapp fell in love with and married a young girl— "a mere doll," according to Garrison, "feeble in mind and fond of dress—who was in every respect unfitted to his situation and wants."[31]

Garrison and his associates were patient with their old friend.[32] Knapp was allowed to continue printing *The Liberator* at a job price, his own terms being accepted. Oliver Johnson was brought in as general agent of the state society to supervise the paper's finances. Then two years later, in the first issue for 1840, it was reported that Knapp had transferred his interest in the subscription list to Garrison for a period of two years and a committee was to be saddled with the financial responsibility of the paper. There had been so many complaints, Garrison said, from those who had been sustaining *The Liberator* for years that either a new arrangement had to be made or the paper dropped altogether. An impartial committee met with Knapp, who reluctantly agreed to a settlement.[33] But he felt so embittered that for some time he and Garrison did not speak. Garrison told Elizabeth Pease of his great reluctance and pain in separating from Knapp. "I exerted myself to the utmost to retain him as printer of the *Liberator*—that I greatly compassionated his forlorn condition, and did every thing in his behalf that friendship and sympathy could suggest—is simply to assert the truth. . . . But *the existence of the Liberator depended upon this new arrangement;* and justice to those who had to sustain it required that it should be made."

Although there is little record of contact between the former partners during the two-year moratorium, Garrison did make efforts to retrieve Knapp's character. He urged him to respect himself and to show his good faith by going to work. Garrison collected for Knapp's relief between thirty and forty dollars from faraway friends—those close at hand would not assist a drunkard and a gambler. He even took the Knapps into his own house for a period of several weeks, hoping that closer association with them would have a beneficial effect. But Knapp continued to drink and gamble. He wandered aimlessly about, hardly knowing where to sleep at night. Nothing Garrison could say or do had any effect. It was a sorry return for kindness rendered, "but my heart yearns over him, and I cannot reproach him," Garrison said.

About six months before the two-year period had expired Knapp failed completely in business and assigned all of his assets to his creditors. *The Liberator* committee, convinced more than ever of Knapp's complete inefficiency as publisher (the paper without Knapp's assistance had run without a deficit in 1841), negotiated with the creditors to buy out whatever interest might remain in their hands.[34] When the creditors agreed to settle for $25, the Knapp incident seemed to be closed.

But in the fall of 1841 there were indications that Knapp was not yet through fighting. He saw Garrison and expressed his desire to buy back his share of *The Liberator,* threatening to set up a rival sheet if need be. In December Garrison received a circular from Knapp, complaining that he had been defrauded of his interest in the paper. On 8 January appeared *Knapp's Liberator*, an unadorned, four-page paper that bore a typographical resemblance to *The Liberator* of 1831. At the top of the first column was a quotation from Garrison himself: "There is no spirit so hostile to us as that which has gone out from us. Original pro-slavery is mercy to it." Then followed the comment: "True, Mr. Garrison; for your former associates know the most about you." Less than two columns of the issue were written by Knapp, who referred in general terms to "the selfish and deceptive conduct of Mr. Garrison," and who explained that he had not written more owing to "the state of my mind, the situation of my family, and other considerations, and partly to the fact that I preferred to let the statements of others appear, and to say what I have to say in some future number."

The "others" seem to have been Hamlett Bates, formerly a clerk in the Anti-Slavery Office, John Cutts Smith, who had been one of the founders of the New-England Anti-Slavery Society, and Joel Prentiss Bishop, a person of more substance than the other two.[35] Bishop also had been a clerk in the office and had subsequently been associated in some way with Charles T. Torrey and with Henry B. Stanton, although there is no real evidence that anyone of their caliber was involved in Knapp's altercation. Knapp's supporters appear to have been motivated more by hatred of Garrison than by love of Knapp. In the rest of their paper they quibbled over Garrison's relationship with various men, trying to stir up trouble between him and his closest associates, men like Samuel J. May, Henry C. Wright, and Nathaniel P. Rogers.[36] No further number of the paper was forthcoming.

Through no fault of Knapp and his associates trouble ultimately did arise between Garrison and Rogers, and the latter had to be sacrificed. We have seen what intimate and congenial friends the two men were on their trip to Britain in 1840. Their friendship continued on their return to this country. Toward the end of 1840 Garrison spoke of Rogers as "a moral Richard Coeur de Lion" who exchanged blows with the opponents of slavery thick and fast, both as editor of the *Herald of Freedom* (Concord, New Hampshire) and as writer for the *National Anti-Slavery Standard*.[37]

Among others Rogers was exchanging blows with Whittier, and Garrison was publicizing the encounter in *The Liberator,* supporting Rogers in every round.[38] In the spring of 1841 Garrison had been busy with a series of antislavery lectures in Massachusetts, Connecticut, and New Hampshire, with the annual meeting of the national society in New York, and with an excursion with Rogers to Philadelphia. In the summer Rogers fulfilled a promise made to Garrison in the Scottish Highlands the year before.[39] He took Garrison on an excursion through the White Mountains of New Hampshire. During this excursion, even though Garrison made himself rather obnoxious trying to cure his friend of the bad habit of smoking ("anti-slavery wants her mouths for other uses than to be flues for besotting tobacco smoke!"), the friendship between the two men deepened.

The following summer when Rogers became involved in a controversy with the Quakers, Garrison staunchly supported him in *The Liberator,* in spite of the violence of the Quaker reaction.[40]

In the summer of 1844 Rogers' real trouble began. When in July Garrison heard that the publication of the *Herald of Freedom* had been suspended, he praised Rogers. Rogers and the paper must be sustained, Garrison insisted. "His pen *talks* with the fluency, ease and simplicity of childhood, yet always with vigor and raciness." [41] He also lauded the paper, marveling at its survival in New Hampshire, which, to judge from its attitude toward slavery, might have been appropriately located somewhere between Texas and Louisiana. Almost as soon as Garrison had completed his editorial, the publication of the paper was resumed "under the auspices of the Board of Managers of the New-Hampshire Anti-Slavery Society."

At the annual meeting of the New Hampshire society Rogers caused a considerable disturbance by objecting to the business of electing officers. He claimed in a whining editorial that good antislavery discussion was interrupted for this business and that officers at this juncture were of little or no value anyway. Garrison was astonished at Rogers' childish pique and pointed out that his friend was really calling for the disbanding of the New Hampshire society and in effect for the liquidation of his employers, since the board of the society had undertaken the publication of the *Herald.* Carried to its logical conclusion, Rogers' no-organization doctrine would abolish the American, the Massachusetts, and all other societies, organizations which Garrison considered "highly essential to a vigorous and systematic warfare against slavery." Although he considered Rogers unduly fastidious on the issue in question, Garrison respected his thinking, perhaps recognizing it as a logical projection of his own nonresistance doctrine. He trusted that Rogers would understand the spirit in which his remarks were made. "It is not for true-hearted friends to apologize to each other for a difference of opinion on questions of this character. A difference in the choice of instrumentalities, or modes of action, is not a difference in spirit." [42]

Before Garrison could hear directly from Rogers, the latter was seriously ill and the paper was under the control of his daughter's fiancé, the printer John R. French. French promptly substituted his name as publisher for the name of the society. A special fact-finding committee, appointed by the board and approved by French, including Wendell Phillips, Edmund Quincy, and Garrison as chairman, exonerated the board in all its dealings with French. The committee, however, expressed the hope that Rogers would continue as editor.[43]

When the *Herald* refused to publish the committee's report, Garrison was astonished: "I confess, I was almost disposed to doubt the evidence of my own senses," he said.[44] The New Hampshire society was denied publication of its official proceedings in its own paper—the very paper Garrison had recently eulogized for its courage and independence! Garrison hoped with all his heart that Rogers was ignorant of his printer's dereliction. But soon it was apparent that Rogers was openly supporting French, and the break between the old friends was complete.

A group of abolitionists remained loyal supporters of Rogers and even seemed to rejoice that another prominent reformer had broken with the Garrison clique. Henry Clapp, suspect as recent convert to the cause and editor of the *Lynn Pioneer* (later the *Essex County Washingtonian*), published in his paper letters from Rogers and attacks on Garrison. James C. Jackson, former Garrisonian, now a devotee of political action and editor of the Albany *Patriot,* commented on the controversy, his analysis of Garrison's character containing more than a modicum of truth. Under the heading "THE SIAMESE TWINS," he explained that

Garrison and Rogers had been severed. "He knew but little of Mr. Garrison, who thought him a *twin* to any thing. He is not capable of *twin-ship*. He lives in himself, and never formed a friendship yet, and never will, that is not one of *convenience*. Those are his friends who *do* as he *says;* those his enemies who differ from him in the management of the anti-slavery enter-prise." [45]

It was difficult for the Garrisonians to understand what had happened. As Edmund Quincy pointed out, Rogers had for some years been the darling of the abolitionists. All the Garrison group had liked him and admired his wit and humor and his ability as publicist. In fact, Quincy thought Rogers had been thoroughly spoiled both by the Garrisonians and his own large family—espe-cially by his red-headed daughter Frances. Frances it was who urged him to support her fiancé, John R. French. In the face of unaccustomed criticism, Quincy said, Rogers became mentally unbalanced, the Don Quixote of the cause. [46]

By the summer of 1845 Garrison described Rogers as a mono-maniac on the subject of no-organization, a man who had made the descent from a "high and responsible anti-slavery position" to "the abyss of self-infatuation" with astounding rapidity. His pres-ent course Garrison characterized as destitute of gratitude and magnanimity and "unprincipled and desperate in purpose." [47] Such a man must be sacrificed no matter how great the pain. And so Rogers joined the community of friends turned enemies. [48]

Although the break with Rogers caused Garrison considerable anguish, as had the break with Knapp, alienation of friends and associates formed a significant pattern in his life. It was a pattern that applied to some extent even to his relationships with his mother and with his wife. He had a curious tendency to turn on those closest to him, those on whom he was most dependent, as though they threatened his own insecure ego. He could remain on friendly and intimate terms with subordinates, but it was dif-ficult for him to continue relationships with equals or superiors. When he repudiated a former friend or patron, there was always a more or less rational explanation for his conduct. But that ex-planation never fully accounted for the emotional fervor which accompanied the alienation. He needed a mother, a father, a wife, friends, and associates, and he wanted them to care for him, to help with his work, to provide money for his needs, to stimulate his ideas. But in the last analysis he never felt entirely comfortable with those to whom he was most indebted. He could accept only a certain quantum of obligation to others. When the debt grew excessive, he could regain his equilibrium only by finding a rationalization for canceling part of it. It was inevitable that he quarrel with Allen and Cushing because he owed them more than he could comfortably admit. The Tappan brothers were suspect for the same reason as well as for their ideological disagreement with him and their challenge to his leadership in the cause. With Phelps, Stanton, Childs, and Smith the break came over differences regarding the importance of political action. With Rogers and Knapp the break was more personal and more painful.

Having by 1845 renounced so many former friends and associates, Garrison was more convinced than ever of his own extraordinary rectitude. And, like Ibsen's Master Builder, he was certain that he was strongest who stood alone.

CHAPTER XVII

———◆◆◆———

Undiscovered Country

L I K E Bostonians even today, Garrison instinctively turned East rather than West. By 1846 he had made three trips to Great Britain but none to Ohio. Ever since the mid-1830's, the time of Theodore D. Weld's active agency, western New York and Ohio had been the province of the abolitionists who believed in political action; and by the 1840's this territory was dominated by Liberty party men. At the New England convention in the spring of 1843 plans were laid for loyal Garrisonians to abolitionize the West. Originator of the idea and leader of the campaign was John A. Collins, general agent of the Massachusetts society. There were to be one hundred conventions in the western states. Lecturers for the cause—not, however, including Garrison—set out in two parallel columns, holding meetings in countless towns through central and western New York, in Ohio, in Indiana, and back through Ohio into Pennsylvania. Occasionally they joined forces for a major engagement, and finally in Philadelphia they held a victory meeting to recapitulate their successes.[1] In Boston Edmund Quincy wrote in *The Liberator* that a new tie would bind the East and West. "The hardy virtues of the young West are precisely those to carry forward this warfare of liberty against slavery. Anti-slavery is the true Patriotism, the genuine Humanity, of this age and country." Surely ultimate victory could not be far distant if East and West truly united.[2]

In 1847 Garrison himself became involved in this *Anschluss* of East and West, when he announced in *The Liberator* that he had "long been importuned, by our friends and coadjutors at the West, to make them a visit." He said that he had hoped to go to Ohio the previous summer, but his transatlantic mission had prevented it. Now he resolved without fail to go West about the first of August.[3] By mid-July his plans for the trip were complete. He would go by the southern route, attending on the way the annual meeting of the Eastern Pennsylvania Anti-Slavery Society. In Philadelphia Frederick Douglass would join him. From there the two men would lecture their way west, to Harrisburg, to Pittsburgh, and to New Lyme, Ohio, for the annual meeting of the Western Anti-Slavery Society. After four weeks in Ohio they would return by the northern route through Buffalo—Garrison looked forward to seeing Niagara Falls—Rochester, Auburn, Syracuse, and Albany. Garrison outlined his itinerary for his readers, even giving definite dates for lectures. He was pleased and excited over plans for his first western trip and hoped his mission would prove as pleasant and profitable as the trip to England the year before. Here was another opportunity to serve the cause of liberty and equality, to widen his circle of friends—he was more interested in breadth than depth—and to make "converts to the vital doctrine of 'NO UNION WITH SLAVEHOLDERS.' "[4]

Even Quincy, who as volunteer editor of *The Liberator* was to feel most intensely Garrison's absence, was elated over the new mission. He announced to his readers that Garrison's visit to the great West would be "of incalculable value to the cause"; for he would make new friends of old enemies. "Men marvel to find the desperate Jacobin, the fanatic infidel, the visionary enthusiast, he that would turn the world upside down, in the apostolic, bland, cheerful, considerate benevolent individual, whose most marked characteristics, which strike every observing eye at first sight, are the coolest-headed sagacity and the most practical common-sense." Garrison, Quincy was certain, "will help bind together that true Union, which should indeed be 'one and indissoluble, now and forever,' the union of honest hearts for the removal of National Crimes."[5]

Garrison's colleague for the mission was to be thirty-year-old Frederick Douglass. Douglass was a commanding figure of a man— over six feet tall, half a foot taller than Garrison, with brown skin, frizzy hair combed in long thick masses, leonine head with large impressive features—nose aquiline, lips thick but well shaped, eyes piercing and deeply set beneath a furrowed brow. He had been born in Maryland, the son of a slave mother and an unknown white father, rumored to be his master. As a house servant in Baltimore, he had learned to write, and in 1838 he had managed to escape to New York City, where he married a free colored woman. They settled in New Bedford, Massachusetts, where he became a menial laborer. But he had been reading *The Liberator* in his spare time, and in August 1841 he attended the convention of the Massachusetts Anti-Slavery Society in Nantucket. There his career as antislavery orator began. He spoke to the convention hesitantly and occasionally stammered, but the effect was stunning to an audience taken completely by surprise. Garrison himself found the speech unforgettable.[6] Here was the reality they had all desired—a chattel become a man.

At the suggestion of Edmund Quincy, Douglass was employed at once as an agent of the Massachusetts society and became in 1843 the central figure in the One Hundred Conventions. But some of those who heard Douglass speak began to doubt his story, and so in 1845 he published the famous *Narrative of the Life of Frederick Douglass, an American Slave,* such a daring account of life among the slaves that Wendell Phillips urged him to burn the manuscript lest the book lead to his re-enslavement. After the *Narrative* was published Douglass did take the precaution of going to Britain for two years.[7] There he and Garrison appeared often on the same platform in the summer of 1846. Garrison's letters home reported that Douglass "creates a deep sensation, and makes a powerful impression."[8] Moreover, he did well financially, "as he sells his Narrative very readily, and receives aid in donations and presents, to some extent."[9] In fact, by the time he returned to America he had accumulated enough money to purchase his freedom, and one of his friends, Mrs. Ellen Richardson of Newcastle, had opened a subscription drive for further funds. Five hundred pounds was subsequently raised and sent to Douglass with the provision that if he had no immediate use for the money, it should be invested by trustees chosen by him for the benefit of himself and his children, but that if he should consider it desirable to establish his own newspaper, the entire capital should be available.[10]

When Douglass returned to this country in April of 1847, he had grown in stature as an abolitionist leader, just as Garrison had following his trip of 1833. Quincy said, "It is like an American actor receiving the approbation of the London theatres." [11] Shortly after his return "a highly respectable audience" gathered in Boston at the Belknap Street Church to do him honor. Garrison and Phillips ushered him to the platform. Speeches and resolutions lauding him for his achievements abroad filled the evening.[12] Henceforth, Douglass' position in the cause virtually rivaled that of Garrison and Phillips themselves. He was in a position to talk on equal terms with them and all of the Boston clique. They discussed among other things Douglass' plan to start his own newspaper, Garrison and others pointing out that there were already four American abolitionist papers edited by colored men, three of them having been founded within the last year. Douglass, they said, had insufficient editorial experience to run a newspaper. They felt that his great powers would find their fullest expression on the lecture platform rather than in the editorial chair, but if he wanted to write, numerous antislavery papers would gladly publish all he could produce.

By the end of June Douglass seemed to have been persuaded that his friends were right.[13] In *The Liberator* for 9 July Douglass definitely renounced his plans for establishing a new paper, and a week later Garrison underlined the renunciation by saying there had never been on any topic more unanimous agreement among friends of the cause than on the issue of whether Douglass should start his own paper. For several weeks, however, Douglass and his paper remained a topic of discussion in the pages of *The Liberator*.[14] Then on 30 July, as though to terminate all rumors that he and the eloquent fugitive from slavery disagreed, Garrison announced in *The Liberator* that he and Douglass would leave together on the western antislavery mission early in August.

The trip began according to schedule. Garrison went to Philadelphia, met Douglass, and the two attended the three-day meeting of the Eastern Pennsylvania Anti-Slavery Society. Men and women, thoroughgoing in antislavery spirit and solid of character, came up from Philadelphia and crowded into the meetings. On the second day Douglass appeared on the platform, "the 'lion' of the occasion." Thomas Earle, biographer of Lundy and opponent of disunion, was there to heckle, and panes of glass were shattered. But all in all the meetings passed off better than could have been expected, and Garrison was content. He wrote home, happy that one week of the eight that separated him from Helen had already passed.[15]

Before they had left Philadelphia Garrison and his companion were made aware of the prejudice against the colored race that was to hound them throughout the western trip. On the Saturday morning of their departure Douglass had seated himself inconspicuously toward the rear of the coach and started to look out of the window—perhaps thinking of his recent cordial reception by the English—when a raucous, slave-driving voice broke into his reverie: "Get out of that seat!" Teetering on unsteady legs, a man —later identified as a citizen of Harrisburg—was showing off to his lady companion. Douglass, startled but poised, indicated "that if he would make his demand in the form of a gentlemanly request, he would readily vacate his seat." But the would-be slave-driver grabbed Douglass and dragged him out of the car. Douglass submitted to the outrage like a good nonresistant and quietly informed his assailant that he was behaving like such a bully that he himself was precluded "from meeting him with his own weapons." Threats of having his teeth knocked down his throat did not disturb the composure of the dignified Douglass. But it was an ominous foretaste of violence to come.[16]

Soon the cars started up and Garrison and Douglass bounced westward, remarking how old and uncomfortable the coaches seemed compared to those in New England. But the countryside impressed them as opulently beautiful, an interesting contrast to rocky Massachusetts, and the journey passed quickly. At the Harrisburg station a loyal subscriber to *The Liberator* was waiting, and the traveling abolitionists were treated like celebrities. That evening the city—formerly apathetic to lecturers on abolition— jammed the courthouse, "some of the most respectable citizens being present." The audience listened quietly and attentively to Garrison—no matter how stringent and severe his remarks. But as soon as Douglass rose on the platform, "the spirit of rowdyism began to show itself outside of the building." It was the first time a "nigger" had had the audacity to speak publicly in Harrisburg. Brickbats, rotten eggs, and firecrackers shattered the windows. One of the malodorous eggs hit Garrison full on the back and dripped down his coat. A stone thudded against Douglass' back, and a brickbat grazed his head. Yells of "Out with the damned nigger!" reverberated through the building. Garrison spoke quietly, firmly, announcing that if this were a sample of "Harrisburg decorum and love of liberty," he and Douglass would shake the dust of the city off their feet and waste no further breath. They paused the next day, however, to speak to the colored citizens of the town, who received them with fitting gentility.[17]

Early in the morning of Monday, 9 August, they took the train for Chambersburg, some fifty-four miles away and the end of the railroad line. Here they faced two days and two nights by stage to Pittsburgh. It proved a tedious, strenuous, and lonely journey, since they found the tickets which they had bought in Harrisburg were on different stages. Douglass was permitted to take the connecting stage at two o'clock, but Garrison had to wait until eleven o'clock that night. Douglass was banished from the eating table during the whole trip and "for two days and nights," Garrison said, "scarcely tasted a morsel of food." Garrison was angry to think of the shocking contrast with his reception in Great Britain. Even for Garrison the trip from Chambersburg to Pittsburgh "seemed . . . almost interminable—almost equal to a trip across the Atlantic." And as in the voyage of 1840, Garrison was arriving late at his destination. At Pittsburgh, a city that reminded Garrison of the manufacturing towns in England, a committee of twenty, white and colored, accompanied by a blaring band met Douglass' coach when it arrived at three o'clock Wednesday morning. Garrison's stage arrived quietly toward evening; he had missed not only the rousing welcome but a meeting at Temperance Hall in the afternoon. There was nothing to do but soak in a hot bath to restore tired muscles and frayed nerves.

Open-air meetings during the day on Thursday and one that night restored Garrison's waning enthusiasm. "I have seen nothing like to it on this side of the Atlantic. The place seems to be electrified, and the hearts of many are leaping for joy." There followed in succeeding days a round of activities in Pittsburgh and neighboring towns and villages that must have reminded him of British tours. "Company without end—meetings continuously from day to day—little or no sleep—it is with the greatest difficulty," he wrote Helen, "I can find time to send you a single line in regard to my tour." But in spite of everything he had to confess, "I am in good health, enjoying myself exceedingly." [18]

From Pittsburgh they took a steamer northwest up the Ohio River about thirty miles to Beaver, which became a center for further antislavery activity. At nearby New Brighton several hundred persons gathered in the upper room of a large store, the only place available for a meeting. Overhead along the rafters were piled many barrels of flour. "While we were speaking, the mice were busy in nibbling at them, causing their contents to whiten some of our dresses, and thinking, perchance, that our speeches needed to be a little more *floury*." But even with the help of the rodents the abolitionizing in the area was not altogether successful. The people were generally so priest-ridden, Garrison said, that they "remained incorrigible." Douglass, moreover, was getting increasingly exhausted and was speaking with what Garrison described as "much physical debility." Garrison himself, though he enjoyed lecturing and meeting old and new friends, was feeling the strain of excessive activity in the exceedingly hot weather. He had never perspired so freely. It seemed as though his solid flesh would melt away. It was about this time that Garrison and Douglass were joined by another veteran abolitionist, Stephen S. Foster; it was to be hoped that he could help share the burden of the strenuous tour.

On Saturday, 21 August, accompanied by Dr. Peck, a recent colored graduate of Rush Medical College in Chicago, the abolitionist party took the canal boat for Youngstown, Ohio, forty miles away. Colored persons were not ordinarily allowed to eat at the table, "even on board of these paltry canal boats"; but Garrison persuaded the captain to make an exception in Douglass' case. By three o'clock on Sunday morning they were at the Mansion House in Youngstown, paradoxically a "rum tavern," even though kept by an abolitionist who furnished free lodgings to antislavery lecturers. Garrison charitably refrained from withering comment. Three meetings were held during the day, the speaking burden falling chiefly on Garrison. "Thus far," he reported to his wife, "I have stood the fatigues of the tour better than I anticipated." [19]

After Youngstown the next major objective in Ohio was New Lyme, site of the anniversary convention of the Western Anti-

Slavery Society. En route Garrison lectured briefly on phonography, the miraculous new method of shorthand, "and thus enabled the good folks to take a peep at the 'elephant' but without his 'trunk.' " Reaching New Lyme Tuesday afternoon, the 17th, Garrison had no sooner inspected the great tent (capacity 4,000) erected for the convention than a great storm came up, blowing it down and reducing the temperature so drastically that a fire was needed for comfort.

But abolitionists were not to be daunted by the vicissitudes of the weather; early Wednesday morning a great variety of vehicles rolled into the village. Festivities began with a poetical welcome to Garrison, Douglass, and Stephen S. Foster sung by a choir with such feeling that many eyes were as moist as the surrounding landscape. Garrison spoke at length; Douglass, his voice regained for the occasion, gave "a capital speech." A watch was kept on the tent during the night lest vandals destroy it. By the second day 4,000 people were in attendance, listening to debates on the disunion question. Joshua R. Giddings and Daniel R. Tilden, congressmen from Ohio, opposed Garrison but without offending him, for he continued to respect them as among the few able and honorable politicians. The third day of the convention was devoted to spirited discussions that held the immense audience until formal adjournment at two-thirty in the afternoon. Then came the long round of shaking hands and bidding farewell. "When the dense mass moved off in their long array of vehicles, dispersing in every direction to their several homes, some a distance of ten, others of twenty, others of forty, others of eighty, and others of a hundred miles, it was a wonderful spectacle. One man (colored) rode three hundred miles on horseback to be at the meeting!"

Following the great convention Garrison and Douglass held meetings at various neighboring villages. Among the most important was Painesville, where Garrison did most of the talking, since "Frederick's voice was much impaired, and he had to have a bad tooth extracted during the meeting." Everywhere "multitudes crowded around us to give us their blessing and God speed, and to express the strong gratification they felt to see us in the flesh. A great many antislavery publications were sold, subscribers obtained for newspapers, &c. &c." [20]

But in spite of his exceptional endurance the arduous schedule was beginning to tell on Garrison. He complained that so many meetings were planned by antislavery friends there was no time left for rest. He regretted that Douglass' hoarseness—his vocal cords seemed incapable of sustained effort—redoubled his own burden. He was sorry there was no time to write anything worthy of *The Liberator*. But he continued the regular but "hasty scrawls" to Helen, waiting patiently for weeks to hear in reply.[21] For her he described the journey, the countryside, the meetings, the people— abolitionists in particular, Westerners in general. "The manners of the people are primitive and simple. The country, of course, looks like a newly settled one, as compared with our New-England States, but it is comparatively thickly settled on this Western Reserve. In regard to contributing money towards carrying forward our cause, they are not so liberal as we are at the East; indeed, money here is not usually plenty, although they have every thing else in abundance." For Helen he promised to be as prudent as possible in this strange and strenuous land.[22]

By 26 August Garrison had arrived at Oberlin, the place in Ohio which he wanted most to see. Oberlin had been founded originally to combine communal living with education. Each colonist had agreed to run his holdings for the common good, to eat only plain food, and to avoid tobacco, tea, coffee, and elaborate dress, especially tight lacing. All had agreed to give their children the best of Christian educations and to care for widows, orphans, and all the needy. The educational institution had been given life by the influx of both professors and students from Lane Seminary following the revolt against the oppression of the trustees in the fall of 1834, thanks to financial support from the Tappan brothers and other New York philanthropists.[23] Oberlin had been one of the first colleges to admit Negroes and women as students. It had done much, Garrison pointed out, to help fugitive slaves, and its church had refused fellowship with slaveholding and proslavery churches. Garrison had been sufficiently impressed with the record as early as 1840 to do what he could to help a fund-raising mission that was in England at the same time he was.

Garrison arrived at Oberlin at the propitious moment, in time for the graduation of the theological students. He found at least 4,000 people present in a meetinghouse as large as the Broadway Tabernacle in New York. He listened to the speeches of the graduates. Two of them, alas, denounced "the fanaticism of Come-outerism and Disunionism" and the infidelity of abolitionists. Professor Charles G. Finney, however, put them to rights by advising the graduates to espouse "all the reforms of the age," and be "anti-devil all over." If they were unready for such a course, he suggested that they become laborers or farmers rather than ministers. Although he was pleased with this advice, Garrison considered it unrealistic: "If those young men should attempt to carry his advice into practice, where could they hope to find congregations and salaries?" Among the graduates it was not the young men but a firm and independent young woman who impressed Garrison. She was Lucy Stone from Brookfield, Massachusetts, a superior little person with a soul "as free as the air." Already she was determined to consecrate her life to the vindication of woman's rights.

After the commencement came four enthusiastic antislavery meetings—three the first day and one the next morning. Garrison and Douglass spoke to 3,000 persons in the Oberlin meetinghouse, discussing radical religious and political reforms and getting into a debate on the nature of the Constitution with the president of the seminary, Asa Mahan. Garrison commended the gentleman for being "perfectly respectful," though as a disputant he considered him "neither vigorous nor profound." [24]

Less exciting, though more strenuous, than the visit to Oberlin were the series of meetings that followed in neighboring villages—Richfield, Massillon, Leesburg, Zoar, Augusta, and finally Salem. In Leesburg there was what Garrison described as "a rich scene," when a Methodist minister insisted on knowing whether Garrison "believed in the inspiration of the Bible." In Salem a letter from Helen awaited him. He devoured every word and sat right down under the eaves of the house of Benjamin S. Jones (the poet whose song had welcomed the eastern abolitionists to the convention of the Western Anti-Slavery Society at New Lyme) to finish a letter to her. He told her of the four immense meetings at Salem—5,000 in attendance—his old optimism breaking forth: "Our friends are in the best possible spirits. The tide of anti-slavery is rising daily. Every thing looks encouraging." Even a torrential thunderstorm failed to disperse the vast audience. "We looked the storm out of countenance, & wound up gloriously." He assured her that though he was "excessively faded out," his health was good.[25]

From Salem the campaign progressed village by village until on 11 September Garrison and Douglass arrived at Cleveland, a city of 12,000 and the terminal point of the Ohio mission. After three meetings—the last of them held outdoors and during intermittent showers—Garrison collapsed. Douglass was persuaded to continue the mission alone since it was apparent that his partner would be incapacitated for a few days. Garrison's sickness developed rapidly after Douglass' departure. His tongue swelled up, his brain became inflamed, and his whole body ached. Soon he was flat on his back, "helpless as an infant" and feeling "indescribably wretched." He took a lobelia emetic, "but nothing particularly offensive was ejected." In the evening he put himself under the care of "a skilful homoeopathic physician," who diagnosed his illness as bilious, intermittent fever tending toward typhoid. For three days Garrison tossed with incessant fever that reminded him of the scarlatina. Then he started to improve, and a week after his arrival in Cleveland he was well enough to write Helen a letter of reassurance. (He had been disturbed by an alarming report of his illness printed in some of the eastern papers.) He speculated over the distance between them—two hundred miles by steamboat across Lake Erie and six hundred by rail from Buffalo to Boston. "This would be formidable indeed, without the power of steam." He sent her a thousand kisses and a thousand more for the children and signed the letter "Your improving husband." [26]

But Garrison was unduly optimistic about his improvement. Ten days later he was still confined and the trip home was only an uncertain hope. Quincy referred to his illness in *The Liberator,* commending Cleveland friends for their services to Garrison, which he considered "services of the highest nature rendered to the Cause itself." He urged Garrison not to return to Boston in too great haste, assuring him that those editing the paper were not restive in their duties.[27]

By October Garrison was well enough to worry about paying the expenses of his illness. In a shaky hand he wrote a pathetic appeal to Stephen S. Foster: "I have been examining afresh the probable expenses of my illness; and I am satisfied that they will not be one farthing less than one hundred dollars. Do not let the friends subject me to the mortification of being necessitated to say to any to whom I am indebted, 'I have no money to pay you now, but my friends will settle with you hereafter.' Spare me that necessity. I want everything settled, cash down, before I leave Cleveland." He went on to instruct Foster quite precisely what to do. He told him to make an effective appeal at the meeting at Randolph and then to have Samuel Brooke and J. W. Walker, leaders among western abolitionists, "take up such contributions as the friends may be disposed to make." Then he suggested that Brooke take in trust the amount collected, ascertaining how far it fell short of the required $100. The letter closed with a postscript: "I have no doubt that every thing will be done that I require. My only apprehension has been, as to the promptness with which the settlement might be made. You must all pardon my sensibility on this point. I am weak and nervous." 28

In the meantime, Henry Wright, just back from England and pleased to have another excuse for escaping his family, was steaming toward Cleveland to come to Garrison's aid, his travel expenses paid by friends of the cause.29 On the 14th, as though he had descended from the clouds, Wright appeared at Garrison's bedside. The two friends talked at length of the past weeks and years—of the crucifying schedule of the western tour, of Garrison's illness, of Douglass' departure, of Wright's experiences in Europe, of his homeward voyage, and of his trip to Cleveland as soon as he heard of Garrison's fever. During the next several days Wright produced a number of letters for *The Liberator,* while Garrison sat in his chair dozing and dictating.30 The two speculated far into the night over love and truth, over war and slavery. And they talked of Garrison's position in the cause. As Wright put it, Garrison had "laid his life on the altar of God and Humanity," and he had become "emphatically *the* leader of the anti-slavery host," a leader who would fall only when God willed that his work was done. Garrison must expect to absent himself from felicity until the slaves were free.

On the 18th the friends interrupted their moralistic reflections long enough for Garrison to take his first carriage ride in five weeks. They saw the beautiful town and marveled over the commanding view of the great inland sea of Lake Erie. They even

William Lloyd Garrison, 1825; from a portrait by William Swain

Garrison, about 1855

Helen Benson Garrison, about 1853

called at a shop for Garrison to be weighed and found that he had lost twenty pounds during his illness. That night, at Garrison's insistence, Wright hustled off to Buffalo to represent the abolitionists at the National Liberty Party Convention. Garrison instructed him to "watch the Convention as cat does a mouse" and to put down in a notebook "everything worth recording."

Garrison, rejuvenated by Wright's visit, felt well enough on the 19th to write Helen the first letter in over a month, and the same day he received a letter from her. The next morning, though writing was still a great effort, he wrote her again, his letter full of happiness that all was well at home, that friends had been thoughtful, that the children were well and progressing at school. One thing he was sorry about: "I rather regret that you have weaned dear Lizzy at so early a period, but perhaps you have decided wisely. I was thinking that about the middle of December would be the most suitable time." [31]

By the 21st Garrison was well enough to start the homeward journey. Stephen S. Foster accompanied him to Buffalo. "Treacherous Erie," which had prolonged Wright's westward voyage for seventy-five hours, remained calm, as though out of respect for the recuperating Garrison; and the passage from Cleveland to Buffalo was short and pleasant. In Buffalo Henry Wright was waiting. On the 23rd the railroad conveyed Garrison and Wright to Rochester—it was a "jarring, jolting, and rocking" journey, one "hardly fitted to make a sick man well." But kind attentions of friends in Rochester soon revived Garrison, and he and Wright were able to see something of "one of our largest, and most flourishing cities, the staple business of which is making wheat into flour." It was a glorious and growing city, Wright reported, and "it annually furnishes many an English table with nourishing four pound loaves." From Rochester they went on to Waterloo, then to Syracuse, a town of 1,200 inhabitants, where they stayed two days with Samuel J. May. Here Garrison had time to write Helen again to assure her that he was bearing up surprisingly well under the strain of traveling. He told her that they expected to arrive in Boston on Saturday, the 30th, and that she should prepare a comfortable bedroom for Henry and "let only a very few friends know of" their arrival—"such as the Jacksons, Mrs. Meriam, Mr. and Mrs. Wallcut, W. Phillips, &c.—as I must see the friends generally by degrees, and I wish to have a very quiet Sunday at home." [32]

On Wednesday, the 27th, the railroad took them from Syracuse to Albany, 153 uncomfortable miles. It was a wonder to Wright that such an uneven track could be laid on such level ground. "The rails seem to be thrown down hap-hazard, and the cars pitch and tumble like a ship in a storm, as they trundle and rattle over, hobbling up and down, and swaying from side to side, producing a strong feeling of sea-sickness and apprehension of danger." Everywhere along the whole route "the tide of emigrants rolling West" was noticeable. Wright reported meeting "one train in which were packed about 1,000, all from Europe, going to plant themselves in the all-receiving West." Thursday they rolled two hundred miles over level New England tracks, arriving at Boston two days ahead of schedule.[33]

Garrison took his family completely by surprise. One can imagine the long round of kisses and embraces as the father, "still weak and trembling," greeted his wife and six children (Lizzy, ten months, Fanny, not yet three, Charles Follen, five, Wendell Phillips, seven, William, Jr., nine, and George Thompson, eleven). He was always happy to return home, but this time, after the "fiery ordeal" in the West, he was ecstatic.

In the meantime, Frederick Douglass, having left Garrison ill in Cleveland on 14 September, had followed the itinerary which they had planned for New York State. He fully expected that Garrison would catch up with him any day, but week after week passed. Garrison could not understand why Douglass had not at least written to inquire after his health. Then when he read in a Cleveland paper that his friend had decided after all to found a newspaper, to be called *The North Star*, he felt betrayed. He wrote to Helen that Douglass "never opened to me his lips on the subject, nor asked my advice in any particular whatever. Such conduct grieves me to the heart." Douglass' conduct he considered "impulsive, inconsiderate, and highly inconsistent with his decision in Boston. What will his English friends say of such a strange somerset?" Garrison regretted that Quincy had not expressed himself more strongly against the project in *The Liberator*.[34]

The first issue of *The North Star* was published in Rochester, New York, 3 December 1847. Douglass explained in his leading editorial that it had long been his "anxious wish" to establish a paper "under the complete control and direction of the immediate victims of slavery and oppression," since he felt that they could perform for themselves a service "impossible for our white friends to do for us"—no matter how sincere and how able they may be. It was only common sense to affirm "that the man who has *suffered the wrong* is the man to demand redress,—that the man STRUCK is the man to CRY OUT—and that he who has *endured the cruel pangs of Slavery* is the man to *advocate Liberty*." In fact, he continued, it was "right and essential" in the great struggle for human freedom "that there should arise in our ranks authors and editors, as well as orators, for it is in these capacities that the most permanent good can be rendered to our cause." Douglass modestly explained that he had had few opportunities for education and training since it was only nine years ago that he was an insignificant slave. But "we shall be the advocates of learning, from the very want of it, and shall most readily yield the deference due to men of education among us." *The North Star,* he announced, shall be dedicated chiefly to the cause of the slave, but its columns shall be open also to "candid and decorous discussion" of other moral and humane subjects, such as temperance, peace, capital punishment, and education.

In appearance as well as in content *The North Star* resembled *The Liberator*. It was a four-page sheet, with simple format much like Garrison's paper in the early years. As in *The Liberator* the meat of the sandwich was the editorials on the inner pages, the outer pages consisting chiefly of speeches by prominent abolitionists and reprints from other papers—a generous number taken from *The Liberator* itself. After the second issue, which followed the first in a month, the new paper was published weekly.

The chief difference between the two papers lay in the editorials themselves. Garrison's were always direct, enthusiastic, and often vituperative and abusive. Douglass', on the other hand, were polite and restrained; they lacked the abandon, the spontaneity which made Garrison's, whether one agreed with the ideas or not, such good reading. Quincy described *The North Star* as not above the average of antislavery papers. He said that Douglass made the mistake of trying to please all men—of wearing like the crown prince of Lilliput one high and one low heel. "The temptation to conciliate is tremendous to a person in the position and with the disposition of Douglass." No ultra reform paper supports itself, he said, and surely a milk-and-water one cannot. Unfortunately, Quincy lamented, in this country we are smothered with a plethora of newspapers. Would that Douglass had not become "infected with this *cacoethes scribendi*"; he and the cause would have been better off if he had spent his time lecturing.[35]

But though they might criticize Douglass and his paper in private, both Quincy and Garrison gave their public approval to his project. An open break with a prominent Negro would have been too impolitic even for Garrison. As soon as he had read the first issue of *The North Star,* Quincy wrote an editorial commending Douglass for his handsome, well-printed, well-edited paper. "Mr. Douglass," he said, "has our sincere good wishes for the highest degree of prosperity and usefulness in his new career." [36] Garrison, his tone perhaps slightly patronizing, paid his respects after four numbers had appeared, marveling at the facility with which Douglass "has adapted himself to his new and responsible situation," and commending his accurate typography, orthography, and grammar as superior to "that of any other paper ever published by a colored man." "Success to our friends, even beyond their most sanguine anticipations, or the warmest wishes of their co-adjutors!" [37]

The year 1847 had been significant for Garrison. In that year he had for the first time learned something of the compass of his own country; he had found that exploring the far reaches of New York and Ohio was comparable to a voyage across the ocean. He had spent days and weeks in close contact with a former slave who, though he was sometimes difficult and did not take advice, was so eloquent that, vocal cords permitting, he challenged Garrison's pre-eminence on the lecture platform. It was satisfying proof that a Negro could be a man. In 1847 Garrison had also approached perilously close to "that undiscovered country from whose bourne no traveller returns," for he had lain deathly sick for five weeks. But even his illness was not without its compensation, for it had demonstrated the generosity of many friends and the devotion of one. The year 1847 had broadened Garrison's experiences and deepened his sensibilities.

It was a full two months after his return to Boston before Garrison resumed his editorial duties. Since they were months of relative quiet for the cause, he spent much of his time at his home on Pine Street, surrounded by devoted family and friends. But, as Quincy put it, "It really seems as if the Devil always would put his foot in it, whenever the Anti-Slavery cause has got into a tolerable position, so as to keep it in hot water," [38] for it was during this period that Garrison and Wright planned a new attack on the institution of the Sabbath.

This time the convention was planned by Garrison himself. It all began in "Helen's parlor," as Wright called the room. There the Boston clique (Mrs. Chapman, Wright, Phillips and Quincy, the Fosters, and even the Reverend Theodore Parker) assembled to hear Garrison's ideas: there must be a call signed by a thousand or even two thousand; there must be essays on various aspects of the topic written and delivered by leading reformers.[39] Talk continued at the Garrison house on a number of occasions and on various topics. There was discussion of Frederick Douglass and the new paper. Wright had little confidence in his firmness. It was agreed that one could not tell by reading *The North Star* how he stood on the Liberty party or the dissolution of the Union. There was talk, also, about more frivolous subjects, such as the séance Wright and Garrison had recently attended, but mostly they talked to "mesmerize the Sabbath," as Wright said. Out of these meetings emerged plans for a great convention in March.[40]

But there was other excitement before March. In Tremont Hall, or Tremont Temple as it was sometimes called, a building maintained by the Baptists and readily available for reform meetings, there was a meeting of nonresistants on 28 December. Garrison himself spoke briefly two or three times, but he was not yet entirely well. "It makes his head ache to speak," Wright said.[41]

Garrison spent a good deal of time toward the end of the year soliciting signatures for the call to the Anti-Sabbath Convention. He secured not the two thousand he had extravagantly contemplated but two dozen. It seemed that the Garrisonians generally were less enthusiastic about the project than were Wright and Garrison themselves. Most of them felt that they were making sufficient contribution by scheduling meetings on Sunday and generally acting as if there were nothing sacred about the day. Even Phillips refused to sign the call, and Quincy signed only with the clear understanding that no service would be expected of him. "I was content to ring the bell, but not to do any part of the preaching or evangelizing." [42]

But Garrison and Wright did not need the active support of Phillips and Quincy. They printed the call with its signatures in *The Liberator* for 21 January and waited for the public reaction, which left nothing to be desired; Garrison was furnished with abundant editorial fodder. He chuckled over the response from newspapers and individuals: "The developments," he said, "are instructive—in some instances, startling. It is well to have some test, by which it can be easily determined in what estimation the rights of conscience are held, and what is the liberty of the people, in this country." [43]

Garrison and Wright decided that the convention should not be a free meeting. The series of essays contemplated earlier were to be read on various aspects of the Sabbath question; Abby Folsom, psychotic pest of reform meetings, would be removed if she caused trouble. The Melodeon—built as the Lion Theatre in 1836 and since 1839 a popular concert and lecture hall—was selected for the meeting. March 23 came, "a furious stormy day"; snow and rain mingled and poured into the Boston streets. Wright and Garrison were in the hall early, ensconced at the table on the platform. Lucretia Mott, Stephen S. Foster, Theodore Parker, Francis Jackson, and others appeared promptly in spite of the weather. Abby was there too, "looking desperate, moody, & wretched." The Chapmans and Westons came also. Charles C. Burleigh, "a good & powerful man," came striding down the aisle after the meeting had begun, his long, curly red hair flowing over his shoulders and his red beard "down long upon his breast." It was "a sternly just & truthful body of men & women." George Benson, Garrison's alter ego, was in the chair.[44] Garrison himself was soon on the platform, reading a letter sent to the convention from Connecticut and formulating resolutions. The third speaker was Theodore Parker, whom Wright described as "a little, plain, meek looking man," who stood and talked on fluently, tracing the history of the first-day Sabbath. It was a powerful talk; the house was full and breathless with interest, as two reporters took notes. After Parker, Garrison took the floor again and read from an old English book, *"Judgements on Sabbath-breakers."* Then came Bronson Alcott, who spoke with feeling and power, urging that it was men and women who were imperial, not crowns, scepters, cities and kingdoms. Following Alcott, Garrison was up again—for the third time—but only to move adjournment till after dinner.

In the evening the whole crowd returned. Buffum spoke and then Burleigh, his broad shoulders concealed beneath the mighty hair. He rolled out his thoughts with the rushing power of Niagara's cataract, his great "under jaw going up & down & the Beard moving and shaking & his head shaking from side to side, & back & forward—making those long, curled Ringlets shaking and flying about his shoulders like a horses *Mane,* & his voice clear & loud & his logic & earnestness—eloquence irresistable [*sic*]." Stephen S. Foster thundered away after Burleigh, proclaiming that only God and Man are holy; there are no holy days. The house was getting fuller and fuller. Abby was beginning to stalk up and down the aisle. Sabbatarian rowdies urged her to action, and she started to shout and yell but in a minute went out of the meeting of her own volition. Garrison was on his feet again, "asking pity and indulgence for poor Abby." Wright regretted there would be no opportunity for Lucretia Mott to speak that night, for the time was passing rapidly.

The next morning—Wright had spent a refreshing night at Garrison's house—the meeting was resumed. There was some agitation for greater freedom of speech at the convention, and Foster insisted that the doors should be thrown open to all who wished to speak. Garrison explained why the convention must have restricting rules. Abby proved his point by starting to rant again. Wright thought Foster crotchety and hated wasting time over mere questions of order. George Benson spoke; then Wright himself took the platform and after speaking for half an hour said he would give way to Lucretia Mott if she had anything to say. He looked down to where she sat. In a moment she faced the audience. "Not a *breath* nor *movement* is heard in this house—but Lucretia's sweet, firm, clear, eloquent & calm voice—as she is advocating the sanctity and consecration of *Man* rather than of days & places. We ought not to bind ourselves to any authority—but to the authority of Truth." The audience was entranced—such "radical sentiments" from such a beautiful and charming woman!

In the afternoon Burleigh and Wright spoke again, and then

came Garrison—for the fifth time. Increasingly apparent during the meeting was an emaciated, white-bearded, round-faced chap— "one of the original Cape Cod Comeouters," who had walked the one hundred miles from his home to attend the convention. He showed his approval of the ultra doctrines being advanced by crying at frequent intervals, "Truth—Amen!" "Go it, brother!" "Amen—Truth—Praise the Lord!" Wright thought him "a queer one."

At the final meeting that evening the house was overflowing with people. Parker Pillsbury said some low and bitter things against the priesthood. Samuel May, Jr., and even Elizur Wright spoke. Garrison read a series of resolutions, and some twenty-five were adopted. Abby Folsom tried to get in, but Francis Jackson was at the door to stop her, in spite of all the abuse that Sabbatarians could heap upon him. The heroine of the evening—indeed of the whole convention—was Lucretia Mott, who spoke for an hour— more eloquently than ever. "The vast concourse . . . [hung] upon her lips in deep & profound attention." It was "a powerful & telling speech. We are all better men for what she has said. She has illuminated many minds." Garrison made a "closing speech— & an efficient & telling one. He is in his glory," Wright said. "I have never seen Garrison appear better than in this meeting. He has stood erect & cheerful—even when opposed to his dearest personal friends. One strange man—with long grey beard—& a hat on . . . says nearly every sentence uttered—'Truth—Truth— Truth.' " [45]

Although Garrison thoroughly enjoyed the excitement and notoriety surrounding the Anti-Sabbath Convention, he did not enjoy the criticism of some of his friends. As we have seen, neither Phillips nor Quincy was entirely happy with his religious excursions. Elizabeth Pease, his English Quaker friend and benefactor, was even less enthusiastic. She wrote letters to Garrison, Wright, and Phillips, describing *The Liberator* as the most interesting paper she received, but one she hesitated to leave lying around for fear some innocent person might be corrupted by reading the many heresies it contained. Garrison was seriously concerned. There was no one whom he liked and admired more than Elizabeth Pease. He wrote her a twenty-page letter of gentle, earnest remonstrance. It was his duty, he said, to present in an independent paper like *The Liberator* both sides of all questions. He suggested that those who feared having their position probed felt insecure in their conviction. Men should learn—and this he was trying to teach his children—to accept nothing on authority; they should analyze all sides of an issue before committing themselves. Even the Bible should be subjected to analysis and be judged according to its intrinsic merits—the erroneous, the obsolete, the visionary, and the contradictory should be discarded. "I am sorry, dear friend, to have caused you any grief or uneasiness, but I must be true to my convictions of duty, and trust you will ever be true to yours." [46]

Following the Anti-Sabbath Convention, the Garrison house was "little better than a hospital," as influenza spread impartially through the family. Garrison had a high fever, a deep cough, "and great pressure upon the brain," as well as erysipelatoid swelling and itching in face, hands, and feet. Helen, as well as her sister Sarah, who was visting the household, was also sick. Of the children Lizzy Pease, the sixteen-month-old baby, was most seriously affected. Lizzy had been frail ever since she had been weaned—prematurely, Garrison was certain now; she had grown slowly and had had great difficulty teething. In her case the flu became lung-fever (pneumonia). Dr. Geist, a homoeopathic friend, was called to attend her. Although the fever continued, she seemed to improve. The night of 19 April she slept so well that her father went to the office in the morning "with an elastic step and a joyous spirit." But when he returned late in the evening, Helen's face was solemn. The baby was worse. Helen and Lloyd spent the night by her side. "Soon after midnight, she drew her last breath so gently, that no one perceived it:—'Night dews fall not more gently to the ground,/Nor weary, worn-out winds expire so soft.' " [47]

It was their first loss of a child. Garrison gazed at the placid face, "so beautiful in death," reminded himself that death was a part of the law of life, and reaffirmed his belief in the immortality of the human soul. Helen, less philosophical, mourned. "To see the cradle vacant—to be unable to clasp her babe to her bosom—to wake up in the night, and find no little one nestling by her side—all this seems to leave her almost solitary, although there are still five others left."

A number of friends were invited to the funeral. Wendell Phillips, Theodore Parker, and others said appropriate words. Two or three cherished daguerreotypes were taken of the dead child. The Garrisons had survived "the first breach" in their family circle.

Garrison himself continued so unwell during the spring that he seemed on the verge of becoming a chronic semi-invalid. The serious illness in Ohio the previous fall had been only the culmination of a long series of complaints. His letters and the editorial section of *The Liberator* are filled with references to the myriad ills that his flesh was heir to. There were fevers by the dozen, swellings of all sorts, some of them scrofulous; colds, flus, spinal attacks; pains in arms, shoulders, knees, teeth; dysenteries, catarrhs, headaches, and bouts of insomnia; coughs, liver complaints, and scarlet fever. For a time following the scarlet fever he had a swelling in his chest that he used to speak of "as an animal or devil . . . busy about his heart, which will soon put an end to him." (Dr. Warren, a surgeon of international reputation, regarded the ailment as nothing serious—not so the homoeopaths and hydropaths in whom Garrison had confidence.) Quincy thought it not surprising that once or twice a year Garrison had "regular turns of illness." "What with steaming in rooms heated with a furnace or stoves, eating all manner of things, & then falling back upon the hell-broths of Thompsonianism [sic] [48] for cure, it is a marvel that he & any of his children yet survive." Garrison must have, Quincy said, an iron constitution to withstand his own ignorance of physiology and the quantity of patent medicines he consumed—some of them stimulatingly alcoholic.[49]

When in the summer of 1848 Garrison was convinced that he must do something about his health, Wright had suggested a three-month water cure.[50] Perhaps it would do him as much good as a trip abroad. Dr. David Ruggles, a self-educated, blind colored man who had several years before established a water-cure infirmary in Northampton,[51] had been urging him to take a free course of hydropathic treatments, and George Benson also had been eager to have him come to Northampton.[52] Always susceptible to the advice of the layman and the eccentric rather than the professional (if traditional church and state were suspect, why not traditional medicine?), Garrison accepted Ruggle's offer. On 17

July he arrived in Northampton, where he was greeted with fervent hugs and kisses from his six-year-old son, Charley, who had been visiting the Bensons.[53]

On the day following his arrival the myriad applications of *aqua pura* began. At five in the morning came a half bath, which Garrison thought a bath and a quarter, then a rubdown, followed at eleven o'clock by a soaking with a wet sheet wrapped around the body. At four P.M. came a sitz bath; Garrison thought it an amusing sight—twelve or thirteen of the men sitting in their baths "like a desperate, as well as unnatural, effort at incubation." Before bedtime there was a foot bath. And scheduled between these various ablutions were various forms of exercise. On subsequent days the regime was intensified with douches and sprays and all manner of internal applications, until in a week water had been administered in forty different ways. The diet also was rigorous: "no coffee, no tea, no butter, no milk, (a spoonful or two of cream,) no meat, (except a lean slice by special permission,) no hot bread, no warm dish of any kind," but there was water—water in abundance—and cereal and bread.

Garrison observed the other patients, as though they were fellow passengers on a transatlantic voyage. But he found them a dull lot. "As there is not a single dogmatic controversial spirit among us, it is not only impossible to get up a breeze, but it is difficult to raise even a zephyr, on any subject." All they could do was agree: that there is no medicine like water; that their appetites were "alarmingly good"; that they were all making progress in the cure; "that our worthy doctor (being blind, you know) is a very *feeling* man, and has much physiological knowledge at his fingers' *ends*"; that Northampton is romantically beautiful; that the weather is perfect; and that the moon waxes in size and splendor.

Agreeable companions and beautiful scenery were not enough for Garrison. "There is nothing in all this region," he complained, "to stimulate the mind." As he sat in his baths, images of the atrocities of slavery flickered through his head. He felt guilty and bored. At the doctor's insistence he limited his correspondence, but he continued to read newspapers, without which, he insisted, he would be more nervous and excited than ever. Reading newspapers relieved "the otherwise intolerable monotony of my situation."

Early in August the monotony was relieved further, when Garrison's family joined him in Northampton. By fall there was abundant evidence that he was getting well, for he had had two or three "flattering crises," which evidently took the form of acute attacks of boils and piles. He hoped to be entirely cured by November, but Helen was so far advanced in pregnancy that she had to take the family back to Boston several weeks earlier.

After the family's departure Garrison felt lost and alone—worse than he had before they came to Northampton; it was as though he had suffered "a general bereavement." He fretted over Helen's letters and all their details of life apart from him. He was thankful that there were friends to help her. He was glad that George had been a good boy and helpful to his mother. Money and credit were what worried him most. There was a bill for $45 for one month's supply of meat and groceries—he didn't see how it could be so high! His salary was in no sense guaranteed; no committee was responsible. When the subscribers were slow in making payment, Garrison's allotment was simply not available.

It was a precarious and harassing livelihood for a man with a large and still growing family. But he had always made headway against wind and tide, and he would do so again. "I throw myself on the promise, which, this far, has never failed me—'trust in the Lord, and do good, and verily thou shalt be fed.' " [54]

At the end of October Garrison returned home, feeling much better for his ordeal at Northampton.[55] He arrived just in time to be present for the birth of another child. A black-haired dark-eyed baby, its "cheeks like thumping red potatoes," weighing ten and a half pounds, arrived about two A.M. on the 29th. Garrison reported to his brother-in-law: "Heigh-ho! The *boys* have it, out of all proportion—five to one! Should they all 'live to grow up,' the *Garrisons* will at last be strongly *manned*." [56] Garrison's latest— and as it happened his last—child was named for Francis Jackson, loyal colleague and benefactor, though Lloyd and Helen were tempted to show their love for Henry C. Wright or Samuel J. May. If only their names had been shorter or—one suspects—their purses larger!

The Garrisons lived out the winter at 13 Pine Street and in March moved to another house—more commodious, it was to be hoped—at 65 Suffolk Street (later Shawmut Avenue).

In April occurred an event that was to try Garrison's faith.

Charles Follen Garrison, the handsome, robust six-year-old who had greeted his father so affectionately when he arrived at Northampton, complained of feeling sick to his stomach. His face looked flushed, and it hurt him to move his arms and legs. They tried various treatments. They wrapped him in a wet sheet three or four times; they gave him homoeopathic prescriptions, following directions in a book, which described similar symptoms and their cure. On Wednesday, 4 April—the illness had begun the preceding Saturday—Garrison was at the office getting *The Liberator* ready for the press, when he received a note from Helen, urging him to come home quickly, that Charley was worse.

Garrison hesitated, wondering whether to go for a doctor, but a friend told him to try a vapor bath and offered his wife's services "to administer it, as she had given it with great success in a multitude of cases." Convinced that the child was suffering from rheumatic fever and needed to perspire more freely, Garrison decided to try this treatment. He found a suitable chair and the proper apparatus and waited for his friend's wife to come over in the evening. By the time she appeared, Charles, though still conscious and rational, was lethargic except that he screamed with pain when his arms or legs were moved. When he was put into the chair, he became frantic—"his screams were appalling—and he begged most piteously to be released. No other person was in the room, except the lady and myself. She endeavored to soothe him as much as possible, and I appealed to his little manhood in the best way I could, thinking he was nervously affected, and urging him to bear it all with fortitude, as he would undoubtedly be benefitted by the operation." When they removed him from the chair they "found that the poor boy had been horribly scalded," especially on the buttocks, the skin on one side of which was entirely destroyed.

After the vapor bath he was delirious for four days. By Sunday he seemed a little quieter. His father, for reasons difficult to understand, bent down close to his ear and said distinctly, "Dear Charley is dying!" The child seemed to sigh gently. "Charley will soon be with our darling Lizzie," Garrison said, remembering how fond he had been of his baby sister and how often he had expressed the wish to be with her. There was a look of recognition. Later in the evening, just before he died, the child rallied once more, saw his mother by the bed, and smiled.[57]

The whole family was shocked by Charley's death. Four-year-old

Fanny had lost "her oracle and champion." Though her father had taught her not to fear death, tears often came to her eyes in the days to come when she thought of her big brother, and she had to remind herself "he is now with dear Lizzie." Helen, although she was always brave and uncomplaining, was difficult to console. She agreed with her husband "it is well with the child," but she could not help wondering whether this death were really necessary. Garrison himself felt more than a modicum of guilt. Their beautiful, intelligent, vigorous boy, who had "seemed born to take a century upon his shoulders without stooping," was gone, and perhaps he himself had been at fault. But Garrison could console himself: "O, how glorious is the thought of immortality! how glorious are the visions of eternity! 'O Death, where is thy sting? O Grave, where is thy victory?' "

There was also more mundane hope for the future of Garrison and his family. Just about the time of Charley's death Garrison discovered that his friends were busy raising a fund for the benefit of himself and his family. Writing to Elizabeth Pease, he thanked her for her contribution to the fund and protested that he did not deserve such generosity, for he had simply done his duty. "Whatever the sum may be, I do not mean or desire to have any thing to do with its expenditure. In the hands of the faithful friends who have kindly consented to act as trustees, it will find a safe deposit, and be appropriated in the most judicious manner. May my future course be such as to give no contributor regret that he ever assisted me in my necessities!" [58] It was the passive side of Garrison speaking out. He needed help, and he was quite willing—even eager—to accept it.

CHAPTER XVIII

⸻ ◆ ⸻

At Mid-Century

FAMILY matters were not the only things that concerned Garrison at mid-century. There were various foreign visitors to be received and sometimes deplored, and there were alarming political developments.

In July 1849 Father Theobald Mathew, whom Garrison in 1841 had called "the most remarkable man of the age," [1] had landed in New York on a temperance mission. Soon his visit assumed unexpected prominence as politicians covetous of the Irish vote at forthcoming elections vied with each other in showing him attention. He was even entertained by President Taylor at the White House. In New York and Brooklyn he was a great success, for twenty thousand people at his instigation took the pledge of total abstinence. When he approached Boston on 24 July, he was met at the city line by a municipal committee in a barouche with four horses. He was subsequently welcomed by Governor Briggs. Multitudes thronged the Common to hear him speak. In one street, according to Wendell Phillips, his mere presence closed all but three of sixteen grog-shops.[2]

Garrison recognized Father Mathew as a vehicle for priceless antislavery publicity. It seemed most appropriate that the Massachusetts Anti-Slavery Society should join in his welcome. Fortunately, the right occasion was at hand, the anniversary of emancipation in the British West Indies, to be celebrated in Worcester on 3 August. Garrison, as chairman of a reception committee, drew up an elaborate letter of invitation, urging his participation in the celebration. In order to be certain that the letter was brought to his attention, Garrison, along with Dr. Henry I. Bowditch, called upon Father Mathew at the Adams House. When Mathew indicated that he was familiar with his name, Garrison characteristically admitted that he was "somewhat notorious, though not as yet very popular." Garrison shook him by the hand and, presenting him with the letter, summarized its contents. Mathew seemed embarrassed; "I have as much as I can do to save men from slavery of intemperance, without attempting the overthrow of any other kind of slavery," he said, as though criticizing Garrison's penchant for universal reform. Garrison reminded Father Mathew that along with Daniel O'Connell he had in 1842 signed an appeal to the Irish in America which described slavery as "a sin against God and man," stating that "all who are not for it must be against it—none can be neutral." Mathew recalled having signed the appeal. In parting, Garrison urged Mathew to read the letter carefully and answer it as soon as possible.

When no answer came, Garrison determined to make the most of another *cause célèbre*. In *The Liberator* for 10 August he printed the letter of invitation, his report of the interview with Father Mathew, and other editorial comments about him, including a favorable one from Frederick Douglass' *North Star*. For the nine weeks following he printed a series of rebukes to the well-meaning priest, including five more letters of his own, reprints from many papers, including some in the South, and even the opinion (supporting his own point of view) of Mathew's fellow countryman, James Haughton. Father Mathew had the good sense to remain silent throughout the controversy.

While Garrison was doing his best to chastise Father Mathew, more important events were unfolding on the national scene. Congress, composed of a distinguished group (though perhaps not according to Garrison's standards), including Henry Clay, John C. Calhoun, Daniel Webster, Stephen Douglas, Jefferson Davis, William H. Seward, and Alexander H. Stephens, was seeking a solution to the problem of slavery in the territories. Henry Clay had taken the lead in January 1850 with a series of resolutions providing for the admission of free California in return for the absence of restrictions on slavery in the land acquired from the Mexican War and the establishment of an enforceable federal fugitive slave law. Although he abhorred the very word compromise, Garrison was not at all surprised at the recommendations of "the great Satanic Compromiser."

In a letter written to Garrison from Ohio in February Henry C. Wright linked Father Mathew and Henry Clay. They were to Wright men of equal turpitude since they both endeavored to protect slavery.[3] The first of March Garrison published his own editorial on Clay and his compromises. He compared the year 1850 with 1835. In 1835 a comprehensive attempt had been made to crush the antislavery cause by a "mobocratic movement throughout the country." Law and order had been abrogated, and the friends of the slave were hunted down "with the fury of a whirlwind." As a result, the antislavery enterprise acquired many new converts and received a tremendous forward impetus. At the present time, Garrison insisted, the slavocratic power in the North "is attempting to play the same old game, under a new phase and for a new object. . . . The idol that is now to be worshipped is the AMERICAN UNION: and whoso falls not down before it, and gives not to it his homage, is to be held up to popular execration." Garrison prophesied doom for those who trifled with the higher law of freedom in order to maintain "an agreement with hell" and called again for "NO UNION WITH SLAVEHOLDERS!"

The following week Garrison wrote a long, indignant editorial condemning a report on the Wilmot Proviso and Compromise presented by a joint special committee to the Massachusetts legislature. Point by point, he made his views clear. The denial of representation of the slave population in Congress, except by the three-fifths formula which merely increased Southern white representation, he agreed with John Quincy Adams, was a "perfect exemplification of the art of committing the lamb to the tender custody of the wolf." The provisions for hunting fugitive slaves in the North—again to use the words of Adams—was "positively prohibited by the laws of God." He was particularly annoyed by the reverence for the framers of the Constitution shown in the report. Men who would sacrifice right and justice to establish a Union were hardly to be revered, Garrison thought. "They were not men of integrity, they were not lovers of liberty for all mankind, their 'patriotism' was marked by intense selfishness . . . they were recreant to their own heaven-attested principles; and by their unrighteous example, they have cursed their descendants with a grievous curse." [4]

On 15 March Garrison reprinted Calhoun's famous last speech, commenting that "he has no breadth of character, no greatness of spirit, no generosity of purpose, no comprehensiveness of view. . . . The real dimensions of a man are to be known by the size of his heart, rather than by the volume of his brain," and Calhoun has no heart. "He is made of iron, not flesh; he is hybridous, not natural." A month later, after Calhoun's death, Garrison proved himself somewhat deficient in heart when he said: "His memory shall rot, or be remembered by future generations only to be execrated for his tyrannical and impious principles." [5]

Garrison was not surprised when three days after Calhoun's speech Webster also spoke in the Senate, modifying Calhoun's position but in essence approving Clay's basic compromises, for Webster had long since forfeited Garrison's respect. However, he insisted that Webster was not equivalent to Massachusetts, that it was time for the people to declare themselves, for they were as capable of forming their own opinions on the great issue of slavery extension or prohibition as were Webster and Clay. "Let it be shown, on their part, by a movement almost as rapid as that of the lightning of heaven, that Mr. Webster receives no endorsement at their hands; that he has not spoken their sentiments; and that they regard him as worthy of official censure." Such a movement could be launched, he suggested, by circulating a memorial to the state legislature; and he supplied the draft of an appropriate statement.[6]

The condemnation that followed Webster's speech was a source of great satisfaction to Garrison. In this instance he was quite willing to follow the crowd. He reprinted in subsequent issues of The Liberator every notice and review of the speech which he thought appropriate. Never in the twenty-four years of his editorial experience, he averred, had a speech in either house of Congress "so powerfully shocked the moral sense, or so grievously insulted the intelligence of the people of the North, or received such strong and general condemnation on the part of religious and political journals." Garrison was especially gratified that even the religious journals, which he ordinarily considered pusillanimous, had arraigned Webster "as a moral culprit."

The excitement attending the Congressional discussions of the Compromise had an immediate and tangible effect on the anti-slavery movement. Early in May, the month for the anniversary meetings of the American Anti-Slavery Society, the New York papers, under the leadership of James Gordon Bennett of the *Herald,* released a barrage against the abolitionists. Waspish Bennett, perhaps the only man of the day who could equal Garrison in journalistic invective, told the merchants and businessmen of the city that they "should frown down the meetings of these mad people, if they would save themselves." He claimed that the ravings of the abolitionists, if unrestrained, would ruin the prosperity of the city, making New York an "arena of blood and murder" and "an object of horror to the whole South. . . . Let all of our honest citizens, who respect themselves, their wives, their mothers, their sisters and daughters, and, of course, the honor and dignity of the city in which they reside, go on Tuesday morning to the Tabernacle, and there look at the black and white brethren and sisters, fraternizing, slobbering over each other, speaking, praying, singing, blaspheming, and cursing the Constitution of our glorious Union, and then say whether these things shall go forth to the South and the world as the feeling of the great city of New York." [7]

On 6 May, the day before the meeting, Bennett selected *The Liberator* and its radical doctrines for special condemnation. The next day he paid his disrespects to Garrison himself, accusing him of taking up abolition through political ambitions. He said that nothing was sacred to Garrison except the ideal Negro intellect. In order to establish his own prejudiced views of human liberty he would abolish the government and the Constitution, annihilate the Union, and virtually subvert all legal and divine order. Never, even in the time of the French Revolution, were there such "blasphemous atheism" and such malevolent wickedness as that espoused by Garrison. Compared to him Robespierre was constructive. Garrison's "only object is to destroy."

The meeting opened at ten A.M., 7 May. As Garrison stepped into the Congregational Tabernacle, he looked from head to foot the proper president of a great society. He had even exchanged his usual old-fashioned turn-down collar for the modish stand-up variety.[8] He stepped onto the platform in the great square hall, tiers of seats rising before and behind, those in the rear merging with the gallery. After presiding over the business part of the meeting, Garrison turned the chairmanship over to Francis Jackson and prepared to speak, holding in his hand notes for his discourse. He talked about the relationship between abolition and Christianity, insisting that the members of his society considered the antislavery movement the chief Christian movement of the day. His manner was calm and dignified. He spoke simply and without humor or bitterness. He criticized various religious denominations for ignoring the sins of the nation, mentioning specifically the Roman Catholic Church. At this point questions calculated to embarrass emanated from the gallery behind the speaker. But Garrison plowed on with his speech, discussing Jesus and how belief in Him could no longer be considered an adequate test of a man's religion or his morality. The questions continued. Garrison was asked whether he knew that slaves in the South had prayer meetings honoring Christ. His reply: "Not a slaveholding or a slave-breeding Jesus!" The audience seethed. Garrison went on to suggest that Jesus had become totally respectable, that He even sits in the President's chair of the United States, explaining that Zachary Taylor who believes in war and "gave the Mexicans hell" believes in Jesus.[9]

At this point the chief disturber in the gallery behind Garrison jumped up with a howl, rushed down the steps to the platform, and after him, like Satan's cohorts swarming from Hell, came his followers. The leader was one "Captain" Isaiah Rynders, formerly a boatman on the Hudson River and currently proprietor of a Democratic sporting-house called the Empire Club, a man of some power in Tammany Hall. Emphatically shaking his fist, Rynders made it clear that he would not allow Garrison to insult the President of the United States. The audience participated in the fray. There were shouts of "Turn him out! turn him out! turn him out!" In his calmest voice Garrison informed Rynders that he ought not to interrupt the meeting, but offered to keep order while Rynders spoke.

The excitement did not diminish even when the Hutchinsons, famous antislavery singers, tried ministering to the mob. Ultimately, Francis Jackson formally offered the floor to Rynders, and the hisses, groans, and yells stopped. Rynders stepped back on the platform to await his turn. Garrison, unperturbed, finished his speech, "a glorious speech—one of the most radical & effective I have ever heard," according to Henry C. Wright.[10] At the end of his speech Garrison offered a resolution to the effect that the antislavery movement, far from being infidel, is truly Christian. Then he resumed the presidency of the meeting. Instead of speaking himself, Rynders selected as deputy one "Professor" Grant, who elected to follow the speech of a dignified Unitarian clergyman. Grant, whom Garrison recognized as a former pressman for *The Liberator,* was a pathetic-looking figure, standing there in his seedy clothes, a dirty cotton cloth wound around one of his hands. He spoke so ludicrously on the topic that Negroes are not men but members of the monkey tribe, that even his own supporters laughed.

It was appropriate that Frederick Douglass should be the next speaker. He asked the audience, seeming to enjoy the whole procedure, "Am I a man?" There was a great uproar, but Douglass kept the audience laughing and hit out at the mobocrats when they interrupted him. Rynders remained standing on the platform behind the speaker, too ill at ease to leave. Douglass referred to him as his half-brother, and when the crowd tried to break up the meeting, he said: "It's of no use, *I've Captain Rynders here to back me.*" By the time Douglass had completed his triumphant performance, the captain of police and fifteen or twenty armed men were on the platform. The police captain whispered to Garrison: "I'll take these disturbers of your meeting into custody soon as you say the word." "Let them alone," Garrison said, "and we will take care of them." Take care of them they did.

Garrison and Wright ate heartily that night at a restaurant on Canal Street. "There we sat," said Henry "& had a nice, cozy, quiet time—got a good dinner & had to pay *one shilling* each— cheap enough. It was very pleasant to get Garrison alone & talk over his private & family affairs. & also the great agitations that are going on. He says there would have been a Mob—a regular knock down & drag out Mob, had there been the least show of fight on the part of any of the colored people or of the abolitionists."

After dinner the meeting continued and Garrison, "powerfully wrought up," spoke on Webster and Union. The following day the meeting opened again, with Rynders and gang still in attendance. Charles C. Burleigh, whose flowing beard and eccentric dress were enough to inspire smiles even from his friends, took quite a ribbing. Someone shouted: "Shave that tall Christ and make a wig for Garrison!" Even Wendell Phillips, in spite of his eloquence, was not immune to taunts from the audience. When he said that some day the people would put the Constitution where it belonged—under foot, stamping on the platform as though to desecrate that instrument—a veritable tornado broke loose. There were "Three cheers for the Constitution!" And then three more. There were three cheers for Washington. Then Garrison proposed "three more cheers for Washington, who died an abolitionist."

Excited momentum filled the great hall. Rynders jumped onto the platform again, holding up a resolution which denied the need for antislavery agitation. It was carried by a vote of his associates, the meeting proper remaining silent. Rynders stood by Burleigh, put his arm round his neck, and stroked his beard. There was a great uproar: noise, confusion, yells, cries, laughter. The Hutchinsons tried again to quiet the mob, but were drowned out by cries and obscenities. The hall reverberated with sound. All through the pandemonium Henry C. Wright sat on the platform calmly writing a journal to his current love, hugely enjoying himself and wishing she and her family were there. "Now there is a rush to the platform," he wrote, "& a great commotion—I am jostled & hustled & can scarcely write. The women sit like glorious martyrs; & flinch not. Indeed, they are worthy the days that try men's souls."

By this time the chief of police and a large force had entered the hall. The trustees of the library located over the hall, fearing damage to the books and to the building, sent a sheriff to consult with Garrison, who, "under protest," declared the meeting of the American Anti-Slavery Society adjourned without further delay.

Henry Wright went to the same eating house on Canal Street that noon to dine with the wealthy Charles F. Hovey and have "a pleasant chat." By four o'clock an adjourned meeting was in session in the large dining room of William P. Powell, and Garrison had left to write resolutions in regard to the mob. By seven o'clock the next morning all were assembled in Powell's parlor having what Wright described as "a merry time." Two hours later the meeting was in progress in the dining room. Wright reported: "Samuel Brook is speaking & says—'I grew out of Stephen Foster's brain—' 'I hope—says Stephen—my brain never brought forth such a *fanatic.*' 'Stephen cannot *Brook* that—' said Garrison. 'Eh-h-h William—I say, thou wouldst make a *pun* if it was thy last breath.' "

By five o'clock Garrison, Wright, and Burleigh were seated in the seclusion of Powell's parlor, their host asleep in his easy chair as Henry continued his journal, and Garrison, feeling almost as young as he had in 1835, wrote the official version of the exciting meeting for the New York papers.

The following September the various measures to be known as the Compromise of 1850 became law. In its effect on the anti-slavery movement the most important provision of the Compromise was the stringent Fugitive Slave Law. Opposition to this law in the North was so general that it served to unify the various branches of the movement and to give great impetus to the development of the Underground Railroad. Helping fugitive slaves to escape to free Canada became virtually a fashionable occupation after 1850. Nearly every year thereafter had its celebrated case, among the more significant in Boston being those of Ellen and William Crafts, Thomas Sims, and Anthony Burns; there were more than eighty major cases in the country during the decade of the fifties.[11] Although Garrison gave many pages of publicity to the famous cases, he never participated directly and enthusiastically in the activities of the Underground Railroad. He made his point of view clear in a speech at Westchester, Pennsylvania, on 26 October 1852:

A great deal is said at the present time, and perhaps not too much, in regard to the Fugitive Slave Law. Many persons glory in their hostility to it, and upon this capital they set up an antislavery reputation. But opposition to that law is no proof in itself of anti-slavery fidelity. That law is merely incidental to slavery, and there is no merit in opposition which extends no further than to its provisions. Our warfare is not against slave-hunting alone, but against the existence of slavery.[12]

As a nonresistant Garrison had additional logical reasons to avoid activities so fraught with force and violence, but, one suspects, he had other more compelling personal reasons. Always independent and proud of sponsoring unpopular causes, he may have felt that assisting fugitives to escape had become almost too respectable to be attractive. Moreover, he was always on the prowl for events, like the raucous meeting of the American Anti-Slavery Society, which could be heroically publicized, whereas most of the duties concerned with helping slaves to escape required secrecy.

By 9 August Garrison was condemning the views of Calhoun's successor in the Senate, Robert Barnwell Rhett. In *The Liberator* for that date he published in the Refuge of Oppression extracts from a secessionist speech of Rhett's. He said that Rhett, like the frog trying to swell himself into the size of an ox, was trying desperately to fill the place of Calhoun. His speech was incendiary and full of incentive for bloody insurrection in South Carolina, for that state with its majority of slave population was one of the weakest and poorest in the nation and therefore utterly dependent on the Union for its very existence. Indeed, Garrison was confident that if South Carolina seceded for a single day, insurrection of her slave population would be inevitable. When in his speech Rhett posed as a champion of liberty, linking himself with the revolutionists of 1776, Garrison called it the raving of a madman. At this time Garrison did not comment on the fact that both he and Rhett were advocating disunion, although he was later to be embarrassed by the similarity of their views.

On 29 October there occurred an event that interested Garrison far more than the antics of any fanatical Southerner. George Thompson returned to the United States for a visit.[13] Garrison was overjoyed that his old British friend seemed as young and energetic as he had sixteen years before, and he resolved that this should be a very different visit from the earlier one. Unfortunately, no amount of favorable publicity in *The Liberator* could quell the hostility that broke up the reception meeting at Faneuil Hall in Boston,[14] though later meetings, especially one in January on the twentieth anniversary of the founding of *The Liberator,* were all that could have been desired.

At the January meeting Garrison was the guest of honor and Edmund Quincy was in the chair. After dinner Quincy in a gay and witty speech proposed honor to *The Liberator*—both the paper and the man. Garrison replied with the sentiments that had become a cliché for him: that a man who starts any great reform is hated at first and loved later, whereas in fact both blame and praise are inappropriate, for he had merely done his duty to God and to his fellow man. Then came the speech of George Thompson, who eulogized Garrison, developing the theme suggested by Garrison's most famous words, "I am in earnest. I will not equivocate." At the close of his speech he presented Garrison with a gold watch as a gift from his friends. Garrison said that he was as surprised by the gift as he would have been by "the falling of the stars from the heavens." He only wished that he had a gold watch to present to each member of the audience.

Then characteristically Garrison launched into a discussion of religion and extraneous reform, claiming—one fears, with a touch of the disingenuous—that he had never discriminated against anyone for his religious or other nonabolitionist views. Before he finished, Garrison had an opportunity to commend Thompson once more. He said that Thompson had praised him for his three English missions, but that actually his success was owing largely to Thompson's support. The meeting proved the perfect vehicle to express the admiration which the two men felt for each other.

Thompson's visit continued pleasant for the most part, and he was ultimately honored at a farewell soirée—over a thousand plates—which provided Garrison with three pages of panegyric in *The Liberator* for 27 June 1851.

Another champion of freedom greatly admired by Garrison, though he could not approve his use of armed force, was Louis Kossuth, hero of the Hungarian revolution. In the summer of 1849, when the outcome of that valiant attempt to break away from the Austrian empire was still in doubt, Garrison had editorialized on Kossuth as the Washington of his country, a man valorous and eloquent, whose electric appeals inspired his countrymen to do the impossible.[15]

In *The Liberator* for 21 November 1851 Garrison announced that the exiled Kossuth was about to come to the United States, but he expressed his apprehension "for his fidelity to the cause of freedom in this country." Soon after Kossuth landed, it was apparent that Garrison's fears had not been misfounded, for the Hungarian patriot made it quite plain that his mission was on behalf of Hungarian and European liberty and that he would maintain a strict policy of neutrality in regard to domestic affairs. In *The Liberator* for 19 December Garrison lamented that Kossuth was evidently determined to remain "deaf, dumb, and blind" in regard to American slavery.

This was precisely the kind of issue Garrison loved to feature. In the same issue of his paper in which he announced the downfall of Kossuth he reprinted a long poem on the Hungarian patriot, which he had written on his own birthday the year before and which appeared in the *Liberty Bell* for 1852. The poem, urging Kossuth to be courageous and declare himself properly on the slavery issue, appeared ironic in its current context.

Then in February of 1852 he published as the official pronouncement of the American Anti-Slavery Society his one hundred and twelve page *Letter to Louis Kossuth* (next to the *Thoughts on African Colonization* the most elaborate work he was to produce). Garrison's method in this pamphlet is so characteristic as to be worth describing. First, he castigates Kossuth in general terms for his silence on the slavery issue:

"Deplorable as it is, the relation of your countrymen to the Austrian government is incomparably more hopeful, a million times less appalling, than that of our slave population to the American government." He accuses him of collecting money for the Hungarian cause by dishonest means, by allying himself with tyrants. He accuses him of being "doubly criminal" because he has also eulogized the Union, the Constitution, and the various free and humane institutions of this country. Lest this general attack have insufficient effect, he devotes seven double-column pages of small type to listing on the left a series of quotations concerning freedom and liberty from Kossuth's speeches and on the right some statements of fact concerning the slave systems. He then shames Kossuth with nearly twelve closely printed pages of quotations regarding slavery from the speeches of another foreign patriot, the Irish Daniel O'Connell. The remaining section of the pamphlet—about eighty pages—consists of a series of disconnected facts, letters, poems, and reprints concerning freedom and slavery from every conceivable source, the whole ending climactically with Garrison's latest rather insipid poem on Kossuth.

This was still not the end of the Kossuth case. There were more speeches, more editorials, more attacks, until the Hungarian, engulfed by a web of contradictory charges, felt so sorry for himself that he was hardly more dignified than Garrison.

Garrison's procedure in the Kossuth case was typical of his tendency to use his heaviest artillery to demolish a butterfly. As we have observed before, he operated most energetically on the personal level. A *cause célèbre,* a personal controversy, such as the one with Mathew or with Kossuth, could absorb his attention and inspire an intensity of response worthy of a more critical issue.

Garrison's personal ire was aroused again in March of 1852 when he read an editorial in the Washington *Union* that accused him and Rhett of being allies, since they both advocated dissolution of the Union. "Extremes meet. The disunionists of the North and of the South train in the same company, and are marching to effect the same object." The solution, the editorial suggested, is to take the middle course. But, said Garrison, though extremes may meet, this does not mean that they coalesce or that they are ever identical. How can one assume a middle course between Christ and Belial, between liberty and slavery, between right and wrong? "We affirm slavery to be morally wrong, the acme of human transgression, an utter violation of inalienable rights; and, therefore, we are morally precluded from treating it as a question of personal accommodation, circumstantial toleration, or necessary endurance." In fact, Garrison assured his readers, the South Carolinian and he resembled each other not in the slightest. The one advocated disunion because he thought it would provide greater security to the slave system; the other professed it because the Constitution on which the Union was based protected slavery. Rhett, moreover, willingly occupied a seat in the United States Senate at the same time that he advocated disunion, whereas Garrison stood outside of the government, repudiating the elective franchise and all allegiance to the Union. "The disunionism of the South is 'as empty as the whistling wind.' That of the North is based upon absolute justice, the claims of suffering humanity, unchanging principle, and a deep religious sentiment. . . . The spirit which animates it is identical with that which has characterized every apostolic and martyr movement since the reformation of a fallen world began." [16]

On 20 March, the week following the editorial on Rhett, Harriet Beecher Stowe's *Uncle Tom's Cabin* was published in book form (it had the year before been serialized in the *National Era*). On the 26th Garrison reviewed it in *The Liberator*. He spoke first of the "thrilling interest" already created by its serial publication. He praised Mrs. Stowe's "rare descriptive powers," her familiarity with the slave system, her "uncommon moral and philosophical acumen, the facility with which she expressed "feelings and emotions of the strongest character." He admitted that her vivid narrative made his eyes water and his nerves tremble. He anticipated that *Uncle Tom's Cabin* would "awaken the strongest compassion for the oppressed and the utmost abhorrence of the system which grinds them to dust."

The book appealed to Garrison for another reason. The character of Uncle Tom, which he thought "sketched with great power and rare religious perception . . . triumphantly exemplifies the nature, tendency and results of CHRISTIAN NON-RESISTANCE." [17] Garrison's only serious objection to the book was that "towards its conclusion, [it] contains some objectionable sentiments respecting African colonization."

Although their association was never close, Garrison and Mrs. Stowe met on a number of occasions and even exchanged letters.[18] At their first meeting Mrs. Stowe asked the question which was always uppermost in her mind in regard to the abolitionist, "Are you a Christian?" [19] She considered his paper, which she read regularly, of great value for "its frankness, fearlessness, truthfulness, and independence." What she feared was "that it will take from poor Uncle Tom his Bible, and give him nothing in its place." [20]

Approximately a year before the book publication of *Uncle Tom's Cabin*, Charles Sumner was elected to the Senate for the first time. Garrison had followed Sumner's distinguished career as lawyer and lecturer since his first great speech in Boston on the Fourth of July, 1845. He had featured many of his speeches in *The Liberator* and had praised his liberal point of view in regard to slavery and the Negro. He was especially pleased at the brilliance of his argument before the Massachusetts Supreme Court on behalf of a colored child who had been obliged to attend a segregated public school in Boston. Garrison also approved of his stand in regard to the Mexican War.[21]

Garrison expected Sumner to speak out in the Senate against slavery and the Fugitive Slave Law soon after his election. But weeks and months passed; and he remained silent, though he spoke on other issues. By April Garrison, who had been known before to change his opinion of a man, berated Sumner in an editorial entitled "Inquiry after a 'Back-Bone.'" Following his usual formula for such matters he admitted: "It is a most unpleasant task to rebuke . . . ; yet sometimes this becomes an indispensable duty, to avoid the appearance of partiality, and to be true to principle." Garrison complained that Sumner had been in Washington more than four months but, whereas many other senators had committed themselves, Sumner "has yet to utter his first word of disapproval of slavery in general, or the Fugitive Slave Law in particular!" Then, giving him the same treatment he had Kossuth, Garrison quoted a long antislavery passage from one of Sumner's earlier speeches.[22]

Garrison's opposition to Sumner was not limited to editorializing in *The Liberator*. In April at the annual meeting of the New York City Anti-Slavery Society he introduced a resolution condemning Sumner's silence in the Senate as contrary to his professions. Although opposed by both Wendell Phillips and William I. Bowditch, the resolution passed. Bowditch felt sufficiently concerned to write Sumner, expressing his confidence in him as an abolitionist and characterizing Garrison as follows: "Much as I honor and love him, Mr. Garrison's *passion* sometimes, seems to be to attack single individuals rather than the system of slavery,— and it frequently happens that his attacks fall on those who sympathize very fully, tho not entirely with his views." [23]

By August, Sumner having remained silent for another four months, Garrison was convinced that "he has clearly demonstrated his unfitness to take upon himself the championship of the antislavery cause in the American Senate." A month later, after Sumner had spoken in support of his motion to repeal the Fugitive Slave Law—a speech many thought fearless and radical—Garrison reprinted the speech with grudging praise, regretting that Sumner had failed to grapple with the crucial issue of "the entire and immediate abolition of slavery." [24]

On 30 May 1854 the Kansas-Nebraska Act was passed, nullifying the Missouri Compromise of 1820 and opening up the territory of Kansas and Nebraska to settlement on the basis of popular sovereignty, so that local settlers could determine whether the territory were to be slave or free.

The following Fourth of July Garrison spoke at Framingham, Massachusetts. The platform was appropriately decorated. There was an insignia of Virginia hung with ribbons of triumph; there was the motto "Redeem Massachusetts" "hung with the crepe of servitude, while above them were two white flags, bearing the names of 'Nebraska' and 'Kansas.' The American flag hung above the platform, Union down, draped in black."

After the preliminary business, Garrison rose to speak. He started with his usual Independence Day theme of the ironic contrast between the profession of the Declaration of Independence and the practice of slavery, though his rhetorical balance seemed more measured, his pace more compelling than usual. "The history of mankind," he began, "is a record of the saddest mistakes, the wildest aberrations, the most melancholy inconsistencies, the bloodiest crimes." He lamented that American greed had become insatiable, American rapacity boundless, injustice profligate, that "we have degenerated in regard to our reverence for the higher law of God, for what is morally obligatory, for the cause of liberty." The government, he regretted, was in the control of "party demagogues . . . who are themselves the tools and vassals of the Slave Power." [25] Then he produced a copy of the Fugitive Slave Law and, holding it up before the audience, named the document. Striking a match, he lighted the paper and watched silently as it burned to ashes. After that he burned several other documents. Finally, holding up the United States Constitution he pronounced it the source of all atrocities—"a covenant with death, and an agreement with hell." With gusto he applied the torch, and the Constitution blazed with a bright flame. "So perish all compromises with tyranny!" pronounced Garrison. "And let all the people say, Amen!" A tremendous shout filled the countryside. "Amen!" "Amen!" The hisses were hardly perceptible. It remained to sing a hymn and to partake of refreshments.[26]

CHAPTER XIX

———•·•———

Violence and Forbearance

For many years nonresistance and its corollary disunionism had been Garrison's most compelling ideas. Nonresistance was a principle which he maintained with stern persistence in spite of his own instinctive belligerence as a publicist. In fact, being a nonresistant had enabled him to face the world with the serenity of a martyr, even though he was almost constantly engaged in the most violent controversy. Because he was in the last analysis a nonresistant, he felt that he could remain aloof and untarnished no matter how bitter his own or another's invective. Thus, the doctrine of nonresistance had provided Garrison with the central rationalization of his life. National events in the later 1850's, however, were to challenge Garrison's basic principle with such intensity that he was to become in effect the belligerent rather than the nonresistant.

By the mid-fifties an increasing number of men in both North and South were resorting to force to achieve their ends. Since the Kansas-Nebraska Act had provided that popular sovereignty was to decide the status of slavery in Kansas, Northerners and Southerners vied with each other to settle there first. Missourians swarmed across the border. Yankee migrations were subsidized in the North, and free-soil settlers were armed with Sharp's rifles or "Beecher's Bibles" as they were called after the famous clergyman. Missourians blockaded the Missouri River and in May 1856 sacked the first Northern settlement at Lawrence. John Brown retaliated with the Pottawatamie massacre.

In the same month a violent act was perpetrated even on the floor of the United States Senate. On the 19th Charles Sumner had won Garrison's complete respect—if not envy, for his abusive invective was worthy of the abolitionist himself—by his "Crime Against Kansas" speech. Two days later Congressman Preston S. Brooks, nephew of South Carolina Senator Andrew Pickens Butler, whom Sumner had attacked in his speech as a Don Quixote courting the harlot Slavery, rushed into the Senate chamber, found Sumner at his seat, and beat him over the head so viciously that Sumner was incapacitated for three and a half years. Sumner lying bleeding on the Senate floor was a potent image for publicity in *The Liberator*. During the summer and into the fall Garrison manufactured eulogy for the stricken hero.[1]

Although his sympathies were entirely with the free-soil settlers in Kansas, it was difficult for Garrison to stomach their use of force, even to kill the Missouri bandits. He said in February 1856 that if force were ever justified, it was in Kansas. "But we insist on the inviolability of human life; on the duty of returning good for evil, at whatever hazard; on the immense superiority of the Martyr spirit to that of armed resistance." [2] By March he was sufficiently sympathetic with the free-soil settlers to admit that they "have shown rare circumspection and great forbearance; and, from a 'patriotic' stand-point, they deserve to be ranked with the men of '76."

But still the old nonresistant was troubled. He could not help feeling that the Northern settlers were suffering "in consequence of their own sanguinary code. . . . They unanimously reject the doctrine of non-resistance as fanatical. . . . They believe that the end sanctifies the means. . . . Is it not plain, that the cure for all this is to be found in a recognition of the sacredness of human life, from which principle no possible violence or wrong can flow, but to the rejection of which every kind of outrage may be unerringly traced?" After all, who would be safe, he questioned in one of his lighter moments, if we were convinced it was right to shoot human beings? Where would the carnage begin? With the President and his cabinet—perhaps—for they would certainly have to be disposed of—as would hordes of doctors, judges, editors (especially of New York papers). There was such a multitude of

Henry C. Wright, about 1847   *Edmund Quincy, about 1868*

Garrison, George Thompson, and Wendell Phillips, 1852

Banners used in antislavery celebrations

"conspirators against the liberty, peace, happiness and safety of the republic," that where would one begin and where stop? [3]

By July, struggling to remain aloof from the violent events in Kansas, Garrison shifted the emphasis of his argument from non-resistance to disunion:

To me, the path is plain. Today, I disown the American flag as the symbol of unequalled hypocrisy and transcendent oppression. . . . To-day, I renew my accusation against the American Constitution, that it is 'a covenant with death and an agreement with hell,' which ought to be annulled now and forever. To-day, I pronounce the American Union a league of despotism, to perpetuate which is a crime against our common humanity, and sin against God. To-day, I affirm the 'Higher Law' to be the rightful and paramount law of the land, to the subversion of every statute, agreement and compromise, inimical to human freedom. To-day, I stand outside of this tyrannical government, a seceder on principle, a revolutionist with Hancock, and Otis, and Warren, but upon a broader platform, with a loftier spirit, with better weapons, and for a nobler object.

Then pronouncing the magical incantation, he concluded that there was only one solution: *"The North must separate from the South,* and organize her own institutions on a sure basis." [4]

For Garrison the supreme test of nonresistance principles came following Brown's raid on Harper's Ferry in October 1859. He and Brown had come into contact no more than twice before the raid—once at Theodore Parker's house one Sunday evening in January 1857, where Brown had impressed Garrison as "a tall, spare, farmer-like man, with head disproportionately small, and that inflexible mouth which as yet no beard concealed." As one might have expected, the two men talked about violence and nonresistance, Brown citing the Old Testament, and Garrison the New. They may have seen each other also at the New-England Anti-Slavery Convention in Boston in May 1859, after which Brown was heard to say: "These men are all talk; what is needed is action—action!" [5]

On 28 October, twelve days after the raid, Garrison wrote his first editorial on Brown, referring to his dramatic action as "well-intended but sadly misguided." He testified to Brown's honesty, truthfulness, and bravery; and he accepted the sincerity of Brown's conviction that he was "raised up by God to deliver the oppressed in this country, in the way he has chosen, as did Moses in relation to the deliverance of the captive Israelites." He associated him with the heroes of the Revolution, none of whom could have answered the question put to Brown by Senator Mason and others "more wisely, more impressively, more courageously, or with greater moral dignity." Finally, with an exuberance that fore-shadowed his later support of the war, Garrison prophesied that the execution of Brown and his followers "will be sowing seed broadcast for a harvest retribution. Their blood will cry trumpet-tongued from the ground, and that cry will be responded to by tens of thousands in a manner that shall cause the knees of the Southern slave-mongers to smite together as did those of Balshazzar of old!" [6]

The issues of *The Liberator* for the rest of the year overflowed with material concerning John Brown. Garrison's own fullest state-ment on the man and his action was reserved for a speech de-livered at Tremont Temple on the day of Brown's execution, 2 December.[7] He opened belligerently with the statement that be-tween Virginia and himself there is an " 'irrepressible conflict,' . . . and I am for carrying it on until it is finished in victory or death." He described Brown as a Cromwellian of Puritan stock, a believer in God—no infidel, though his enemies wished he were —who also believed in the efficacy of dry powder. He commended Brown's restraint at Harper's Ferry, indicating that his raid might have been successful if he had been less humane with his prisoners. He accepted readily Brown's assertion that his men were armed merely for defensive purposes and that they had furnished the freed slaves with arms only to protect them in their exodus from Virginia. Brown's trial he considered "an awful mockery, before heaven and earth! . . . It was the trial of the lamb by the wolf— nothing less." "Was John Brown justified in his attempt? Yes, if Washington was in his; if Warren and Hancock were in theirs. If men are justified in striking a blow for freedom, when the ques-tion is one of a three penny tax on tea, then, I say, they are a thousand times more justified, when it is to save fathers, mothers, wives and children from the slave-coffle and the auction-block, and to restore to them their God-given rights." Judged by the Ameri-can standard, surely Brown was justified.

In this speech Garrison virtually ignored the nonresistance principles which had for so many years been the gyroscope of his thinking. Only in a single paragraph tucked away in the middle of his speech did Garrison grapple with his conscience. He admitted that as a nonresistant, he believed "in the inviolability of human life, under all circumstances." If possible, he would have disarmed John Brown, but he would also have disarmed "every slaveholder and tyrant in the world." He asked the audience how many nonresistants were present, but only one admitted such principles. "Nevertheless, I am a non-resistant, and I not only desire, but have labored unremittingly to effect the peaceful abolition of slavery, by an appeal to the reason and conscience of the slaveholder; yet, as a peace man—an 'ultra peace man—I am prepared to say, 'Success to every slave insurrection at the South, and in every slave country.' . . . And I do not see how I compromise or stain my peace profession in making that declaration." He went on to say that he was thankful when men believing in the use of "carnal weapons are so far advanced that they will take those weapons out of the scale of despotism, and throw them into the scale of freedom. . . . Give me, as a non-resistant, Bunker Hill, and Lexington, and Concord, rather than the cowardice and servility of a Southern slave plantation." Garrison even rationalized that the use of arms for freedom rather than despotism "is an indication of progress, and a positive moral growth; it is one way to get up to the sublime platform of non-resistance; and it is God's method of dealing retribution upon the head of the tyrant."

Although Garrison might abhor violence, at least in principle and for himself, he was sufficiently passive to wish things done for him as long as he was not implicated in the doing. Perhaps it could be said that John Brown as an activist was making the kind of attack on slavery which Garrison himself unconsciously would like to have made, but which his previously proclaimed principles and his passivity prevented. Consequently, he could rationalize his support of John Brown [8] in much the same way that he had explained his support of disunion.

The great champion of the Union, Abraham Lincoln, was first referred to in *The Liberator* in the summer of 1860. The initial pronouncement was a hostile editorial by Wendell Phillips, entitled "Abraham Lincoln, the Slave-Hound of Illinois," in which an attempt was made "to gibbet a Northern hound . . . side by side with the infamous Mason of Virginia." Phillips had dug up in the Congressional records the fact that Lincoln had in 1849 sponsored a fugitive slave law for the District of Columbia. But he failed to mention that at the same time Lincoln was proposing a law to abolish slavery in the same area. Such an abolition proposal could hardly have passed without some provision for protecting the interests of the slaveholders in surrounding states.

On the other hand, Garrison's early attitude toward Lincoln was neutral. He referred to him in a letter in August 1860, assuming that Lincoln would be elected but regretting that he would probably "do nothing to offend the South." [9] He referred to him first in *The Liberator* just before the election, proclaiming that "standing aloof from all political parties acting under the American Constitution, because in its pro-slavery compromises it is 'a covenant wth death and an agreement with hell,' we reiterate the cry, 'NO UNION WITH SLAVEHOLDERS.' " [10]

In spite of his indifference to Lincoln, Garrison could not, after the election, disguise his satisfaction with the Republican victory. The Southern reaction delighted him: "The brutal dastards and blood-minded tyrants, who have so long ruled the country with impunity, are now furiously foaming at the mouth, gnawing their tongues for pain, indulging in the most horrid blasphemies, uttering the wildest threats and avowing the most treasonable designs. . . . They rave just as fiercely as though he were another John Brown, armed for Southern invasion and universal emancipation!" And yet, Garrison pointed out, Lincoln is a conservative on every critical issue.[11]

On the first anniversary of John Brown's death a meeting was held in Boston's Tremont Temple. But a large crowd of well-dressed men, some of whom could be recognized as State Street merchants—like the mob of 1835 "gentlemen of property and standing," *The Liberator* said—were determined to halt the meeting. There was a great tapping of canes and stomping of feet and kicking of seats. There were cheers for Tennessee, for Virginia, for everything Southern. Again and again there were three cheers for Bell and Everett, who were candidates for President and Vice President on the Constitutional Union ticket, latest incarnation of the old Whig party. Two mob chairmen took over the meeting. They were thoroughly heckled by Frederick Douglass and Stephen S. Foster, but the purpose of the meeting, to honor John Brown, went largely unfulfilled.[12]

Within a month following Lincoln's election South Carolina seceded from the Union. A few days later Garrison rejoiced that "all Union-saving efforts are simply idiotic. At last, 'The covenant with death' is annulled . . . —at least, by the action of South Carolina, and, ere long, by all the slaveholding States, for their doom is one. . . . Hail the approaching jubilee, ye millions who are wearing the galling chains of slavery; for, assuredly, the day of your redemption draws nigh, bringing liberty to you, and salvation to the whole land!" [13]

Inevitably, some of Garrison's critics again suggested that there was no difference between the disunion position of the abolitionists and the secession of the Southern states. By April, after the fall of Fort Sumter and the secession of several more states, Garrison was busy answering this charge. On the 19th he denied categorically that there was any analogy between the two positions: "The Parties stand at antipodes in their ideas of government, moral obligation, human relationship, individual or 'State sovereignty.' " [14] The distinction between the two could be explained in constitutional and moral terms. The Southern states were claiming the right to secede from the Union because it had failed or was failing to protect their property rights and thus to promote the general welfare for which the Constitution was instituted. On the other hand, there was in existence no constitutional reason for secession, because the Constitution did not recognize any such right. Further, the Constitution specifically protected the very rights which the South would assert, since it took cognizance of slavery. The only just reason, therefore, for breaking the Union would be a revolutionary one, by appeal to the Declaration of Independence. But, "the South has rent the Union asunder without being able to show a bruise or a scratch, or an outrage of any kind. She may not, therefore, take refuge in the example of our revolutionary fathers, nor quote in her defense the doctrines laid down by them in the Declaration of Independence." As a result, the actions of the South in confiscating federal property, in bombarding and capturing Fort Sumter, in beginning a cruel civil war, in abrogating freedom of speech and press, constituted most outrageous offenses. In fact, the Southern states were "the most lawless, desperate, barbarous, mobocratic, tyrannical and profligate body of wrongdoers, to be found in the world."

Northern abolitionists were to be otherwise judged. They urged peaceful disunion through the right of revolution following the dictates of the Declaration of Independence. They "are justified in all that they demand, by every principle of justice, every claim of humanity, every law of God, by the patriotism of 1776 and the Christianity of the first century." [15] In short, the abolitionist appeal for disunion "is based upon the eternal fitness of things, and animated by a noble, disinterested, and philanthropic spirit," whereas the secession of the South "is the concentration of all diabolism." [16]

In the meantime, Lincoln had been inaugurated. Garrison was pleased with his dignity and self-respect and with his manly bearing. He reprinted the Inaugural Address in *The Liberator* with favorable comments. Although he thought the speech marked with moderation toward the secessionists, he had to concede that Lincoln had "met the trying emergency with rare self-possession and equanimity." He was impressed with Lincoln's style, said that he was "no word-monger," that he avoided circumlocution, and that he was able to compress into a sentence what others would require paragraphs to express.[17]

At the time of the inauguration Garrison was insisting that civil war was unnecessary, and that there should be a peaceful separation between the free and the slave states. Less than two months later, aware that "the country is aflame," he shouted the battle cry with an enthusiasm hardly befitting the nonresistant. He reported an uprising in every city and hamlet of the North that seemed "like a general resurrection from the dead." Fife and drum corps were recruiting by the thousands. "So mighty and irresistible is the popular feeling since the capture of Fort Sumter [that the effect] is total, wonderful, indescribable—uniting the most discordant, and reconciling the most estranged." [18]

In spite of his willingness to modify and even compromise his nonresistance principles, it is difficult to explain Garrison's sudden shift from proponent of disunion to enthusiastic supporter of a war to preserve the Union. It may be that pressure had been exerted by a number of staunch Republicans with whom he had been on good terms during the early months of 1861. Men like Senators Charles Sumner and Henry Wilson, like Governor John Albion Andrew, a supporter of John Brown who had been re-elected on the same ticket that elected Lincoln, like Dr. Samuel Gridley Howe, founder of the Perkins Institution for the Blind and husband of Julia Ward Howe, may have flattered and per-suaded, exerting no little influence on Garrison during this crucial period in his career.[19] More significant than any such pressure, however, may have been the force of Garrison's own conscience. It would seem that he really had become convinced that a popular war could effect quickly and with a minimum loss of life the total extirpation of slavery, a goal which his method of moral suasion had been unable to attain in thirty years. If the war could bring about such a result, it would seem that almost any principle ex-cept that of freedom could be justifiably compromised. Perhaps in the last analysis, Garrison was acute enough to realize that there were really only two choices—the North or the South. The latter was unthinkable and support of the North was easier to rationalize than it might have been because the South had fired the first shot.

As the weeks passed, Garrison urged that slavery, the real cause of the war, must not be overlooked in the enthusiasm to support the government and preserve the Union. It was evident, he thought, that with the preponderant strength of the North in population and resources, as well as in energy and courage, the war could not last long. However, the outcome must not be the subjugation of the South, but the abolition of slavery. Such a result would make the war more glorious in the history of our country than the Revolution itself.[20] Garrison also discussed the relation-ship of the abolitionists to the war, pointing out that the number of nonresistants among the group was small and that even they—thinking specifically of himself and what John Brown had taught him—must not blench at the violence, though it led (as seemed probable) to insurrection of the slaves. If the slaves do revolt, all abolitionists, Garrison insisted, must give them their sympathies just as they give them now to the government. Garrison's optimism flared up like a torch. All the signs told him "that a death-blow has been given to the accursed slave system" and the way "opened for a glorious redemption. Complexional prejudice shall . . . swiftly disappear, injurious distinctions cease, and peace and good will every where reign." [21]

Garrison's ebullient optimism during the first years of the war betrayed his eagerness for the successful termination of his great crusade to free the slave and his inability to plan logically for the future. All during his life, or at least up to the end of the war, he had a naïve confidence that once the immediate goal had been attained, all subordinate problems would automatically be solved. Free the slave, and he will immediately be the equal of other American citizens!

During 1861 Garrison was busy writing his friends and associates in the cause, advising caution and inaction, urging them to "stand still, and see the salvation of God," saying that they must not criticize Lincoln and the Republican party, for they are fighting the forces of evil. "We need great circumspection and consummate wisdom in regard to what we say and do, under these unparalleled circumstances. We are rather, for the time being, to note the events transpiring, than seek to control them. There must be no needless turning of popular violence upon ourselves, by any false step of our own." [22] In short, "let us *all* stand aside, when the North is rushing like a tornado in the right direction." [23] He even advised the postponement of the annual meeting of the American Anti-Slavery Society; "for the present, at least, the abolitionists are justified in suspending their usual operations." [24]

But *sub rosa* Garrison and his abolitionists were busy planning a campaign to influence public opinion. There were consultations in Boston, meetings in the office of Dr. Samuel Gridley Howe and elsewhere. Garrison and his clique were contemplating "a wide use of the newspaper press in the publication of able and telling articles, simultaneously, printed on slips, and sent privately for insertion—all bearing upon the extinction of slavery by the exercise of the war power" (ironically, that power of the federal government which had made Garrison a no-government man).[25]

However, Lincoln's reluctance to use his war power to exterminate slavery caused Garrison's view of the President to shift. As the summer of 1862 passed into autumn and winter, Garrison became restless and pessimistic. In *The Liberator* of 20 September he branded Lincoln's virtual annulment of General Frémont's emancipation of the slaves in Missouri as "a serious dereliction of duty. Either the government must abolish slavery, or the independence of the Southern Confederacy must be recognized." Resenting Lincoln's Message to Congress in December because it had no reference to slavery, he pronounced it "very feeble and rambling" —"ridiculous as a State paper, which ought to be high-toned, vigorous, comprehensive, and historically important." [26] In a letter to Oliver Johnson he was more blunt: "What a wishy-washy message from the President! It is more and more evident that he is a man of very small calibre, and had better be at his old business of splitting rails than at the head of a government like ours, especially in such a crisis." Garrison regretted that Lincoln was no abolitionist and had no sympathy for the slaves.[27] He pronounced the President's scheme for colonizing the colored population on some foreign territory absurd: "Lincoln may colonize himself if he choose, but it is an impertinent act, on his part to propose the getting rid of those who are as good as himself." [28] He was unenthusiastic about the President's Message to Congress in March for its recommendation of gradual rather than immediate emancipation and for its style, which he considered inappropriate for an official document. "The Cabinet should help the President to mend his phraseology." [29] It is puzzling that Garrison no longer had an ear for Lincoln's laconic style.

Another evidence that abolition of slavery was paramount to Garrison is the fact that toward the end of 1861 he had quietly changed the superscription at the head of the right-hand column of the first page of his paper, from "The United States Constitution is 'a covenant with death, and an agreement with hell' " to "Proclaim Liberty throughout all the land, to all the inhabitants thereof." In almost no time the *Journal of Commerce,* Garrison's abomination among New York papers, called *The Liberator* to task for denying "its old faith." In a full-dress reply, entitled "A Change of Position, but not of Principle," Garrison explained that before the rebellion the South had recognized the authority of the Constitution and sought its protection for slavery. But now that the South had withdrawn from the Union and organized a separate government, she could no longer seek protection for slavery under the Constitution. Consequently, "it is not only the right, but plainly the solemn duty and exalted privilege of the

Government, UNDER THE WAR POWER, in this terrible emergency, as a matter of self-preservation, to seek the utter suppression of the rebellion through the abolition of slavery, its murderous cause." Such being the case, it would hardly have been proper for the paper to have continued its old motto at the same time that it was denouncing "the Government for not proclaiming emancipation." [30] In concluding the same argument in a subsequent speech, Garrison quotes Shakespeare's Benedick as saying, "When I said I would die a bachelor, I did not think I would live to get married." [31] "And when I said I would not sustain the Constitution, because it was 'a covenant with death and an agreement with hell,' *I had no idea that* I would live to see death and hell secede." [32]

On 14 January 1862 Garrison was to speak at Cooper Union in New York on the topic "The Abolitionists and their Relations to the War." The Sunday before his lecture Henry Ward Beecher announced from his pulpit:

It seems a little unmanly for me to speak in his [Garrison's] favor now, when all the community are beginning to have some sense of that heroism which has sustained him against the most violent public opinion, in the Church and out of the Church, in the State and out of the State, for more than thirty years. . . . This man has stood fearless and faithful amid universal defections for many years; but the days are soon coming when men will mention his name only with praise.[33]

Shortly before Garrison appeared in the auditorium, a woman rose from one of the seats on the platform and placed a bouquet of flowers and a wreath of ivy beside the speaker's desk. The audience burst into spontaneous applause. At eight o'clock Garrison was escorted to the platform by Theodore Tilton, capable young managing editor of *The Independent,* who introduced him to the large audience as "a genuine Yankee"—he could hardly have chosen a description which Garrison would have liked better. There was a long round of applause. Garrison said that he knew of no reason for such response other "than that I am an original uncompromising, irrepressible, out-and-out, unmistakeable, Garrison Abolitionist." The house shook with approval. Garrison exulted in the instantaneous rapport with a sympathetic audience.

Here was the adulation he had feared and longed for. He could say no wrong as far as the audience was concerned, and for many minutes of talk he said very little. Cheers followed one pious exhortation after another.

Finally Garrison approached the topic of his speech. What of the abolitionists today? They are, Garrison attested, the most loyal men in the country—more loyal even than Lincoln, who, Garrison now thought, lacked backbone and was disposed "to make some compromise with slavery." But even though Lincoln may have been "nearer Jeff. Davis than I am," we are "both so bad that I suppose if we should go amicably together down South, we never should come back again." The audience laughed and cheered. Continuing more seriously, Garrison suggested that the loyal abolitionists had the great responsibility to educate the country to the tremendous importance of emancipation, the solution to all ills. Never before, he said, has a government had the opportunity to accomplish such philanthropy and justice. "Emancipation is to destroy nothing but evil; it is to establish good, it is to transform human beings from things into men; it is to make freedom, and education, and invention, and enterprise, and prosperity, and peace, and a true Union possible and sure. . . . Blow the trumpet of jubilee." Emancipation, Garrison was convinced, would even solve military problems. With the slaves freed and protected by the government, there would be little need even for a federal army in the South; the freedmen would "take care of" their rebel masters, and soon the rebellion would collapse.[34]

However, during the winter of 1861–1862 Garrison was making a more significant contribution to his country than the pious and often illogical utterances in his speeches and editorials. He was writing letters to George Thompson regarding the British misunderstanding of the American Civil War. Garrison found it difficult to understand why so many Britons sympathized with the South, thinking that the North had no more right to control the destiny of the South than Germany had to control Austria. But Garrison pointed out in three open letters to Thompson [35] the close relationship between the antislavery cause and the war and did his best to persuade British abolitionists that they must support the antislavery North rather than the slaveholding South. Reports in *The Liberator* of Thompson's activities make it clear not only that he agreed with his American friend, but also that he spoke for the Northern cause on many occasions.[36]

In the spring of 1862 Garrison received a letter from a charming, high-spirited, striking-looking, nineteen-year-old Philadelphia girl named Anna E. Dickinson, asking to trespass on the offer of help which he had extended when they met the preceding fall. In December she had been discharged from the Philadelphia Mint for accusing General McClellan of treason. Since that time she had given several successful lectures on woman's rights and the national crisis. She asked Garrison to schedule speaking engagements in New England for her. He arranged that she should speak first on 28 April, but she arrived in Boston ahead of schedule and, with almost no notice, substituted at another meeting for Wendell Phillips, who was ill. There were four to five thousand people in the audience, and the young lady charmed them all. Garrison was "overrun with thanks" for finding her.

Anna Dickinson's letters, in particular one to her sister, provide an interesting glimpse of the Garrison family at the time. She told how Garrison treated her "like a father," and how the family as a whole had done everything to make her stay pleasant. She agreed with Wendell Phillips that his twenty-one-year-old namesake was the handsomest and most intelligent of the children, though she did not find him "especially lovable." Willie, twenty-four, witty, gifted, "splendid . . . a specimen, of simple, natural, dignified,—attractive manhood," was her favorite. She was almost inclined to fall in love with him. The eldest, twenty-six-year-old George she found kind but reserved, "the 'most stillest' young gentleman I know." Fanny, seventeen, she considered "handsome, talented & cultivated, . . . simple & unpretending, . . . full of life." The youngest, Frankie, thirteen, was a special pet, "the beauty and genius of the family," and very lovable. Mrs. Garrison, who seemed to interest her less than the others, she described simply as "motherly." [37]

During the spring and summer of 1862 Garrison continued to press for emancipation and to reprimand leaders in the government, especially systematic General McClellan, for dilatory tactics. He was particularly upset when Lincoln vetoed General Hunter's emancipation order. David Hunter, who had been in command of

the Department of the South, had on 9 May pr⌐
tion of all slaves in Georgia, South Carolina,
action, though pleasing to the abolitionists, had c⌐
sternation in the border states and in Congress. A
Lincoln annulled Hunter's order on the grounds that h⌐
ceeded his authority. Despite Garrison's disappointment, h⌐
cism of Lincoln was surprisingly restrained: "The President is ⌐
disposed to treat the dragon of slavery as though it was only a
wayward colt." [38]

On 22 September, following the rather indecisive federal victory
at Antietam, Lincoln issued his preliminary proclamation declaring
all slaves in states or parts of states still in rebellion on the First of
January to be free. The proclamation also emphasized that the
restoration of the Union was the objective of the war and that the
President would make further efforts to provide compensation for
slaveholders who freed—either immediately or gradually—their
slaves. Garrison's enthusiasm was grudging. The proclamation, he
said, was a "step in the right direction," but not all "the exigency
of the times and the consequent duty of the government require."
However, the proclamation, Garrison said, made the duty of all
abolitionists who are not nonresistants clear—they should stand
"loyally by the government." [39] A few days later, as the conservative
press that had been supporting Lincoln's moderate policy condemned the proclamation, Garrison's respect for that document
increased, and he felt sufficiently relieved to go off for a fortnight's
rest in Vermont.[40] He considered it "a great and historical event,
sublime in its magnitude, momentous and beneficent in its far-
reaching consequences, and eminently just and right alike to the
oppressor and the oppressed." He prophesied that it would be
sustained by the people, that it would inspire the army, and that
it would fill the South with consternation.[41]

Garrison's reaction can be contrasted with the radical Republican point of view as expressed, for instance, in *The Commonwealth,* where various weaknesses and inconsistencies are specified
and the proclamation condemned as follows: "It must have required considerable ingenuity to give two and a half millions of
human beings the priceless boon of liberty in such a cold ungrace-
ful way." [42]

Garrison reprinted the text of the proclamation frequently in

The Liberator; and, although he still felt that it was not sufficiently far-reaching, he did on occasion defend the document against attack, especially from the English.[43]

During the 1860's differences of opinion between the two leading New England abolitionists, Wendell Phillips and Garrison, were gradually becoming apparent. For years the two men had admired each other. As we know, Garrison had named one of his sons for his colleague, and Phillips in return had provided for the young Garrison's education at Harvard as well as contributed generously —both directly and indirectly—to Garrison's own support.[44] Six years younger than Garrison, Phillips had entered the cause later and had been quite willing to follow Garrison's lead on crucial issues before 1861.

After Lincoln's election, however, divergence of opinion brought increasing, though at first almost imperceptible, strain between the two abolitionists. Officially, they were congenial associates. In *The Liberator* Garrison defended Phillips against attacks by the New York *Tribune,* the Newburyport *Herald,* and the New York *Herald.*[45] He reprinted many of Phillips' speeches between 1861 and 1864. Both men were made trustees of the abolition bequest under the will of Francis Jackson.[46] But in his letters Garrison became increasingly critical of his younger colleague. He was disappointed in his speech at New Bedford in April of 1861.[47] He was slightly miffed that Phillips wanted to rewrite his own statement in regard to the abolitionists and the war for the Executive Committee of the American Anti-Slavery Society and was annoyed that he was so slow in making the revision.[48] He spoke of his lecture in the Music Hall in December 1861 as "of course, able and instructive, and well received, but not so brilliant and effective as some of his efforts."[49] He was amused and annoyed at the extent of Phillips' revisions of a New York speech, even after two columns were in type. Garrison suggested sending "his altered 'slips' to Barnum as a remarkable curiosity."[50] When the following summer Phillips told Garrison that he would not speak more than ten minutes at the August first celebration, Garrison was perturbed.[51] All of these indications of annoyance, though unimportant in themselves, were of cumulative significance.

Differences between the two men were most obvious in their reactions to Lincoln. During the early years of the administration,

Garrison tended to show greater forbearance and understanding of Lincoln than Phillips did. The proclamation both approved.[52]

In 1864, Lincoln's campaign for re-election occasioned a series of dramatic and public exchanges between Garrison and Phillips. The first occurred at the annual meeting of the Massachusetts Anti-Slavery Society, 28 January, where there was quibbling about the wording of a resolution critical of the government. Phillips introduced a resolution censuring Lincoln, whom he thought ready to make a peace "in disregard of the negro." Garrison explained that his opinion of Lincoln had changed, that he was unwilling to censure the administration so severely as Phillips wished, and that, in fact, he believed, "The re-election of Abraham Lincoln to the Presidency . . . would be the safest and wisest course." Garrison said that Lincoln accurately represented the sentiment of the people, that he had advanced as far and as fast "as the people were ready to endorse him," and that he "must be judged by his possibilities, rather than by our wishes, or by the highest abstract moral standard." But the Phillips resolution carried.

The Commonwealth, which was following the dispute closely, characterized Garrison as more optimistic because less experienced in politics than Phillips, concluding that "Mr. Phillips better indicates the true policy for abolitionists than Mr. Garrison does." [53] In other words, Phillips was closer to the radical Republican point of view than Garrison was.

Three weeks later Garrison assured his readers that he felt no ill will toward Phillips. He attested to his honesty, his adherence to principle, his great service to the cause of freedom for more than twenty-five years, and his generous self-sacrificing spirit. "We are not willing to accept of any compliment at his expense. In matters of opinion and comparison of views, we sometimes differ from him; but in an uncompromising adherence to principle, we have always seen eye to eye." [54]

However, the friction between Garrison and Phillips smoldered during the early spring, and burst into open flame again in May— first at meetings at Cooper Institute in New York, where Garrison hoped "nothing fell from my lips which was deemed personal or unkind by dear Phillips." Then came a more dramatic debate at the meeting of the American Anti-Slavery Society in New York on the 10th and 11th.

The meeting opened with a long speech by Phillips, emphasizing the terrible loss and expense of the war, speculating on the staggering efforts of future generations to pay the accumulated debt. The war, he expected, would last many months. But even after it ended, the more important ideological struggle would continue. For there was a basic conflict of ideas, of institutions, a difference as obvious as that between the eagle and the fish, which must live in different elements. It was the postwar problems that concerned him: "I contend that . . . the government has shown a willingness to let the white race and the black race, and their relations, remain, after the war, as nearly what they were before as possible." There were, he said, only two possible avenues for reconstructing the Union. Either the rebel states must be relegated to the status of territories for twenty years until the present white generation has died out, or the Negro must be given the vote at once, so that he could protect himself against the vengeful whites and himself help reform the Union.

Following Phillips' speech, though as president of the society he was the chairman of the meeting, Garrison spoke up for Lincoln, saying that no man is so much hated by the rebels and their sympathizers as he and that Lincoln is quite capable of running the machine for another four years—perhaps much longer. Repeating his favorite point, he said that the people must realize that they have not been "one hair's breadth in advance of Abraham Lincoln." Then he listed the President's accomplishments: With a precarious majority in the North he had freed three million slaves; he had expressed a desire for total abolition; he had implored the border states to abolish slavery; he had recognized the citizenship of the colored population of the country; he had armed more than 100,000 Negroes; he had recognized the independence of Liberia and Haiti; he had granted the right to search vessels in order to abolish the foreign slave trade; and he had nearly won the war. "I do not feel disposed, for one, to take this occasion, or any occasion to say anything very harshly against Abraham Lincoln." Garrison's statement brought loud and prolonged applause.

Then Garrison's old friend and supporter, George Thompson, who had returned to the United States in February 1864, spoke with considerable tact, complimenting Phillips, but reminding him that "men in public office cannot always do what they would."

He said that "there is not a name to conjure with so powerful in England as the name of Abraham Lincoln."

Stephen S. Foster spoke in defense of Phillips. He said bluntly: "Men who did not and would not vote ought to say nothing upon public affairs. He had not voted himself, neither was Mr. Garrison a voter. Ought, [not] therefore, their mouths to be closed?"

Again Garrison seemed unable to restrain himself. He went on speaking of Lincoln. "The difficulties and embarrassments of his situation have been such as no man in that position has ever experienced. He deserves charitable and generous consideration, rather than wholesale, indiscriminate censure."

On the first day of the meeting Phillips had the final word. He said that he "would have sooner severed my right hand than taken the responsibility" Garrison had of insisting that the slave's fate is certain. He said that no one hundred men together could have as much influence as Garrison "in determining the future of the government and country," and that an article of his on Lincoln in *The Liberator* was worth more than a million dollars in publicity to the administration.

However, this was not the end of the dispute. The next day Phillips, in a rather disjointed speech, led off by saying that Lincoln had acquired his international reputation by doing precisely what the American Anti-Slavery Society had been urging for a quarter of a century. Offended, as though he felt deprived of something rightfully his, he said: "I am asking you to remember how our work has been taken out of our hands." Then, directing his fire at Thompson, he started talking about England as a second-rate power. For several minutes hisses and applause dominated the meeting. Phillips explained that he meant that the *government* of England was second-rate. The war seemed a safer subject. He urged an energetic, prompt, decisive prosecution of the war—Grant's method, not McClellan's. His final sentence reverted to Lincoln: "The day of his election I shall consider the end of the Union in my day, or its reconstruction on terms worse than Disunion."

Garrison took the platform. He said that Phillips' speech had begun with brightness and ended with darkness, and that he would begin in the same way as his colleague, but end as brightly as possible. "Tell me not the blood that flows! It cannot be otherwise.

Tell me not of the cost of the war! It is inevitable." But we have before us a "magnificent spectacle" of "a nation struggling to be free, and learning the lesson of impartial justice through divine retribution. The future before us, with liberty, is bright and glorious; and we are to have liberty." "It is said that the war must be conducted upon war principles. . . . Granted—*Grant*-ed!" There was laughter at Garrison's pun. Instead of lamenting that more has not been done by the administration, he said, let us realize how much has been done. "The work of a quarter of a century done in a single year should make us hopeful and patient." The situation today is totally different from the situation three years ago, when Wendell Phillips "had to be escorted from the Music Hall to his home by a strong body-guard to prevent his assassination." It was a good-humored, confident speech, which changed the whole tone of the meeting.

Garrison still hoped to give the impression that the break between Phillips and himself was superficial. In the same issue of *The Liberator* in which he reported the second day's meeting, he attacked the Springfield *Republican* for writing an editorial on the "schism between Phillips and Garrison." It was no schism because he and Phillips were still united in purpose. "Mr. Phillips is as free to be criticised as he is to criticise; and so are we. Abolitionists are the last persons to make any man their oracle, or to merge their individuality in that of any living being." His words struck close to home, because many would think that Garrison had always wanted to be the oracle whose words should not be questioned.

Feelings between the two abolitionists were hardly cordial two weeks later at the meeting of the New-England Anti-Slavery Convention in Boston. At the final session Phillips attacked Lincoln at length. Garrison tried to restrain himself, but before Phillips had ended, rose to say: "I do not think that our friend Mr. Phillips wishes to monopolize the hours of this short evening." As though stunned, Phillips suddenly became aware of the time and sat down.

The audience was confused. There was applause, and there were hisses. Some called for Phillips, some for Garrison. The evening closed with relatively short speeches by both Garrison and Thompson, exonerating Lincoln and his administration from the charges alleged by Phillips.[55]

Garrison reported to his wife, about three weeks later, that his associate was more passionately confirmed in his opposition to Lincoln than ever and that he had been so brash as to forbid the treasurer of the national society to pay a cent toward sustaining the *Standard*, official organ of the "Society, by resolution, against the administration—ergo, the Standard ought to conform to its decision!" The matter had to be taken to the Executive Committee; Garrison feared that his opponent had the majority.[56] But the committee, though containing two anti-Lincoln men, decided that the *Standard* "had been conducted with remarkable fairness and impartiality." No instructions were given to the editors, though they were advised to use care not to be partial to the re-election of Lincoln.[57]

Senator Henry Wilson had been urging Garrison, who had never been to the capital city, to visit Washington ever since February 1864.[58] Finally, Garrison decided to include Washington in the itinerary of a trip to the annual meeting of the Progressive Friends at Longwood, near Philadelphia. Before coming to Washington he also attended at Baltimore the national convention at which Lincoln was renominated. On 9 June Theodore Tilton, editor of the New York *Independent* and the man with whom Garrison had been traveling, introduced Garrison to Lincoln. The President, who had been receiving a group of delegates to the Baltimore convention, greeted Garrison heartily, showed surprise at how youthful he was, and mentioned his imprisonment in Baltimore thirty-four years before. "Then you could not get out of prison; now [the old building having been demolished] you cannot get in." The next day in an hour's private interview Garrison forswore diplomatic congratulations on the renomination and probed Lincoln's convictions as an abolitionist. He told the President he had made mistakes: limiting the proclamation, which should have been universal; wickedly mistreating colored troops; vetoing Frémont's proclamation, and so on. Garrison was delighted with Lincoln's response, with "the familiar and candid way in which he unbosomed himself." He concluded that the President was determined to do all he thought right and possible "to uproot slavery, and give fair play to the emancipated."

During his visit to Washington Garrison also had a long interview with Stanton, who impressed him as a thoroughgoing abolitionist. While Congress was in session he visited the Capitol, where Sumner and Wilson took him onto the Senate floor. "Quite a sensation was produced by my presence. Sumner and Wilson were exceedingly marked in their attentions." Wilson even went to the trouble of getting Garrison a room in his hotel, when it was reported that all the hotels were full.[59]

In the weeks following his visit to Washington Garrison was more than ever committed to Lincoln and his administration. Sumner, Wilson, Stanton, and Lincoln himself had personally insured Garrison's support in the forthcoming election. When on 20 October Wendell Phillips launched his final pre-election attack on Lincoln at Tremont Temple in Boston, Garrison thought "much of his criticism of Mr. Lincoln to be not only exceedingly ill-timed, but severely unjust." Phillips seemed determined, he said, to present Lincoln in the "worst possible light."[60]

Phillips' long speech at the meeting of the American Anti-Slavery Society in New York contained a passage that may help to explain his frenetic opposition to Lincoln:

You know, every one of you, that I have stood on this platform, and so have my friends, year after year, and have quoted to you the good words that Mr. Lincoln whispered to Mr. Sumner, the excellent promises that he made to Mr. Wilson, the charming words he said to me. Why, when we saw him, he promised so much, we could not get hold of him anywhere. He anticipated everything we would ask, by saying he had already decided to do it,—yet we have never heard of those things since. As a citizen, therefore, I refuse to commit my future to the pleasant words of Mr. Abraham Lincoln.[61]

Edmund Quincy felt certain that Phillips' animosity to Lincoln was personal. This was his reasoning: Shortly after Lincoln's inauguration Phillips went to Washington where he was kindly received by Lincoln and other leaders in the government; hence his relative approval of the first two years of the administration and his enthusiasm over the Emancipation Proclamation. After the proclamation had been issued, he appeared again in Washington, no doubt thinking, Quincy said, that it was time for him to make his influence felt in the government, time for him to be taken into the confidence of the President "& be the Power behind the Throne." Quincy thought that his first demand of Lincoln was "the removal of Seward. And I have not the least doubt that the

President snubbed him roundly, told him, virtually, to mind his own business. For from that time forward he seems to have been animated by the bitterest personal hostility to Lincoln. He could do & say nothing right & the lies of the press were caught up by him & set forth with all the charms of his eloquence as authentic facts." [62]

Thus, the reactions to Lincoln of both Phillips and Garrison may have been basically personal. Whereas Phillips may have felt insulted by Lincoln's indifference, Garrison was flattered by the President's attention. He had found Lincoln open, confidential, humorous, kindly, and human. He may have felt a kinship with a man who had risen from a humble background—an origin even more modest than Garrison's own—to a position of such eminence. On the other hand, Phillips resented Lincoln's proficiency as a politician and like many of the well-born abolitionists may have been suspicious of a humble man who was also a representative of the new industrial ruling class.[63] He was doubtless also convinced, along with the radical Republicans, that Lincoln was too soft on the slavery issue.

The results of the election left Garrison ecstatic: "It shows how great is the confidence of the people in the honesty, sagacity, administrative ability, and patriotic integrity of Abraham Lincoln." It indicates that "the government is stable beyond all precedent," and that no quarter will be given to the rebels. In fact, the victory for Lincoln, Garrison thought, constituted "a re-affirmation of the republican form of government." [64]

As the day of Jubilee approached, Garrison met the challenge of the times with a flexibility, with a forbearance and understanding hitherto alien to his nature. He modified his nonresistance principles, God knows with what anguish, so that he could conscientiously accept with a minimum of rationalization all those developments of the age that led in the direction of his own vision. He welcomed John Brown and Abraham Lincoln. He became a violent partisan of Northern justice as it fought on the battlefield. He discovered respect for the Constitution which he had once sneeringly burned in public. He supported the Union, once his abomination. It was as though he had absorbed by osmosis some of the humility and wisdom of Lincoln himself. He had, in effect, the grace and the strength to come of age at the very moment when the uncompromising reformer was no longer needed.

CHAPTER XX

━━━◆◆◆━━━

Jubilee

THREE weeks after the 1864 election Garrison was urging the passage of a constitutional amendment prohibiting slavery. "The Constitution of the United States is the supreme law of the land," he said. "Let it declare slavery forever abolished in the republic, and that no man can hold property in his fellowman beneath the American flag, and all that disturbs and rends the country will be effectually removed out of the way." [1] In December he praised Lincoln's Message to Congress as "commendably brief," simple, and direct. "Its tone is firm, yet conciliatory, and on the subject of slavery radical and inexorable." Lincoln's recommendation of an amendment abolishing slavery he thought especially commendable. [2]

Less than two months later, on the first of February, there passed through Congress a resolution to submit to the states the Thirteenth Amendment. Garrison could hardly contain his emotions on receipt of the exciting news. In an editorial in *The Liberator* on the 3rd, headed "LAUS DEO!—HALLELUJAH!" he described the event as the "most important . . . in the history of congressional legislation" and "better than all the military and naval victories of the war." As he walked the streets, friends and strangers greeted him with personal congratulations. On the 4th an enthusiastic Grand Jubilee Meeting assembled at Music Hall to hear him speak:

At last, after eighty years of wandering and darkness,—of cruelty and oppression, on a colossal scale, towards a helpless and an unoffending

race—of recreancy to all the Heaven-attested principles enunciated by
our revolutionary sires in justification of their course; through righteous
judgment and fiery retribution; through national dismemberment and
civil war; through suffering, bereavement and lamentation, extending
to every city, town, village and hamlet, almost every household in the
land; through a whole generation of Anti-Slavery warning, expostula-
tion and rebuke, resulting in wide spread contrition and repentance;
the nation, rising in the majesty of its moral power and political sovereignty, has decreed that LIBERTY shall be "PROCLAIMED THROUGHOUT
ALL THE LAND, TO ALL THE INHABITANTS THEREOF," and that henceforth
no such anomalous being as slaveholder or slave shall exist beneath the
"stars and stripes," within the domains of the republic.[3]

The audience broke out in cheers. Garrison paused in satisfaction. Then he continued to say that there has been recorded no
change of feeling and sentiment comparable to that of the last
four years. He confessed that he felt disposed, like a Methodist,
"at the top of my voice, and to the utmost stretch of my lungs,
to shout 'Glory!' 'Amen and amen!' " There must have been some
Methodists in the audience, for the applause was rapturous, and
cries of "Glory!" "Alleluia!" and "Amen and amen!" echoed spontaneously through the hall.

One evening about the same time as the Jubilee meeting he and
the son named for him attended a supper party at Mrs. Brigham's,
where George Thompson boarded. The party had been arranged
so that Garrison, Thompson, and Phillips could meet. Soon after
Garrison's arrival Thompson came down from his room; Phillips
appeared some minutes later, after the party had been seated at the
table. After greeting the group, he went up to Garrison and said:
"I congratulate you on the amendment. I was on the Hudson near
Roundout when I got the news, & would have telegraphed congratulations at once but could not get near the wires." The whole
evening passed agreeably in spite of bantering remarks about the
differences between the three lions tossed out by one of the women
guests. Garrison's son reported: "Two or three times the foiling
was keen & expert on both sides, Mr. Phillips turning her thrusts
with gentlemanly instinct, father making exertions to be entertaining & Thompson shielding himself behind his then happy
deafness." After dinner Thompson, who refrained from his usual
snuff-taking in deference to his hostess, told "some capital stories"

which stimulated both Phillips and Garrison to their best efforts at conversation. There was little talk of politics, much discussion of spiritualism, which always fascinated Garrison, and the three men seemed as cordial and friendly as ever.[4]

However, the strain between Garrison and Phillips showed clearly again over the reconstruction policy initiated in Louisiana by General Nathaniel P. Banks as military governor of the Department of the Gulf. General Banks had tried to form a provisional state government and as early as January and February of 1864 had set down rules for establishing suffrage, adopting a new state constitution, and seeking recognition in Washington for the new government. Radical Republicans and some abolitionists had objected to so prompt an attempt to reconstruct the state and had especially condemned Banks's method of controlling the employment of the freed Negroes—apparently a sensible system that provided the newly freed laborers with fair wages and with shelter for themselves and families.

About the middle of February at an Emancipation Jubilee held by the colored citizens of Boston (curiously, few colored attended) [5] Phillips denounced the "ingenious malice" of General Banks and condemned his reconstruction policy in Louisiana. Garrison spoke up, defending Banks and quoting from a letter which Banks had addressed to him.[6] Phillips said that he would not believe a word Banks might utter. "Very well," said Garrison, "your charge is then that Banks is an unmitigated liar!" Saying that he considered Banks "the friend, the benefactor & the liberator of the colored people of Louisiana," he challenged Phillips to produce some proof. Phillips had no reply.[7]

Early in April, shortly after the fall of Richmond, Garrison attended a Freedmen's Aid meeting in Chelsea. Featured prominently in the décor were some steps formerly leading to a slave auction block. Across the steps was draped a Confederate flag that had been captured by the Massachusetts 55th, the colored regiment to which George Thompson Garrison was attached. Just as Garrison was mounting the steps, a telegram was put into his hand. He climbed to the platform and read aloud to the audience a dispatch from the secretary of war, inviting him to be the official guest of the government at a flag-raising ceremony at Fort Sumter on 14 April, the anniversary of the surrender. The wildly enthusiastic applause seemed to formulate Garrison's reply to the invitation. In fact, the universal enthusiasm over Garrison's projected trip to Charleston convinced him more than almost anything else "that slavery is annihilated beyond any hope of resurrection." [8]

By the 7th he was in New York, where he received another telegram from Stanton, with the joyful news that Captain George T. Garrison (actually he was a lieutenant) was to be granted a furlough while his father was in Charleston. On the 8th Garrison and Thompson, who, thanks to Senator Henry Wilson, had also been invited to participate in the ceremony, steamed out of New York Harbor on the *Arago*. The sky was bright, the wind fair, the sea calm. The vessel contained many dignitaries in addition to the abolitionists—judges, generals, statesmen, ministers, professors, merchants, and editors. Henry Ward Beecher and Major General Robert Anderson, formerly in command of Fort Sumter, were there. Everyone, Garrison self-consciously reported, was courteous and attentive to Thompson and himself. Despite the heterogeneity of the groups, "there was entire harmony on the slavery question." [9]

The vessel sailed to Charleston through magical, moon-filled nights, arriving on the 11th, and then continued on to Savannah, described by Garrison as "a city of mingled gentility and squalor, but entirely dead in regard to all business affairs." [10] From Savannah they circled back to Charleston, arriving on the same morning as news of General Lee's surrender. One of the boats bringing passengers to the flag-raising threaded its way through the fleet assembled in the harbor, calling out the news: "General Lee has surrendered! . . . General Lee has surrendered!" There was universal shouting from all ships. Bands struck up the national anthem. The harbor rang with "The Star-Spangled Banner" and "Rally Round the Flag."

By noon they had reached Fort Sumter—"brown, battered, silent, lonely, in the quiet waves," its ruined walls scarred by battle, its narrow beach thick with "balls and broken iron," no flag fluttering on its tall staff, though all the other fortifications in the harbor flew the American flag. The distinguished visitors mounted the fort, descending to the inner bowl. General Anderson stood silent for a moment at the head of the stairs, overcome with emo-

tion at the first glimpse of the inner fortress where he had fought
four years before.

The ceremony which followed greatly impressed Garrison. First,
Anderson spoke, briefly, but with deep feeling. Then the ragged
flag, the same that the general had lowered in defeat in 1861, was
opened to the breeze, and the halyard passed from Anderson to a
dozen others on the platform who laid hold with determined
energy. "Was not that a good pull for John Bull?" said Thompson.
"When the flag reached the apex, the whole bay thundered with
such a volley of cannon from ship and shore, that one might
imagine the old battle of the Monitors renewed again. Then we
grasped hands, shouted, embraced, and wept for joy." The speaker
of the day, Henry Ward Beecher, like Edward Everett at Gettysburg, was hardly worthy of the occasion.[11]

Before dinner time Garrison and the others had entered Charleston itself. The once fashionable Battery, center of the residential
section, showed the full devastation of the war. The broken pave-
ment was pockmarked with shell holes. Once-elegant mansions,
now roofless, windowless, and riddled with cannon balls, were
tenanted only by scattered Negroes. Marble mantels lay hap-
hazardly strewn about ruined parlors. The financial buildings on
Broad Street were open to the weather—"their fronts burst
through with shells—their floors covered knee-deep with scattered
bankbooks, checks and drafts—and the street in front grown with
grass and weeds among the shattered pavements." The cashier of
the Bank of Charleston—one of the few able-bodied white men
still in town—stood in line at the commissary, along with refugee
Negroes, to receive his rations of bread and rice. Only the persistent fragrance of roses and mock orange evoked the image of
prewar Charleston.[12]

But Garrison seemed indifferent to the ravages of war, for his
own account makes no reference to the ruins of Charleston. He
was firmly convinced that no punishment was too terrible for the
sinful slaveholders. Such desolation was only fitting retribution.
Following the ceremony at Fort Sumter, he and the other special
guests were entertained at dinner by General Gillmore at the
Charleston Hotel. George Thompson spoke briefly first, telling of
his great joy on the occasion and saying that he felt like an American rather than an Englishman that night.[13] Then Theodore

Tilton spoke, and, finally, came Garrison. He told the audience that he was so unaccustomed to speaking in Charleston that he rose "with feeling natural to a first appearance." The audience laughed and cheered. He went on to contrast 1835 with 1865, recounting how he had been mobbed in Boston and cheered in Charleston. "Yes, we are living in altered times. To me it is something like the translation from death to life—from the cerements of the grave to the robes of heaven." In 1829 he had been, he said, stretching the facts a little, imprisoned in Baltimore for preaching immediate emancipation, and today "Maryland has adopted Garrisonian Abolitionism, and accepted a Constitution endorsing every principle and idea that I have advocated in behalf of the slave." Even "that noble man, Abraham Lincoln," had been converted. "Either he has become a Garrisonian Abolitionist or I have become a Lincoln Emancipationist, for I know that we blend together, like kindred drops, into one, and his brave heart beats for human freedom everywhere." (It must have been almost precisely at this moment in Ford's Theatre that John Wilkes Booth fired the fatal shot.)

The next morning, the morning of Lincoln's death, Garrison stood in front of St. Michael's Church as the 127th Regiment came down Meeting Street, playing "John Brown's Body." Garrison said: "Only listen to that in Charleston streets!" and burst into tears.[14] He visited also the other great eighteenth-century church, St. Philip's, and the graveyard, where he stood by an impressive, though simple, tomb—a great marble slab, raised on supporting walls of brick. On the face of the marble was one word, CALHOUN. Garrison laid his hand on the marble and the words rolled out: "Down into a deeper grave than this slavery has gone, and for it there is no resurrection."

Scheduled for this same morning was a mass meeting of the freedmen and women; crowds estimated as high as ten thousand assembled in Citadel Square by eleven o'clock. When Garrison appeared, he was borne in on the shoulders of the cheering multitudes. The superintendent of public instruction introduced him to two thousand Negro children. As soon as they realized who he was, they gathered around him, threw their hats and caps in the air, shouted welcome, and fairly turned somersaults in greeting. Their elders were hardly less enthusiastic, so that Garrison with difficulty made his way to Zion's Church, where the main meeting was to be held. Four thousand squeezed their way inside, three fourths of them former slaves. From the pulpit Garrison received a tribute from one of the freedmen who spoke, it was said, as well as a Harvard graduate. The Negro pointed to two neatly dressed little girls: "Now, sir, through your labors and those of your noble co-adjutors, they are mine, and no man can take them from me. Accept these flowers as the token of our gratitude and love, and take them with you to your home, and keep them as a simple offering from those for whom you have done so much." Garrison, Thompson, Wilson, and others spoke. In his usual vein, Garrison referred to his past efforts, giving God credit for the results; and he advised the freed people to be frugal, industrious, and ambitious to educate themselves. The patriarch stood before his people; they listened with an intense enthusiasm.[15] Following the meeting a procession of about two thousand led the speakers back to the hotel.

Toward evening Garrison visited the camp of the 55th Massachusetts Regiment, about three miles from the city. There at last he saw his eldest son. George had enlisted two years earlier with only the faintest objection from his nonresistant father, who wished that his son had been conscientiously able to adopt peace principles.[16] The regiment had the night before returned to Charleston with 1200 freed plantation slaves. These poor freemen formed as ragged a group as the followers of Falstaff himself. The men gathered curiously around Garrison when they heard that he had always been their friend. Sensing the opportunity for another Jubilee meeting, Garrison spoke to them: "Well, my friends, you are free at last—let us give three cheers for freedom!" He led off with the first cheer, but the Negroes looked at each other and at him in silence. All three cheers were solo performances. Garrison concluded that they were so underprivileged that they did not even know how to cheer.[17]

That same night the *Arago* sailed north from Charleston, carrying most of the visitors back home. But Garrison remained behind, planning a trip with the Henry Ward Beechers and Senator Wilson to Beaufort, Savannah, and St. Augustine. They arrived at Beaufort and were about to go ashore when a telegram came for Senator Wilson. Beecher joked with the messenger as he walked toward the senator's cabin. In a moment Senator Wilson hurried on deck and said: "Good God! the President is killed!" In half an hour the ship had wheeled upon its keel and was plowing North. Beecher reported: "It was not grief, it was sickness that I felt. . . . We could see no more sights. We had no more heart for pleasure. The heavens seemed dark. Nothing was left . . . but God and his immutable providence, and his decrees." All minds were dominated by thought of Lincoln's death.[18]

Despite Lincoln's death, which was soon to bring into the open the factionalism regarding the future of the freed slaves, Garrison was convinced by his trip to Charleston and the various Jubilee celebrations that emancipation was, practically speaking, complete and that the various agencies and papers dedicated to that goal were now obsolete. However, a group of abolitionists led by Phillips, who had accepted the radical Republican point of view on Reconstruction, emphatically disagreed with him.[19] They reasoned that the slave was not really free until he had all the rights of citizenship, including especially the right to vote. Until such time, they thought, all the extant antislavery societies were needed to agitate on his behalf.

Consequently, Garrison returned from Charleston to face again the issue of whether antislavery societies should be discontinued. At the May anniversary of the American Anti-Slavery Society in New York Phillips spoke first, referring only obliquely to the crucial issue. Then came Thompson, who introduced President Garrison. Garrison spoke with the best of humor, contrasting his lot with that of Jefferson Davis. A reward of $100,000 was available for the apprehension of the ex-president of the Confederacy, but he himself had had only $5,000 on his head in Georgia, and the other day when he was down there, no one would give sixpence for him.[20]

Then Garrison approached the crucial issue. He said he rejoiced that he was no longer "an isolated Abolitionist." He thanked God that "the guns of the American Anti-Slavery Society . . . are spiked, because slavery is abolished." Americans are now a "people, united in sentiment as against slavery. . . . Let us mingle with the millions of our fellow countrymen," and, therefore, abolish the now happily obsolete antislavery society.

These speeches by Garrison, Phillips, and Thompson were only the beginning. For two days the issue of dissolution was debated.[21] Charles L. Remond, distinguished-looking mulatto, urged the continuation of the society, citing from his own experience many examples of prejudice against the colored. Henry C. Wright insisted that the question was solely whether slavery had been abolished. The society was founded to abolish slavery; therefore, if slavery had been abolished, there was no reason for the society. At this point Wendell Phillips broke in to challenge Wright, and the debate ricocheted back and forth among Phillips, Wright, and Remond, the latter saying at one point: "I do not blame those who are growing old, like myself, for their desire to retire." Garrison was offended by this innuendo: "I do not ask the Society to *permit* me to retire. That is language I do not understand on this platform. I shall retire when I think proper, and I shall think proper to do so at the end of this anniversary."

When a question involving interpretation of the Declaration of Sentiments arose, Garrison was piqued again: "I think I am competent to interpret the language of the Declaration of Sentiments, if any man living be. I was the author of it!" He explained vehemently that the declaration provided only incidentally for the vindication of the rights of the free colored and that it was concerned primarily with abolition.

The abolitionists, Garrison said, are a small minority, with no particular qualifications for elevating the colored people. Now "we have the million with us. . . . We mingle now, thank God, with the great mass of our fellow-citizens." Loyal audiences and the loyal press will readily admit the right of the colored man to vote. "Let us mingle with the mass, then, and endeavor to work with the mass, and not affect isolation or singularity, nor assume to say, 'Stand by, we are holier than you,' when we are no better."

Garrison himself had foreseen the outcome of the meeting. The final vote went 118 to 48 against him. But the nominating committee did him the honor of proposing his name for re-election as president. When he declined to serve, Phillips was elected in his place, and a resolution was passed commending the retiring president.

The fact was, it would seem, that John Brown, Abraham Lincoln, and the war itself had demonstrated to Garrison that great social and economic changes could be most surely effected through widespread popular movements rather than through agitation by a minority. It was appropriate for an unpopular cause to be launched through the moral suasion of a small persecuted group, but that same minority was impotent when pleading a popular cause.[22]

There were more obscure personal reasons why Garrison was eager to disband the society and retire, whereas Phillips was anxious to go on. Garrison's goal had been reached. He had been heard. He had made a place for himself in a world that had seemed likely to ignore his talents. There had been abundant recognition for years of unselfish labor in a noble cause. He was loved and respected by a large and energetic family and by the general public in the North. What more could be desired? But for Phillips there had been wealth and position since birth. He had been bred to a kind of leadership no longer readily available in the new industrial age, and he had married an invalid who needed his career as much as he did. For him there was more to be desired. He must become the leading reformer of the age, a goal within sight now that Garrison had retired.

Although Garrison had insufficient power to dissolve the national society, the discontinuation of *The Liberator* was his decision. During 1864 there had been some discussion of the termination of the paper. By October he was considering the possibility of merging *The Liberator* and the *Standard,* a proposal favored by his family, since they thought it would relieve him of responsibility and give him much needed rest.[23] A month later, however, Garrison had decided that with the election of Lincoln the Jubilee was at hand and that it would be unnecessary to combine the papers. Moreover, he hated to sacrifice the historic position and the moral prestige of his paper until the Thirteenth Amendment had been passed.[24] He raised the subscription rate to $3.50 and resolved to continue *The Liberator* through the year, announcing officially on 24 March that the paper would be discontinued in December. But even with the raise in the subscription rate it was apparent that there would be a substantial deficit, and so Garrison set out to lecture in the West during November and the first week of December.

Garrison had never enjoyed a strenuous lecture tour, and he approached this one with less than usual enthusiasm, since his subject, "The Past, Present, and Future of our Country," lacked the compelling significance of the antislavery lectures and since his motivation was largely financial. He ranged as far west as Chicago, lecturing as often as five or six times a week for fees ranging from $25 to $100, the average being $75; his total receipts were $1,400.[25] Although for the most part he was well received, he was honestly disappointed in some of his performances, and he was eager to be home again.[26]

As the tour continued, his false teeth, acquired the preceding July, became loose and made clear enunciation difficult.[27] Also, his throat became hoarse, and his eyes sore. But he was still able to appreciate the great spectacle of travel westward: "The West is a mighty theatre for enterprise, labor, business of every kind. It is a vast empire in process of rapid development, and its capacity for growth and prosperity seems boundless. Every thing is in the gristle, but a solid and gigantic growth is sure. Our East is fossilized in contrast. We have gone to seed." [28] Of Chicago he said it "outruns my highest anticipations. With a great deal that is embryotic, rough, unfinished, cheaply built, it contains edifices which, in point of size, architectural taste, and magnificence, will compare favorably with the finest in Boston, New York, or Philadelphia. It has a population nearly as large as that of Boston; yet, when I commenced *The Liberator,* Chicago had scarcely a house or an inhabitant and gave no sign of ever having an existence in the future!" [29] He found Springfield almost as interesting as Chicago, because he stayed with William H. Herndon, who took him to Lincoln's grave and told him "many interesting facts and anecdotes about him." [30] To Henry Villard, his daughter's fiancé, he reported that he had "gazed wonderingly at the seemingly interminable prairies till my very spectacles ached." [31]

Garrison returned to Boston in time to celebrate the official ratification of the Thirteenth Amendment in the penultimate issue of *The Liberator.* Secretary Seward issued the proclamation with the exciting announcement on 18 December. Garrison took up the composing stick once more and himself set up the proclamation for insertion in the issue for 22 December. With his most florid rhetoric he saluted regenerated America: "Hail, North and South, East and West! Hail the cause of Peace, of Liberty, of Righteousness, thus mightily strengthened and signally glorified! Hail, the

Present, with its transcendent claims, its new duties, its imperative obligations, its sublime opportunities! Hail, the Future, with its pregnant hopes, its glorious promises, its illimitable powers of expansion and development!"

The final issue of *The Liberator* appeared 29 December 1865. Conspicuous on its pages were congratulatory letters to Garrison from Samuel E. Sewall, Samuel J. May, Henry C. Wright, Oliver Johnson, Theodore Tilton, and others, some of them specifically solicited by Garrison himself.[32]

Also featured in this final issue was Garrison's own Valedictory, the contents of which could have been anticipated by those who had followed his editorial career. First, he summarized his career as editor and reformer, concluding that at his time of life it was doubtful that he would begin a new journal "with the certainty of struggling against wind and tide, as I have done in the past." He confessed proudly that just as he had begun *The Liberator* without a single subscriber, so he ended it "without a farthing" to show for thirty-five years of toil. He expressed at length his conviction that the paper had been conducted with absolute "fairness and impartiality." He expressed his surprise that some had asserted that this was not the time to discontinue *The Liberator*. "As I commenced its publication without asking leave of anyone, so I claim to be competent to decide when it may fitly close its career." He firmly believed, moerover, that he was entitled "to take a little repose in my advanced years," admitting that he was delighted "to be no longer in conflict with the mass of my fellow-countrymen on the subject of slavery. For no man of any refinement or sensibility can be indifferent to the approbation of his fellow-men, if it be rightly earned." The valedictory closed with romantic flourish: "Farewell, tried and faithful patrons! Farewell, generous benefactors . . . Farewell, noble men and women who have wrought so long and so successfully, under God, to break every yoke! Hail, ye ransomed millions! Hail, year of jubilee!"

A few days after the appearance of the last issue of *The Liberator*, Garrison wrote a generous letter to his old friend and recent opponent, Wendell Phillips. He explained that he wrote with difficulty since he was not well, but he wanted Phillips to know how grateful he was "for . . . numerous acts of kindness, and . . . generous pecuniary aid." He was especially indebted for his having sent Wendell Phillips Garrison to college. Although he knew that he and Phillips had differed on occasion, he was confident that "in our principles, our desires, and our claims for equal and exact justice to the colored race as to the white, we blend together as fully now as ever." He hoped that their friendship would "be as perpetual as sun, moon and stars." [33]

But Garrison's New Year's Day truce proved ineffectual. Before the end of the month the two men clashed again at the meeting of the Massachusetts Anti-Slavery Society. Edmund Quincy, president of the society, laid before the meeting the vote of the Board of Managers which recommended dissolution on the grounds that slavery had been abolished. Garrison spoke briefly, favoring dissolution. Then Phillips spoke at length, denying that emancipation was complete and urging continuance of the society. Garrison sputtered in a letter to his daughter: "Of course, as the whole thing is a farce, I care nothing for it." [34] He also wrote a letter to *The Independent* on 3 February defending his position and attacking Phillips'. He explained that he had no intention of retiring from the struggle to elevate the Negro. "The work of educating, elevating, protecting, and vindicating the mancipated millions . . . is not done; IT IS ONLY JUST BEGUN; and . . . I and those opprobriously associated with me by Phillips, take as deep and absorbing an interest, and expect to participate as earnestly, as himself." It is Phillips, he said, who has deserted the cause, with "personal antagonism," "egotistical assumption," and "swollen self-complacency." [35]

In a personal letter Garrison admitted that the break between Phillips and himself was open and permanent. "It is inexpressibly painful to my feelings to have this breach occur, but the responsibility rests with him. We shall probably never meet again as of old." [36] Unconsciously, Garrison may have sensed a satisfaction in this canceling of the debts to one of his chief benefactors.

Eighteen sixty-five was the year of Jubilee, the year when, everywhere from Boston to Charleston, the panegyric which Garrison had been fearing and longing for pressed in upon him. It was the year when Lee surrendered at Appomattox, when the resolution submitting the Thirteenth Amendment to the states passed through Congress and was subsequently ratified by the states. It was the climactic year of *The Liberator*. It was the year, according to

Garrison, when the Massachusetts and the national societies should have been dissolved. But it was a bittersweet year too—unmitigated Jubilee would have been too much happiness—for Abraham Lincoln died and Wendell Phillips failed to accept his elder colleague's judgment. But for Garrison it was the year of ultimate justification, the year of adulation, the year he became a highly respected gentleman, a man of family and standing.

CHAPTER XXI

Gentleman Reformer

Although in 1864 Garrison was still a happily married man of family, his life had not lacked its tragic elements. Not only had he lost a son and a daughter but, even sadder, his wife had become a chronic invalid. On the night of Tuesday, 29 December 1863, Helen Garrison had gone to bed in vigorous health. She had seemed more fresh and rosy than usual during the day, but shortly after midnight she had a severe attack that paralyzed her left side. Within twenty-four hours she began to recognize the members of the family and to speak a little. By Friday, her speech seemed normal, although for several days she did not know what had happened to her, assuming that she had had rheumatic fever and "that her left arm & side belonged to some one else." This had not been the first attack, the family remembered, for Helen had been stricken in April a year before, though the resulting slight paralysis had lasted only an hour.[1]

Gradually Helen Garrison improved, and within a few days it was apparent that she would live. For a time Garrison, who was totally dependent on his unselfish, efficient wife, thought that she would make a complete recovery. He reported in February that she was a little better, in March that she was slowly recovering. But by May he referred to her as his "invalid wife," though when he returned home from a short absence in June, he thought that she had improved. By September she was trying the healing powers of a Mrs. French. Garrison urged, in a letter from New York State: "Let the experiment be fairly made, and mix as much faith with it as you can; for strong belief has often much to do with surprising cures." The following spring she went to Providence for electrical treatments. "Have a shocking time," Garrison advised. But by the end of 1865 she was still disabled—left arm useless, left knee stiff—and though in excellent general health, she spent most of her time upstairs alone. Garrison was convinced that she would never recover.[2]

For the rest of her life (she lived for twelve years after her stroke) Helen Garrison remained an invalid—self-conscious and humiliated at her own helplessness. She was glad when, shortly after her attack, the family moved from Dix Place in Boston, where the sky was never visible, to Highland Avenue in Roxbury, where the house was attractively situated on rock ledges thirty feet above the street. She spent much of her time sitting at a front window looking out at the garden or awaiting the post boy, who might bring a letter from Fanny or Wendell. Garrison always found her at the window when he returned from a meeting or a trip. Through inactivity she grew fat, and by the end of 1866 she weighed two hundred pounds; as her hair greyed, she used many bottles of restorative. It was a sad life for a woman who had once been so energetic and so efficient.[3]

In the same month when Garrison retired as editor of *The Liberator,* two of his children were married—Wendell to Lucy McKim, daughter of the Philadelphia abolitionist, J. Miller McKim, and a sister of the architect Charles McKim; Fanny to Henry Villard, a journalist and, later, a businessman. The year before, William, Jr., had married Ellen Wright, and thus only two sons remained with the family, the eldest and the youngest, George Thompson and Francis Jackson.

George was always a problem; for, though he was steady and conscientious, he was slow and diffident and lacked intelligence and initiative. He had had a series of insignificant jobs, usually acquired through the influence of father or brother and often lost through his own inertia. He had for a time worked at *The Liberator* office. During the Kansas excitement he had announced that he was sick of the town and all the people in it and wanted to go West to seek his fortune, but the same year he returned home, saying that the West was in a state of collapse. Perhaps his greatest achievement in life was to become a lieutenant in the Massachusetts 55th—his mother was proud that he was considered "the purest man in camp." Characteristically, George had been engaged as early as 1864, but waited ten years for the marriage.[4]

The brightest and most independent of the sons was Wendell, as Phillips was fond of mentioning.[5] He was scholarly and intellectual, and by 1865 he had made a place for himself in New York as one of the subeditors of *The Nation*. Wendell had even had the temerity to differ with his father over the re-election of Lincoln. In the spring of 1864 he had written his sister: "I think Mr. Lincoln by his Amnesty and Reconstructive Policy has betrayed the Republic; . . . I think he has fastened upon us long years of vexations and unnecessary agitation to secure the black man his rights as a citizen; . . . he has thus delayed the woman's rights movement; . . . he has endangered the State by admitting to a return to power the discomfited rebels." [6]

The businessman among the Garrison sons was William Lloyd, Jr., who had been a cashier of a bank and by 1865 was a wool broker.[7] It was William who acted as his father's banker, receiving and depositing checks for him and generally looking after his financial matters. Although William's business, like any other, had its ups and downs, he was over the years successful and became the stabilizing influence that the family needed.

The favorite of both parents was Fanny, a handsome and attractive young woman who gave music lessons before her marriage and who became a charming New York hostess in later years. In one of Helen's letters to her daughter is an enticing image of Garrison hanging pictures in the Roxbury house—all the nicest ones going into Fanny's room. It was Fanny who made the brilliant marriage in the family to Henry Villard, an intelligent German of aristocratic family background, who was full of expansive and imaginative business ideas that won him three fortunes and lost him only two.

Last to marry was the faithful youngest son, Francis Jackson Garrison, a boy of seventeen when Garrison retired. He became his father's constant companion and close associate, almost taking his mother's place in the daily routine of the household. He was conscientious, unimaginative, a great keeper of routine journals, and a great writer of pedestrian letters. He refrained from the attractions of women until he was almost too old to enjoy them, becoming engaged the year his father died, but he finally married an eccentric Christian Scientist shortly thereafter.

Garrison may have been a man of family, but he was certainly not a man of property in 1865. In 1861 Henry C. Wright had wanted to show his friendship by giving the Garrisons some money. However, Helen discouraged him, saying that her husband always had said that if he did his duty, God would provide for all his and his family's wants.[8]

Garrison's philosophy proved efficacious. During the final months of *The Liberator* many of his friends had become concerned about his finances. George Thompson, who had been in the United States since February of 1864, had told mutual friends that "the wolf is at Mr. Garrison's door," testifying that as a guest at his house he had in the past often observed that Garrison had difficulty in meeting his necessary expenses. Edmund Quincy discussed the matter in a letter to Richard Davis Webb, saying that Garrison was considering a salaried post in connection with the Freedmen's Aid movement and that he was planning to lecture. But Quincy thought that "there should be a testimonial raised sufficient to put him at ease for the rest of his life." [9] The Reverend Samuel May, Jr., cousin of Samuel J. May, was also eager to help Garrison with his financial problems. Early in 1866 it was definitely decided that there should be a National Testimonial to raise at least $50,000 for Garrison.[10] On 22 March formal printed invitations were sent to sixteen gentlemen to appear the evening of the 18th at the house of Dr. Henry I. Bowditch "to meet Ex-Governor *ANDREW* and a few other gentlemen . . . to consider the propriety of a National Testimonial to *WM. LLOYD GARRISON.*" At the meeting, in addition to Andrew and Bowditch, were Josiah Quincy, Samuel May, Jr., and others.[11] Governor Andrew spoke of Garrison as "The prophetic leader of a great movement" who had "sought no property" in his thirty-five years of labor as an abolitionist. "It would," he said, "be only an act of justice, on the part of the country, to take care that the remaining days of this true and brave friend of humanity should be set free from anxiety and care, so far as the possession of a fair competency could do this." A standing committee of seven was chosen to supervise the raising of funds: Governor Andrew, Jonathan I. Bowditch, Samuel E. Sewell, Robert C. Waterston, William Endicott, Jr., Edmund

Quincy, and William E. Coffin. Samuel May, Jr., was subsequently named the paid agent and secretary of the committee. Several meetings occurred in the two weeks before Garrison heard of the project. He wrote to his wife early in April that, although he was much pleased that such an attempt should be made, he had little hope of its success, since so many similar ventures, including one for George Thompson and another for John Brown's family, had failed so completely.[12]

But the hard-working committees were determined not to fail. They organized their efforts with all the precision essential for successful fund-raising. On 6 April, equipped with letters of introduction from Governor Andrew, May set out to interest prominent men in New York, Philadelphia, and Washington. By the 25th he had secured eighty-five signatures to a circular announcing the drive. The list read like a highly selected *Who's Who*. There were two members of the cabinet, two governors, several ex-governors, seventeen United States senators from sixteen states, fourteen members of Congress from three states, six distinguished men of letters (Emerson, Whittier, Longfellow, Lowell, Child, Bryant), five editors, and about thirty-five businessmen, many of them men of wealth. A letter from Chief Justice Salmon P. Chase and another from Charles Sumner were printed with the circular; a thousand copies were sent "to prominent persons & those known to feel an interest in the Antislavery Reform." Subsequently the circular was published in major newspapers throughout the country. A large group of local agents—May wrote to 175—was recruited.

The first contributions came in before the end of April. Five hundred dollars each from Gerrit Smith and R. Warren Weston set the pace. Mrs. Maria W. Chapman gave $200, as did Samuel May, Jr., whose father gave $500. By the end of June more than $5,000 had been raised, and the committee paid off the $3,000 mortgage on Garrison's house. During the summer and fall the contributions poured in rapidly. Virtually all of Garrison's associates and many prominent political and literary figures made their contributions.[13] The largest single gift, £100 ($688.89), came from Elizabeth Pease Nichol in Edinburgh. There were also modest contributions from humble and even illiterate people. For example, a policeman with five children sent one dollar, saying that lots of money could be acquired if there were a way for a poor man to subscribe without having to hunt up Mr. May or to torture himself by writing a letter. A colored washwoman sent him another dollar, which she wrote as $100 and said: "If I were a milionaire [*sic*] by the God's I would give him $1000,000 & make him President of the United States When he dies his destiny is the Heaven of Heavens."

As might have been expected, a high percentage of the contributions came from the Boston area, New England, and the Atlantic seaboard, but there were scattered gifts from New York State, South Carolina, Virginia,[14] Ohio, Michigan, Indiana, Illinois (especially Chicago), Texas, and California, as well as England, Scotland, and Ireland.[15]

The total gross amount raised was, by May 1870, $35,275.99, leaving a net figure after expenses of $33,010.23. From time to time during the accumulation of this fund, Garrison was paid interest on the amount collected, and twice, in addition to the payment of the mortgage in the spring of 1866, he was given payments of $1,000. Although the fund had been placed to his credit the year before, Garrison was formally presented with it on 10 March 1868, in a letter signed by all members of the Standing Committee, except Governor Andrew, who had died in the interim. The committee called the money "the gift of a grateful country" and expressed the hope that it would cheer the Garrisons for the rest of their lives.[16]

And so by the spring of 1867 the man of family had become as well a man of property. God had—with generous assistance from Samuel May, Jr., Governor Andrew, and others—provided for the aging reformer.

The portrait of postwar Garrison which has become traditional in recent biographies is of a feeble old man, devoid of reforming energy, sitting in his house in Roxbury hunched over his newspaper, pasting clippings in scrapbooks, playing whist, or talking with friends.[17] Such a picture of the man is inaccurate, as one of the early commentators on the reform movement, Thomas Wentworth Higginson, was aware. In an article on Wendell Phillips for the *Nation* in 1884, he contrasted the response of various abolitionists to emancipation. Quincy, he said, retired to comfort with his family, living a full and cultured life but no longer concerned with reform. Phillips seemed to be restless, always seeking like

Shakespeare's Hotspur "for some new tournament." But Garrison "with his usual serene and unabated vigor, went on contending for the rights of the freedmen and of women, as before, for those of the slaves." [18]

It is true that Garrison never lost his instinct for reform, though he worked in slightly different areas from Phillips. While Phillips considered agitation for Negro suffrage the most important activity immediately after the war and worked through the antislavery societies for that purpose, Garrison considered it more important to educate the freedmen. By April of 1865, nine months before the discontinuance of *The Liberator,* Garrison was a vice president of the New-England Freedmen's Aid Society.[19] This society had been organized in Boston in February 1862 in order to furnish teachers for an experiment in Negro education at Port Royal, one of the Sea Islands off South Carolina. Two years later branch societies were being formed. By January 1865 there were twenty-two of them.[20] The purpose of the various societies was to raise funds, locate teachers, and furnish books and clothing for the freedmen. When the Freedmen's Bureau was organized under the War Department in May 1865, the already extant private societies were urged to continue their work and to cooperate with the national bureau.[21]

By October 1865 Garrison had been named the first vice president of the New England society. In November he spoke to "an intelligent and fashionable audience" at the Academy of Music in Philadelphia. In the meantime, when the various branch societies had grouped themselves together into two main national groups, the American Freedmen's Aid Union and the American Union Commission (later called simply the Freedmen's Union Commission), Garrison was again selected as a vice president and made a member of the Executive Committee.[22]

In February Garrison went to Washington, ostensibly for recreation, but he spoke to "a very respectable and intelligent audience in the Union League hall," and he talked to a Negro congregation about the freedmen and their problems. He also was able to observe the mounting hostility between President Johnson and Congress. He was a visitor in the gallery on the 19th when the President's message vetoing the proposed extension of the powers and the duration of the Freedmen's Bureau was presented and when

Congress failed to supersede the veto by only two votes. "As God lives," he said, "what the veto intends to put down, it will in essence and substance put up—that is, the cause of impartial justice and universal liberty. It will rejoice none but the brutal contemptuous enemies of the hapless negro race." Garrison also listened to radical Democrat Senator Lyman Trumbull from Connecticut, sponsor of the bill, speak in refutation of the veto, a performance so clear, so logical, so powerful that it alone, he thought, was worth the trip to Washington. In addition, he happened to hear the President harangue a motley crowd in front of the White House on the 22nd. It turned his stomach.[23]

First-hand observation in Washington as well as the influence of Sumner and Wilson did much to convert Garrison from the moderate position, espoused while defending Lincoln, to the radical point of view. Even before he returned to Boston, he sounded like a radical Republican; for he attacked the President in a speech at the Academy of Music in Brooklyn shortly after he had heard Johnson's speech to the mob at the White House. The *Standard* reported: "If Wendell Phillips chastises Andrew Johnson with whips, Garrison laid on with thongs of twisted scorpions." [24] In this speech Garrison disclaimed being an optimist, though he still thought that the American Anti-Slavery Society should be discontinued, for the majority was now on the side of the Negro, and the rebellious element in the South "is to be grappled with, not by an insignificant body of Abolitionists, but by the whole loyal strength of the country, and held in subjection until rendered powerless." He said that the liberated bondsmen must have complete citizenship, "with the right to own land, to inherit and bequeath property, to be justly remunerated for their labor, to sue and be sued, to testify in all courts, to be represented and vote for representation, as do the whites." [25]

Following the Washington trip Garrison fell while running for a train and was, as he said, *"hors de combat"* until the first of the year,[26] but nevertheless he went on record in *The Independent* to urge the President's impeachment.[27]

By January he was feeling assertive again, and he wrote of the President: "He is manifestly as obstinate as he is unprincipled, and as self-conceited as he has proved himself perfidious. It is idle to say that the results of the recent elections [the people had overwhelmingly supported Congress rather than the President when appealed to in the Congressional elections the preceding fall] will be to sober his judgment and restrain his power. . . . All his plans, his appointments, his commands will have but one object— the restoration of Southern rule in the councils of the nation or the overthrow of the Union." [28] In February he was attacking William H. Seward, conservative secretary of state, as the "lost leader," who had sunk even lower than Johnson. "He is by far the more guilty of the two; he has sinned against principles which the former never professed. In all the loyal ranks there is now 'none so poor as to do him reverence.' " [29]

In March there was another important speech in Brooklyn, in which he discussed the condition of the freedmen. He said that it was ridiculous to argue that the constitutional amendment was null because there had been crime and suffering in the South. The freedmen were not worse off than the chattel slaves. The difference was that we now had direct knowledge of what had happened; before we were ignorant. He espoused the radical Republican position that the states were no longer really states, that they were so totally in ruins that the South belonged to the dark ages rather than the nineteenth century. "The South must be kept under the wise and beneficent guardianism of the General government for an indefinite period; that is, until she is civilized and preponderantly loyal, be that period what it may. Till then, she must not be allowed any Senators or Representatives in Congress. There must be no bargaining with her for impartial suffrage in exchange for universal amnesty. That amnesty she ought not to be granted; that suffrage, if pledged, she would speedily revoke." The first important step to be taken, he insisted, was the impeachment of the President.[30]

For several years there had been talk of Garrison's writing a history of the antislavery movement. Boston publishers Ticknor and Fields had apparently approached him during the last ten days of *The Liberator*.[31] In March 1866 they repeated their request in more specific terms, and Garrison agreed to write a two-volume work, the first volume to be published in October—*The Commonwealth* said, in the winter.[32] Late in the summer Ticknor and Fields were advertising the book as if it were already in the press. However, Garrison never began the work. He was full of excuses:

he had been ill, he had no diary to draw from, his memory was defective, he was too closely associated with the cause to write about it objectively.[33] But in fact he was—always had been—a man of action and a publicist, not an intellectual and a scholar. He much preferred activities connected with the freedmen's cause and even lecturing, though he had complained about the burden of that.

Garrison was so eager for the freedmen's societies to prosper that he himself raised funds for them,[34] and he did his best to have a large portion of the Francis Jackson bequest given to them. His activities as a member of the board in charge of the distribution of the Jackson fund brought him again into direct conflict with Phillips, who wanted the money used to sustain the *Standard,* which was campaigning for Negro suffrage. The trustees had met in January and agreed on a compromise, that of the total fund of $9,200, $4,200 should go to the American Anti-Slavery Society and $5,000 to the Freedman's Society. By May Garrison had decided that suffrage had already been given to the Negro by a reconstruction act recently voted by Congress and that therefore the earlier compromise regarding the Jackson bequest was no longer in force. Phillips accused him of acting as though he were the only trustee. All the leading New England abolitionists were drawn into the controversy. Mrs. Chapman and Edmund Quincy favored Garrison's stand. The court eventually ordered the money paid over to the Freedman's Commission, but even then the trustees disagreed and voted four to three against complying with the order. Robert Purvis, prominent colored reformer, went so far as to bait the two principals at a meeting of the Progressive Friends in Longwood, Pennsylvania. When Garrison refused to rise to the bait, Purvis' eyes flashed fire, his voice rose to a high pitch, and he accused Garrison of "being to the Anti-Slavery cause what *Benedict Arnold* was to the Revolutionary struggle and Judas Iscariot was to Jesus"![35] It was a ridiculous and extravagant controversy that seemed the *reductio ad absurdum* of the many personal quarrels which had beset the antislavery movement for three decades.[36]

One of the unfortunate results of the controversy over the Jackson legacy was that it resulted in a total break between Garrison and Phillips. Both men showed during the late 1860's that they were more alike than anyone had realized. They were both headstrong, both inflexible once they had made up their minds. It was impossible to say who was wrong. Both were. It was a mock-heroic struggle, a burlesque battle of the frogs. No one was victorious. But the break with Phillips did fit the pattern of the alienation of friends that is found in Garrison's life.

In the spring of 1867, at the height of the controversy, Garrison must have been thankful to be selected as delegate of the American Freedmen's Union Commission to the Paris Anti-Slavery Conference. He was able to go abroad and be with the Henry Villards (his daughter was getting acquainted with her new family in Bavaria) and his son Frank. He took with him George Thompson, who had not seen his own country for three years, money having been collected to pay Thompson's passage by Lucretia Mott.[37] Once more he escaped nagging family responsibilities at home.

The *Cuba* was to sail from Boston on 8 May.[38] It was to be a festive day, for the fund-raising committee of the Garrison testimonial had planned a formal presentation, the sum having reached by that date approximately $29,000. The night before the sailing, Thompson came to Rockledge to say goodbye to Helen. Garrison himself was in such a whirl that there was little time for tearful farewells.

On the morning of the 8th—the vessel was scheduled to sail at one o'clock—he worked frantically answering letters until the latest possible minute. By the time Garrison's hired cab reached East Boston at twelve o'clock, the rain was emptying out of the heavens in torrents. The steamer was crowded and people struggling in opposite directions were wedged together in the passageways. A large deputation of notables was to come by private tug to see the vessel off, but only some fourteen of Garrison's closest associates arrived. Three of them found Garrison jammed firmly into the dining room. Formalities were dispensed with. Mr. Waterston whispered a few words into Garrison's ear, and Garrison, relieved because he had not prepared a formal acceptance, spoke briefly. Nobody—not even William, Jr., who was within a foot of his father—heard a word that he said.

Just at that moment the cry "Shore!" was heard, and the crowds bolted for the gangway. Edmund Quincy "chuckled & smiled"— his jokes dry in spite of the rain. "Mrs. Chapman, kept her pace like Cleopatra, serene & oblivious to all around her." Others smiled through the moisture. Some who had come from a distance were much disappointed not to have a glimpse of the great man. All the friends huddled together on board the tug. There was a heavy breeze, though the sea was light; occasionally the rain stopped, so that umbrellas could be shut and the *Cuba* could be seen. Then came the signal gun, and the great steamer backed out. Suddenly Thompson was visible, hat in hand, rushing toward the stern, Garrison following close behind; they "waved their hats, kissed their hands & called out blessings & adieux." A Copperhead, who had unaccountably got aboard the tug, turned to Edmund Quincy: "What's all this fuss about?" "Why don't you know?" Quincy said, "It's all for Garrison, he's cock of the walk now!"

Except for the usual seasickness on the voyage, Garrison's health, as he had expected, greatly improved on the trip. Some of his English friends told him that his appearance had not changed since his last visit in 1846. But Garrison knew better: "It is my baldness, however, that looks as young as it did twenty-one years ago; 'only this, and nothing more.' " He spent four weeks in Paris —his first experience in the great continental capital; and though his letters indicated that he felt he should disapprove of Paris, he found it difficult not to be enthusiastic. There was lots of drinking, but few drunkards. He was thankful that Harry Villard was abstemious. He was fascinated by Versailles. Even the military display at the Bois de Boulogne race-course, though reprehensible from a moral point of view, was "as a spectacle . . . the most gorgeous and the most imposing of any I have ever witnessed, or ever expect to witness." [39] He visited the Exposition, where he marveled at the series of fountains that cost $3 per hour to operate and where he was delighted to be recognized and greeted by two colored waiters who worked at the American restaurant. He also spent an evening with William Cullen Bryant, whom he had not met before. And he dined with Turgenev. His only regret in Paris was that he did not speak the language.[40]

From France Garrison proceeded to Great Britain. Although he had resolved to limit himself on this trip to social activities, he could not avoid participation in several public breakfasts in his honor, and he functioned as an ambassador of good will between England and America. The most impressive of the public entertainments was at St. James's Hall, London, on 29 June. Chairman was the Duke of Argyll, who moved hearty congratulations to the distinguished guest of honor and characterized the cause of Negro emancipation in America as "the greatest cause which, in ancient or in modern times, has been pleaded at the bar of the moral judgment of mankind." [41] Also among the speakers were John Bright and John Stuart Mill. Garrison himself gave his best jubilee-type of address, bringing laughter, cheers, and applause. He spoke seriously for peace and forbearance between England and the United States, so that together they "may lead the world to freedom and glory." [42]

There was an interesting meeting at Victoria Hall in Leeds, where Garrison told how emancipation was "destined to make the United States of America a grand, homogeneous, prosperous nation." He said that Great Britain had already generously contributed £100,000 to the freedmen and that the nation would receive back in trade a guinea for every shilling contributed. "If the United States have been hitherto your best customer, remember you have only half that mighty republic to deal with, and you are soon to have the whole." [43]

During his stay in England, Garrison received many honors and many invitations. Perhaps he was proudest of the attention bestowed upon him by the Dowager Duchess of Sutherland, who wrote him a note and insisted that he have luncheon at her house, though she had been quite ill for a month. He was ushered into the Duchess' chamber on his arrival at the house and again as he was departing. She received him with great warmth of feeling. He visited the House of Commons, where he heard speeches by Bright, Disraeli, and Gladstone. He disputed with Anthony Trollope at the house of Lord Houghton, Trollope having a low ethnological opinion of the Negro.[44]

In Scotland Garrison visited Edinburgh, where he stayed for a week with his old friend and benefactor, Elizabeth Pease Nichol, and where he received the freedom of the city. From Huntley Lodge, the Nichol home, he wrote to friends and family of the many honors that had been thrust upon him, confessing that, far from expanding, he was shriveling up with it all. But he was pleased at the evidence of "peace and good will between England and the United States by this interchange of fraternal sentiments." [45] To his wife he said: "If I had not long ago crucified myself to the opinions of men, I might be in peril of slumbering on enchanted ground for the rest of my life, or moved from my feet by self-inflation." At Glasgow he stayed with a nephew of Arthur Tappan and participated in the third public breakfast in his honor.[46]

After a brief stay in London, Garrison returned to Paris for the International Anti-Slavery Conference. But again he was greatly handicapped by his ignorance of the language, for he could understand little of what he heard, and few could understand his forty-minute speech.

From Paris, toward the end of August, Garrison and party went to Switzerland, which he found "all witchery and enchantment." There on his thirty-third wedding anniversary he sat by the Lake of Geneva, close by the Castle of Chillon (Byron's poem in his mind), and, letting his thoughts range freely, he remembered the beginning of his correspondence with Helen. He remembered the happy hours and days of their courtship, the marriage ceremony in Brooklyn, Connecticut, the birth of their first child, the deaths of Charley and of Lizzy Pease, and all the happiness and sorrow of the intervening years. And he thought of the present, with the great Atlantic Ocean separating man and wife, he seeking rest and refreshment, she suffering patiently in helpless paralysis. He yearned, nonetheless, to be by her side once more and he remembered her perfection as a wife—loving, faithful, unselfish, helpful. He recalled the ceaseless struggle against wind and tide and how steadfast she had been. He remembered as well her qualities as a mother—affectionate, devoted, unwearied. He would crown her, he said, as the best of wives and of mothers.[47]

There was more than a month in restful Switzerland—restful but for the mountain climbing and the resulting sore feet—and then Garrison had a few days in Germany before returning to London to sail "on Saturday, 26th [October], . . . for Rockledge, via the Atlantic Ocean, Halifax, and Boston Common!" Then the arrival at Rockledge: The house was brightly lighted "with all that the gas fixings could do," Helen, rosy and fair, was waiting impatiently at her window, the parlor and sitting room were handsomely decorated with special bouquets of flowers. It all seemed so natural that Garrison felt "as if there had been neither separation nor lapse of time." [48]

Not all of Garrison's remaining days were spent close to the family hearth with Helen. The habits of a lifetime reasserted themselves even during the downward course of years. In the late sixties and the seventies Garrison remained a devotee of freedom and of reform. Now that he had become a man of property and standing, his words on current reforms and even on politics were considered oracular and worth paying for. At least eighty-three of his utterances were published in the New York *Independent,* his favorite paper, during the decade following the termination of *The Liberator.*[49] At times he wrote about familiar topics. On 19 March 1868 he attacked once more the American Colonization Society, the Executive Committee of which had memorialized the United States Senate for funds to help Negroes desirous of colonizing go to Liberia. Garrison insisted that the freedmen wanted justice, not banishment, and he made one of his more moderate statements about the postwar South: "Now that her old system of slavery has passed away— . . . let her bring all the zeal, determination, and effort that she evinced in its behalf to the system of free labor and the cause of impartial liberty, with its inspiring motives and sure rewards, its growing intelligence and rapid development, its shining virtues and its thronging blessings."

Of prejudice against the Negro he had a good deal to say. At first, his point of view was that "prejudice is born of slavery and will ultimately be buried in the same grave of infamy. It is most violent among the most degraded of the whites, and always as vulgar and ungentlemanly as it is unchristian." [50]

Later he realized that prejudice was a persistent phenomenon, and he became impatient that there were not more serious and systematic efforts to fight it. He was indignant that great sums were being spent to send missionaries to foreign lands when we had as bad a caste system here as in India. Fifty thousand pulpits should be crying out against the sin of colorphobia, but the church was playing a negative role just as it had done in the slavery controversy.[51] Even the federal government was not beyond criticism in this matter. Garrison was shocked at the persecution of the first colored cadet to be admitted to West Point. "I should rejoice to see the Military Academy at West Point blotted out; but, while it exists, the Government is to be held strictly responsible for its management." Certainly all students at the academy are entitled to equal and unprejudiced treatment. Garrison categorically denied the statement of Senator Allen G. Thurman of Ohio that social equality in the public school system would mark the end of that system. On the contrary, said Garrison, the whites would not have their children remain uneducated while the colored were being educated. "The experiment of abolishing all complexional distinctions in the common schools, wherever tried, has proved not only successful, but an unexpectedly easy transition." [52]

In regard to woman's rights he used much the same arguments that he had early employed for the abolition of slavery. At the end of 1868 he was hopeful that woman would soon be given the vote: "Why, there is less opposition to her voting at the polls—nay, to her being voted into office—than there was thirty years ago to her being a member of a business committee, or one of the speakers at a public meeting! . . . Yes, Galileo, 'the world moves!' " [53] But the world did not move fast enough; a year and three months later he felt called upon to launch a full-dress argument on behalf of woman suffrage. He explained that great reforms always meet with opposition, the greatest current reform being woman suffrage. He said that those who oppose giving the vote to women do so on the grounds that woman is basically inferior to man—an obvious absurdity. [54]

Garrison's effectiveness in the movement for woman's rights was diminished by the fact that by 1867 he had little use for either Elizabeth Cady Stanton or Susan B. Anthony, two of the leading proponents of the cause. He was offended at them both for their progression around the country in 1867 with eccentric George Francis Train, advocating human rights but also denouncing, he claimed, Republicanism with Copperhead enthusiasm. [55] And by 1870 he was convinced they were "untruthful, unscrupulous, and selfishly ambitious"—women with whom he could not possibly cooperate. [56] When early in 1877 Miss Anthony requested that he write a letter approving a woman's suffrage amendment, he refused, saying that the petition for the amendment was premature, and that it would be rejected by every state in the Union. [57]

Garrison's concern over the rights of woman was not limited to this country. He grew excited over the British Contagious Diseases

Act of 1866 and 1869, which provided for the examination in garrison towns of prostitutes or any women whom the police chose to implicate, in order to protect the health of the servicemen. "Of course," Garrison said, "such a prurient power, lodged in such hands, leaves every woman at the mercy of official lewdness, cupidity, or malice; and . . . is a wanton assault upon personal inviolability, a dastardly subjection to shameful exposure of one sex avowedly for the licentious protection of the other, and an audacious governmental sanction of prostitution as a legitimate vocation." [58]

In the spring of 1869 Garrison became actively interested in free trade, a doctrine advocated for years by many of his English friends and acquaintances. In March, in a letter to his son Wendell, who had disapproved of his being vice president of the American Free Trade League, he indicated that he knew something "of the fundamental principles, and of the laws of political economy, and these have long since brought me to the side of free trade as against what is deceptively called the protective policy." [59] In April he spoke at a free-trade meeting,[60] and in May (the 20th) he wrote for *The Independent* an editorial, propounding principles of free trade. He said that historically protection has too often been "the shelter which the wolf gives to the lamb," but that it is ridiculous to protect the strong against the weak. "Have we not the best educated and most intelligent population on earth? . . . Have we not a country unrivaled in the variety and abundance of its natural resources? . . . What is free trade but the assertion of common human interests the world over? . . . It harmonizes with free speech, a free press, free institutions."

During this period of his life, Garrison became the champion of two racial groups which he thought were being discriminated against in much the same way that the Negro had been—the Indians and the Chinese. He was terribly shocked, in the spring of 1870, by the brutal massacre of the Piegans, which because of alleged provocation had been approved by General Sheridan and even by General Sherman. He insisted that unprovoked atrocity has almost never been proved in the whole history of white-Indian relations.[61] Three years later when revenge was being sought for the death of two members of the Indian Peace Commission, Garrison said that like the slave population a few years before, the Indians had been looked upon as having no rights that the white men needed to respect. "Their wrongs have been grievous and insupportable. They have been corrupted, defrauded, plundered, betrayed, insulted, driven from one reservation to another, only to be again compelled to undergo a fresh exodus; hunted and shot down like bears and buffaloes, and at times massacred by wholesale. Our Government has repeatedly violated its plighted word to them, shamelessly disregarded one treaty after another." [62]

Garrison also became vehement about attempts to discriminate against and even exclude the Chinese. In the summer of 1870 a shoe manufacturer in North Adams, Massachusetts, contracted to employ seventy-five Chinese from San Francisco. When working men in the area menaced the merchant for employing Chinese, Garrison insisted that the Chinese have the same rights as any foreign immigrants and that America can readily absorb untold quantities of immigrants. We have only ten persons to the square mile of our area, whereas Belgium thrives on five hundred. He said: "Our ports are open to all comers. . . . We call ourselves Americans; but we are fast becoming cosmopolitan. . . . All the nations of the earth are more or less strongly represented on our soil, and we are still attracting the oppressed and laboring millions by an irresistible magnetic power. . . . If preference be shown to any, let it be to the class or race most needy to be raised in the scale of civilization and Christianity." [63]

Garrison's interest in issues specifically political did not diminish during his last years, though some might question his judgment—especially in supporting Grant from first to last. He had favored him for President in 1868, partly because he was so disgusted with Johnson, and partly because he felt certain that Grant would implement a harsh policy of Reconstruction. He wavered in his support of Grant when he wanted to annex Santo Domingo, even questioning his motives. But the rest of Grant's expansionist program he seemed to ignore, in spite of his own emphatic rejection of the policy of Manifest Destiny.[64] In January 1872 Garrison wrote an article on the approaching presidential election, citing as evidence in favor of Grant Democratic opposition to him. He felt that Grant had followed the views of the popular majority. "On the whole . . . I think it may be fairly claimed that no administration has excelled his own since the days of Washington." He praised his handling of the Indian problem and his peaceful settlement of the difference with Great Britain growing out of the war. A few months later he commented that Grant's great strength was that "the mass of the people" supported him.[65]

When, shortly before the Republican convention, Sumner attacked Grant for the terrible corruption in his administration, Garrison was appalled and said that it sounded as though Sumner were talking about some other man, and he wrote Sumner a letter insisting that he did not express the views of his constituents.[66] Shortly thereafter, his son Wendell mentioned in a letter Grant's corruption and regretted the "despicable choice" between him and Horace Greeley. Ignoring the allegation of corruption, Garrison answered that it was essential that Grant be re-elected because of the "impending crisis." [67] Of Greeley he was scornful, branding him "the most mischievous person in the whole country" and one whose somersault in turning against the Republican party and President Grant he found impossible to understand, as he did also General Banks's reversal.[68]

It is difficult to understand Garrison's myopia regarding Grant's effectiveness as President. How could the man who showed such remarkably good judgment in recognizing Lincoln's greatness be so far wrong about Grant? He may have been attracted by the glamour surrounding Grant, which the common man found so compelling. He certainly knew little about the malpractices of his government and probably discounted as mere rumor what he did hear, though one would have expected him to be hypersensitive to such charges. The main reason he supported Grant apparently was that he abhorred the Democratic party, and he considered Grant a radical Republican who wielded a firm hand with the rebellious elements in the South.

When in March of 1873 a letter was sent to Garrison signed by thirty-nine of his close associates (virtually all those still alive except Phillips), asking him to write his autobiography, he gave a noncommittal reply but referred again to the plan to write an antislavery history, modestly suggesting that the project "exceeds my ability." He also confessed: "I feel no interest in any history

of it [the antislavery movement] that may be written. It is enough
for me that every yoke is broken and every bondman set free." [69]
In December of this same year Garrison was certain that he had
made the right decision when a medium in reply to his inquiry
denied it was his mission to write the history, saying: "Others
could attend to the dead past, but I was needed for the present." [70]
In short, Garrison was a man of action, not a philosopher.

A few months before his death, on an issue obviously analogous
to antislavery and one with which he felt completely at home,
Garrison showed more dependable judgment. He carried on
in the New York *Tribune* a spirited controversy with Senator
James G. Blaine. He upbraided the senator for advocating a bill
to restrict Chinese immigration further than already provided by
treaty, accusing him of supporting the "hateful spirit of caste"
which Garrison himself had opposed for a period of fifty years.
"The Chinese," he said, "are our fellow-men, and are entitled
to every consideration that our common humanity may justly
claim. In numbers they constitute one-third of mankind. Of existing kingdoms theirs is the oldest, the most peaceable, and apparently the most stable. Education is widely diffused among
them, and they are a remarkably ingenious, industrious, thrifty,
and well-behaved people." As a result of his part in this controversy, Garrison received many letters, including a grateful one
from the Chinese minister in Washington.[71]

By 1874 Garrison's contributions to *The Independent* had
virtually ceased. His rheumatism made writing too burdensome.
In the summer of that year he spent several weeks in Providence
at Dr. Dow's water-cure establishment,[72] where he derived greater
satisfaction from the séances conducted by a patient named Mrs.
Currier than he did from the treatments by water and electricity.
One morning at breakfast Garrison showed his fellow sufferers a
very special photograph—a picture of himself on which was super-
imposed the spirit image of Charles Sumner, dangling broken
chains across his chest. The table lifted up several times to confirm
the authenticity of the photograph. Soon the group was having
séances with all meals. On one occasion, while Mrs. Currier was
receiving electric treatment, some insistent rappings were heard.
The spirit proved to be none other than Dr. Benjamin Rush, the
celebrated eighteenth-century Philadelphia physician. Dr. Rush

indicated on this and other occasions that electrical treatment was not suitable for Garrison's case. He advised a change. "On Dr. Dow suggesting various things, a strong negative was given in every case. At last he emphatically rapped his approval of Dr. Soule's Oriental Pills for the blood." [73] The prescribed medicine was administered with little success. Garrison went home before the end of August, through with the treatment, if not with the disease.

Garrison's failing health and his stubborn faith in eccentric cures during his last years were quite a trial to his family. His daughter on one occasion wrote Wendell: "He is as full of quack notions as ever & talks first of trying one thing & then another. He has given up Dr. Dunham & is trying a medicine given him by Dr. Tabor. . . . I wish he could be persuaded to try one thing a reasonable length of time. However, opposition to his varied medicinal fancies only makes him cling to them the closer & he will pursue his own way any way." [74]

Also it was becoming increasingly difficult for Garrison to nurse his invalid wife. Even after he himself was far from strong, he continued to try to care for her. They slept in the same room, and he did all he could to be helpful. When Fanny told her mother that it was no longer right for him to share her room, Helen was hurt. She told her daughter that she "was utterly mistaken in supposing that Father could be induced to sleep out of her room." [75]

If Garrison's health was poor, his wife's was worse. On 29 December 1875, the twelfth anniversary of her first serious stroke, Garrison described her as "very feeble." [76] Soon thereafter, she developed pneumonia, her condition remaining critical for several weeks. On the morning of 25 January she seemed relieved from her heavy suffering. Fanny and Frank stood at each side of her bed, doing all they could to make their mother comfortable. Ellie, her daughter-in-law, sat in front and removed tenderly the froth and phlegm from her mouth. And Garrison stood by, feverish and coughing. Gradually the end approached. [77]

Garrison went from the death chamber to his own bedroom. He was too ill to attend the funeral, at which Wendell Phillips, forgetting past differences, [78] assisted Samuel May, Jr. A month later Garrison could be seen wandering aimlessly from room to room, as if he were looking for his wife. It did not seem possible that he could no longer find her lying in bed or sitting by the front window.

Garrison received many letters of sympathy. One of them, from Whittier, read: "I would fain reach out a hand to thee. I know what it is to sit alone, like a stranger, at my own hearth; but as time passes on, the memory of my dear friends grows more sweet & precious, & the hope of soon meeting them makes the great inevitable change more tolerable to contemplate." [79] But the most wonderful letters were the yellowed batch Fanny found—Helen's love letters. He devoured them with a bitter-sweet excitement.[80]

During the winter months Garrison devoutly prepared for the press a small volume honoring Helen.[81] It contained a thirty-six page "In Memoriam" by himself, the remarks of May and Phillips at the funeral, as well as some twenty pages of personal tributes from letters by various friends.

It was on the following Fourth of July, the one hundredth anniversary of the Declaration of Independence, that Garrison wrote one of his last editorials for *The Independent,* its tone perhaps made more somber by his wife's death.[82] He admitted that it was important to celebrate all that is "noble and self-sacrificing in the conduct of the men of Revolutionary fame," but he considered it no less important to recall to what extent they were untrue to the "Heaven-attested theory" of the Declaration of Independence. "It is not a gracious task to make this examination, and its performance cannot fail to give offense; nevertheless, our national career, from 1776 to the present Centennial period, calls for deep humiliation before God, and penitent confession that we have been guilty of dissimulation, perfidy, and oppression on a frightful scale." In fact, "the whole naval and military power of the nation was mortgaged for the security of the slave system and the traffickers in human flesh." In 1861 came—fitting punishment for our sins—Civil War and the slaughter of thousands upon thousands. As a glorious result of the war the slaves were emancipated, but the luster even of that great event was mitigated by the fact that it was done specifically as "a military necessity," and in order to preserve the Union. Moreover, "the South is still insolent and brutal to the race it once held in abject bondage," and, in effect, denies Negroes and their sympathizers freedom of speech and press.

Today, Garrison said, we are guilty of mistreating the Indians; of taxing, without consent and without representation, "one-half of the American people . . . solely on the grounds of sex (a disability which admits of no relief)." Thus, Garrison felt forced to conclude that this was no "time for special jubilation." We can only rejoice "that we have not been utterly consumed."

Garrison looked upon this editorial as courageous and daring. He expected that " 'patriotic' vials of wrath" would be heaped upon his head, and he wrote his son Wendell that he hoped he would send him "any animadversions upon my article in your exchange papers," fairly smacking his lips over the prospect,[83] but no avalanche ensued. The nation knew Garrison as a conscientious patriarch and could accept or ignore his tirade.

During 1876 Garrison's health remained feeble, if not precarious. He complained of a rheumatic knee, chronic catarrh, and kidney trouble with "too frequent and too copious urinal discharges." [84] But he attended some concerts, frequently played whist in the evening, and occasionally met young admirers.[85]

Early in 1877 Garrison's family, remembering how their father's health had responded to earlier trips, urged a change of scene for the spring. It was a choice between California with the Villards and Europe with Frank. Garrison chose the latter in order to see old friends and to save money, since there would be so much free hospitality in England.[86] He promised that he would avoid public meetings, and that the trip would be purely for rest and relaxation.[87]

Just as plans for the trip were being completed, Wendell's frail wife, Lucy, was stricken with paralysis and epilepsy; in two weeks she was dead. Garrison moralized on the uncertainty of life, but did not regret her death since she would have been paralyzed if she had lived.[88] He went to New York for the funeral and stayed on waiting for the *Algeria* to sail, sputtering in his letters about President Hayes and his betrayal of public trust through his amiable credulousness. He planned to write him a letter of complaint, but did not find the time.[89]

The day before the boat sailed, Garrison learned of the sudden death of Edmund Quincy, which startled him greatly because

Quincy had seemed well the last time he saw him. In a letter to May, Garrison paid tribute to Quincy for his uncompromising courage, his trenchant wit, "his indomitable spirit, his unswerving adherence to principle, his noble disregard of high social distinctions and the spirit of caste, his cheerful readiness to encounter all manner of ridicule, defamation and ostracism for the slave's sake!" [90] He "was for many years with his pen what Wendell Phillips was with his voice to the Anti-Slavery cause." [91]

Garrison had no sooner landed in Liverpool, after a voyage devoid of the usual seasickness, than he reported improving health. He saw old friends. He enjoyed social activities, avoided all public functions—except for a few semi-public breakfasts— and actually gained weight on the trip.[92] He found George Thompson "greatly debilitated"—his body so weak that he tottered when he walked, his deafness increased, and his vocal cords partially paralyzed, making conversation difficult. "Of course, we were both deeply affected at our first meeting, and particularly when we bade farewell to each other, there being no probability of our ever again meeting on earth." [93]

When he returned home, Garrison seemed to have new vigor. He was able to write to the New York *Times* [94] the letter condemning President Hayes. There were anniversaries to mark: the sixtieth of his apprenticeship in Newburyport by setting in type three of his earlier sonnets; the forty-third of the mobbing in Boston; and his own last birthday. More significant, there was the exchange, already described, with Senator Blaine. Also in February 1879, he attended with relish another séance. "George Thompson spoke audibly his name to me, grasped my hand, and gave me other tokens of his presence. So did your mother," he wrote his skeptical daughter.[95]

By spring it was apparent that his health was definitely deteriorating. His kidney trouble was especially difficult and painful. Fanny persuaded him in April to come to New York for treatment. Before the end of the month the daily use of the catheter was necessary. He continued to write his sons Frank and William until 7 May. The last of his autographs to be preserved (dated 8 May) was the following adaptation of Burns's poem:

> Though woman never can be man,
> By change of sex, and a' that,

> To equal rights, 'gainst class or clan,
>   Her claim is just, for a' that.
> For a' that, and a' that,
>   Her Eden slip, and a' that;
> In all that makes a living soul
>   She matches man, for a' that! [96]

During the several weeks to follow, Fanny sent Frank daily bulletins about their father's health.[97] The middle of the month Garrison managed to get a copy of the *Tribune,* which reported him as in critical condition. The next day Fanny reported: "Father is making steady progress now." Reporters came from the *Tribune,* the *Post,* and the *Times.* The one from the *Tribune*—"a gentleman," according to Fanny—reported that Garrison is "nearly recovered." His recuperation continued until the 19th. By the 20th, the day that Frank wrote his last letter to his father, Fanny wired: "Father failing rapidly Lose no time and all take first train you can and come."

On the morning of the 23rd his doctor asked: "What do you want, Mr. Garrison?" The reply: "To finish it up!" That evening his children—all of them with him—sang his favorite hymns, as he beat time with his hands and feet. The final struggle began at ten-thirty. Garrison remained unconscious for twenty-four hours and died shortly after eleven on Saturday evening, 24 May 1879.

At his funeral on the 28th Samuel May, Lucy Stone, and Theodore D. Weld spoke. But the major address was by Wendell Phillips, who paid tribute to Garrison's common sense and said that he made fewer mistakes during his fifty years of agitation than any other American. "The world," Phillips said, "suffers its grandest changes not by genius, but by the more potent control of *character.* His was an earnestness that would take no denial, that consumed opposition in the intensity of its convictions, that knew nothing but right. . . . His was the happiest life I ever saw. . . . To the day of his death he was as ready as in his boyhood to confront and defy a mad majority. . . . He showed nothing either of the intellectual sluggishness or the timidity of age." [98]

The malcontented Newburyport boy had traveled far since the days of his apprenticeship. There had been a long struggle against wind and tide, with passionate, self-righteous, sometimes in-discriminate exhortation and abuse. But for a generation, as central publicist, as Liberator of the reform movement, he had been the leading abolitionist, the universal reformer. The name of William Lloyd Garrison had become a symbol of the prophetic New England conscience. The unsubstantial dream of evil over-thrown had become the fabric of reality.

NOTES

———◆———

INDEX

ABBREVIATIONS

CSmH	Henry E. Huntington Library and Art Gallery, San Marino, California
DLC	Library of Congress, Washington, D.C.
MB	Boston Public Library, Boston, Massachusetts
MH	Harvard University, Cambridge, Massachusetts
MHi	Massachusetts Historical Society, Boston, Massachusetts
MNS	Smith College Library, Northampton, Massachusetts
MSaE	Essex Institute, Salem, Massachusetts
MWA	American Antiquarian Society, Worcester, Massachusetts
MeHi	Maine Historical Society, Portland, Maine
NN	New York Public Library, New York, New York
NSU	Syracuse University, Syracuse, New York
PPHi	Historical Society of Pennsylvania, Philadelphia, Pennsylvania
PSC	Swarthmore College, Swarthmore, Pennsylvania
PSC-F	Friends Historical Library, Swarthmore College, Swarthmore, Pennsylvania

NOTES

———————◆◆◆———————

INTRODUCTION

1. See "The Antislavery Myth," *The American Scholar,* XXXI (Spring 1962), pp. 312–328.

I. SON AND APPRENTICE

1. Although it now seems quite certain that Garrison was born in 1805, the day of his birth is still uncertain. Until his trip to New Brunswick in the summer of 1835, Garrison (hereinafter referred to as WLG) thought he had been born 10 Dec. 1804, but his aunt corrected the year to 1805 (WLG to Helen Garrison, 25 July 1835, MB). Since WLG is known to have been born in Newburyport, further evidence that he was born in 1805 is provided by a letter from Abijah Garrison, 4 April 1805, from Granville, Nova Scotia (see *W. P. and F. J. Garrison, William Lloyd Garrison,* New York, 1885–1889, I, 17ff.; hereinafter referred to as *Life*), announcing that the family is about to move to Newburyport. Additional proof is provided by entries copied by James H. Garrison from the family Bible (information provided by Miss Fanny Garrison), where the same date is given. WLG himself decided in the spring of 1867, when he examined the town records in Newburyport, that he was born 12 Dec. 1804 (WLG to F. J. Garrison, 23 April 1867, MB; see also WLG to W. P. Garrison, 10 Dec. 1867, MB; WLG to W. P. Garrison 12 Dec. 1867, MB; WLG to W. P. Garrison, 13 Dec. 1870, MB; and WLG to William Newhall, 10 Nov. 1873, copy, MB). During the last years of his life, WLG grew concerned over whether he were celebrating the proper birthday. When W. P. Garrison questioned if the letter from Abijah were conclusive (WLG to Fanny Villard, 30 Jan. 1877, MNS; WLG to W. P. Garrison, 11 Dec. 1877, MB), WLG examined carefully the Newburyport record, concluding that "the town records at that time were kept in a very loose disjointed manner, furnishing ample scope for blunders as to dates" (WLG to W. P. Garrison, 29 March 1878, MB).

2. Knowledge of WLG's paternal ancestry, in spite of rigorous search by a son and a grandson, goes no further back than Joseph Garrison, the abolitionist's grandfather, who some ten or twelve years before the Revolution settled among a group of New Englanders, mostly from Essex County, Massachusetts, along the Jemseg River in what was later New Brunswick. A family tradition (stated in various letters found among the correspondence of W. P. Garrison in the Villard Papers at Harvard) suggests that the first Garrisons in this country were three or four brothers who immigrated from the western part of England to New Jersey in 1700 or slightly earlier. One of these brothers is said to have moved to Virginia, another up the Hudson, and a third to Long Island.

From these three brothers three main branches of the family are said to have sprung—the Southern branch, some of whom fought on the Confederate side during the Civil War; the New York financiers; and the New England branch, from which Joseph Garrison descended. To what extent this tradition is based on fact, it is difficult to say. I have been unable to find any clues in historical societies in New Jersey, Long Island, and Massachusetts which would make it possible to trace Joseph Garrison back to the brothers in question. And the Hudson River branch of the family claims to be descended directly from Isaac Garrison, who immigrated from France to New York, where he was naturalized in 1705. I am reasonably certain, however, that the name Garrison was originally Huguenot French, and that different branches of the family at various times migrated from France to England, Holland, Canada, and the United States.

3. For descriptions of Newburyport in the days of Garrison's childhood and youth see the following: John J. Currier, *History of Newburyport, Massachusetts, 1764–1905* (Newburyport, Mass., 1906); Caleb Cushing, *The History and Present State of the Town of Newburyport* (Newburyport, 1826); Joshua Coffin, *A Sketch of the History of Newburyport* (Boston, 1845); Mrs. E. Vale Smith, *History of Newburyport* (Newburyport, 1854); and George Wood, "Early Recollections of Newburyport," a series of thirteen sketches in the Newburyport *Herald,* which terminated 20 March 1863 (to be found in a scrapbook at Essex Institute).

4. Abijah Garrison to Joseph Garrison, 3 April 1806. This is a copy in the hand of W. P. Garrison, MH.

5. It has been rumored that Abijah subsequently remarried, and without waiting for the death of his first wife. According to a member of the Garrison family, W. P. Garrison discovered the church records of that bigamous union in an Episcopal church in St. John, New Brunswick. Unfortunately, the appropriate records for Trinity Church, the only Episcopal church functioning in St. John during the early nineteenth century, were destroyed by fire; and the W. P. Garrison papers (MH) contain no trace of the bigamous union, although there is a suspicious gap in the otherwise complete correspondence between W. P. Garrison and O. G. Villard. (There is a frequent exchange of letters between the two men until W. P. Garrison takes his trip to New Brunswick during the summer of 1906. Then after a card announcing that he is going to St. John tomorrow, there is no further communication from him until some weeks later when he has returned from the trip.)

6. 4 Aug. 1814, in author's possession. All of the extant autographs of Fanny Lloyd Garrison are in the author's possession. Extracts from a few more of her letters, in the hand of W. P. Garrison, have been preserved at Harvard.

7. W. P. Garrison's copy, MH.

8. In 1810 the population was over 46,000; by 1820 it had reached 63,000. See John Bach McMaster, *A History of the People of the United States* (New York, 1905), IV, 524.

9. Fanny Garrison to Martha Farnham, 7 Sept. 1816, W. P. Garrison's copy, MH. For a letter from Mrs. Timothy Pickering to Mrs. Garrison, expressing her gratitude to Fanny for her excellent nursing of her daughter, who unfortunately had died, see Charles W. Upham, *The Life of Timothy Pickering* (Boston, 1873), IV, 319.

10. Fanny Garrison to Martha Farnham, 7 Sept. 1816, W. P. Garrison's copy, MH.

11. Fanny Garrison to Martha Farnham, 18 April 1816, W. P. Garrison's copy, MH.

12. Walter M. Merrill, ed., *Behold Me Once More* . . . (Boston, 1954).

13. Fanny Garrison to Martha Farnham, 30 April 1817, W. P. Garrison's copy, MH.

14. See WLG editorial in the *Genius of Universal Emancipation*, 1 Jan. 1830 (mislabeled 1829 on the editorial page). In this article WLG rather pathetically sets his thirteenth birthday in the context of his family, although he was no longer living with either his mother or his father at that time.

15. For a brief characterization of E. W. Allen, see Mrs. E. Vale Smith, *History of Newburyport*, p. 261.

16. Speech at the Franklin Club in Boston, 14 Oct. 1878. The speech was reported fully in the Boston *Traveller* for 15 Oct. from which the passage here is transcribed.

17. See the speech at the Franklin Club referred to above, as well as *Life*, I, 41. Miller was later active in New Hampshire as editor, publisher, and minister. See John W. Moore, *Historical, Biographical* . . . *Gatherings* . . . *relative to Printers* (Concord, N.Y., 1886), pp. 512–513.

18. See *Life*, I, 73. Unfortunately, I have not been able to find a copy of this book or any official notice of its publication. Bennett did have some little fame as the author of *A Voyage from the United States to South America* . . . (Newburyport, 1823).

19. 12 May 1820, in author's possession.

20. Fanny Garrison to Martha Farnham, 20 July 1820, W. P. Garrison's copy, MH.

21. 21 May 1822. See Chap. V for a discussion of WLG's ideas on marriage.

22. Newburyport *Herald*, 22 April 1823.

23. 26 May 1823, MB. I believe this is the earliest extant WLG autograph.

24. Fanny Garrison to WLG, 1 July 1821, W. P. Garrison's copy, MH. The correct date is probably 1 July 1822, since WLG did not write for the *Herald* until that year.

26. WLG to Helen Benson, 21 June 1834, MB.

II. YOUNG EDITOR

1. See *The Free Press* for 9 Dec. 1826.

2. *The Free Press*, 13 July 1826.

3. *Life*, I, 67.

4. For the text of most of these early poems see Walter M. Merrill, ed., "Uncollected Early Poems by John Greenleaf Whittier," Essex Institute *Historical Collections*, XCI (April 1955), 128ff.

5. *The Free Press*, 18 May 1826.

6. *The Free Press*, 29 June 1826.

7. *The Free Press*, 29 March 1826.

8. *The Free Press*, 20 July 1826. Ironically, WLG was destined to be even less consistent than Allen. About twenty years later (*The Liberator*, 21 Nov. 1845; hereinafter abbreviated *Lib.*) he was enthusiastic about the religious writings of the most notorious of American deists, Tom Paine.

9. *The Free Press*, 27 July 1826.

10. John H. Harris, as his obituary notice in the Gloucester *Telegraph* (27 Oct. 1875) indicates, was at this time a printer some two years older than

WLG. He had already had several jobs and was, in fact, destined to spend his life moving from one paper to another.

11. *The Free Press,* 5 Oct. 1826.

12. Haverhill *Gazette & Essex Patriot,* 28 Oct. 1826.

13. Although I have found no direct proof of WLG's statement, it is true that Cushing had a new law partner named Robert Cross—as can be seen by reading the notice in *The Free Press* for 10 Aug. and for many subsequent dates, which states that Caleb Cushing and Robert Cross "have formed a connexion for the transaction of Law Business at Newburyport and Amesbury Mills." Moreover, in May of 1824 Cross had been one of the publishers of the *Northern Chronicler* (predecessor of *The Free Press*). It is a fact, also, that *The Free Press* was discontinued on 9 Dec., just a month and three days after Cushing's defeat at the polls.

14. Diligent search through Newburyport, Haverhill, and Salem papers has revealed no report of WLG's attack on Cushing; but both the Garrison brothers (*Life,* I, 72) and Dr. Claude M. Fuess (*The Life of Caleb Cushing,* New York, 1923, I, 78) insist that it took place.

15. *National Philanthropist,* 11 Jan. 1828.

16. *National Philanthropist,* 20 June 1828. The method of answering a critic by means of footnotes WLG used increasingly as the years passed. That he was at this time rewriting some of his correspondents' letters is indicated by "A Mechanic's" reply in the issue for 28 June. He says he wants to thank WLG "for the new dress you gave my first child, and the conspicuous place he filled in your columns," and admits he himself has little time and less ability for newspaper writing.

17. See the *National Philanthropist* for 8, 15, 29 Feb. 1828. Almost invariably in his literary criticism, WLG's ultimate emphasis is on moral content.

18. See WLG to Stephen Foster, 30 March 1829, MeHi.

19. It is ironic that WLG should have undertaken to electioneer for Adams since in the campaign of 1824 he had had little to say in his favor, much preferring the Southern slaveholder, William H. Crawford. See Newburyport *Herald,* 25 Jan. 1825.

20. Throughout this paper WLG's resolve to be a reformer is evident. See especially his poems, "The Resolve" (12 Dec.) and "The Birthday" (26 Dec.). Benjamin Lundy, whom WLG met in 1828, helped in this resolution. See the discussion of Lundy in Chap. III.

21. *Journal of the Times,* 31 Oct. 1828.

22. *Journal of the Times,* 7 Nov. 1828. This editorial was to be a source for his first important public address on slavery. See p. 29. The imagery of the speech often echoes that of the editorial.

23. *Journal of the Times,* 13 March 1829.

24. *Journal of the Times,* 27 March 1829.

25. Horace Greeley (*The American Conflict . . . ,* New York, 1864, I, 115) praised the *Journal of the Times* as "about the ablest and most interesting newspaper ever issued in Vermont."

III. HIGHER ENTERPRISES

1. *Lib.,* 20 Sept. 1839.

2. *Journal of the Times,* 12 Dec. 1828.

3. This was the William R. Collier who had been one of the proprietors of the *National Philanthropist*. See editorial page of that paper in the issue of 21 March 1828.

4. WLG to Stephen Foster, 30 March 1829, MeHi. This letter belies the statement of WLG's sons, that "the winter which he spent in Bennington was a very happy one to Mr. Garrison. He was relieved, from the outset, of all pecuniary responsibility and anxiety . . ." (*Life*, I, 115). It is true that the editorials in his papers would give no indications of his discontent, for he often praised Vermont and Vermonters as in the one for 14 Nov. 1828.

5. As can be seen in Chap. VII below, the Mary Cunningham WLG loves is probably from Massachusetts rather than Vermont. Since he was writing in praise of her in the first issue of the *Journal of the Times* and since she seems to have been well known to his Boston friends, it hardly seems possible that he had not met her until he came to Vermont.

6. WLG to Jacob Horton, 27 June 1829, MB.

7. WLG to Jacob Horton, 27 June 1829, MB.

8. WLG, *Writings and Speeches of* . . . (Boston, 1852), pp. 42–61.

9. *Genius of Universal Emancipation*, 25 Sept. 1829.

10. *Genius*, 16 Oct. 1829.

11. *Genius*, 30 Oct. 1829.

12. Actually, it was his twenty-fourth birthday, but WLG thought he was born in 1804 until he discovered otherwise on a trip to New Brunswick in 1834.

13. *Genius of Universal Emancipation*, 5 March 1830.

14. *Lib.*, 5 Feb. 1831.

15. WLG to Mrs. Jacob Horton, 12 May 1830, copy in possession of Miss Fanny Garrison. The original letter, which I have been unable to locate, is supposed to be in the possession of Miss H. Therese Horton, a granddaughter of Mrs. Jacob Horton. WLG apparently wrote several letters to friends on 12 May. One, written to Joseph T. Buckingham, the editor of the Boston *Courier*, and printed in that paper, 24 May 1830 (reprinted partly in *Life*, I, 179–180), used substantially the same first two paragraphs as this one. He may also have written in much the same way to Whittier (see *Life*, I, 189), although I have been unable to find either the manuscript or a copy of it.

16. A second edition of *A Brief Sketch of the Trial of Wm. Lloyd Garrison for an Alleged Libel on Francis Todd* was published in Boston in 1834.

17. *Brief Sketch*, p. iii.

18. Newburyport *Herald*, 11 June 1830.

19. *Life*, I, 190–191.

20. The letter (MB) was addressed "To the Friends of the Anti-Slavery Cause," and it contained a postscript, indicating that WLG was to show the letter to anyone he saw fit.

21. Lewis Tappan, *The Life of Arthur Tappan* (New York and Cambridge, Mass., 1870), p. 163.

22. WLG to Ebenezer Dole, 14 July 1830; printed in *Life*, I, 192–195. WLG sent an IOU with his letter, which Dole promptly canceled.

23. *Lib.*, 1 Jan. 1831. This is probably the first direct statement of the martyr impulse which was to animate WLG.

NOTES TO CHAPTER IV

IV. THE LIBERATOR

1. David Donald, *Lincoln Reconsidered* (New York, 1956), p. 33. Mr. Donald has made a statistical study of the abolitionist leaders and reached the following conclusion about them: "Descended from old and socially dominant Northeastern families, reared in a faith of aggressive piety and moral endeavor, educated for conservative leadership, these young men and women who reached maturity in the 1830's faced a strange and hostile world. Social and economic leadership was being transferred from the country to the city; from the farmer to the manufacturer; from the preacher to the corporation attorney. Too distinguished a family, too gentle an education, too nice a morality were handicaps in a bustling world of business. Expecting to lead, these young people found no followers. They were an elite without function, a displaced class in American Society."

2. Samuel J. May, *Some Recollections of our Anti-Slavery Conflict* (Boston, 1869), p. 19.

3. May, *Some Recollections*, pp. 20ff.

4. Samuel E. Sewall to WLG, 27 Oct. 1830, MB.

5. WLG remembered his great debt to May and Sewall in the last issue of *The Liberator*, 29 Dec. 1865.

6. Frederick Jackson Turner, *The United States, 1830–1850* (New York, 1935), p. 42; see also p. 75.

7. Foster was listed as the printer of *The Liberator* for the first three issues. Thereafter another arrangement was made, for Knapp and Garrison acquired some second-hand type and their own handpress. (See *Lib.*, 5 Nov. 1831, for Foster's obituary.)

8. Unfortunately, these letters have not been preserved, although some of the answers to them can be found at Boston Public Library.

9. Charles W. Denison to WLG, 5 March 1831, MB.

10. George Cary to WLG, 6 June 1831, MB.

11. WLG to S. J. May, 14 Feb. 1831, MB; and WLG to S. S. Jocelyn, 31 May 1830, MB.

12. It has been suggested (Russel Nye, *William Lloyd Garrison and the Humanitarian Reformers*, Boston, 1955, p. 48) that WLG adapted this motto from Thomas Paine, but WLG claims not to have read Paine until 1845 (*Lib.*, 21 Nov. 1845).

13. Frederick Jackson Turner (*The United States, 1830–1850*, p. 85) described this passage as "a voice from the early days of intolerant Puritanism, in the spirit of the martyrs refusing to enter into treaty with what was believed to be wickedness and convinced of the responsibility of the community for sin."

14. *Lib.*, 29 Jan. 1831.

15. *Lib.*, 5 Feb. 1831. In the issue for 24 Sept. 1831 WLG appears more receptive to Whitcomb's ideas; for he approves his address to the "Working-Men's Society of Dedham," commending Whitcomb as "a self-made man, who deserves great credit for his industry and talents," and admitting that "it is a lamentable truth, that wealth has more power than knowledge or merit in society. Every moral effort, therefore, which is made to reverse this unnatural superiority, deserves praise."

16. *Lib.*, 12 Feb. 1831.

17. *Lib.*, 8 Jan. 1831.

18. *Lib.*, 13 Aug. 1831.

19. *Lib.*, 17 Sept. 1831. There are a number of other references to Colonel Johnson in WLG's paper during the next several years as the practical amalgamator who became Vice President and who WLG feared might become President. See *The Liberator* for the following dates: 20 June 1835, 4 July 1835, 1 Aug. 1835, 28 Jan. 1837, 11 March 1837, 7 April 1837, and 3 Nov. 1837.

20. The full title is *Walker's Appeal in four articles together with a Preamble to the Colored Citizens of the World, but in particular and very expressly to those of the United States of America.*

21. *Lib.*, 8 Jan. 1831.

22. See the following issues of *Lib.* for 1831: 29 Jan., 30 April, 14 May, 28 May.

23. See the following issues of *Lib.* for 1831: 10 Sept., 17 Sept., 29 Oct., 5 Nov., 12 Nov., 19 Nov., 26 Nov., 3 Dec., 17 Dec.

24. The *National Intelligencer,* by the way, refused to print WLG's long letter. See WLG's comment in *Lib.*, 15 Oct. 1831.

25. WLG to Henry E. Benson, 19 Oct. 1831, MB.

26. *Lib.*, 29 Oct. 1831.

27. *Lib.*, 17 Dec. 1831.

28. See *Lib.*, 24 Dec. 1831.

29. *Lib.*, 15 Oct. 1831.

30. *Lib.*, 10 Dec. 1831.

V. BRISK TRADE

1. *Lib.*, 18 June 1831.

2. *Lib.*, 25 June and 17 Nov. 1832.

3. *Lib.*, 14 June 1834. See also following issues: 19 Feb., 2 April, 14 May, 21 May, 29 Oct. 1831; 21 Jan., 10 March, 1 Dec. 1832; 25 Jan., 1 Feb., 22 Feb., 15 March, 18 July 1834.

4. *Lib.*, 17 Dec. 1831.

5. WLG to Henry Benson, MB. Oliver Johnson gave WLG credit for realizing, even before he started *The Liberator,* the necessity for antislavery societies (*William Lloyd Garrison and His Times,* Boston, 1880, p. 82). Johnson's book is the chief source for firsthand material about the founding of the New-England Anti-Slavery Society.

6. *Lib.*, 18 Feb. 1832.

7. Oliver Johnson calls him "George C." (*Garrison and His Times,* p. 87), whereas WLG reports his name as "James C." (*Lib.*, 18 Feb. 1832).

8. See Ian Lewis, "Biographical Sketch," *The Poetical Works of Alonzo Lewis* (Boston, 1883), pp. xvii–xxiii.

9. WLG was not the only one who thought of the founders of the New-England Anti-Slavery Society as apostles. Johnson said (*Garrison and His Times,* p. 88): "If our cause, like Christianity, started with the union of twelve men, so also, our twelve, like that of Jesus, had its one traitor." Johnson was referring to Robert B. Hall, a theological student, who when he entered the ministry, "found the cross of abolitionism too heavy to bear, as it interfered with his clerical ambitions, and so he threw it off." Later as a Know-Nothing congressman, however, he redeemed himself by voting properly on antislavery issues.

10. Johnson reported (*Garrison and His Times*, p. 92): "It seems ludicrous now, but I remember that the least enthusiastic of our number thought it would not take more than ten years at the utmost to abolish slavery!"

11. In Kendrick's obituary (*Lib.*, 8 June 1833) WLG reported that he had given $600 to the New-England Anti-Slavery Society and $100 toward a manual-labor school.

12. Benjamin Thomas agrees with Garrison (*Theodore Weld, Crusader for Freedom*, New Brunswick, N.J., 1950, p. 68) that colonization was "the major hindrance to the beginning of the abolition movement."

13. *Thoughts on African Colonization . . .* (Boston, 1832), p. 124.

14. *Thoughts on African Colonization*, p. 141.

15. *Thoughts on African Colonization*, p. 151ff.

16. WLG to [John B. Vashon?], 15 Aug. 1832, copy, MH. See also WLG to Robert Purvis, 30 May 1832, MB; WLG to Henry E. Benson, 31 May 1832, MB; WLG to Robert Purvis, 22 June 1832, MB; WLG to Ebenezer Dole, 29 June 1832, copy, MB; and WLG to Henry [E. Benson?], 7 July 1832, MB.

17. *Lib.*, 4 Aug., 8 Dec. 1832; 16 Feb. 1833.

18. See *Life*, I, 299.

19. MB.

20. *Lib.*, 18 Oct. 1834. WLG mistakes the name of the sonnet, calling it *"On the detraction which followed upon my writing certain Treatises."*

21. See the letter from WLG, 10 June 1831, printed in *Lib.*, 18 June 1831, as well as the report in the issue for 9 July 1831.

22. See *Lib.*, 24 Sept. and 29 Oct. 1831.

VI. TO ENGLAND AND BEYOND

1. Communications from Cropper are published in *Lib.* for 15 Dec. 1832, 16 Feb., 20 April, 12 Oct. 1833, and 22 Feb. 1834. Garrison's sons suggest (*Life*, I, 146) that "it was doubtless to . . . [James Cropper], an active supporter of Wilberforce and Buxton in the English anti-slavery movement, that Lundy and Garrison were indebted for a frequent supply of reports and other publications showing the progress of the agitation for West-India emancipation."

2. Gilbert H. Barnes said depreciatingly (*The Antislavery Impulse 1830–1844*, New York, 1933, p. 42ff.): "Upon Garrison these British contacts had a revolutionary effect. His ardent, suggestible imagination seized upon the abstract absolutes of the radical pamphleteers of immediate abolition, and he made them his own. Unfortunately his formal education had been meager, and he possessed no background of general knowledge to balance the radical doctrine of the British extremists."

3. The Tappans had employed Theodore D. Weld to tour the schools and colleges of the country and report to the society. See Benjamin P. Thomas, *Theodore D. Weld, Crusader for Freedom*, pp. 38–42. The manual-labor idea was later responsible for the formation of many of the land-grant colleges. See Chap. X below.

4. See *Lib.*, 29 Sept. 1832.

5. The list of donors is given in *Lib.*, 1 June 1833; $326.50 of the total is clearly labeled as from the colored. Gilbert Barnes is incorrect in asserting (*The Antislavery Impulse*, p. 220), "Less than half the total amount was given by Negroes."

6. The main source for information about this period of WLG's life is a

typed document (MB) entitled "Extracts from letters from W.L.G. to 'In-quirers after Truth,' at Derry, N.H., and to Miss Harriet Minot of Haverhill, Mass., 1833," dating from 4 March to 1 May.

7. "Extracts from letters," 9 April 1833.

8. "Extracts from letters," 4 March 1833.

9. *Lib.*, 6 July 1833. The letter is dated from Liverpool, 23 May. See also a letter, dated 20 June, in *Lib.*, 31 Aug., where WLG writes: "I have had fre-quent consultations with our abolition friends, as to the objects of my mission. The plan and object of our School excite their admiration; and as soon as the question relative to colonial slavery is finally settled in this country, they promise to give us liberal and constant assistance. It is their purpose to organize societies for the abolition of slavery throughout the world."

10. WLG, "Speech of . . . ," *Proceedings at the Public Breakfast Held in Honor of William Lloyd Garrison, Esq. . . .* (London, 1868), p. 38.

11. *Lib.*, 6 July 1833.

12. The challenge and other information he reprinted from the *Second An-nual Report of the New-England Anti-Slavery Society*, in *Life*, I, 352ff. Cresson was not unknown to WLG at this time, for his career as a colonizationist had been followed fairly closely in the pages of *The Liberator*. See the issues for 1 Oct., 10 Dec. 1831; 14 April, 22 Dec. 1832. If one may judge by the account of his life in *DNB*, Cresson was not such a scoundrel as the abolitionists would have him. He is classified as "a Quaker merchant and philanthropist," and he did give large sums of money to many charities.

13. For a full report of this meeting see *Lib.*, 10 Aug. 1833.

14. See WLG's letter, dated 20 June, printed in *Lib.*, 31 Aug. 1833.

15. *Lib.*, 7 Sept. 1833.

16. WLG's speech is fully reported in *Lib.*, 9 Nov. 1833. The rest of the Exeter Hall meeting is reported in subsequent issues for 16 Nov., 23 Nov., 30 Nov., and 7 Dec. 1833.

17. For the rest of two of his letters to the *London Patriot* see *Lib.*, 26 Oct. and 12 Dec. 1833.

18. WLG was not the only one in England who had been attacking the Colonization Society. Charles Stuart, born in Jamaica as the son of a British army officer, had been laboring effectively against the society and against El-liott Cresson since 1831. (See *DNB* and Barnes, *The Antislavery Impulse*, pp. 36–37.)

19. See *Lib.*, 19 Oct. 1833.

20. Whether Paul and the colored men for whom he had raised the money were ever repaid the £40 is a moot question. Paul arranged that WLG should reimburse Arthur Tappan, upon whom Paul could then draw. But WLG with his usual vagueness in regard to financial matters did not make the situation clear to Tappan until a subsequent lawsuit brought forth an explanation. The most pertinent information about this matter is to be found in two letters from WLG to Lewis Tappan, 17 Dec. 1835 and 29 Feb. 1836, DLC. As usual, Barnes interprets the matter (p. 221) in the way most unfavorable to WLG, and he misdates the second letter to Tappan as 24 Feb.

21. See *Lib.*, 12 Oct. 1833, for a reprint from the *Courier and Enquirer*.

22. WLG apparently remained on board, perhaps in quarantine, between the 29th and the 2nd. See *Life*, I, 382.

23. *Lib.*, 12 Oct. 1833.

24. *Lib.*, 12 Oct. 1833.

25. *Lib.*, 12 Oct. 1833.
26. *Lib.*, 12 Oct. 1833.
27. *Lib.*, 2 Nov. 1833.
28. *Lib.*, 28 Dec. 1833.
29. WLG to John B. Vashon, 5 Nov. 1833, a typed copy, MH. The main purpose of the letter is to thank Vashon for contributing "sixty dollars as a gift to my partner and myself." WLG insists that Vashon consider this gift a loan and that he and Knapp will repay it as soon as they are able. The following spring (see form letter dated 15 April 1834, MB), WLG proposed selling stock in *Lib.*, though this scheme was apparently abandoned.
30. See *Lib.*, 28 May 1831. Barnes (*The Antislavery Impulse*, p. 54) accuses WLG of urging the formation of the national society in 1833 so that he could appeal to it for funds—an accusation inconsistent with WLG's having advocated such a society since 1831.
31. See the letter from Arnold Buffum printed in *Lib.*, 4 May 1833, and May, *Some Recollections of our Anti-Slavery Conflict*, p. 80.
32. May, pp. 81–82. May considered this episode characteristic. "Those who have only heard of Mr. Garrison, and have believed the misrepresentations of his enemies, have supposed him to be 'a roaring lion, seeking whom he may devour.' But those who have become most intimately acquainted with him have found him to be 'as harmless as a dove,' though indeed 'as wise as a serpent.'" May is the most important source for information about the convention.
33. John G. Whittier, "The Antislavery Convention of 1833," *Atlantic Monthly*, XXXIII (February 1833), 169.
34. May, p. 87.
35. May, p. 89.
36. *Lib.*, 21 Dec. 1833.

VII. A PASSIONATE ATTACHMENT

1. In the Villard Papers at Harvard is to be found the most important source for this chapter, the correspondence between WLG and Helen Benson, dating from 18 Jan. to 29 Aug. 1834. All references, unless otherwise specified, will be to this correspondence.
2. Newburyport *Herald*, 3 Jan. 1826.
3. See the letter written to Edwin Harriman from Boston in 1829, Samuel T. Pickard, *Life and Letters of John Greenleaf Whittier* (Cambridge, Mass., 1895), I, 94.
4. WLG to Stephen Foster, 30 March 1829, MeHi.
5. WLG, *Helen Eliza Garrison, A Memorial* (Cambridge, Mass., 1876), p. 18.
6. For a description of the Benson farm see the advertisement for its sale in *Lib.*, Sept. 1839. The name "Friendship's Vale" was supplied by Prudence Crandall, who found the Benson home a refuge in her trouble.
7. This attitude about the conflict between earthly and heavenly love was shared by other pious lovers of the period. Theodore D. Weld wrote to his fiancée, Angelina Grimké: "I *do* love the Lord our righteousness *better* than I love you. And it is *because* I love him *better* that I love you *as* I do." (Gilbert H. Barnes and Dwight L. Dumond, eds., *Letters of Theodore Dwight Weld, Angelina Grimké Weld and Sarah Grimké, 1822–1844*, New York, 1934, II, 533.)

8. See, in addition to the love letters (MH), WLG's letter to Anna Benson, 14 April 1834, MB.

9. See Sarah M. Fell, *Genealogy of the Fell Family in America* . . . (Philadelphia, 1891), p. 138. This genealogy reports that Leah had been talented and promising as a young woman, but that "soon after arriving at womanhood . . . her mind became clouded, which terminated in later years in insanity." She married David Moore, 18 Oct. 1843, and lived until 1887, surviving her husband by nearly 33 years and Garrison by 8.

10. The wife of the Reverend Samuel J. May of Brooklyn, Connecticut, the minister who married Helen and Lloyd.

11. WLG was sufficiently enamored of these cat puns to repeat them with variations in letters to Helen's two brothers. On 10 July 1834 (MB), he wrote to George: "The Canterburians lately killed a cat, cut her throat, and hung her by the neck to Prudence's gate. We may say to the victim, Requies-*cat* in pace—and to the perpetrators of the murderous deed, 'You have added another black act to the long *cat*-alogue of your offences.' The *cat*-astrophe will be duly chronicled, not *dog*-matically but *cat*-egorically." On 24 Aug. 1835 (MB), he wrote to Henry: "Is puss drowned yet? If so, write me the particulars of the *cat*-astrophe. Poor thing! in sincerity we will exclaim, 'Requies-*cat* in pace.' "

12. MB.

13. WLG to George W. Benson, 4 Sept. 1835, MB.

14. For the record of the wedding day we are indebted to Mrs. George W. Benson's confinement. Since she was expecting a baby, George was unable to attend the ceremony, and WLG wrote to him, 12 Sept., to describe the events of the day (MB).

15. MB. Actually, Eliza was attended by the doctor twice a day for a week, as WLG reported in the letter to George on 12 Sept.

VIII. MAGNETS OF ATTRACTION

1. See the letter written by WLG to his wife on her fiftieth birthday, printed in *Helen Eliza Garrison, A Memorial* (Cambridge, Mass., 1876), p. 30.

2. See *Life*, I, p. 502, footnote 2.

3. This verse is attached to the letter dated 31 May 1835, MB.

4. WLG to Henry Benson, 24 Aug. 1835, MB.

5. WLG to George W. Benson, 4 Sept. 1835, MB.

6. WLG to George W. Benson, 12 Sept. 1835, MB.

7. In his preface to Thompson's *Lectures* ([Boston, 1836], p. xviii) WLG goes further: "His mission would be, physically and spiritually, intellectually and morally, the identical mission of the Son of God . . ."

8. This description of Thompson is drawn largely from material which WLG reprinted (*Lib.*, 6 Dec. 1824) from the Manchester (England) *Times*. Henry C. Wright appraised Thompson frankly ("Autobiography," an unpublished fragment, MH): He was "a man of good and kindly feelings, of ardent and enthusiastic and excitable temperament; of vivid imagination; of a powerful talent for satire and ridicule; of great oratorical powers." But Wright thought him lacking in judgment, for he tried to run every meeting he attended and he joined the Garrison group so closely that he antagonized Garrison's opponents, including much of the clergy and many of the moderate abolitionists.

9. *Lib.*, 6 Dec. 1834.

10. *Lib.*, 6 Dec. 1834.

11. See Thompson's correspondence with Robert Purvis and Isaac Knapp in addition to that with WLG in the various antislavery papers, MB, as well as May, *Some Recollections of our Anti-Slavery Conflict*, pp. 123ff.

12. George Thompson to WLG, *Lib.*, 15 Nov. 1835.

13. WLG to Henry Benson, 3 Sept. 1835, MB.

14. Garrison's sons (*Life*, I, 519, footnote 1) give the date as the 17th, basing their assumption on the fact that the gallows episode had been referred to in *The Liberator* for the 18th as on "Thursday night," but in that issue Garrison himself editorializes on the incident and since he was in Brooklyn, he could not possibly have replied to the news of the gallows in time to meet the deadline for publication of the paper on Friday, the 18th. In their later publication, *The Words of Garrison* (Boston, 1905), they give the correct date, the 10th.

15. *Lib.*, 19 Dec. 1835.

16. Pickard, *Life and Letters of John Greenleaf Whittier*, I, 144.

17. George Thompson to WLG, 15 Sept. 1835, MB.

IX. HURRICANE EXCITEMENT

1. The manuscript of the threat (MB) is written in a bold hand that—ironically enough—closely resembles George Thompson's.

2. Keeping order in Boston in 1835 offered practical difficulties. Although the population of the city was 78,603, law was enforced during the day by only 15 constables who spent most of their time serving writs and subpoenas—only five of them usually were on duty to patrol disorderly quarters in the city. During the night order was entrusted to 30 night watchmen, most of them teamsters and truckmen by day, who went on duty alternate nights. The mayor alerted all of the watch—60 men—for duty on the night of the 21st. (See Theodore Lyman, III, ed., *Papers Relating to the Garrison Mob*, Boston, 1870, pp. 52–53.)

3. *Lib.*, 24 Oct. 1835.

4. There is some question about the exact time; C. C. Burleigh, who wrote the eye-witness account of the mob, gave the time (*Lib.*, 31 Oct.), as two o'clock, whereas WLG said it was two-forty. In describing the events of the day, I have tried wherever possible to use the earliest accounts of the riot, although I have had to depend for many of the details on WLG's later (*Lib.*, 7 Nov.) and in part highly editorialized version.

5. *Lib.*, 7 Nov. 1835.

6. Maria W. Chapman, *Right and Wrong in Massachusetts* (Boston, 1839), p. 33.

7. WLG and other abolitionists resented the desecration of their sign, which they considered a symbol to be protected at all costs. They attacked the mayor unmercifully for his action in removing the sign, but there seems little evidence that he acted with any malice or even that he intended to throw it to the lions. Indeed his conduct in the whole affair, though it may have lacked the force that a more powerful man would have exerted, seems to have been conscientious.

8. Two of these bodyguards were Aaron and Daniel Cooley, of a well-known trucking firm. It is unknown why they acted as they did. Mrs. Garrison suggested in the letter quoted below that they must have been bribed. Possibly they were encouraged by some loyal Garrisonians to protect their leader.

9. *Lib.*, 7 Nov. 1835.

10. *Lib.*, 7 Nov. 1835. The inscription presumably remained until the jail was demolished in 1852.

11. See Nina Moore Tiffany, *Samuel E. Sewall, a Memoir* (Boston, 1898), p. 47.

12. Helen Garrison to Caroline Weston, 31 Oct. 1835, MB.

13. *Lib.*, 19 Oct. 1833.

14. WLG to George W. Benson, 17 Sept. 1835, MB.

15. WLG to Samuel E. Sewall, 24 Oct. 1835, MHi. Of course the martyr complex is a commonplace among reformers. Harriet Martineau was so struck with the martyr spirit among the abolitionists whom she met during a trip to America that she wrote for the *London and Westminster Review* (Dec. 1838) "The Martyr Age of the United States of America . . ." This article was subsequently published as a small book (Newcastle-Upon-Tyne, 1840). Recently, Hazel Wolfe published *On Freedom's Altar, the Martyr Complex in the Abolition Movement* (Madison, 1952). But this book, in spite of its subtitle, contains no psychological analysis of the martyr complex. A far more perceptive work is Eric Hoffer's *The True Believer* (New York, 1951). Although this book is primarily concerned with the nature of mass movements, it contains (pp. 60ff.) the fullest and most thoughtful analysis of the martyr complex that I have read. Hoffer's description of the motivation of leaders of mass movements might almost be a description of Garrison's psychological peculiarities.

16. WLG's attitude toward the mayor's behavior during the mobbing changed decisively after he had developed his official picture of the mob. Samuel E. Sewall reported in his letter of 22 Oct. (Tiffany, *Samuel E. Sewall*, p. 50): "Garrison thinks he owes his life to the mayor's interposition on this occasion." George Benson, WLG's father-in-law, wrote to his son, 23 Oct. (*Life*, II, 35): "The mayor of Boston was very friendly to Garrison."

17. Vincent Y. Bowditch, *Life and Correspondence of Henry Ingersoll Bowditch* (Boston, 1902), p. 100.

18. Edward L. Pierce, *Memoir and Letters of Charles Sumner* (Boston, 1877), I, 173. See also Lyman, ed., *The Garrison Mob*, pp. 6–7.

19. See his manuscript journal, which is deposited in the Massachusetts Historical Society.

20. WLG to Samuel E. Sewall, 24 Oct. 1835, MHi.

21. WLG to Helen Garrison, 4 Nov. 1835, MB.

22. WLG to Helen Garrison, 7 Nov. 1835, MB.

23. WLG to Helen Garrison, 11 Nov. 1835, MB. Both these votes and the number of new subscribers being added to *The Liberator's* list at this time were doubtless the result of publicity in connection with the recent mobbing. See also WLG to Helen Garrison, 9 Nov. 1835, MB.

24. WLG to Helen Garrison, 7 Nov. 1835, MB.

25. WLG to Helen Garrison, 14 Nov. 1835, MB. The house was not rented until January. See WLG to Henry Benson, 26 Jan. 1835, MB.

26. WLG to Helen Garrison, 14 Nov. 1835, MB.

27. WLG to George W. Benson, 27 Nov. 1835, MB.

28. WLG to Amos A. Phelps, 16 Dec. 1835, MH.

29. 11 Jan. 1835, MB.

30. WLG to Henry Benson, 16 Jan. 1835, MB.

31. WLG to Henry Benson, 26 Jan. 1835, MB. WLG's instructions were: "Should the Lynn Record publish a piece of poetry headed, 'There were

some little souls,' &c let it be copied into the Liberator" (16 Jan. 1835, MB). WLG may have planted the poem there; for he said: "The accompanying packet for the editor of the Lynn Record, I wish you would drop immediately into the Boston Post Office, paying the postage upon it, and charging the same to my account." For the complete text of the poem see *Lib.*, 13 Feb. 1836.

32. WLG to Henry Benson, 9 Jan. 1836, MB.
33. WLG to Henry Benson, 9 Jan. 1836, MB.
34. WLG to Samuel J. May, 17 Jan. 1836, MB.
35. WLG to Henry Benson, 26 Jan. 1836, MB.
36. See *Life*, II, 99, as well as WLG to Mrs. George Benson, 20 Jan. 1838, MH.
37. George Benson to Henry Benson, 13 Feb. 1836. This manuscript is in the possession of Miss Fanny Garrison.

X. CENTRAL LUMINARY

1. Thomas, *Theodore Weld*, pp. 6ff. This book is the source for much of the information concerned with Weld in this chapter.
2. As quoted in Thomas, p. 35.
3. Thomas, pp. 36–37. Subsequently, as one of the leaders of the New York abolitionists, Wright was to become one of Garrison's chief opponents.
4. Weld had written WLG as early as 2 Jan. 1833 (Barnes and Dumond, eds., *The Letters of Theodore D. Weld* . . . , New York, 1934, I, 97).
5. WLG to Helen Garrison, 11 May 1835, MB.
6. 11 Nov. 1835, MB.
7. *The Letters of* . . . , I, 286–287.
8. Reports of the number in attendance vary. *The Emancipator* (15 Dec. 1836) said 40; Garrison (to Henry Benson, 3 Dec. 1836, MB) said 30. Perhaps the number of agents enrolled at the meeting increased between the 3rd and the 15th.
9. WLG to Henry Benson, 3 Dec. 1836, MB.
10. WLG to Henry Benson, 22 Nov. 1836. See also *Lib.*, 13 Oct. 1837.
11. *Lib.*, 19 Sept. 1835.
12. See also WLG to George Benson, 12 Sept. 1835.

XI. THE CLERGY MILITANT

1. During the first years of *The Liberator* Garrison seemed more conservative about the meaning of the term "immediate emancipation" than he was later. He said in *The Liberator* for 7 Jan. 1832: "Immediate abolition does not mean that the slaves shall immediately exercise the right of suffrage, or be eligible to any office, or be emancipated from law, or be free from the benevolent restraints of guardianship." In the issue for 8 Dec. the same year he said that he did not mean by the term that slaves should "be turned loose . . . to roam as vagabonds," nor that "they shall be instantly invested with all political rights and privileges," though he would have them protected under law, employed as free laborers and have them "placed under a benevolent and disinterested supervision."
2. WLG to Henry Benson, 11 Aug. 1836, MB.
3. WLG to William Ellery Channing, 20 Jan. 1834, copy, MB.
4. William Ellery Channing, *Slavery* (Boston, 1835), p. 3.

5. Channing, *Slavery*, p. 54.
6. Channing, *Slavery*, p. 127.
7. Channing, *Slavery*, p. 131.
8. Channing, *Slavery*, p. 134.
9. Channing, *Slavery*, pp. 138–139.
10. WLG to Henry Benson, 10 Dec. 1835, MB.
11. WLG to Amos A. Phelps, 16 Dec. 1835, MB.
12. Barnes points out (*The Antislavery Impulse*, p. 165; see also footnote 10, p. 277) that in June of 1837 Birney urged that Channing become the leader of a new group of moderate Massachusetts abolitionists.
13. See the following issues of *Lib.*: 17 Sept., 22 Oct. 1831; 3 March 1832; 3 Jan., 17 Jan., 13 June, 11 July 1835; 12 March, 25 June, 23 July 1836.
14. For expressions of WLG's outrage over various desecrations of the Sabbath see the following issues of *Lib.*: 19 March, 9 April, 16 April 1831; 14 Jan. 1832; 28 June, 30 Aug. 1834; 31 Jan., 4 July 1835.
15. *Lib.*, 23 July 1836.
16. 21 Aug. 1836, MB.
17. *Lib.*, 23 July 1836.
18. Barnes points out (*The Antislavery Impulse*, p. 93) that WLG brought about the end of an important institution because the Congregational churches had for years been community forums.
19. *Life*, II, 114.
20. The meeting between Noyes and WLG is described in *Life*, II, 144–145, the original source being the *American Socialist*, 12 June 1879.
21. See *Lib.*, 9, 16 June 1837.
22. *Lib.*, 7 July 1837.
23. *Lib.*, 11 Aug. 1837.
24. *Lib.*, 25 Aug. 1837.
25. WLG to Isaac Knapp, 9 Aug. 1837, MB.
26. WLG may have acquired his doctrine of the unity of truth and the conviction that the reformer must support all good causes from Abby Kelley, who wrote him (20 Oct. 1837, MB): "I trust the time is now *fully* come, when thou wilt take a decided stand for *all truths*, under the conviction that the whole are necessary to the permanent establishment of any *single one;* for, altho' some or rather, many of our Abolitionists are fearful of the result of such a course, it appears to me that such have never yet comprehended the *nature of truth*—and yet, how perfectly simple and easy to be understood it is, to the unsophisticated child of nature."
27. *Lib.*, 22 Sept. 1837.
28. 10 Oct. 1837, MB. This letter appears to have been crumpled up, as in anger, and then to have been straightened out. See also E. Wright to WLG, 6 Nov. 1837, MB, where Wright continues his plea. "Still I do beg of you, as a brother, to let other subjects alone till slavery is finished, because this is the work you have taken in hand, it is the most pressing, and needs your whole energy." What if WLG does not live to proclaim his "peculiar views of peace, Human Government, Theology, &c., will wisdom die with you?" Wright very much fears his friend will be sucked "into a vortex of spiritual Quixotism," where his precious energy will be depleted. See also Wright's letter to Mrs. Chapman, 15 Sept. 1837, MB.
29. 23 Aug. 1839.
30. For the best analysis to date of this controversy among the abolitionists

see Russel B. Nye, *William Lloyd Garrison and the Humanitarian Reformers* (Boston, 1955), pp. 110ff.

31. See *Lib.*, 29 Sept. 1837.

32. 20 Oct. 1837.

33. Ever since 1833 *The Liberator* had been operating with an annual deficit of approximately $1,000. In 1837 the managers of the state society agreed to assume pecuniary responsibility for the paper for a period of one year. In March (see form letter signed by Isaac Winslow, Ellis Gray Loring, Samuel Philbrick, *et al.*, dated 8 March 1837, MB), they circularized the local societies, telling of the new arrangement and asking them to inform the state society as to how many copies each would be responsible for selling.

34. WLG to George W. Benson, 10 Oct. 1837, MB.

35. See *Lib.*, 5 Jan. 1838.

36. A few years later (*Lib.*, 15 Oct. 1841), WLG stated his perfectionist views more explicitly: "The central question is," he says, "whether there is any such thing as a union of Christ and Belial, light and darkness, holiness and sin! . . ." The answer was in the negative. "May not men dwell in God, and God in them, here, as elsewhere—in the body, as well as out of it?" Garrison continued. "How or why is it impossible to be delivered from all sin on earth? How can one serve two masters—God and Mammon—and be a loyal subject of both? . . . The argument is clear. If men cannot be wholly free from sin at any time in this life, then they are not responsible for their sinful acts. If they can be, then to deny the possibility of it is to speak falsely, and to reject Christ." It is possible that in addition to being directly influenced by Noyes WLG may have been influenced by his writings, since he may have been reading Noyes's monthly paper, *The Perfectionist,* from its inception in 1834. See *Life,* II, 114, 144–145.

XII. TOWARD CRASHING UNANIMITY

1. For information about Lovejoy and the Alton riot see *Lib.*, 24 Nov. 1837, and for the three weeks following; see also Joseph C. and Owen Lovejoy, *Memoir of the Reverend E. P. Lovejoy* (New York, 1838); Edward Beecher, *Narrative of Riots at Alton* (Alton, Ill., 1838); Henry Tanner, *History of the Rise and Progress of the Alton Riots . . .* (Buffalo, N.Y., 1878); John Gill, *Tide Without Turning: Elijah P. Lovejoy and Freedom of the Press* (Boston, 1958); Herman R. Muelder, *Fighters for Freedom* (New York, 1959).

2. WLG to Mrs. George Benson, 20 Jan. 1838, MHi.

3. See Sarah Grimké's defense of woman's rights, *Lib.*, 6 Oct. 1837.

4. *Lib.*, 8 Sept. 1837.

5. WLG to Samuel J. May, 24 April 1838, MB.

6. Thomas, *Theodore Weld*, p. 142.

7. WLG to Helen Garrison, 12 May 1838, MB.

8. As early as the fall of 1837 (*Lib.*, 8 Sept.) WLG had said: "I hope to be more deeply engaged in the cause of Peace by and by, than I can at present; and unless they alter their present course, the first thing I shall do will be to serve our Peace Societies, as I have done the Colonization Societies."

9. See James Garrison's description (Merrill, ed., *Behold Me Once More,* p. 110): "Miss Kelly [*sic*] lecture'd on slavery in the evening. She is a noble masculine looking woman, with stentorian lungs which would put some of our Naval Boatswains to the blush."

10. For his informal report of the convention see WLG's letter to Helen Garrison, 21 Sept. 1838, MB.

11. See the entry for 22 Sept., MHi.

12. 24 Sept. 1838, MB. I am quoting from the final and most interesting paragraph of the letter, which is omitted from the version published in *Life*, II, 237.

13. WLG to Mary Benson, 23 Dec. 1838, MB.

14. MB.

15. 14 Jan. 1839, MB.

16. For the full text of the resolutions see *Lib.*, 1 Feb. 1839.

17. The fullest account of this meeting is to be found in Maria W. Chapman, *Right and Wrong in Massachusetts* (Boston, 1839), pp. 93ff. This is a highly colored and rhetorical account, written with a strong bias toward WLG's side of the controversy. Appended to the text are three letters from Torrey to May, in which he tries to persuade WLG's friend to use his efforts to establish the official paper for the Massachusetts Anti-Slavery Society. Although Torrey questioned the authenticity of these documents in a letter to Mrs. Chapman, the latter indicated in *Lib.*, 29 Nov. 1839, that she would attest to their authenticity through legal affidavit.

18. *Lib.*, 12 Aug. 1842.

19. Phelps did not take part in the meeting as he was ill. See Whittier's letter to WLG, *Lib.*, 8 March 1839.

20. Chapman, p. 98.

21. Chapman, pp. 100–101.

22. WLG gives the figure 180 but suggests that it may have been as much as 190 (*Lib.*, 1 Feb. 1839). Mrs. Chapman, however (p. 113), gives the number 183.

23. *Lib.*, 1 Feb. 1839. WLG would have been surprised could he have foreseen the rest of C. T. Torrey's career. In 1842 he was jailed in Annapolis, Maryland, for attending and reporting a convention of slaveholders and WLG (*Lib.* 21 Jan. 1842; see also issue for 15 April) appealed to the people of Massachusetts to make common cause in such a case. Torrey was released after a few days, but two years later got into trouble again for helping fugitive slaves escape across the Maryland and Virginia borders. He was imprisoned, convicted, and sentenced to six years of hard labor, after about a year of which he died of tuberculosis. WLG devoted the columns of *The Liberator* to several appeals during the year of Torrey's imprisonment. (See *Lib.*, 26 July, 9 Aug., 23 Aug., 13 Sept., 27 Sept., 13 Dec., 27 Dec. 1844.) He even wrote two impersonal sonnets on the occasion of his imprisonment (*Lib.*, 10 Jan. 1845). After Torrey's death WLG, at a New-England Anti-Slavery Convention, called him "the late victim of American Christianity—alias Slavery" (see *Lib.*, 22 May 1846). But when the free colored of Boston planned a monument for Torrey, WLG advised them to think of the living rather than the dead (*Lib.*, 10 July 1845). A year later J. C. Lovejoy, brother of the martyred E. P. Lovejoy, published a memoir of Torrey.

24. *Lib.*, 22 Feb. 1839.

25. *Lib.*, 8 March 1839.

26. *Lib.*, 12 July 1839.

27. *Lib.*, 12 July 1839.

28. DLC.

29. *Lib.*, 16 Aug. 1839.

30. Quoted (*Lib.*, 19 July 1839) from his Fourth of July address at South Scituate, Mass.

31. See Barnes, *The Antislavery Impulse,* p. 265.

32. *Lib.*, 22 March 1839.

33. See the "Address to the Abolitionists of Massachusetts" signed by the Managers of the Massachusetts Society, *Lib.*, 1 March 1839.

34. *Lib.*, 31 May 1839.

35. *Lib.*, 14 Feb. 1840.

36. DLC.

37. See Lewis Tappan to Seth Gates, 21 March 1840, letterbook, DLC. Tappan suggests that Garrison may be strong enough to turn the Executive Committee out at the annual meeting, and that it may be time to disband the society since "abolitionism is now so soaked into the community that it will live. Perhaps a central committee . . . might be formed to carry on the enterprise in this city. So many isms & hobbies have been attached to the antislavery cause that the National Organization can not carry the load." See also Lewis Tappan to Joshua R. Giddings, 24 April 1840, letterbook, DLC.

38. 16 Jan. 1840.

39. 18 Feb. 1840.

40. Samuel D. Hastings to Lewis Tappan, 29 April 1840, DLC. See also Samuel D. Hastings to Lewis Tappan, 23 April 1840, DLC. Hastings felt greatly embarrassed because people would think, not knowing he had been absent from the meeting, that he had voted for the female delegates. He also feared that "Garrison will make use of the appointment for his own purposes."

41. *Lib.*, 10 April 1840.

42. WLG to Helen Garrison, 5 May 1840, MB.

43. Lewis Tappan to Theodore D. Weld, 4 May 1840, letterbook, DLC.

44. *Lib.*, 15 May 1840. The description of the antislavery boatload is quoted from a letter from WLG to his paper.

45. WLG in a letter to his wife (16 May 1840, MB) gives the figures as 560 to 450; but 557 to 451 are the figures to be found in the report of the meeting in *Lib.*, 22 May 1840, as well as in the official journal of the new national society, *The American and Foreign Anti-Slavery Reporter* (June 1840) and Lewis Tappan, *The Life of Arthur Tappan* (New York, 1870), p. 303.

46. *The American and Foreign Anti-Slavery Reporter,* June 1840.

47. WLG to Helen Garrison, 16 May 1840, MB. According to Edmund Quincy (to Richard D. Webb, 27 June 1843, MHi), it was three years before the old society was able to dedicate its annual meeting to abolition rather than to fighting new organizations. At the meeting in 1842, according to Quincy, WLG suffered a setback when he advocated that the headquarters of the society be moved to Boston. He was opposed by what Quincy called the Boston Clique (Wendell Phillips and Caroline Weston in addition to himself), who insisted that moving to Boston would be equivalent to dissolution and said they would not support the organization if it moved. "Garrison dilated his nostrils like a warhorse, & snuffed indignation at us," Quincy reported. As a compromise measure it was decided that a quorum of the executive committee of the society be appointed from Boston so that the business could be done there. At Quincy's suggestion, moreover, WLG was appointed president. Quincy explained to Webb that "Garrison makes an excellent President at a public meeting where the order of the speakers is in some measure arranged, as he has great felicity in introductory & interlocutory

remarks, but at a meeting for debate he does not answer so well, as he is rather too apt, with all the innocence & simplicity in the world, to do all the talking himself. This, moreover, we shall arrange by having Francis Jackson to act as V.P. on such occasions."

XIII. ABROAD AGAIN

1. See WLG to George Bradburn, 24 April 1840, copy, MB, and WLG to Lucretia Mott, 28 April 1840, PSC.

2. Reprinted in *Lib.*, 8 May 1840.

3. *Lib.*, 8 May 1840. The issue the following week definitely informed his readers that he was going to London.

4. For a full description of WLG's negotiations see Merrill, ed., *Behold Me Once More*, pp. 101ff.

5. Merrill, ed., *Behold Me Once More.*

6. WLG gives interesting information regarding the expenses of trans-Atlantic travel in 1840. Passage on an ordinary ship cost $60, on a fast packet, $100, and on a steam packet, $140. WLG estimated that the total cost of sending a delegate to the World's Convention was between $400 and $500. See *Lib.*, 28 Feb. and 20 March 1840.

7. WLG to Helen Garrison, 28 May 1840, MB.

8. 13 June 1840, MNS.

9. MHi. Extracts from many of WLG's private letters, even those to his wife, were printed, with WLG's explicit permission (see letter to Helen Garrison, 29 June 1840, MB), in *The Liberator*. The passage here quoted is from a letter dated 12 June 1840 and is printed in *Lib.*, 31 July 1840.

10. MB.

11. WLG to Helen Garrison, 15–16 June 1840, MB.

12. Dwight L. Dumond, ed., *Letters of James Gillespie Birney, 1831–1857* (New York, 1938), I, 557.

13. See his letter to *The Liberator*, dated 22 May and published in the issue for 29 May 1840.

14. The opinion of Charles Stuart, expressed a year later (to Gerrit Smith, 15 Aug. 1841, NSU), was typical of the British reaction: "If the Garrison party would cease to ridicule and abuse those abolitionists who think it not right for women to mingle with men in public debate etc., much would be accomplished towards a reunion of abolitionists." See the *Calendar of the Gerrit Smith Papers in the Syracuse University Library* (Albany, 1941–42).

15. C. Marshall Taylor ("Whittier vs. Garrison," Essex Institute *Historical Collections*, LXXXII, July 1946, 273) says that although the official grounds for excluding the female delegates was that they were women, the real reason was that they were members of the wrong branch of the Society of Friends. Lucretia Mott makes it quite clear in the diary kept during her trip that she is being discriminated against because of her religious views, mentioning that in Glasgow some orthodox Friends went so far as to publish in the newspaper the fact "that we hold no religious fellowship with Lucretia Mott, nor with the body in the United States (called Hicksites), to which she belongs: they not being recognized by the Society of Friends in the United Kingdom, nor by those Friends with whom we are in connection in America" (Anna Davis Hallowell, ed., *James and Lucretia Mott, Life and Letters*, Boston, 1884, pp. 175–176). WLG on his return to America mentioned (*Lib.*, 28 Aug.

1840) that Lucretia Mott was a Hicksite Quaker, whereas the majority of the London Committee was orthodox. "To gratify their bigotry on one point, they did not scruple to act against their principles by joining in a crusade against the admission of women with those whom on other occasions they call 'hireling priests.'" William Howlitt in a letter to Mrs. Mott (Hallowell, pp. 175–176) agreed that the women were excluded as Hicksites, not as women. (See WLG to Helen Garrison, 3 July 1840, MB.) Whittier disagreed (*Lib.*, 27 Nov. 1840). See also Lewis Tappan to Joseph Sturge, 5 May 1840, letterbook, DLC, which indicates that Sturge had urged that orthodox Quakers be sent to the London convention.

16. Mrs. Mott recorded in her journal on the 9th of June (*Life and Letters*, p. 151): "W. D. Crewdson and W. Ball came with official information that women were to be rejected."

17. *Lib.*, 24 July 1840. For a full report of the proceedings of the convention see *Proceedings of the General Anti-Slavery Convention* (London, 1840).

18. *Lib.*, 24 July 1840.

19. WLG to Helen Garrison, 29 June 1840, MB.

20. For laudatory comments on Garrison's action see Nathaniel P. Rogers, *A Collection from the Miscellaneous Writings of . . .* (Boston, 1840), p. 100, and Rogers' communication in *Lib.*, 28 Aug. 1840. For less favorable comment see *Lib.*, 27 Nov. 1840, where Whittier grants WLG's right to remain aloof from the meeting if his conscience so dictated, but questions his right to condemn the whole convention for its rejection of women.

21. Rogers in *Lib.*, 28 Aug. 1840.

22. Letter to Sarah Grimké and Angelina G. Weld, 25 June 1840, DLC.

23. WLG to Helen Garrison, 3 July 1840, MB.

24. Alexander P. D. Penrose, ed., *The Autobiography and Memoirs of Benjamin Robert Haydon* (New York, 1929), p. 532. Haydon saw WLG right after his visit to the duchess.

25. *Herald of Freedom*, 16 Oct. 1840.

26. WLG to Helen Garrison, 3 July 1840, MB.

27. George Thompson to WLG, 15 Sept. 1840, printed in *Life*, I, 520.

28. WLG and Rogers had known each other for a number of years; they had been in correspondence at least since February 1834. See *Lib.*, 8 March 1834.

29. *Herald of Freedom*, 16 Oct. 1840, reprinted in *Miscellaneous Writings*, p. 106.

30. WLG to Helen Garrison, 23 July 1840, MB.

31. *Herald of Freedom*, 30 Oct. 1840, reprinted in *Miscellaneous Writings*, p. 118.

32. 23 July 1840, MB. This self-righteous passage is deleted from the letter as printed in *Life*, II, 397.

33. *Lib.*, 4 Sept. 1840.

34. *Lib.*, 28 Aug. 1840.

35. WLG explained (*Lib.*, 18 Dec. 1840) all the circumstances surrounding this episode and defended himself against a subsequent Chartist attack in another handbill.

36. See the editorial on "Working Men" in the first issue of the *Lib.* (1 Jan. 1831), as well as subsequent comments (*Lib.*, 29 Jan. 1831).

37. He said (*Lib.*, 23 Oct. 1840): "We scarcely found an abolitionist in

England, who was ready to avow himself a chartist, or who expressed any sympathy in that movement."

38. See *Lib.*, 21 Aug. 1840.

39. WLG to R. D. Webb, 27 Feb. 1842, MB.

40. WLG to Elizabeth Pease, 31 Aug. 1840, MB. This letter is full of information about the return voyage.

41. Edmund Quincy corroborates WLG's statement by calling this voyage "the shortest passage ever made between the Continents." See entry in his Journal for 17 Aug. 1840, MHi.

42. See especially WLG to Henry C. Wright, 23 [?] Aug. 1840, MB, and *Lib.*, 21 Aug. 1840.

43. Barnes, *The Antislavery Impulse*, p. 173.

44. Barnes, pp. 173ff. See also *Lib.*, 19 March, 21 May, 4, 25 June, 6, 27 Aug. 1841.

45. Barnes, pp. 175–176.

XIV. SMILING AT SATAN'S RAGE

1. Thoreau writes in *Walden* (Modern Library College Edition, pp. 69–70): "If anything ail a man, so that he does not perform his functions, . . . he forthwith sets about reforming—the world. . . . I believe that what so saddens the reformer is not his sympathy with his fellows in distress, but, though he be the holiest son of God, is his private ail. Let this be righted, let the spring come to him, the morning rise over his couch, and he will forsake his generous companions without apology."

2. Merrill, ed., *Behold Me Once More*, p. 28, see also pp. 117ff.

3. WLG to George W. Benson, 1 Nov. 1840, MB. WLG disclaims (*Lib.*, 29 Jan. 1841) credit for the Sabbath Convention; Edmund Quincy takes full responsibility in a letter to WLG (*Lib.*, 19 March 1841).

4. For WLG's most complete report of the convention see his letter to John A. Collins, 1 Dec. 1840, MB. WLG was active in another Sabbath convention in the spring of 1848; see especially *Lib.*, 21 April and 2 June 1848.

5. See entry for 17 Nov., MHi.

6. R. W. Emerson, "The Chardon Street Convention," *Lectures and Biographical Sketches* (Boston, 1884), p. 354.

7. For WLG's brief report of the proceedings see *Lib.*, 27 Nov. 1840; for a fuller and, according to WLG, "tolerably accurate" report from the *New York Observer* see *Lib.*, 4 Dec. 1840; for a lively though perhaps prejudiced account from the Portland *Advertiser* see *Lib.*, 25 Dec. 1840.

8. See *Lib.*, 29 Jan. 1841, for quotations from Colver's letters as well as WLG's response. WLG explains that his informant is "a highly respectable member of the Society of Friends in England." In *Life* (II, 429) the estimable Quaker is identified, doubtless correctly, as Elizabeth Pease.

9. *Lib.*, 28 July 1841.

10. The letter is also printed in *American Socialist*, 12 June 1879, and in an edited version in *Life*, II, 144–145.

11. *Lib.*, 27 Oct. 1841. In a letter to R. D. Webb (27 June 1843, MHi) Edmund Quincy described WLG's perfectionism, saying that the perfectionists are "a sect whose general doctrines he receives though he does not belong to it or any."

12. WLG to George W. Benson, 11 Oct. 1842, MB.

13. 2 May 1842, DLC.

14. *Lib.*, 5 May 1843. That WLG never sympathized with Noyes's views on multiple marriage as practiced in his communities is indicated in a long editorial, "Marriage—Perfectionism." Torrey had challenged WLG on this issue, and the response was unequivocal: "The marriage institution is divine," WLG said, "and none the less divine because the initiatory rites vary in nearly every country on the face of the globe" (*Lib.*, 26 Nov. 1841).

15. *Lib.*, 1 Dec. 1843.

16. In July, however, WLG was still reading Noyes's *Perfectionist* (WLG to Maria W. Chapman, 7 July 1843, MB), although not uncritically.

17. *Lib.*, 3 Jan. 1835; see also 5 Jan. 1844 and 3 Oct. 1845.

18. But WLG seems to deny particular providence entirely. See WLG to Eliza F. Eddy, 3 Oct. 1848, MB, and *Lib.*, 28 Dec. 1848.

19. *Lib.*, 21 Nov. 1845. In this discussion of Paine WLG really avows himself a moderate deist, though he would perhaps have been shocked that anyone should use this term in reference to his religious views.

20. WLG also gives James and Lucretia Mott great credit for liberalizing his religious views (*Lib.*, 9 Nov. 1849).

21. In 1842 Wright published in Boston under the title *A Kiss for a Blow* a collection of stories he had written to teach children the principles of non-resistance. Edmund Quincy reported in a letter to R. D. Webb (27 June 1843, letterbook, MHi) that Wright had made a great hit with the Rogers' children and told this story: "One day two of the children quarrelled & the little boy struck the little girl. Rogers, as in duty bound, endeavored to impress upon his mind the enormity of his offense & by way of bringing it home to him said, 'Now, should you have liked to have had Mr. Wright see you strike your little sister?' " The boy admitted he would not have liked Mr. Wright to see him, and so the father continued: "But though Mr. Wright did not see you, GOD did, & you ought to be much more afraid of doing wrong before him than before Mr. Wright.' 'Oh, but Charley,' exclaimed the little girl looking up & smiling through her tears, 'you needn't mind God's seeing you, for *he* isn't half as good as Mr. Wright!' 'What *do* you mean, my dear?' demanded the petrified papa, horror struck at this result of all his religious instructions. 'Why you know that God once killed a man & a woman for telling a lie, & Mr. Wright wouldn't do such a wicked thing!' "

22. Henry Clarke Wright, *Human Life: Illustrated in my Individual Experience as a Child, a Youth, and a Man* (Boston, 1849), p. 192.

23. *Human Life*, p. 331.

24. *Human Life*, p. 341.

25. *Human Life*, pp. 363–364.

26. *Human Life*, p. 378.

27. WLG's sons, although suggesting (*Life*, IV, 335) that "the one man who stood next to my father in a bond of warm and romantic friendship, was unquestionably George Thompson," admit that Wright stood closer to him than Quincy or Phillips. Garrison told Wright in a letter a few years later (1 Oct. 1844, MB): "There is no one on this wide earth, among the great circles of my friends, for whom I entertain greater love and respect. Your views of the nature, spirit and design of Christianity,—of the brotherhood of the human race—of the corruption of existing political, religious and governmental institutions—are more nearly identical with my own, than those

of almost any other individual. In your welfare—in all your labors and trials—in all that you are endeavoring to accomplish in behalf of the human family—I take a deep abiding, thrilling interest. God be with you to the end of the conflict here below and bless you eternally." In a letter to Edmund Quincy (15 Feb. 1868, MB) R. D. Webb confirms the fact that Garrison was not intimate socially with the Quincys, that Garrison had, in fact, never seen Quincy's son. "It was the strongest proof I ever got of the existence of the same kind of class separation amongst you which rules every thing in these old countries where the separation of people into classes is universal."

28. WLG to Henry E. Benson, 16 Jan. 1836, MB; WLG to Samuel J. May, 17 Jan. 1836, MB.

29. WLG tells Wright (12 April 1842, MB) that he is having great difficulty raising funds for the English mission, partly because so many abolitionists think him too valuable in this country to be spared. See also WLG to George W. Benson, 13 May 1842, MB, and *Lib.*, 25 March, 15 April, 22 April, 15 July 1842.

30. R. D. Webb, curious to know why Wright was so content to be away from his home and family, inquired of Quincy the reason. Quincy said (28 Mar. 1847, letterbook, MHi): "I never saw his wife but once, nor her daughters but once or twice, but from what I remember of them my impression is that I should be quite [as] willing to live away from them as with them. His wife is many years older than he; & you know they took the wrong side on the Rogers matter [i.e., sided with Rogers against Garrison], which is a pretty sure criterion of their characters."

31. See Wright to WLG, 18 March 1843, MB; *Lib.*, 5 May, 15 Sept. 1843; 9 Feb. 1844. Wright's speeches resembled WLG's not only in idea but sometimes in imagery. In the speech reported in *Lib.* for 15 Sept. 1843, for example, he used one of WLG's favorite allusions—to the line from Colley Cibber's version of *Richard III*, "Conscience, avaunt! Richard's himself again!"—when he said that O'Connell "showed himself more than Richard again." WLG had made use of this very allusion in a letter to Wright in 1840 (23 [?] Aug., MB), where he rejoiced that George Thompson was with them once more. " 'Richard's himself again,' and nobly will he do battle for us." The same phrase appears in the editorial section of *The Liberator* for 19 Oct. 1838. See also Wright's letter (*Lib.*, 9 Feb. 1844) where he refers to O'Connell as "the observed of all observers," using one of WLG's favorite phrases from *Hamlet*. For WLG's use of the phrase see his letter to Helen Benson, 11 May 1835, MB, and the editorial section of *Lib.* for 29 Aug. 1845 and 26 March 1847.

32. As a preface to a poem on the subject, Whittier reprinted the words of the judge in passing sentence. See *The Poetical Works of* . . . (Boston, 1904), III, 90. Whittier reports that Brown had already married the young lady, but this is not the usual version of the story.

33. For a full report and reprints from various newspapers see *Lib.*, 26 April 1844, the day set for Brown's execution. WLG resented the almost complete indifference of the American political and religious press on the subject.

34. *Lib.*, 17 May 1844.

35. Thomas Clarkson to Lewis Tappan, 31 July 1844, DLC. This letter is to be found in the Tappan papers.

36. Lewis Tappan to Thomas Clarkson, 14 Sept. 1844, DLC.

37. More than eighty letters were printed in the paper between the spring of 1844 and the spring of 1846, which meant that Wright was in effect WLG's foreign correspondent.

38. For reference to the counterattacks against the two abolitionists see letters from Wright to WLG published in *Lib.*, 27 June and 1 Aug. 1845.

39. *Lib.*, 29 May 1846.

40. Funds collected totaled $949.25 by the end of November. See *Lib.*, 27 Nov. 1846. Of this amount $100 each had been given by Wendell Phillips, Francis Jackson, Edmund Jackson, C. F. Hovey, and Andrew Robeson; $50 from Samuel May, Jr.; $25 from Nathaniel Barney; and $20 from Ellis Gray Loring.

41. *Lib.*, 24 July 1846.

42. Edmund Quincy, "Journal," 16 July 1846, MHi. In a letter to R. D. Webb (14 July 1846, MHi) Quincy explained that he was going to town to see WLG off. "I expect to see him rushing down to the Steamer, carpetbag in hand, just as she is pushing off."

43. Edmund Quincy, "Journal," 13 July 1846, MHi.

44. *Lib.*, 24 July 1846.

45. 14 July 1846, MHi.

46. For descriptions of the voyage see WLG to Helen Garrison, 18 July 1846, MB, printed in *Lib.*, 7 Aug. 1846, and WLG to Helen Garrison, 26–31 July [mislabeled Aug. on the first page] 1846, MB.

47. 1 [possibly 4] Aug. 1846, MB.

48. 1 [possibly 4] Aug. 1846, MB.

49. WLG to Helen Garrison, 11 Aug. 1846, MB.

50. WLG to Helen Garrison, 4 Aug. 1846, MB. Toward the end of his life WLG opposed the Contagious Diseases acts in England (see Chapter XX); he also wrote against licensing prostitution in the *Womans Journal* for 4 Jan. 1878.

51. The fullest report of the episode is to be found in the extracts from a letter written by WLG to his wife, dated 4 Aug. 1846, in *Lib.*, 11 Sept. 1846. The original manuscript of the letter apparently was destroyed.

52. *Lib.*, 18 Sept. 1846.

53. 18 Aug. 1846, MB.

54. WLG reported the matter to his wife, 17 Sept. 1846, MB. Mrs. Howitt's own comment on the biographical sketch was: "I did not say all I felt, because I feared many readers would think me extravagant. To my mind there is no impropriety in comparing to Christ men who have striven to follow His example. All do not see it so, and as we write for the many, I have been contented to mention facts and leave them to speak for themselves." (Margaret Howitt, ed., *Mary Howitt, an Autobiography*, Boston & New York, II, 40.)

55. For a full description of the various people he cultivated see the letter to Quincy, dated 14 Aug., in *Lib.*, 11 Sept. 1846, and letters to his wife, dated 3 Sept., 17 Sept., and one undated, though undoubtedly written in Sept. of the same year. See also footnote in *Life*, III, 159.

56. WLG to Edmund Quincy, dated 18 Sept., in *Lib.*, 9 Oct. 1846. See also the letter to Quincy, dated 3 Oct., in *Lib.*, 30 Oct. 1846.

57. The duty became a subject of controversy in the pages of *The Liberator*, WLG claiming that duty should never be attached to *"a token of personal and public regard."* See *Lib.*, 25 Dec. 1846. Friends of the cause subse-

quently reimbursed WLG for the total amount of the duty. In the letter of thanks to Mrs. Ellis Gray Loring for her $10 contribution (30 July 1847) he told how much he hated customs houses and how thoroughly he believed in free trade. For a public acknowledgment of the reimbursement see *Lib.*, 30 July 1847; for WLG's analysis of free trade, see Chapter XX.

58. *Lib.*, 30 Oct. 1846.

59. 7 Oct. 1846, letterbook, DLC.

60. WLG to George W. Benson, 11 Dec. 1846, MB.

61. 19 Dec. 1846, MB.

62. WLG indicated in *Lib.* for 22 Nov. 1834 that there would shortly be an exhibition of articles contributed by ladies for the benefit of the New-England Anti-Slavery Society. When the articles were sold on 16 December, $300 was raised for the society (see *Lib.*, 20 Dec. 1834). The next year the fair netted $350 (*Lib.*, 9 Jan. 1836). As the earnings of the fairs increased from year to year, WLG and his associates began to plan far in advance for the forthcoming fairs, eventually starting to work on the next year's fair as soon as the last year's had ended. Meetings were held by the antislavery ladies through the spring and summer. Articles were collected for sale from friends in England, Scotland, Ireland, and even France (mementos from Paris seemed especially popular). By 1845 the fair—then called a bazaar—was held in Faneuil Hall, and the receipts reached $3,700 (*Lib.*, 9 Jan. 1846). The amount raised stayed approximately the same in 1847 (*Lib.*, 7 Jan. 1848). Then the receipts fell off gradually (*Lib.*, 5 Jan. 1848, 25 Jan. 1850, 17 Jan. 1851, 2 Jan. 1852) until 1853, when it rose to $4,256 (*Lib.*, 20 Jan. 1854). By 1856 a record $5,250 was raised (*Lib.*, 30 Jan. 1857). In 1857 the figure dropped abruptly to $3,500 (*Lib.*, 1 Jan. 1858). The following year the bazaar was discontinued in favor of a National Anti-Slavery-Subscription Anniversary, at which $6,117.02 was raised (*Lib.*, 18 Feb. 1859; see also *Lib.*, 26 Nov. 1859). During the war the total contributed gradually diminished with the exception of 1864, when $4,500 was collected (*Lib.*, 19 Feb. 1864; see also *Lib.*, 10 Feb. 1860, 15 Feb. 1861, 14 Feb. 1862, 20 Feb. 1863). In 1865 only $3,300 was raised (*Lib.*, 3 March 1865). The bazaars and the subscription anniversaries, during the last twenty years of the antislavery agitation, represented the most important devices for raising funds to support the movement.

63. See WLG to Helen Garrison, 10 Sept. 1846, MB. In his letter to Elizabeth Pease on 15 Nov. WLG reported: "There are several boxes of articles for the Bazaar in the Acadia."

64. Henry C. Wright, "Diary," MB.

65. The full description of the various articles to be sold at the bazaar is in *Lib.*, 25 Dec. 1846. For the most complete report following the bazaar see *Lib.*, 29 Jan. 1847.

66. *Lib.*, 1 Jan. 1847.

67. James Miller McKim, abolitionist editor of the *Pennsylvania Freeman* and the father of Wendell P. Garrison's future wife.

68. WLG reprinted this long poem, which had previously been published anonymously in the *Pennsylvania Freeman*, in *Lib.*, for 8 Jan. 1847, recognizing the poet as Lowell. I have quoted from James Russell Lowell, *The Poetical Works* (Cambridge, Mass., 1904), I, 317–318.

XV. THE NATIONAL SCENE

1. *Lib.,* 24 July 1846.
2. *Lib.,* 13 Oct. 1832.
3. *Lib.,* 20 Dec. 1834.
4. *Lib.,* 20 Dec. 1834.
5. *Lib.,* 3 Jan. 1840. WLG's campaign against the formation of a third party was doubtless given impetus by James G. Birney's having been offered the presidential nomination at a state convention at Warsaw, New York, 13 Nov. 1839.
6. *Lib.,* 31 Jan. 1840.
7. *Lib.,* 13 March 1840.
8. After Birney had freed his slaves and resigned from the American Colonization Society in 1834, WLG reprinted his letter from the Lexington *Kentucky Intelligencer,* calling it "one of the most important documents of the American antislavery cause" (*Lib.,* 16 Aug. 1834). WLG admired greatly Birney's courage in agitating for emancipation in the South (*Lib.,* 15 Aug. 1835); and he followed closely in the pages of *The Liberator* Birney's attempt to found an antislavery paper and his flight from Kentucky to Ohio (see *Lib.,* 26 Sept., 10 Oct., 26 Dec. 1835; 13 Feb., 13 Aug., 10 Sept., 17 Sept. 1835). Birney's persecution, WLG said, was the perfect answer to the query, "Why don't you go South?" (see *Lib.,* 16 June 1837).
9. Garrison said in 1841 (*Lib.,* 15 Jan.): "Third partyism is but another form of new organization—grew out of it, was devised by it, lives upon it, is controlled by it—and the leaders in the one, are the leaders in the other." Two years later Edmund Quincy wrote (*Lib.,* 22 Sept.) that it was impossible to trust politically those who had been untrue abolitionists.
10. A recent work on the subject (Howard P. Nash, Jr., *Third Parties in American Politics,* Washington, D.C., 1959, p. 28) indicates: "The Albany meeting . . . was attended by a bare 100 delegates from New York and less than 30 from five other states." Garrison gave a total figure of 121, with 104 from New York.
11. *Lib.,* 10 April 1840.
12. *Lib.,* 1 Oct. 1841.
13. *Lib.,* 16 Sept. 1842.
14. *Lib.,* 10 Oct. 1845.
15. *Lib.,* 6 March 1846.
16. *Lib.,* 13 March 1846.
17. *Lib.,* 13 March 1846.
18. *Lib.,* 13 March 1846. In a sense WLG's argument here resembles that of the South, which can also be stated in terms of the majority-minority problem.
19. For a discussion of the constitutional argument used by the abolitionists and others see Jacobus tenBroek, *The Antislavery Origins of the Fourteenth Amendment* (Berkeley, Calif., 1951), p. 31: "If slaves were things, chattels, property, then the purpose of government, the right to protection, the idea of equality, the due process and just compensation clauses of the Fifth Amendment—were all applicable to their owners as citizens or as persons and were designed to continue the servitude by safeguarding ownership. If the slaves were human beings, individuals with minds and souls, persons, then the just compensation clause was wholly irrelevant to the forcible termination of their

slavery; their liberty was protected by the due process clause; and they were in the class of persons whose equal need for protection and equal possession of inalienable rights gave rise to government." Or to put it more succinctly (p. 110): "To the southerner, the natural right involved was property; to the abolitionist, liberty."

20. 29 Dec. 1832. It is difficult to determine the source of Garrison's constitutional argument. Gerrit Smith insisted in a letter to Whittier (*Lib.*, 31 Aug. 1844) that the nonresistants who considered the Constitution proslavery were greatly influenced by John Quincy Adams and Joshua Giddings. Wendell Phillips, who officially answered Smith's letter (*Lib.*, 6 Sept. 1844), mentions Calhoun, Judge Story, and Webster as in some respects agreeing with the Garrisonians about the Constitution. Garrison himself in his three editorials on Smith's letters (*Lib.*, 20, 27 Sept., 4 Oct. 1844) quotes Adams, Hamilton, and Madison in support of his view. H. L. Pinckney's analysis of the Constitution as protecting slavery may have been influential (see *Lib.*, 4 June 1836). The Reverend John Rankin's letters to his brother, which touch obliquely on the constitutional issue and were so much admired by Garrison that he reprinted them all in *The Liberator* (between 25 Aug. and 17 Nov. 1832) certainly left their impact. It is unlikely that any single source can be found for Garrison's position.

21. *Lib.*, 12 Sept. 1835.

22. See especially *Lib.*, 22 April, 6, 13, 20, 27 May 1842.

23. *Lib.*, 3 Feb. 1843; also printed in *Eleventh Annual Report, Presented to the Massachusetts Anti-Slavery Society* . . . (Boston, 1843), p. 95. At the preceding annual meeting there had apparently been no discussion at all of the Constitution and dissolution (see *Lib.*, 11 Feb. 1842).

24. *Lib.*, 24 May 1844.

25. *Lib.*, 24 May 1844.

26. See TenBroek, *Antislavery Origins*, pp. 118–119.

27. *Lib.*, 31 May 1844.

28. *Lib.*, 31 May 1844.

29. *Lib.*, 31 May 1844.

30. *Lib.*, 14 June 1844.

31. *Lib.*, 14 June 1844.

32. For a full description of the trip to Philadelphia and Norristown and the meeting see *Lib.*, 23 Aug. 1844.

33. *Lib.*, 20 Sept. 1844. The group of British abolitionists now supporting Garrison did not include Joseph Sturge, Charles Stuart, and others who had become disaffected since 1840.

34. *Lib.*, 20, 27 Sept., and 4 Oct. 1844.

35. *Lib.*, 18 July 1845. For the idea that the Constitution and Union are equivalent see also 1 May 1846.

36. *Lib.*, 24 April 1846.

37. *Lib.*, 25 March 1842.

38. *Lib.*, 1 Dec. 1843.

39. *Lib.*, 8 Dec. 1843.

40. *Lib.*, 22, 29 March, 5 April 1844.

41. *Lib.*, 3 May 1844.

42. *Lib.*, 7 Nov. 1845.

43. *Lib.*, 7 March 1846.

44. *Lib.*, 29 May 1846.

45. *Lib.*, 25 Dec. 1846.
46. *Lib.*, 22 Jan. 1847.
47. *Lib.*, 7 May 1847.
48. *Lib.*, 11 Feb. 1848.
49. *Lib.*, 17 Feb. 1849.
50. *Lib.*, 12 March 1847.
51. For a full description of the genesis of the Free-Soil party see Howard P. Nash, Jr., *Third Parties in American Politics* (Washington, 1949), pp. 23–55. For the development of the party in Massachusetts see Frank O. Gatell, " 'Conscience and Judgment'; the Bolt of the Massachusetts Conscience Whigs," *The Historian*, vol. XXI, no. 1 (November 1958), pp. 18–46.
52. 30 Jan., 10 July 1848. Nash is incorrect in saying (p. 43) that Garrison attended the Worcester convention. He must have confused that meeting with the one at Tremont Temple in Boston.
53. *Lib.*, 14 July 1848.
54. *Lib.*, 11 Aug. 1848; see also 18 Aug. 1848.
55. *Lib.*, 10 Nov. 1848. The following week Garrison printed a somewhat more moderate editorial.
56. *Lib.*, 12 Jan. 1849.

XVI. COMMUNITIES, FRIENDS AND ENEMIES

1. MB.
2. See 11 [or 14] April, and 8 July 1842, MB.
3. 3 March and 12 June 1842, MB.
4. WLG to Francis Jackson, 15 July 1843, MB. According to T. D. Seymour Bassett (Donald D. Egbert and Stow Persons, eds., *Socialism and American Life*, Princeton, N.J., 1952, I, 183), the Northampton Association "was perhaps the most thoroughly industrial secular utopian community in American history." The fullest description of the community is to be found in Charles A. Sheffeld, ed., *The History of Florence, Massachusetts* (Florence, Mass., 1895), pp. 65–107.
5. *Lib.*, 5 Jan. 1844.
6. *Lib.*, 19 April 1844.
7. *Lib.*, 26 Feb. 1847.
8. WLG to Henry C. Wright, 1 April 1843, MB. See also WLG to Wright, 1 Oct. 1844, and to R. D. Webb, 1 March 1845, MB.
9. *Lib.*, 5 Jan. 1844. I have found no evidence that he ever did study Fourier.
10. *Lib.*, 3 May 1850.
11. *Lib.*, 1, 15 Aug., 5, 19 Sept., 3, 24 Oct., and 12 Dec. 1845.
12. *Lib.*, 3 May 1850.
13. *Lib.*, 11 Jan. 1850.
14. *Lib.*, 5 Jan. 1844. WLG accused Collins of holding many peculiar beliefs at this time. When he started to edit *The Communist* Collins resigned as general agent of the Massachusetts society.
15. See *Lib.*, 28 Aug. 1846 and 3 Oct. 1851. Edmund Quincy said (letter to R. D. Webb, 14 Jan. 1844, MHi): "The worst thing I know about these associations is that they almost without exception kill out the anti-slavery of their members." The utopian theory was that it was unnecessary for associationists to be abolitionists, because if all men would enter communities, and do their own work, slavery would of course cease.
16. *Lib.*, 1 March 1845.

17. WLG, though he gladly accepted Cushing's help in securing James Garrison's release from the Navy, remained hostile in feeling toward his fellow townsman. He condemned Cushing for attacking nonresistance and woman's rights (*Lib.*, 6 Sept. 1849); he called him "that unscrupulous demagogue, and most servile worshipper of the Slave Power" (*Lib.*, 28 April 1848); "the odorous and odious Gen. Cushing" (*Lib.*, 1 Dec. 1848); and by 1852 he was quite willing to visit upon him the final obloquy of comparing him with Webster (*Lib.*, 18 June 1852).

18. *Lib.*, 1 Aug. 1851. See also *Lib.*, 26 March 1852, where WLG refers to L. Tappan's "milk and water" abolitionism.

19. WLG to George W. Benson, 14 June 1837, MB. Up to 1838 WLG praised both men repeatedly in letters and in *The Liberator*.

20. Mrs. Child retired as editor in May of 1843, and WLG made remarks about how she had made the *Standard* a family paper and how it needed more vigor and spirit (*Lib.*, 19 May 1843). David Child, her husband and successor as editor, lasted for only a year when he resigned on the disunion issue (*Lib.*, 17 and 31 May 1844).

21. *Lib.*, 25 Jan., 15 Feb. 1834; 10, 31 Jan., 7 Feb. 1835.

22. *Lib.*, 16 Jan., 14 May, 2 July 1836.

23. *Lib.*, 24 Dec. 1836; 14 Jan. 1837; 25 Jan. 1839.

24. *Lib.*, 21 Dec. 1838; 31 Jan., 6, 27 March, 24 April 1840.

25. *Lib.*, 30 Aug. 1844. For the four editorials see *Lib.*, 20, 27 Sept., 4 Oct., 15 Nov. 1844.

26. *Lib.*, 2 July 1847. See WLG to Oliver Johnson, 10 March 1863, MB; WLG to Gerrit Smith, 31 Oct. 1863, NSU; WLG to Helen Garrison, 6 Sept. 1864, MB; WLG to Gerrit Smith, 12 Dec. 1870, NSU; WLG to Helen Garrison, 7 July 1871, NSU.

27. *Lib.*, 27 Aug. 1831.

28. See the statement regarding the new arrangement in *Lib.*, 2 Jan. 1836.

29. *Lib.*, 18 Aug. 1837

30. The frankest description of the Knapp episode is to be found in WLG's letter to Elizabeth Pease, dated 15 May 1842, MB, in which he feels compelled to tell the whole story for the benefit of English friends who are being led astray through propaganda from his enemies.

31. In the letter to Elizabeth Pease referred to above, WLG explained that Knapp seemed to dote on his wife's very weaknesses and that "she was unquestionably very strongly attached to him," but that she soon died. "It was a happy release for her. I hope it will not prove detrimental to her bereaved partner. They ought never to have been united together. But 'love is blind,' it is said— and the adage was exactly verified in this instance."

32. See especially the letter Knapp wrote to WLG, 12 Sept. 1838, MB, which is printed in *Life*, II, 255–256.

33. The exact amount is not clear. The letter to Elizabeth Pease of 15 May 1842 reports it as $150, whereas a letter to George W. Benson, 4 Jan. 1840 (misdated 1839), MB, gives $175.

34. See the letter to Elizabeth Pease referred to above. If the negotiation had proved unsuccessful, the committee had resolved to have WLG issue a new paper under the title, "Garrison's Liberator."

35. For references to the three men see the two following letters from WLG to George W. Benson, MB: 6 Dec. 1841, 9 Jan. 1842. See also *Life*, III, 39, footnote 2.

36. It was probably only because the paper had been circulated rather freely

in England by Captain Charles Stuart that WLG took any notice of it by writing the letter to Elizabeth Pease. He was always hypersensitive to criticism abroad.

37. WLG to John A. Collins, 1 Dec. 1840, MB.

38. See *Lib.*, 27 Nov., 18 Dec. 1840; 15 Jan. 1841.

39. See Nathaniel P. Rogers, *A Collection from the Miscellaneous Writings of* . . . (Manchester, N.H., and Boston, 1849), p. 167. This book contains the fullest account of their excursion; see pp. 157ff. See also *Lib.*, 10 Sept. and 15 Oct. 1841.

40. *Lib.*, 15 July, 9 Sept. 1842.

41. *Lib.*, 5 July 1844.

42. *Lib.*, 26 July 1844.

43. *Lib.*, 6 Dec. 1844. Garrison realized that he was in a most delicate position (*Lib.*, 13 Dec. 1844): "As chairman of the committee, I stood in the closest and most endearing relations to Mr. Rogers, not only as an admirer of his brilliant genius, but as deeply smitten with the qualities of his heart. Circumstances had occurred to blend us together, and to cause us to mingle 'like kindred drops, into one.' Among the host of my highly beloved friends in this country and on the other side of the Atlantic, there was no one for whom I cherished a warmer attachment than himself. Hence my situation was a most trying one, as every tender and reflecting mind must readily perceive."

44. *Lib.*, 6 Dec. 1844.

45. *Lib.*, 14 March 1845.

46. In five long letters to R. D. Webb (22 Sept., 14 Dec. 1844; 30 Jan., 29 March 1845; and 28 March 1847, letterbook, MHi) Quincy gave a frank and full account of the entire controversy with Rogers. Both Webb and Quincy considered Rogers the Don Quixote of the cause. "The Knight of La Mancha himself could not be more bent upon transforming windmills into giants & harmless flocks of sheep into armies of the infidel than poor Rogers is upon magnifying molehills into mountains & seeing what is not to be seen. Honest Francis Jackson presiding over an anti-slavery meeting is transformed in his eyes into a truculent slaveholder, with a scourge in one hand & a branding iron in the other. The Mass. A-S Soc'y looks to him like the despotism of Nicholas. . . . The church and clergy even are allowed to rest in comparative quietness while he follows his crusade against Chairmen, business committees and Societies. This strange folly amounts almost or rather quite to a fanaticism. He is not satisfied with being allowed to act by himself without reproach from those who believe that two can do more work than one, but he is unwilling to let them use their method without doing his best to bring it into ridicule & contempt. '*Free Meeting*' or a meeting where everybody may talk about everything all at the same time is his panacea for all earthly ills. To disband our forces & every man *fight 'on his own hook'* seems to him the true way to gain the battle" (22 Sept. 1844). Quincy praised WLG's patience and fairness in dealing with Rogers. Since much had been made of Rogers' poverty, Quincy assured Webb that Rogers was prosperous (30 Jan. 1845); on his death, Quincy said, Rogers left his family approximately $10,000—a substantial fortune in New Hampshire (28 March 1847).

47. *Lib.*, 20 June 1845.

48. In his later years WLG resumed friendly relations with the Childs (WLG to Thomas W. Higginson, 22 Feb. 1868, MB; WLG to Mrs. L. M. Child, 25 Oct. 1874, copy, MB; WLG to Fanny Villard, 7 Feb. 1877, MB; WLG to

Mrs. L. M. Child, 25 Aug. 1878, MB; WLG to John A. Collins, 20 March 1879, copy, MB); and even to some extent with Arthur Tappan (WLG to James M. McKim, 14 Nov. 1863, MB), although not with his brother Lewis.

XVII. UNDISCOVERED COUNTRY

1. See the *Twelfth Annual Report* of the Massachusetts Anti-Slavery Society (Boston, 1844), pp. 34ff.

2. *Lib.*, 29 Sept. 1843. In a letter to R. D. Webb (27 June 1843, MHi) Quincy explained that the plan for the western conventions had been made possible by a gift of £100 from the English abolitionist Thomas Sturge. He said that they were not publicly announcing the gift lest it diminish the response of New England abolitionists.

3. *Lib.*, 19 March 1847.

4. *Lib.*, 30 July 1847.

5. *Lib.*, 13 Aug. 1847.

6. "Preface," *Narrative of the Life of Frederick Douglass, an American Slave* (Boston, 1845), p. iv.

7. Some of the more radical American abolitionists—not including WLG—felt that he should not buy his freedom on the grounds that the very act acknowledged the institution of slavery. See *Lib.*, 29 Jan., 5, 19 March 1847.

8. WLG to Helen Garrison, 10 Sept. 1846 MB.

9. WLG to Helen Garrison, 17 Sept. 1846, MB; see also undated letter to R. D. Webb, which was undoubtedly written in September 1846, MB.

10. Frederic M. Holland, *Frederick Douglass, the Colored Orator* (New York, 1891), pp. 149ff.

11. Edmund Quincy to R. D. Webb, 28 March 1847, in author's possession; the letter is also to be found in the letterbook (MHi). Quincy said further of Douglass: "He is a man of great tact & talent, ability to make the most of what he has, but without a very wide range. We rejoice in his success. It must seem like a fairy land to him, to be sure. I trust it will not spoil him & make him discontented at home" (to R. D. Webb, 13 Dec. 1845, letterbook, MHi). In this letter is a delightful description of Douglass' visit to Quincy's house in Dedham, the first gentleman's house he had ever entered in·the North. It is in this letter that Quincy takes credit for first suggesting that Douglass be employed as an antislavery lecturer.

12. The meeting was on 3 May. See *Lib.*, 21 May 1847.

13. *Lib.*, 27 June 1847.

14. In *Lib.*, 23 July 1847, is to be found the fullest statement on the topic. In next week's paper it was announced that Douglass would accompany WLG on his western mission.

15. WLG to Helen Garrison, 3 Aug. 1847, MB.

16. WLG to Helen Garrison, 9 Aug. 1847, MB.

17. WLG to Helen Garrison, 9 Aug. 1847, MB. WLG had to rush to the station before completing this letter to Helen; the crude hand of a friend provided the last short paragraph.

18. WLG to Helen Garrison, 12 Aug. 1847, MB.

19. WLG to Helen Garrison, 16 Aug. 1847, MB. This letter was left unsealed at the hotel in Youngstown, but the landlord was apparently kind enough to mail it.

20. WLG to Helen Garrison, 25 Aug. 1847. The manuscript of this letter

appears to have been lost, but much of it was printed in *The Liberator,* 10 Sept. 1847.

21. The first letter came to him at New Lyme about three weeks after he left home. See WLG to Helen Garrison, 20 Aug. 1847, MB.

22. WLG to Helen Garrison, 20 Aug. 1847, MB.

23. For an interesting account of the Lane revolt and the founding of Oberlin see Benjamin P. Thomas, *Theodore Weld, Crusader for Freedom* (New Brunswick, N.J., 1950), pp. 70ff.

24. WLG to Helen Garrison, 28 Aug. 1847, MB.

25. The final section of this letter, which WLG started in Oberlin 28 Aug., was finished in Salem, 5 Sept.

26. WLG to Helen Garrison, 18 Sept. 1847, MB.

27. *Lib.,* 8 Oct. 1847.

28. 12 Oct. 1847, MWA.

29. Friends also offered to pay Helen's way to Cleveland, but both she and WLG felt she should remain at home. See WLG to Helen Garrison, 19 Oct. 1847, MB.

30. See *Lib.,* 29 Oct., 5, 12, 19 Nov. 1847. Although several of these letters were addressed to Elizabeth Pease, they were, I believe, intended primarily for publication in *The Liberator.*

31. WLG to Helen Garrison, 19, 20 Oct. 1847, MB.

32. WLG to Helen Garrison, 26 Oct. 1847, MB. Internal evidence indicates that this letter is incorrectly dated; it was probably written a few days later than the 26th.

33. The journey from Buffalo to Boston, which cost $15 each, is described in Wright's letter to Elizabeth Pease, 31 Oct. 1847, *Lib.,* 12 Nov. 1847. Wright emphasized the need for American railroads to have a complete set of double tracks; he thought it dangerous for trains running in opposite directions to have to depend on occasional double tracks to avoid collisions.

34. Postscript to letter, 20 Oct. 1847, MB. WLG chiefly blamed Samuel Brooke, general agent of the Western Anti-Slavery Society, for influencing Douglass' decision. Frederic M. Holland (*Frederick Douglass,* pp. 161ff.) defends Douglass' action by saying both that he was under no further obligation to consult WLG after the talks in Boston and that the violence of WLG's illness "probably caused him to forget what had been told him just before his sickness by Douglass, according to a statement made by the latter that winter."

The Frederick Douglass Papers, located in the Frederick Douglass Memorial Home, Anacostia, D.C., though extensive, consist of materials too late (mostly from the 1880's and 1890's) to be of interest to a biographer of Garrison.

35. See two letters from Edmund Quincy to R. D. Webb, 9 March 1848, letterbook, MHi, and 3 Oct. 1848, in author's possession. The weakness of his vocal cords so apparent on the western trip may have furnished Douglass with one reason for desiring to spend part of his time with editorial work.

36. *Lib.,* 17 Dec. 1847.

37. *Lib.,* 28 Jan. 1848.

38. Edmund Quincy to R. D. Webb, 9 March 1848, letterbook, MHi.

39. Henry C. Wright, "Diary to Maria," 2 Dec. 1847, MB.

40. Wright, "Diary to Maria," 10 Dec. 1847.

41. "Diary to Maria," 29 Dec. 1847. Others spoke more volubly at the convention. Most spectacular was Abby Folsom, the chief disturber of reform

meetings during the middle of the century. Henry Wright was sitting by the table placed in front of the platform and Garrison to his right. Abby, who had been sick for several days—or perhaps resting up for the occasion—writhed about the room like a Pythoness. Wright described her as "a large, liny woman. Wild, unsettled eyes—desperate energy of body, & in a state of perfect phrenzy. She is at this moment screaming at the top of her voice—stalking up & down & around the open space—walking, now up to Garrison, & now up to me, putting her face near ours & screaming against *Chairmen, Secretaries, Committees & Boards of Managers, & Societies*," and all the time quoting Nathaniel P. Rogers as authority for her views. She called Wright and Garrison tyrants and despots, and she yelled and shook her fist and stamped her foot. Garrison looked "grave & sorrowful & kind at the poor lady." Wright wished that he could enjoy the mad scene, but he found the lady more pathetic than humorous. The audience, except for Henry Clapp and the few anti-Garrisonians, sat quietly, as though resigned to let her have her hour in court. Suddenly she sat down, exhausted; and in a few minutes she sallied out of the room, shouting, "Good Bye *Sane* folks—I have done with you—this time."

42. 9 March 1848, letterbook, MHi. Quincy had apparently had enough of such antics at the Chardon Street Convention eight years before. The entries in Quincy's journal for 23 and 24 March indicate that he was indifferent to the convention. Both days he arrived late, and the first day he left early by the side door.

43. *Lib.*, 11 Feb. 1848.

44. George Benson was fired by the Presbyterian owners of the cotton factory in Northampton as a result of the role he had played as president of the Anti-Sabbath Convention; see WLG to Nathaniel Barney, 8 Sept. 1848, in author's possession.

45. Henry C. Wright, "Diary to Maria," 24 March 1848, MB.

46. June 1849, MB. The long section of the letter concerned with religious matters is preserved only in a copy in the hand of R. D. Webb.

47. The fullest report of the death is to be found in a letter to Elizabeth Pease, 3 May 1848, MB; see also three letters the day of the death, 20 April 1848, one to George W. Benson, one to Mrs. Chapman, and one to Theodore Parker, as well as one to Benson on 3 May, MNS.

48. Samuel Thomson, the originator of the best-known unorthodox medical system, prescribed for treatment a variety of herbs, an emetic called lobelia, and steam baths.

49. See the letterbook (MHi), Edmund Quincy to R. D. Webb, 27 June, 26 July 1843; 31 Jan. 1844; 13 Dec. 1845; 13 Jan. 1853.

50. In his diary entry for 15 May (MB), Wright said: "He is a child & needs looking after as one. I have got his promise to go to a Water Cure—this summer 3 months. Edmund Quincy consented to take the Liberator. I am sorry to have G. leave it again but their [sic] is no help."

51. Ruggles had been associated with WLG as early as 1835, when he was a New York agent for *The Liberator*. He had actively assisted Frederick Douglass and other fugitives to escape from slavery. Early in the 1840's he became ill and blind and moved from New York to Northampton, where he joined George Benson's community. Following the principles developed by Dr. Wesselhoeft at Graefenberg, Germany, he treated himself with such beneficial results that patients were soon clamoring for his attention. He started practice in a small house and later built what WLG described as "a large,

NOTES TO CHAPTER XVII

commodious and handsome building, in the vicinity of pure and exhaustless springs of water." For a short biographical sketch see his obituary, *Lib.*, 21 Dec. 1849.

52. WLG to Edmund Quincy, 8 Dec. 1847, MNS; WLG to Geo. W. Benson, 17 Dec. 1847, MB.

53. WLG to Helen Garrison, 18 July 1848, MB. The information about the water cure is to be found in a series of letters written by WLG from Northampton as follows: to Helen Garrison, 23, 26 July; to Francis Jackson, 31 July; to Mrs. E. J. Meriam, 9 Aug.; to Edmund Quincy, 10 Aug., MB; to R. F. Wallcut, 28 Aug., MNS; to Nathaniel Barney, 8 Sept. (in author's possession); and to Elizabeth Pease, 3 Oct., MB.

54. WLG to Helen Garrison, 10, 18 Oct. 1848, MB.

55. Quincy, who had little sympathy for unorthodox medical treatments, had this comment to make about WLG's water cure: "He was removed from all care and anxiety, placed in a beautiful country, his diet and habits regulated by a despotic master, compelled to take exercise in the open air, not allowed to exert his mind and kept well washed. Who would not be better for such a regime?" (to R. D. Webb, 3 Oct. 1848, letterbook, MHi).

56. WLG to George W. Benson, 29 Oct. 1848, MHi.

57. For a full description of Charles Follen Garrison's death see WLG to Elizabeth Pease, 20 June 1849, MB. (Garrison, incidentally, was inconsistent in his correspondence about the spelling of "Lizzie.")

58. WLG to Elizabeth Pease, 20 June 1849, MB. Henry C. Wright refers to this fund in his diary entry for 3 Dec. 1847, MB, for he says that unknown to WLG, J. N. Buffum had started to raise $5,000 to buy WLG a house or to invest for his children's benefit. In a few weeks the total fund, he thinks, had been nearly raised. "Garrison has nothing laid up—he is a pauper—like the rest of us—but I had rather he might have *5000* than get it myself."

XVIII. AT MID-CENTURY

1. *Lib.*, 17 Dec. 1841. In 1844 when Father Mathew was $40,000 in debt WLG had readily indicated (*Lib.*, 29 Nov.) his willingness to be helpful.

2. *Life*, III, 348.

3. *Lib.*, 1 March 1850.

4. *Lib.*, 8 March 1850.

5. *Lib.*, 5 April 1850.

6. *Lib.*, 15 March 1850. A few months later (*Lib.*, 26 July 1850) WLG was more outspoken about Webster: "this lick spittle of the slaverholding oligarchy." "Massachusetts spurns him."

7. See *Lib.*, 10 May 1850.

8. *Life*, III, 286. Much of the available material about his meeting is presented in this biography. But the full source is *The Liberator* itself (issues for 10, 17, 24, 31 May), where various newspaper attacks and WLG's replies are to be found.

9. Most of the details about this section of the meeting come from an article in the New York *Herald*, 8 May 1850, which was reprinted in *The Liberator*, 17 May. Although WLG corrects many of the statements to be found in the reports in New York papers, he does not deny the facts which I have used here.

10. "Diary to Hetty," 7 May 1850, MB. This diary is the source of much of my information about the New York meeting.

11. For the best brief account of the Fugitive Slave Law and its effect on the abolition movement see Russel B. Nye, *William Lloyd Garrison and the Humanitarian Reformers* (Boston, 1955), pp. 156ff. For a longer but ineffective description see William Breyfogle, *Make Free, The Story of the Underground Railroad* (Philadelphia and New York, 1958).

12. As quoted in *Life*, III, 365.

13. WLG's sons admitted (*Life*, III, 313) that "Thompson was the great central fact in Mr. Garrison's inner life and public activity during the eight months of the Englishman's stay in America."

14. *Lib.*, 25 Oct. 1850.

15. *Lib.*, 31 Aug. 1849. Later the same year WLG reprinted Kossuth's farewell address to his country, delivered when he went into exile on the failure of the revolution (see *Lib.*, 7 Dec.).

16. *Lib.*, 12 March 1852.

17. It is true that more than half of WLG's one-column review of the book is devoted to the nonresistant idea, but it hardly seems accurate to suggest as Russel B. Nye does (p. 161) that "its effectiveness as abolitionist propaganda evidently escaped him." WLG indicated quite explicitly in the paragraph quoted above that its effect "must be prodigious."

18. WLG's letters appear not to have been preserved, but most of Mrs. Stowe's are reprinted in *Life*, III, 395ff.

19. *Life*, III, 363.

20. *Life*, III, 396.

21. For the more important references to Sumner in *The Liberator* during these years see the following issues: 11 July, 15, 22 Aug., 5 Dec. 1845; 6, 27 Nov. 1846; 19 Feb., 18 June 1847; 19 May 1848; 1 June, 7 Dec. 1849; 11, 25 Jan. 1850.

22. *Lib.*, 23 April 1852.

23. 23 April 1852, MH. This letter is to be found in the Sumner Papers.

24. *Lib.*, 17 Sept. 1852.

25. *Lib.*, 7 July 1854.

26. *Lib.*, 7 July 1854. Thoreau also spoke at this particular Fourth of July meeting. As WLG put it (*ibid.*), "HENRY THOREAU, of Concord, read a portion of a racy and ably written address, the whole of which will be published in the LIBERATOR." On the 21st Thoreau's speech was printed. It offers as great a contrast to WLG's florid performance as Lincoln's Gettysburg Address did to Edward Everett's major endeavor. For Thoreau's rich and allusive style invigorated all the antislavery clichés he was concerned with. What more could be said, for example, on the subject of moral suasion than the following: "But there is no such thing as sliding up hill. In morals, the only sliders are backsliders." Also his final paragraph, following one in which he had described the scent of the water lily, is worth remembering: "Slavery and servility have produced no sweet-scented flower annually, to charm the senses of men, for they have no real life: they are merely a decaying and a death, offensive to all healthy nostrils. We do not complain that they *live*, but that they do not *get buried*. Let the living bury them; even they are good for manure." (Thoreau's speech under the title "Slavery in Massachusetts" was published also in his volume *A Yankee in Canada, with Anti-Slavery and Reform Papers*, Boston, 1866, pp. 97–116.)

XIX. VIOLENCE AND FORBEARANCE

1. See especially *Lib.*, 6, 13, 20, 27 June; 18 July; 8, 15, 22 Aug.; and 7 Nov. 1856.

2. *Lib.*, 29 Feb. 1856.

3. *Lib.*, 14 March 1856.

4. *Lib.*, 11 July 1856.

5. *Life*, III, 487–488; see also O. G. Villard, *John Brown* (New York, 1943), pp. 271–272.

6. *Lib.*, 28 Oct. 1859. I have found no earlier references to Brown either in WLG's letters or in *The Liberator*.

7. This speech was printed in *Lib.*, 16 Dec. 1859.

8. Toward the end of his life WLG became excited once more about John Brown but for altogether different reasons. In a letter to A. M. Ross, dated 18 Aug. 1875 (copy MB), he thanks Ross for sending him his volume, *Recollections and Experiences of an Abolitionist,* but regrets that he has expressed there some sentiments attributed to Brown that are derogatory to the abolitionists. Even if Brown had actually said these things, he thinks that it would have been expedient to have omitted them from the book. He goes on in the letter to argue against Brown, as if he were disputing with Brown's wild-eyed ghost.

9. WLG to Oliver Johnson, 19 April 1861, MB.

10. 2 Nov. 1860.

11. *Lib.*, 16 Nov. 1860.

12. *Lib.*, 14 Dec. 1860.

13. *Lib.*, 4 Jan. 1861.

14. *Lib.*, 12 April 1861.

15. *Lib.*, 19 April 1861. In the midst of his logical argument concerning the higher law followed by abolitionists, Garrison cannot resist making a highly emotional appeal for the abolitionists. "As God lives, it is impossible that they can fail to be otherwise than honored by posterity. They are neither fanatical nor misled, but in their right minds, faithful in a faithless age, witnessing to the truth, protesting against the wrong, disseminating light and knowledge, and elevating the moral standard of the times."

16. *Lib.*, 19 April 1861.

17. *Lib.*, 8 March 1861.

18. *Lib.*, 26 April 1861.

19. See WLG to Charles Sumner, 26 Feb., 22 March, 6 April 1861, MHi; WLG to Henry Wilson, 26 Feb. 1861, MHi; WLG to John Albion Andrew, 28 Feb., 9 March 1861, MHi; WLG to Samuel Gridley Howe, 1 April 1861, MHi. To Sumner, Wilson, and Andrew he wrote recommending specific individuals for political appointments.

20. *Lib.*, 3 May 1861.

21. See *Lib.*, 10, 17, 24 May 1861.

22. WLG to Oliver Johnson, 19 April 1861, MB.

23. WLG to Oliver Johnson, 23 April 1861, MB.

24. WLG to J. S. Gibbons, 28 April 1861, MSaE. See also WLG to J. M. McKim, 13 Oct. 1861, PPHi.

25. WLG to Henry T. Cheever, 9 Sept. 1861, MWA.

26. *Lib.*, 6 Dec. 1861.

27. 6 Dec. 1861, MB.

28. WLG to Charles Sumner, 20 Dec. 1861, MHi; *Lib.*, 6 Dec. 1861.

29. *Lib.*, 14 March 1862.

30. *Lib.*, 10 Jan. 1862.

31. WLG slightly misquotes the main clause, which should be: "I did not think I should live till I were married."

32. *Lib.*, 24 Jan. 1862.

33. *Lib.*, 24 Jan. 1862.

34. For reprint of speech see *Lib.*, 24 Jan. 1862.

35. *Lib.*, 21, 28 Feb., 7 March 1862.

36. *Lib.*, 28 June 1861; 10, 17 Jan.; 14 March; 18 April; 28 Nov. 1862.

37. Anna E. Dickinson to Susan Dickinson, 28 April 1862, DLC. Although Anna Dickinson became one of the most popular and successful lecturers in the country, and subsequently an actress and playwright, there seems to have been relatively little contact between her and the Garrison family after the spring of 1862. She did send Frankie her picture in the fall of 1863. See his letter of thanks (F. J. Garrison to Anna E. Dickinson, 12 Sept. 1863, DLC).

38. *Lib.*, 23 May 1862.

39. *Lib.*, 26 Sept. 1862.

40. *Lib.*, 3 Oct. 1862.

41. *Lib.*, 2 Jan. 1863.

42. *Lib.*, 10 Jan. 1863.

43. See *Lib.*, 3 April 1863, where he defends Lincoln and the proclamation against the attack of Earl Russell, at the same time offering his own criticism of the document.

44. For example, there is the rough draft of a pathetic letter from Garrison to Phillips, dated January 1851, at the Boston Public Library. Garrison tells that he is $200 in debt, mostly for the past year's expenses. "I am neither a spendthrift nor improvident, but careful and scrupulous, and even anxious to keep out of debt." He cites Helen's frugality and dread of debt. He speaks of the necessity for a certain amount of entertaining and says he has spent nothing "for personal fancy or gratification." He admits that he is very unhappy to call on Phillips again.

45. *Lib.*, 4 Jan. 1861; 4 April, 15 Aug. 1862.

46. *Lib.*, 6 Dec. 1861. When he died on 14 November 1861, Francis Jackson left a bequest of $10,000 for the cause. Garrison and Phillips later clashed over the disposition of the funds.

47. WLG to Oliver Johnson, 19 April 1861, MB.

48. WLG to J. M. McKim, 13 Oct. 1861, PPHi.

49. WLG to Oliver Johnson, 22 Dec. 1861, MB.

50. WLG to Oliver Johnson, 26 Dec. 1861, MB.

51. WLG to Oliver Johnson, 31 July 1862, MB.

52. For the text of Phillips' speech on the subject see *Lib.*, 9 Jan. 1863.

53. *The* [Boston] *Commonwealth*, 12 Feb. 1864. This meeting of the Massachusetts Anti-Slavery Society was fully reported in *The Liberator*, 5 Feb. 1864.

54. *Lib.*, 26 Feb. 1864.

55. The two-day meeting was reported in *The Liberator* for 20 and 27 May 1864.

56. WLG to Samuel May, Jr., 17 June 1864, copy, MB.

57. WLG to Oliver Johnson, 20 June 1864, copy, MB. WLG told Phillips that his own "partisan appeals for Frémont, and his unjust and sweeping accusations" had compelled the defense of Lincoln in the *Standard*.

58. WLG to Henry Wilson, 20 Feb. 1864, MB.

59. Interesting information about the Washington visit is to be found in three of WLG's letters to his wife (9, 10, 11 June 1864, MB), and a letter from W. L. Garrison, Jr., to his fiancée, Ellen Wright (27 June 1864, MNS), as well as in *Lib.*, 6 Jan. 1865.

60. *Lib.*, 28 Oct. 1864. After the election Phillips' venom toward Lincoln seemed to evaporate (*Lib.*, 16 Dec. 1864).

61. *Lib.*, 28 Oct. 1864.

62. Edmund Quincy to R. D. Webb, 16 Oct. 1865, MB.

63. David Donald has observed (*Lincoln Reconsidered*, pp. 33–36) that there was something almost paranoid about the way many abolitionists denounced Lincoln. Mr. Donald offers as partial explanation of that prejudice against Lincoln the fact that the abolitionist leaders as a group were descended from prominent northeastern families, that they were born into a hostile world increasingly under the control of industrial and urban leaders of relatively insignificant social and economic backgrounds, and that Lincoln especially was suspect as a man of humble origin and as a successful corporation lawyer become President.

64. Lib., 18 Nov. 1864.

XX. JUBILEE

1. *Lib.*, 25 Nov. 1864.

2. *Lib.*, 9 Dec. 1864.

3. *Lib.*, 10 Feb. 1865.

4. See WLG, Jr., to Ellen Wright Garrison, 6 Feb. 1865, MNS.

5. See brief report, *Lib.*, 17 Feb. 1865.

6. WLG had been asked by Charles Eliot Norton to write an article for *The North American Review* on Banks's labor system and reconstruction policy in Louisiana. As a result, he had corresponded with the general. See WLG to C. E. Norton, 13 Jan. 1865, MB.

7. See WLG, Jr., to Ellen Wright Garrison, 14 Feb. 1865, MNS.

8. WLG to Helen Garrison, 7 April 1865, MB.

9. WLG to Helen Garrison, 9 April 1865, MB.

10. WLG to Helen Garrison, 15 April 1865, MB.

11. WLG's account appeared in *Lib.*, 28 April 1865. A more colorful account of the day's activities is reprinted in *Lib.*, 5 May 1865, from the New York *Evangelist*.

12. *Lib.*, 5 May 1865, reprint of *Evangelist* article.

13. R. D. Webb in a letter to Edmund Quincy (27 Feb. 1851, MB) indicated that Thompson would be much happier in America than in England: "I think his life with you must be a heaven away from his old home—and the perpetual irksomeness of his false position of an English M.P. without rank or property. . . . I wish he could always live and work in America—I am persuaded that he is eminently suited for labour there and he cannot but do good with such congenial backers. He requires backers—and there is a coldness among the English dilettante philanthropists entirely unsuited to the eagerness and fire of his mind which is much better suited by the real hearty energy inseparable from the action of those in the United States who have real work to do. I do not suppose he has much chance of re-election to Parliament nor do I think he wishes it. It must be his most earnest desire to escape from his ambiguous posi-

tion and there is not a man in England I would be better pleased to see flourishing & happy."

14. *Lib.*, 5 May 1865.

15. Descriptions of the morning's festivities are reprinted in *The Liberator*, from the New York *Tribune* (28 April 1865), from the New York *Independent* (12 May 1865), and from the Charleston *Courier* (5 May 1865).

16. See *Life*, IV, 80, for extracts from a letter from WLG to G. T. Garrison, 11 June 1863, in which he indicates that he will not in any way oppose his son's determination to enlist, much as he might like to have him embrace nonresistance principles. He also said: "Personally, as my son, you will incur some risks at the hands of the rebels that others will not, if it is known that you are my son." (I have not been able to locate the manuscript of this letter.)

17. *Life*, IV, 148–149, and WLG to Helen Garrison, 15 April 1865, MB.

18. *Lib.*, 26 May 1865.

19. *The Commonwealth* went on record against dissolution of the antislavery endeavor as early as 11 February 1865.

20. A report of this meeting is to be found in *Lib.*, 19 May 1865.

21. *Lib.*, 26 May 1865.

22. In a letter to the New York *Independent* Edmund Quincy supported WLG's position. He said that he had voted for WLG's resolution for the dissolution of the society, because he believed that slavery was, practically speaking, abolished. "The sagacious and statesmanlike mind of Mr. Garrison recognized the necessities and proprieties of the case. He refused to be hindered by the machinery he had himself invented, when it had done its work. The Society he had formed had been a sharp threshing instrument in his hands until the harvest was secured. To go on threshing the straw after the grain was out would be a task productive only of dust and noise, and one suited neither to the dignity of his character, nor to his eminently practical good sense." (This letter is reprinted in *Lib.*, 26 May 1865.)

23. Ellen Wright Garrison to Martha Coffin Wright, 31 Oct. 1864, MNS.

24. WLG to Oliver Johnson, 26 Nov. 1864, MB.

25. In a memorandum, which has been preserved at the Boston Public Library, he recorded the fees for all his lectures.

26. He described to his wife (5 Nov. 1865, MB) his lecture at Meadville, Pennsylvania: "Last evening, I lectured to a small audience, in a hall dimly lighted, and never was more stupid in my manner, or more unsatisfactory in my talk. . . . I felt my effort to have been a dead failure, and no one said any thing to the contrary. The truth is, my lecture is crude and disjointed, and I have no time to recast it. It will cause general disappointment, I am quite certain; and that is the reason why I feel so about exacting $75. . . . I am more and more disinclined to public speaking; and it always worries and annoys me when I speak for pay. How I long to get home!"

27. WLG to Helen Garrison, 6 Nov. 1865, MB. His teeth were removed toward the end of July, as letters to his wife (dated 20, 23, 24 July 1865, MB) make clear.

28. WLG to Helen Garrison, 10 Nov. 1865, MB.

29. WLG to Helen Garrison, 17 Nov. 1865, MB.

30. WLG to Helen Garrison, 27 Nov. 1865, MB.

31. WLG to Henry Villard, 10 Dec. 1865, MB.

32. He wrote, for example, to Oliver Johnson (23 Dec. 1865, MB): "Perhaps it would be gratifying to you to send me a congratulatory and farewell letter

for insertion next week. If so, it would be still more gratifying to me to publish it,—bating and omitting all personal panegyric. I merely make the suggestion, as your modesty may hold you back where your desire is strong." See also WLG to Henry C. Wright, 25 Dec. 1865, MB.

33. 1 Jan. 1866, NNC.

34. WLG to Fanny Garrison Villard, 27 Jan. 1866, MB.

35. Published 8 Feb. 1866.

36. WLG to Fanny Villard, 11 Feb. 1866, MB.

XXI. GENTLEMAN REFORMER

1. The fullest description of Mrs. Garrison's attack is in a letter from Samuel May, Jr., to Samuel J. May, 3 Jan. 1864, MB.

2. See the following of WLG's letters: in 1864, to [WPG?], 18 Feb., MB; to Gerrit Smith, 29 March, MHi; to Mrs. H. W. Sewall, 21 May, MB; to Samuel May, Jr., 17 June (copy), MB; to Helen Garrison, 14 Sept., MB; in 1865, to Oliver Johnson, 21 May, MB; to Helen Garrison, 8 June, MB; to Elizabeth Pease Nichol, 9 Oct., MB.

3. One of the main sources of information about Mrs. Garrison's later years and about the Garrison children is her correspondence, in the author's possession.

4. WLG to Thomas Davis, 6 Oct. 1854, MHi; Helen Garrison to W. P. Garrison, 20 Dec. 1863, in author's possession; WLG to Oliver Johnson, 9 April 1873, MB.

5. Wendell Phillips to Elizabeth Pease Nichol, 30 April 1846, in author's possession.

6. W. P. Garrison to Fanny Garrison, 16 May 1864, MH. The most violent difference of opinion between WLG and his second son came in 1878. Wendell, who was critical of his father's opinion of President Hayes's Southern policy, collected clippings from what WLG called (to Fanny Villard, 2 Feb. 1878, MNS) "malignant Southern and Northern journals in fiercest denunciation of me, as evidence that he is in the right, and I am in the wrong!" WLG said: "Such a letter from a son to a father!" In a letter to his son (5 Feb. 1878, MB) he questioned "whether my son is in his right sense." Subsequently in a letter to his daughter (7 Feb. 1878, MNS) he regretted: "Alas the day that he ever became connected with Godkin and the Nation!"

7. Edmund Quincy to R. D. Webb, 16 Oct. 1865, MB.

8. 11 Sept. 1861, in author's possession.

9. 16 Oct. 1865, MB.

10. Undated, unsigned manuscript in the author's possession.

11. Most of the information about the testimonial has been taken from the minutes, correspondence, and other records of the testimonial drive, in the possession of the author.

12. 6 April 1866, MB.

13. Among the more important contributions arranged in order of receipt were the following: Oliver Johnson, $50; Edmund Quincy, $100; Thomas Mott, $500; Andrew Jackson Davis, $50; Charles Sumner, $100; Samuel E. Sewall, $100; Josiah Quincy, $50; Ticknor and Fields, $200; Harriet Beecher Stowe, $50; Frederick Law Olmsted, $50; E. L.. Godkin, $50; Richard Henry Dana, $5; John Bertram, $500; John Albion Andrew, $50; Ralph Waldo Emerson, $10; Henry Wadsworth Longfellow, $50; James Russell Lowell, $50;

Charles Eliot Norton, $50; William Cullen Bryant, $50; Horace Greeley, $50; Henry Ward Beecher, $100; John Lothrop Motley, $100; Henry Wilson, $25. (The records indicate that Wilson never paid anything and that the $25 with which he was officially credited "was paid, five dollars each, by J. I. Bowdith, W. E. Coffin, W. Endicott, Jr., E. Quincy, & S. May Esq.")

14. One each from South Carolina and Virginia.

15. May kept interesting records, arranging the contributions chronologically, numerically (according to the size of the gift), and geographically.

16. WLG was worried that the committee might put his fund in trust rather than give him complete control over it. He told his son William (11 Sept. 1867, MHi) that he thought he would rather never receive any of the money than to be told in effect that he was being put under guardianship because he was too incompetent or too extravagant to manage it himself. "If there is anything in my character or habits that renders it inexpedient or unsafe for me to receive it in full, then it ceases to be a Testimonial, and ought not to be so proffered, but only as a charitable contribution to save me from want!"

17. See Ralph Korngold, *Two Friends of Man* (Boston, 1950), and Russel B. Nye, *William Lloyd Garrison and the Humanitarian Reformers* (Boston, 1955).

18. See the pamphlet form of the article *Wendell Phillips* (Boston, 1884), pp. xviii–xix.

19. See *The* [Boston] *Freedmen's Record,* April 1865. This periodical was published from 1865 to 1874; Garrison's name appeared as vice president on the list of officers from April 1865 until the last issue. This publication, as well as the organ for the national society (*The American Freedman,* 1866–1869), contains lists of teachers and their supporters, financial statements, lists of contributors, whether towns or individuals, annual reports, reports of meetings of branch and national societies, reports of inspections of schools, letters from teachers and others telling of their experiences, etc.

20. For a history of the various freedmen's organizations see *The Freedmen's Record,* January 1868.

21. *The Freedmen's Record,* August 1865.

22. *The Freedmen's Record,* August 1865. See also *The American Freedman,* April 1866; in the issues of the journal following July 1867 Garrison was listed as among those who had promised occasional contributions to its pages.

23. *The Independent,* 8 March 1866.

24. *National Anti-Slavery Standard,* 3 March 1866.

25. *National Anti-Slavery Standard,* 10 March 1866.

26. WLG to W. P. Garrison, 25 March 1866, MB. See also WLG to F. J. Garrison, 12 April 1866, MB.

27. 29 March 1866.

28. *The Independent,* 10 Jan. 1867; see also the issue for 17 Jan. 1867.

29. *The Independent,* 31 Feb. 1867.

30. *National Anti-Slavery Standard,* 9 March 1867.

31. WLG's sons claimed (*Life,* IV, 178) that Ticknor and Fields had made the request as early as December 1867, though I have found no documentary evidence of the fact.

32. WLG to Helen Garrison, 10 March 1866, MB; WLG to W. P. Garrison, 25 March 1866, MB; and WLG to J. M. McKim, 31 March 1866, NN. See also *The Commonwealth,* 12 May 1866.

33. WLG to Samuel J. May, 18 Sept. 1866, MB. In this letter WLG thanks

May for giving him an insurance policy that has reimbursed him during his six months of disability. See also WLG to Fanny Villard, 21 Sept. 1866, MB.

34. *The Freedmen's Record,* December 1866.

35. WLG to Helen Garrison, 8 June 1868, MB.

36. See the following letters from WLG, written in 1868 and all except the letter to Powell, which is in the author's possession, at the Boston Public Library: to Oliver Johnson, 19 Feb.; to W. P. Garrison, 6 March; to Anne W. Weston, 16 March; to Oliver Johnson, 27 March, to W. I. Bowditch, 28 March; to A. H. Love (copy), 30 March; to Powell, 10 April; to W. P. Garrison, 13 April; to W. P. Garrison, 22 April; to Edmund Jackson, 10 May.

37. See WLG to F. J. Garrison, 27 March, MHi; WLG to Samuel May, Jr., 5 April 1867 (copy), MB.

38. Vivid descriptions of the departure are to be found in two letters at MNS: WLG, Jr., to W. P. Garrison, 9 May 1867, and Ellen Wright Garrison to Martha Coffin Wright, 9 May 1867.

39. WLG to Helen Garrison, 7 June 1867, MB.

40. WLG to Helen Garrison, 7 June 1867, MB, and *Life,* IV, 192–193.

41. *Proceedings at the Public Breakfast Held in Honor of William Lloyd Garrison, Esq . . .* (London, 1868), p. 25.

42. *Proceedings,* pp. 36–37, 46.

43. *The American Freedman,* November 1867.

44. *Life,* IV, 194–195.

45. WLG to Rev. S. A. Steinthal, 15 July 1867, MB.

46. WLG to Elizabeth Pease Nichol, 23 July 1867, MB.

47. WLG to Helen Garrison, 4 Sept. 1867, MB.

48. WLG to Fanny Villard, 12 Nov. 1867, MB.

49. The Garrison sons say (*Life,* IV, 236) that their father contributed one hundred articles, but I have been able to find only eighty-three.

50. *The Independent,* 12 April 1866.

51. *The Independent,* 3 Sept. 1868.

52. *The Independent,* 16 Feb. 1871.

53. *The Independent,* 31 Dec. 1868.

54. *The Independent,* 17 March 1870. See also the issues for 19 Jan., 2 March 1871, and 3 April 1873.

55. WLG to A. H. Love (copy), 18 Dec. 1867, MB.

56. WLG to Theodore Tilton (copy), 5 April 1870, MB.

57. WLG to Susan B. Anthony, 4 Jan. 1877, CSmH.

58. *The Independent,* 31 Aug. 1871.

59. 20 March 1868, MB.

60. WLG to W. P. Garrison, 21 April 1869, MB.

61. *The Independent,* 31 March 1870.

62. *The Independent,* 1 May 1873.

63. *The Independent,* 18 Aug. 1870.

64. *The Independent,* 27 April 1871.

65. *The Independent,* 4 Jan. 1872.

66. *The Independent,* 8 Aug. 1872.

67. *The Independent,* 12 Sept. 1872.

68. *The Independent,* 3 Oct. 1872.

69. Printed copies of both the letter to WLG dated 10 March 1873, and WLG's reply, dated 17 March 1873, are to be found in the Garrison Papers at the Boston Public Library.

70. WLG to W. P. Garrison, 14 Dec. 1873, MB.

71. See the issues of the *Tribune* for 15, 17, 24, 27 Feb. 1879.

72. The description of WLG's stay at Dr. Dow's is to be found in a series of letters to his wife in the Boston Public Library.

73. WLG to Helen Garrison, 15 Aug. 1874, MB.

74. Fanny Villard to W. P. Garrison, 24 Sept. 1870, MH; for Wendell's opinion see his letter to Fanny, 24 Dec. 1872, MH.

75. F. G. Villard to W. P. Garrison, 24 Sept. 1870, MH.

76. WLG to Samuel May, Jr., 31 Dec. 1875, copy, MB.

77. WLG described the scene on the first anniversary of Helen's death, 25 Jan. 1877, MB.

78. Although WLG and Phillips were never close again, a letter written (1 Aug. 1871) by the former to his son Wendell, enclosing a large photograph of Wendell Phillips and asking the son to respect and admire his benefactor in spite of his recent conduct, may indicate that the relationship was less strained.

79. 10 Feb. 1876, PSC-F.

80. WLG to W. P. Garrison, 27 Jan. 1876, MH.

81. *Helen Eliza Garrison, A Memorial* (Cambridge, Mass., 1876).

82. Published 6 July 1876.

83. WLG to W. P. Garrison, 6 [July] 1876, MB. This letter is incorrectly dated June, the proper month being substituted above.

84. WLG to W. P. Garrison, 22 Dec. 1876, MB.

85. There is in the Boston Public Library an interesting extract from a letter written by Hartley Wicksteed to his mother, 24 Sept. 1876, that shows how much impressed "a chance young visitor" was with the generosity, kindness, wisdom, conversation, and memory for the apposite quotation of the distinguished elderly man.

86. WLG to Fanny Villard, 20 Feb. 1877, MB.

87. WLG to Elizabeth Pease Nichol, 6 April 1877, MB.

88. WLG to Maria W. Chapman, 11 May 1877, copy, MB.

89. See especially WLG to W. P. Garrison, 16 May 1877, MB, and WLG to F. J. Garrison, 18 May 1877, MB.

90. WLG to Samuel May, Jr., 22 May 1877, MHi.

91. WLG to Elizabeth Pease Nichol, 5 June 1877, MB.

92. See WLG to Geo. J. Holyoke, 19 Aug. 1877, MB, and WLG to Fanny Villard, 10 Sept. 1877, MB.

93. WLG to Fanny Villard, 10 Sept. 1877, MB. Thompson died the following month. WLG's other intimate friend, Henry C. Wright, had died in the summer of 1870. Since he had had no definite home for some time, it was a problem to know where to bury his body. Finally Garrison consulted a medium in Boston and later one in Providence; as a result the proper lot and cemetery were found, through the dictation of Wright's spirit, in Providence. See *Life,* IV, 253, and WLG to Oliver Johnson, 7 Nov. 1870, MB.

94. 30 Oct. 1877.

95. 7 Feb. 1879, MB.

96. MHi.

97. MHi.

98. "Remarks of Wendell Phillips," *Tributes to William Lloyd Garrison at the Funeral Services* (Boston, 1879), pp. 43, 47, 48.

INDEX

THE FOLLOWING abbreviations are used: AA-SS, American Anti-Slavery Society; *Lib., Liberator;* MA-SS, Massachusetts Anti-Slavery Society; NEA-SS, New England Anti-Slavery Society; WLG, William Lloyd Garrison.

INDEX

American Anti-Slavery Society (*cont.*)
quarrel, 284, 285–288, 290; possible
dissolution, 299–300, 313; Jackson be-
quest, 315
American Anti-Slavery Women, 143
American Colonization Society, 32, 41,
60, 61, 62, 64, 66, 76, 79, 118, 189, 320;
WLG vs. Cresson, 70–72; Birney and,
120, 121
American Free Trade League, 322
American Freedmen's Aid Union, 312
American Peace Society, 20
American Union Commission, 312. *See
also* Freedmen's Union Commission
"An Old Bachelor," WLG's pseudonym,
9, 10, 31, 82
Anderson, Major-General Robert, 295,
296
Andover Theological Seminary, 133, 135,
175, 185
Andrew, Governor John A., 277, 309, 310,
311
Anthony, Susan B., 321
Anti-Sabbath Convention, 243–246, 247
Antislavery. *See* Abolition; Emancipation
Antislavery fairs, 196, 359
Anti-Slavery League (British), 192–193
Anti-Slavery Office, Boston, 100, 103, 104,
106, 132, 222
Antislavery societies, 56, 59, 74, 76, 80,
130, 144, 175, 182, 219; at Lane Semi-
nary, 118; in Ohio, 122; criticize WLG,
146–147; differences over nature of,
153–154; and financial problems of
AA-SS, 154–156; and women, 166;
Rogers on organization, 223–224; post-
war conflict over, 299–300, 301, 305,
312. *See also individual societies*
*Appeal of the Clerical Abolitionists on
Anti-Slavery Measures.* See *Clerical
Appeals*
Apprenticeships, WLG's, 4, 6–12
Argyll, Duke of, 317
Ashurst, William H., 166–167, 194
Associationist movement, WLG on, 216–
217

Ballou, Adin, 216
Baltimore, 4–6, 7, 8–9, 11, 22, 26, 27, 229,
289, 297; WLG in, 30–39; WLG's trial
and imprisonment in, 34–38, 48
Baltimore *Gazette*, 48
Bancroft, George, 208
Banks, General N. P., 294, 324
Baptist church, 132, 243
Baptist Magazine, 71

Barker, Joseph, 194
Bartlett, Deacon Ezekiel, 3, 6, 12, 46
Bassett, William, 147
Bates, Hamlett, 222
Beaver, Ohio, 233
Beecher, Henry Ward, 119, 280, 295, 296,
298, 299
Beecher, Lyman, 42, 119, 120; WLG on,
131–132, 136, 180
Belfast, Ireland, 195
Bell [presidential candidate], 274
Bennett, James Gordon, 257
Bennett, Thomas H., 8, 337
Bennington, Vermont, WLG in, 21–25,
27–28
Benson, Anna, 86, 95, 147
Benson, George, Jr., 91, 99, 113, 114, 147,
181; and Northampton Association,
215, 216; at Anti-Sabbath Convention,
244, 245
Benson, George, Sr., 60, 64, 77, 84, 94,
162, 177
Benson, Helen. *See* Garrison, Helen Ben-
son
Benson, Henry, 57, 62, 95, 98, 99, 112,
114, 115, 132
Benson, Sarah, 247
Bible, 182, 184, 247
Birney, James G., 120, 121, 124, 138, 152,
159, 165, 167, 202, 203
Birth, WLG, 1
Bishop, Joel P., 222
Blaine, James G., 325, 329
Booth, John Wilkes, 297
Boston, 1, 18, 56, 66, 94, 119, 130, 177,
192, 253, 302; WLG lives in, 18–21, 26,
28–30, 38 *et passim;* WLG chooses for
Lib., 43–44; WLG's reception in—*1833,*
73–74, 75, 76; *1835,* 99; *1840,* 174; mob-
bing of WLG, *1835,* 104–108, 109, 110,
111–112, 138, 142, 187, 219, 297, 329,
346; Fr. Mathew in, 253
Boston *Commercial Gazette*, 103, 104
Boston *Courier*, 40
Boston Daily Advertiser, 43
Boston Evening Transcript, 74
Boston Female Anti-Slavery Society, 103–
107, 134; annual reports, *Right and
Wrong in Massachusetts*, 196
Boston *Patriot*, 43
Boston *Recorder*, 183
Boston *Telegraph*, 59
Bourne, George, 30
Bowditch, Dr. Henry I., 111, 254, 309
Bowditch, Jonathan, 309
Bowditch, William, 267

INDEX

Bowring, John, 194
Boycott of slave-labor products, 56, 80
Brice, Judge, 36
Briggs, Governor George N., 211, 212, 253
Brigham, Mrs., 293
Bright, John, 318
Brisbane, Albert, 216, 217
British and Foreign Anti-Slavery Society, 165, 168, 175
British Contagious Diseases Act, 321–322
Brook Farm, 200, 215, 216
Brooke, Samuel, 238, 260
Brooklyn, Conn., 42, 57, 64, 66, 85, 97; WLG on, 98–99; WLG and Helen live in, *1835*, 111–115; James Garrison in, 162, 164, 177
Brooks, Congressman Preston S., 270
Brougham, Lord, 68, 187
Brown, Capt., 32, 33
Brown, John, 52, 269, 274, 275, 277, 300, 310; WLG on, 271–273, 291
Brown, John L., 187–188
Brown University, 84
Bryant, William Cullen, 310, 317
Buffalo, N.Y., 239
Buffum, Arnold, 58, 77
Buffum, James, 197, 245
Burke, Edmund, 48
Burleigh, C. C., 105, 109, 112, 244, 245, 259–260, 261
Burns, Anthony, 261
Burritt, Elihu, 209
Butler, Senator A. P., 270
Buxton, Thomas Powell, 68–69, 71
Byron, Lady Anne Isabella, 168, 169, 197
Byron, George Gordon, Lord, 21, 319

Cabinet-making, WLG apprenticed in, 7
Calhoun, John C., 210, 254, 256, 262, 297
California, 254, 311, 328
Calvinism, 40, 43, 184, 201
Canada, 72, 261
Canterbury, Conn., 64, 85, 113
Cary, George, 44
Chace, Eliza, 92, 94–95
Chandler, Elizabeth Margaret, 31, 45
Channing, William E., 42, 43, 132, 136, 177; *Slavery*, 129–130; WLG on, 130–131
Channing, William H., 177, 197, 216
Chapman, Henry G., 196, 244
Chapman, Maria W., 106, 149, 159, 177, 179, 188, 196, 206, 243, 244, 310, 315, 316
Character, WLG, 4, 12, 16–17, 18, 22–23,

36–37, 45–46, 48, 52–55, 60, 87–88, 93, 95, 96, 109, 128–129, 132, 146, 163, 164, 173, 217–218, 225–226, 252, 273
Chardon Street Chapel, Convention at, *1840*, 177–180
Charleston, S.C., 125, 134, 187, 188; WLG's trip to, 294–299
Chartists: appeal in Glasgow, 172; Vincent, 193, 194
Chase, Justice Salmon P., 310
Chicago, 302, 311
Child, David Lee, 57, 58, 59, 205, 218, 310
Child, Lydia, 159, 218, 226
Chinese, WLG on, 322, 323, 325
Christian Examiner, 44
Christian Soldier, 57
Christianity, 128, 130, 140, 185, 199, 258, 259, 266. *See also* Church; Clergy; Religion
Church: view of emancipation, 128; WLG's view of, 132, 160, 172, 188, 258; nature and authority debated, 177. *See also* Clergy
Cincinnati, 118–120
Civil War, 50, 52, 219, 327; WLG on, 276, 277–278, 288; beginning of, 275; British misunderstanding of, 281; Phillips on postwar problems, 286; effect on WLG, 300–301
Clapp, Henry, 224
Clarke, James Freeman, 197
Clarkson, Thomas, 68, 71, 72, 112, 165–166, 188
Clay, Henry, 20, 41, 151, 153, 254, 255, 256
Clergy, 80; WLG and, 128, 134–140, 143, 146–147, 151, 153, 175, 179, 184, 186, 188, 233; and Chardon Street Convention, 177, 178
Clerical Appeals, 135–136
Cleveland, Ohio, 237–239
Clinton Hall, N.Y., 73, 74
Cobbett, William, 13
Coffin, Joshua, 58, 77
Coffin, William E., 310
College, colored, plans for, 63–64
Collier, William, 27, 28, 44, 339
Collins, John A., 175, 217, 227
Colonization, 123, 185; Lundy on, 26, 31; WLG on, 31, 33, 41, 59, 60, 69–72, 73, 138, 266; opposed by AA-SS, 78; at Lane Seminary, 118, 119, 120; Lincoln's plan, 279
Columbia, S.C., vigilance association, 53
Colver, Rev. Nathaniel, 179–180

INDEX

INDEX

INDEX

INDEX

Jackson, James C., 224
Jefferson, Thomas, 2, 16
Jerrold, Douglas, 193
Jesus, 108, 133, 143, 145, 258
Jocelyn, Nathaniel, 66, 67, 88
Jocelyn, Simeon S., 44, 63, 66
Johnson, Andrew, 312, 313–314, 323
Johnson, Oliver, 57, 58, 66, 136, 146, 147, 177, 220, 279, 303, 341
Johnson, Colonel Richard, 49, 50, 341
Jones, Benjamin S., 236
Journal of Commerce, 279
Journal of the Times, WLG edits, 21–25, 26, 27, 57, 83, 200–201
Julien Hall, Boston, 41, 42

Kansas, 269, 270, 271
Kansas-Nebraska Act, 267–268, 269
Kelley, Abby [Foster], 144, 159, 177, 197, 243, 349
Kendrick, John, 60
Kirk, Rev. Edward Norris, 192, 193
Knapp, Abigail, 92, 95
Knapp, Isaac, 35, 44, 76, 92, 95, 98, 112, 114, 138, 147; and WLG, 219–222, 225, 226
Knapp's Liberator, 222
Kneeland, Abner, 40–41
Kossuth, Louis, 263–265, 267

Labor: WLG and, 47–48, 215; boycott of products by slave, 56, 80; slavery compared to, 172–173
Ladd, William, 20, 42, 145
Lake Erie, 238, 239
Lane Seminary, 124, 235; abolition movement at, 118–121, 128, 131
Lawrence, Kan., 269
Leavitt, Joshua, 124
Lee, General Robert E., 295, 304
Leesburg, Ohio, 236
Leggett, Samuel, 38
Legislature, state, and WLG, 112
Letter to Louis Kossuth (WLG), 264
Leverett Street Jail, 107, 108
Lewis, Alonzo, 58
Lexington, Ky., *Intelligencer*, 121
Libel, WLG's trials for, 34–37, 39, 48
Liberator, The: founding, 43–45; WLG's Manifesto, 45; audience for, 46–47, 55; topics, 47–53; reputation in South, 53–55, 64; financial problems, 75–76, 92–93, 146, 147, 181, 219; disagreements over, 138, 139–140, 148–149, 150, 152, 246–247; new departments, 143; Quincy edits, 190, 228, 237; Mrs. Chapman and,
196; anti-Constitution superscription, 205; and Knapp, 219–222; and Douglass' *North Star*, 241; Bennett on, 257; twentieth anniversary, 262–263; approaching discontinuation, 301–302; final issue and Valedictory, 303
Liberia, 286, 320
Liberty Bell, 188, 197, 264
Liberty League, 219
Liberty party, 183, 200, 202, 203–204, 205, 208, 212, 213, 227, 243
Lieber, Dr. Francis, 111
Lincoln, Governor, 20
Lincoln, Abraham, 275, 277, 297, 300, 301, 313, 372; Phillips on, 274–275; WLG's view, 274, 276, 278–279, 281, 292; vetoes Hunter's emancipation order, 282–283; preliminary emancipation proclamation, 283; and Phillips-Garrison quarrel, 284–285, 286–287, 288–289, 290–291; WLG meets, 289; death, 299, 305
Liquor. *See* Alcohol
Litchfield County, Conn., 184
Liverpool, 68, 164, 191, 194, 329
Lloyd, Charlotte, 94–95, 97
Lloyd inheritance, 97–98, 177
London: WLG in, *1833*, 68–72; reputation in, 73, 75; WLG in, *1840*, 165–170; WLG in, *1846*, 191–192
Longfellow, Henry Wadsworth, 310
Loring, Ellis Gray, 44, 57, 58, 59, 150, 181, 205, 218
Louisiana, 120, 294
Lovejoy, Rev. Elijah P., 111, 141–142, 187
Lovelace, Richard, 34
Lovett, William, 194
Lowell, James R., 198, 310
Lowell, Mass., 100, 110, 111
Lundy, Benjamin, 42, 60, 230; and WLG, 26–28, 30–31, 34, 35, 37–38, 41, 137–138
Lyman, Major Theodore, 103, 105, 106
Lynn, Mass., 3–4, 5, 22, 134
Lynn *Pioneer*, 224
Lynn *Record*, 114

Macauley, Zachary, 71
McClellan, General, 282, 287
McKim, Charles, 307
McKim, J. Miller, 62, 307
Madison, James, 41
Mahan, Asa, 236
Maine, 77
Manifest Destiny, 323
Manual-labor education. *See* Education

INDEX

INDEX

INDEX

INDEX